LIVING ABROAD
FRANCE

AURELIA D'ANDREA

PRIME
LIVING LOCATIONS
IN FRANCE

UNITED KINGDOM

Thames River
⊗ London

English Channel

Haute-
Normandie

Seine

Channel
Islands
(U.K.)

Basse- Normandie

Île
Fr

Chartres

BRITTANY

Brittany

Rennes

Pays de
la Loire

Vannes

Orl

River

Cen

Nantes

Loire

F R A N C

ATLANTIC
OCEAN

Poitiers

Poitou
Charles

Limousin

Île d'Oléron

Limoges

Gironde
Estuary

**BORDEAUX AND THE
DORDOGNE VALLEY**

Bordeaux

Bergerac

Sarlat

Garonne

Lang
Rous

Aquitaine

River

0   100 mi
0   100 km

Bay of Biscay

Pibriac   Blagnac

Midi-Pyrénées   Colomiers   Toulou

Biarritz

Pau

**PAU, TOULOUSE
AND MONTPELLIE**

Lourdes

Pyrénées

SPAIN

ANDORRA

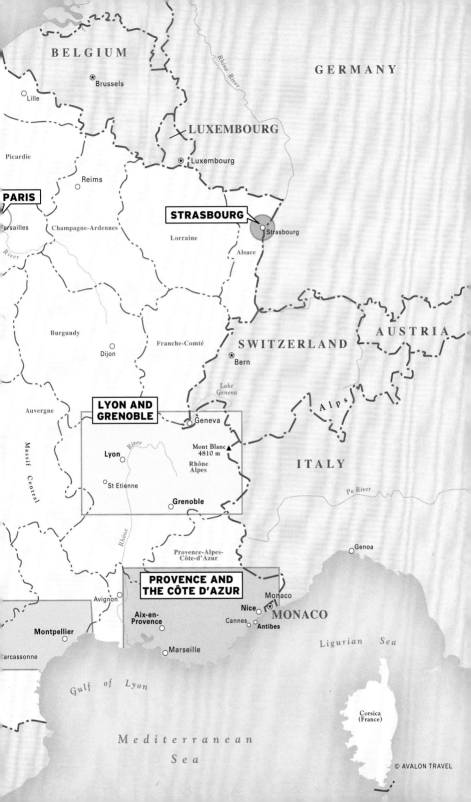

Contents

Poet T. S. Eliot cautioned, "The chief danger about Paris is that it is such a strong stimulant." The same wonderful warning can be applied to all of France, where the everyday sensory experience borders on extravagant. Throughout the country, breathtaking architecture that stretches back to the Middle Ages sets the fairytale tone. Add the luscious scent of warm bread rising in a *boulanger*'s oven, toss in the sound of a distant church bell ringing, and finish with a smattering of outdoor markets bursting with all the colors of the rainbow, and you have a solid sense of the sort of stimulation l'Hexagone has to offer.

As worthy of superlatives as this complex country may be, France is much more than a delicious carnival for the senses. For the roughly 150,000 North American expatriates who call France home, at least part of the country's allure is its renowned quality of life: relaxed, engaged, and fine-tuned to simple pleasures. The French way of living isn't perfect, but it's pretty darn close.

On any day in hundreds of hamlets, villages, and urban metropolises throughout the country, you can follow the yeasty aroma of baking baguettes down a crooked cobblestone alleyway and wind up standing before a dazzling display of culinary wizardry: shiny fruit tarts–their buttery crusts pinched to perfection–sitting in neat little rows between caramel-and-whipped-cream *religieuses* and meringue-topped *tartes au citron*.

Your eyes feast on the tempting patisserie until a familiar melody from a distant accordion coaxes you out of your sugary reverie. Drifting away on an éclair-scented cloud, you hear the music grow louder. Rounding a corner, you spy the source: a mustachioed man in a striped

WELCOME TO FRANCE

INTRODUCTION

There are many ways to describe 21st-century France, but the most fitting might be "traditional." The French cling to their customs with an unrivaled tenacity for reasons as mysterious to foreigners as they are to the locals themselves. Ask why, and you're likely to be met with a rote *"C'est comme ça"*—that's just the way it is. Progress can wait, the French seem to be saying. What's the big hurry?

Change tends to make the French feel a bit uneasy, so forward motion takes place at an Operation Escargot pace. But it is those same timeless, traditional values that attract many of us to France. The French have earned a global reputation for having mastered the art of living, and they deserve it. In a manner that elicits envious sighs around the world, they continue to show us that balancing work and home life isn't just a dream. Here, the motto seems to be "work to live, and live *la belle vie.*" This is particularly evident at lunchtime, when construction crews and suited-up office workers from Picardie to Provence file into homey brasseries to relish their perfectly quotidian three-course lunches—*with* wine. You also see it in the healthcare safety net that guarantees 90 percent of the population is covered by comprehensive medical insurance. And you feel it during the month of August, when entire cities empty out as locals flock to the seashore and the countryside to enjoy their luxuriously long summer vacation. In France, *relaxation* is definitely not a dirty word.

This country of 65 million may have nailed the quality-of-life thing, but there are still a few areas of the French modus operandi that could use a modern makeover. The customer is most certainly *not* always right in France, so even the most mundane tasks—opening a bank account, getting your electricity connected—can serve as an exercise in frustration that will test the patience of the most laid-back émigré. The French are also a guarded bunch, with a very distinct line separating public and private life. Many an American expat laments never having been invited to a French person's home. This is the norm, not the exception, and it's not worth getting offended about. Give your new French friend time—five or six years, perhaps—and you just might find yourself on the receiving end of that most mysterious, coveted dinner invitation.

What seems to matter most here is family, and that's reflected in the social system. Even before a child is born, the social benefits kick in: parents-to-be are entitled to special grants for having a child through biological means or adoption. From 11 days *congé de paternité* for new fathers (new moms get 16 weeks to bond with their offspring) and subsidized childcare for preschool-age kids, adding to the population is rewarded rather than punished. France consistently ranks at the top of the global charts when it comes to the scope and standard of healthcare, and a government-subsidized "family allowance" is given to all families with two or more children, regardless of income. Equally, housing benefits are doled out to all families with children under the age of 20. To the uninitiated, these social benefits might seem excessive, but voters consistently say "yes" to the established welfare system.

In spite of France's deeply held traditional values, there is a sense of transition in the air. In May 2013, with the outspoken support of President François Hollande, the Assemblée Nationale voted to legalize same-sex marriage, and homosexual couples were also granted the right to adopt children. (This shift wasn't without its detractors; thousands flocked to Paris from around the country to march the streets in protest.) Traditionally valued institutions such as marriage continue to wane, while civil unions—including same-sex unions—are on the rise. English is more widely spoken than ever before, and multiculturalism has reached unprecedented levels. Immigrants from North and West Africa, Eastern Europe, and Asia continue to alter the look, feel, and flavor of France, taking the edge off the homogeneity that has long defined the French ethos.

As private, traditional, family-oriented France slowly adapts to its changing landscape, it continues to attract an expatriate community that fortifies itself on those timeless, easily accessible attributes that have stood the test of time: dazzling architecture, towering snowcapped mountains and picture-perfect seashores, unrivaled cuisine, a fascinating history, and an unsurpassed quality of life. There's never been a better time to let this seductive country make its everlasting imprint on the adventurous Francophile.

The French Alps are a popular winter destination.

The Lay of the Land

The largest country in Western Europe, France—nicknamed l'Hexagone for its distinct six-sided geometry—occupies a particularly strategic and resource-rich piece of the European pie. Hemmed in by Belgium, Luxembourg, and Germany to the north and northeast; Switzerland and Italy to the east; and Monaco, Andorra, and Spain to the south; metropolitan France is a bountiful bouquet of geographic diversity, boasting world-renowned beaches, rivers, valleys, and mountain ranges.

To the east, the French Alps lay claim to Western Europe's tallest peak, Mont Blanc. The 15,770-foot-high mountain attracts many thousands of skiers, bikers, climbers, and daring outdoors enthusiasts of every stripe each year, making it the third-most-visited natural monument in the world. To the south, a magnificent cluster of dormant volcanoes forms the Massif Central, a giant swath of rugged, millennia-old mountains and plateaus dotted with thermal hot springs, a reminder that the volcanoes are merely dormant, not extinct.

Butting up against Spain in the far south, France's second mountain range, the Pyrénées, acts as a natural border separating the Iberian Peninsula from the rest of mainland Europe. Like the mountains of the Massif Central, the Pyrénées are dotted with hot springs, around which spas both fancy and utilitarian have been built, each touting the naturally curative benefits of their waters to ailing bodies. (*La sécurité sociale*—or "*sécu*" for short—even covers the cost of some thermal springs "cures.") Winter sports are popular here, and in summer, hiking enthusiasts come in droves to tackle the 500-mile Mediterranean-to-Atlantic footpath known as the GR 10.

The Gallic landscape is crisscrossed by hundreds of rivers that meander between mountains, flow across great stretches of verdant farmland, and wend their way through some of the most picturesque, châteaux-rich valleys in all of Europe. The fabled Seine is surely the best known of all France's *fleuves,* twisting majestically through Paris on its way to the seaport of Le Havre, where it billows out into the rocky waters of the English Channel. However, the Seine is neither the longest nor the most important of the country's waterways. The swift-moving Rhône has served as France's primary internal trade route since Roman times; and, at 620 miles long, the Loire claims the title of France's longest waterway.

At its northernmost point, France meets Belgium on the brutish North Sea, but the coastline relaxes as you travel south, moving along the English Channel and finally to that swath of Atlantic coastline known as the Bay of Biscay, which reaches clear down to the Spanish border. This expanse of windswept land where sea meets sand is flat and marshy, and because of its easy proximity to France's most famous wine-growing region, it's extremely popular for French vacationers during the month of August.

France is blessed with exceptional natural beauty, but the country's prize jewel is easily the Mediterranean coast—more specifically, that exclusive stretch of sundrenched seashore called the Côte d'Azur. Notorious for its 300 days of sunshine per year and more yachts per capita than any other region in the world, the Riviera serves up razzle-dazzle with substance. Over the centuries, the region has played host to waves of invading armies and migrating crusaders, plus a famous artist or two, including Pablo Picasso, Marc Chagall, and Henri Matisse, whose paintings reflect the special flavor of their temporary home base.

Jutting out of the turquoise Mediterranean 100 miles off the Provençal coast is Corsica (known as *Corse* in French), a rugged explosion of jagged mountains and red-tile rooftops. Though closer to Italy than France—and culturally distinct, with its own language and culinary customs—Corsica is considered no less French than any other mainland region. As well as being a major tourist hub, the island is an important agricultural zone, producing many warm-weather fruits (those delicious little Clementine oranges in particular) and vegetables sold throughout France at open-air *marchés* and standard supermarkets.

COUNTRY DIVISIONS

Metropolitan France, or what the locals refer to as La Métropole, is carved into 22 culturally distinct regions, which, after a final vote in the National Assembly in December of 2014, are undergoing a shrinking-and-fusing process that will whittle that regionl figure down to 13. Each of these regions, which includes Corsica, is further divided into 96 *départements,* which are also up on the chopping block—a step that aims to decrease state spending and reduce the size of the government. In the manner of Russian dolls, each department contains *arrondissements, cantons,* and *communes.* For the day-to-day practical purposes of the average expat, knowing your regions and departments is what matters most.

Departments are numbered alphabetically, beginning with Ain (01) and ending with Val d'Oise (95). Corsica is the one anomaly, with two departmental codes—2A and 2B, representing Corse du Sud (southern Corsica) and Haute Corse (northern Corsica)—standing in for 20. In the same way that all French phone numbers begin with a two-digit sequence that indicates the region, French license plates bear the

Mind Your Manners

Snobby. Rude. Elitist. These are some of the nicer adjectives folks who haven't even visited France will casually bandy about to describe an entire nation and its inhabitants. Maybe even a person or two who *has* set foot on French soil will substantiate the pejorative name-calling with an anecdote or two, likely based on a hurried weekend trip to Paris armed with little more than a loud American accent. Give the country's 65 million people half a chance, however, and they'll show you that the negative stereotypes are unfounded.

What many mistake for snootiness is actually an ingrained social formality that, from an outsider's perspective, can feel very old-fashioned. People still greet their neighbors with a cordial *"Bonjour, madame"*; never forget to say *"Au revoir, monsieur"* at the pharmacy, wine shop, and post office; and always hold the door for the person behind them, regardless of gender. A certain attention to dress—nice shoes, for instance—is almost universal in French cities, and only recently has the casual sartorial approach (sweatpants, white gym shoes) inched its way into the fashion sphere. If you want to make a good first impression and feel like a local *tout de suite* (immediately), commit these phrases to memory and employ them liberally.

What to Say	What It Means	When to Say It
Bonjour, madame/ monsieur	Hello, madam/sir	When entering any shop, restaurant, or business during the day
Bon journée, madame/ monsieur	Have a nice day, madam/sir	When leaving any shop, restaurant, or business
Bon soir, madame/ monsieur	Good evening, madam/sir	When greeting shopkeepers and others after dark
Bon soirée, madame/ monsieur	Have a nice evening, madam/sir	When saying goodbye to shopkeepers and others after dark

two-digit departmental number at the end of the seven-character alphanumeric sequence. This indicates where that car was registered and makes for a great game during long-haul road trips.

Each department has its own elected officials and an administrative capital known as a *préfecture*. The *préfets*—the places to go to register a birth, report a death, acquire a driver's or a marriage license, or register a new address—are responsible for carrying out national law on a local level. This system, first instituted under Napoleon I, allows local administrative hubs to function with a certain degree of autonomy within the centralized French government. *Préfectures* are also the primary public administration zone most foreign nationals get to know on an intimate level; expect to spend hours here waiting in line, having your dossier scrutinized, and ultimately registering your legal status as a temporary resident in France.

What to Say	What It Means	When to Say It
Au revoir, madame/ monsieur	Goodbye, madam/sir	When leaving any shop, restaurant, or business (often combined with bon journée or bon soirée)
S'il vous plaît	Please	Before approaching strangers for help, before placing your order at a restaurant, when trying to get someone's attention
Merci bien, madame/ monsieur	Thank you very much, madame/sir	At the close of any transaction
Excusez-moi, s'il vous plaît	Pardon me, please	When asking strangers for directions or other information
Je suis désolé(e) de vous déranger, mais...	I'm so sorry to bother you, but...	When you want to lay it on thick in the gratitude department
Merci, c'est très gentile	Thank you, that's so nice	When you're especially grateful for something
Je suis très désolé(e), mais je ne comprends pas	I'm so sorry, but I don't understand	When you want to elicit sympathy and possibly an English-language response

POPULATION DENSITY

Until the 1950s, half the French population lived rurally. Today, the majority resides in urban areas, with Paris topping the charts as the most dense, accounting for a full 3.5 percent of the country's population. With approximately 65 million inhabitants, France is the fourth-largest country in Europe, falling behind Germany (82.5 million) and just ahead of the United Kingdom (64 million). In only a few major cities—Paris, Marseille, and Lyon in particular—and their suburbs will you feel the suffocating glut of overcrowding, and usually just at rush hour or during one of the many annual public festivals.

France differs from North America in that its suburbs, or *banlieues,* are often as densely populated as the urban centers they skirt. This is a symptom of poor urban planning; to meet the needs of a growing immigrant population in the '70s and '80s, city planners working with local governments hastily erected enormous concrete housing developments called *cites,* which were intended as temporary dwellings to house a population that was expected to return "home" at some point. Some of these *banlieues,* most notably to the north of Paris but also on the periphery of Marseille, have been the sites of police clashes and rioting. In 2005, a weeklong series of riots in the northern Paris suburbs, replete with burning cars and Molotov cocktails, made international headlines and drew attention to the racial issues that had previously been ignored by the mainstream media. Marginalized populations—often discontent second-genera-tion immigrant youth caught between two cultures—are credited as the source of the suburban "problem," but humanizing the structure of suburban communities through better urban planning is seen by many as one possible solution.

Generally, French streets tend to feel lively and functional rather than clogged. Cities and towns usually have a commercial center where you'll find basic necessities, including a post office, a café, a *boulangerie,* and other services. Many towns have user-friendly squares or parks with benches, picnic tables, and children's play areas. Whatever the season and the weather conditions, you're bound to see silver-haired grandmothers out buying bread, fathers ushering their children to school, working women cycling to their offices, and beret-sporting old men out walking their dogs.

After a long spell of declining birthrates, the numbers have charted a steady increase over the past decade, evening out at roughly two children per woman of childbearing age. This increase is due in large part to the continued creation of family-friendly so-cial policies and financial incentives, and because women are entitled to hold their jobs if they choose to, after maternity leave. This is critical, especially when you consider that 85 percent of women in France work outside the home. Life spans in France tend to be on par with the rest of Western Europe: 78.5 years for men, and 84.91 years for women—not bad, considering the number of cigarettes inhaled by the general popu-lation. (One quarter of all French women smoke, and a full third of men.)

WEATHER

It's safe to say that France is a four-season country, but the winter you get in Paris is not the same one you'll experience in Nice (winter in the capital is guaranteed to be considerably colder and a few shades grayer than that of its southern cousin). Often referred to as having a temperate climate, France actually claims four distinct climatic zones wherein the proximity to oceans and mountains dictates the amount of heat or cold you'll experience throughout the year.

The north of France holds the honor of that oft-touted temperate climate, with cool springtime temperatures; warm summers; cold, wet winters; and a mild autumn. You can also expect year-round rain showers—summer in the capital may mean dramatic thun-derstorms and spirited downpours, while Brittany and Normandy are a veritable wet-fest throughout the winter, which makes for a verdant paradise in the warmer months.

The climate along the Atlantic coast stretching down to Bordeaux is classified as "maritime," meaning the sun shines nearly as bright year-round as it does along the Mediterranean, but the North Atlantic Drift moderates the temperatures so it's never extremely hot nor cold. The further you inch along the sandy white beaches toward the Pyrénées, the more rainfall you can expect in winter. The maritime climate also plays host to the "June gloom" phenomenon, which socks those pretty beaches beneath a blanket of fog for the first half of summer.

A mountain climate reigns in the Alps, ushering in bitterly cold winters with gener-ous and predictable snowfall; cool, wet springs; mild summers; and a nippy autumn.

Ski resorts see avalanches regularly in the wintertime, and the southeastern river valleys experience an occasional flash flood in the warmer months.

The renowned Mediterranean climate, consisting of year-round sunshine and mild winters, is tempered by the Mistral, a relentless wind that whips down through the Rhône River Valley most winters and often through the spring. You can see the Mistral's legacy in the cypress trees hugging the Provençal coastline, hunched over like old crones trying to escape the brunt of the wind. While the punishing nature of this unique meteoric phenomenon is known to keep the locals locked indoors for days on end, the wind is, in part, what gives the Mediterranean its prized climate. It blows all the detritus from the air and sucks the moisture out with it, leaving the terrain sun-drenched, dry, and clear.

Giant whirling wind turbines, towering high on the hills above the Western Mediterranean coast, harness the mighty Mistral's winds and generate power for the region, but they're a source of contention among locals. Are they an environmentalist's answer to an impending energy crisis or an eyesore marring the pristine landscape? It depends entirely on whom you ask.

FLORA AND FAUNA

Before the industrial revolution in the mid-19th century, when forests and woodlands were razed to lay the foundation for industrial agriculture and an emerging urban-centric way of life, France teemed with diverse wildlife and plant species. Now, untamed wilderness has given way to structured farming, formal parks and gardens, and concentrated urbanism, but within the human-designed order you can still find natural pockets of biodiversity.

Plane trees dominate the picturesque Parisian streetscape, lining up majestically

Lavender is an important crop for France's perfume industry.

along the Champs-Elysées and every other major thoroughfare in the French capital. But oak, beech, poplar, and chestnut trees are the scene stealers throughout the rest of France. In the mountainous eastern regions, coniferous pines and spruces stretch skyward against an evergreen backdrop, and in the spring and summer, the Alps explode in a riot of wildflowers, inviting the intrepid rambler to take a nature hike among them.

France is an important flower-growing region for the world's perfume industry; the perfume capital of the planet is, inarguably, the Provençal city of Grasse. Lavender, jasmine, and roses are cultivated here, and the city hosts two important flower festivals each year in honor of the aromatic blooms. If you're prone to allergy flare-ups, you can expect them here and elsewhere along the southern coast in the springtime, when the bright yellow mimosa and other pollen-heavy flowers begin to blossom.

To visit an outdoor market in France is to experience the country's edible bounty in miniature. Mushrooms—from the legendary black truffles to woodsy morels and bright yellow girolles—grow wild in every corner of the country and are a point of culinary pride. But don't think about harvesting any you stumble upon without seeking permission. French law dictates that mushrooms belong to owner of the land they grow on, so getting the all-clear before harvesting will help circumvent any unnecessary visits to the *préfecture de police.*

The most beloved crop grown in France is surely the grape, with dozens of varieties produced for both *la table* (table grapes) and for that bottle of *vin rouge* you'll be sipping with your next meal. At outdoor markets, it's customary to sample the wares before buying; just ask for *un petit goût*—especially if the heavenly purple muscat grapes are in season. Apples are the most popular fruit consumed in France, and, like grapes, they are also transformed into beverages including soft and hard cider and that potent elixir called Calvados, both of which have been produced in Normandy for 500 years.

Despite a long tradition of hunting in the countryside, wild boar and deer still manage to survive in French forests, but the wildlife you're most liable to stumble upon throughout the country is the ubiquitous *lapin.* Rabbits have proven to be particularly adaptable creatures, burrowing holes along the runways at Charles de Gaulle airport and proliferating with healthy vigor in urban parks from Strasbourg to Biarritz. The farther you move away from urban centers, the more likely you are to spot the foxes, badgers, hedgehogs, and martens that also make their home here.

Migrating birds—ducks and geese—make temporary pit stops in France along their migratory routes, and pheasant, partridge, and gulls linger as year-round residents. In the southern river delta known as the Carmague, there's even a rare species of pink flamingo that's flourishing, thanks to a bountiful plankton growing in the brackish waters. For those who prefer a more animal-friendly sport than hunting, birdwatching is a superb option, with plentiful opportunities for the would-be ornithologist.

A Kiss is (Not) Just a Kiss

Everyone's heard of a French kiss, but the voracious tongues-and-all method isn't the standardized variety carried out in *la belle France*. From the moment you step off the plane or alight from your train, you'll see what French kissing is really all about (and, perhaps, what it *isn't* about: tongues). The art of the *bisou* begins with identifying who's on the receiving end: If you're of the female persuasion, you'll dole out kisses to everyone. Ditto if you're a child. (They start 'em young here.) Men are typically exempted from kissing other men, unless they're family or extremely close friends. Step two is all about the action: Lean in toward your intended with your right cheek, allowing your respective cheeks to touch gently and momentarily while you make a kissing sound. Step three involves pulling back slightly and repeating the gesture on the left cheek. One or both hands can rest gently on the kissee's shoulders or an arm, or simply keep your mitts to yourself. In some parts of France, this act can be repeated for a total of four kisses; let the Frenchie take the lead if you're uncertain of the local protocol. So what about that other French kiss practiced the world over? Yes, they do it in France, too, but here they call it *un bisou avec la langue*–a kiss with the tongue.

Social Climate

Several years into the Eurozone financial crisis, France is certainly feeling the economic pinch. National unemployment hovers at about 10 percent, petty crime such as pickpocketing and bicycle theft is holding steady, and homelessness in the big cities is on the rise. The French aren't content to simply sit home and complain about these important national concerns; instead, they take it outdoors. Even though union membership is waning, the tradition of the non-violent *grève* (strike) lives on throughout France. The masses—young and old, male and female—take to the streets several times a year to protest the rising retirement age and other threats to the French lifestyle. To the untrained eye, it sometimes looks as if France's social order is spiraling out of control, but it's really just par for the course in a country with a long history of social action and galvanizing for a cause.

When French president Francois Hollande took office in 2012, the French public understood that he would not be picking up where his predecessor, Nicolas Sarkozy, left off. Whereas Sarkozy's political agenda focused on curbing crime and stemming the tide of immigration, Hollande made his focus cutting government and raising taxes on the wealthy. In 2014, after a personal crisis went public and his public-opinion ratings sank to record lows, the president flip-flopped on a number of key political points, announcing a new wave of tax cuts for businesses, and axing several far-left members of his cabinet, leading many French to question whether the ballot they cast was for the right person.

Thankfully, it's not all doom and gloom in the land of the Gauls. In spite of a sluggish economy, free enterprise is finally catching on here as an idea, and relaxed tax laws for small businesses that defer payments for the first three years have spawned a healthy new wave of entrepreneurship. As foreign immigration continues to change the face of France, it is also reshaping ideas inside contemporary art, politics, and social policy, building onto an already impressive foundation. Could the collective chokehold on the past be slowly loosening its grip? Time will tell for certain, but all the elements are in place for a modern French renaissance.

FRANCE AND FOREIGNERS

For centuries, foreigners by the boatload have flocked to France in search of political exile, freedom of artistic expression, and unfettered adventure. Writers from Ernest Hemingway to David Sedaris have parlayed their fabled expatriate experience into a literary canon that continues to enthrall and entice new generations of immigrants, but it's easy to focus on the fantasy and forget the reality of moving abroad. In France, the success of your individual experience hinges greatly on whether or not you make an effort to assimilate quietly into the local culture.

Most French men and women will tell you that their country is a place where tolerance is exercised—if you play by the rules. Tune into the local frequency, and you'll feel the sense of "sameness" that permeates French society, from the standardized education model to the way public parks are designed to the uniform manner in which people dress. Uniqueness isn't a prized quality here in the same way it is in North America; in France, upholding the status quo means maintaining order, and that's the way the French like it. This commitment to homogeneity is palpable on many levels, and it sometimes comes cloaked in the separation-of-church-and-state veil. In a notable example, the 2004 ban on headscarves in French public schools stirred heated public debate, prompting some pundits to call it an act of "neocolonialism."

Since the early 20th century, France has developed repatriation schemes loaded with seductive promises of all-expenses-paid travel and cash bonuses to those willing to commit to quitting the country for good. The truth is that most of these programs target specific populations—unskilled workers, illegal migrants, and other candidates perceived as taking advantage of a generous public welfare system—while immigrants from the United States and other developed nations aren't generally regarded as part of the problem. "White privilege" exists in France, though it is a discreet system of veiled perks and advantages that aren't always obvious to the untrained eye.

Politically, the French public view of the United States shifted with the departure of George W. Bush back in 2009, and you'd be hard-pressed to hear anyone give anything but glowing reviews to American president Barack Obama. Obama's foreign-policy revamp heralded a newfound sense of solidarity between the United States and France, and while culturally, France has long resisted the

McDonald's in Paris

© DENYS KUVAIEV/123RF.COM

Americanization effect inherent in globalization, there's no denying the presence of Starbucks, "McDo's," and even Burger King, nor the popularity of long-running television shows like *The Simpsons* and *Friends*.

Since the French are purveyors of public politesse, you probably won't sense it if they *aren't* in the mood to welcome foreigners. If you swagger into town with a purple mohawk, tattoos, and a face full of piercings, you're likely to garner some down-the-nose looks (this is especially true in Paris, though body modification has recently come into vogue and may be the norm by the time you read this)—but for the most part, your new neighbors will keep their thoughts about your appearance to themselves. The key to ingratiating yourself with the locals is as easy as learning a few key words of the language and always remembering to say *"merci"* (thank you) and *"s'il vous plaît"* (please). If you adopt the unifying national characteristic of formal politeness, the French will warm up to you in no time and will help ease the shock of transitioning to a country that is, indeed, very different from your own.

HISTORY, GOVERNMENT, AND ECONOMY

Wherever you are in France, you are never more than a few paces from some landmark that recalls the rich and illustrious France of antiquity. Majestic arches conjure memories of great battles and conquests, gothic cathedrals recall the legends of martyred saints, and those turreted châteaux stand as reminders of the rise and fall of the French monarchy. Signs of more recent history are evident at every turn, too. It's hard to step across a rough patch of road revealing a cluster of cobblestones without remembering the student uprising of 1968 and its famous freedom cry, "Beneath the cobblestones, the beach!" Plaques commemorating World War II and the names of those who "died for France" are prominently displayed on streets throughout the country, and in churches and squares in most provincial towns. In other words, finding a corner of the country that doesn't overflow with profound historical significance is next to impossible.

Tucked among the symbolic remnants of yore are emblems of modern France that hint at the sort of potential the future holds. In multicultural metropolises, thriving art scenes driven by the younger generations continue to propel France to the forefront of the avant-garde movement. Daring culinary experimentation is staking its claim

amid the old-guard, *très* traditional *cuisine française* in cutting-edge restaurants, and France continues to surprise the rest of the world with its realization of novel ideas that raise the quality of living, from public bicycle networks to public art and the creation of family-friendly green spaces.

Above all, the French themselves represent the spectacular convergence of old and new. Immigrants in traditional West African boubous and dashikis mingle at the markets with men in djellabas and women in hijabs, modern-day reminders of France's colonial past. A population in flux means more diversity: gay, straight, Muslim, Jewish, old, young, conservative, liberal. Active participation in politics, as evidenced by high voter turnout—the 2012 presidential election drew 80 percent of eligible voters, versus 57 percent in the U.S.—reflects an empowered population with a vested interest in creating a 21st-century society that meets the basic needs (and quite often the wants) of every citizen.

History

PREHISTORIC FRANCE

In 1940, four teenage boys spelunking in the bucolic town of Montignac, in the Dordogne Valley, accidentally discovered an ancient treasure trove that put France on the map as an important source of prehistoric riches. The cave paintings of Lascaux, dating back nearly 20,000 years to the upper Paleolithic period, feature larger-than-life-size renderings of horses, bison, bears, and other animals, hinting at the hunter-gatherer civilization's two preoccupations: sourcing an adequate food supply and avoiding becoming someone else's *déjeuner.*

Beyond providing clues about the eating habits of early humans, these vivid murals support the theory that Cro-Magnons were not just modern humankind's closest ancestors but possibly the earliest French aesthetes; decorative objets d'art ranging from primitive statuettes to more ornate pottery have been discovered in many French cave dwellings. Fashion before function? Indeed. Damage from human traffic prompted officials to close the Lascaux caves in the early 1960s, but an artificially re-created Lascaux II, complete with reproduction murals, opened 20 years later. It now welcomes thousands of visitors each year.

The early hunter-gatherer civilization that thrived throughout southern France, from the Dordogne to the Mediterranean, fed on the abundant plant and animal life that flourished along the waterways. *Homo sapiens* mastered the art of tool-making for hunting and ultimately evolved their tools to adapt to a more sedentary agricultural society that followed the hunter-gatherer epoch. It was during this period that *Canis familiaris*—hunter, protector, and friend—was domesticated in France, solidifying its status within the French family structure.

THE CELTS AND THE ROMANS

On the outskirts of the tiny seaside village of Carnac, in the far west region of Brittany, rows upon rows of lichen-covered stones rise up from the grassy fields, looking very much like an army of frozen soldiers standing sentinel over the windswept terrain.

These Celtic megaliths, known as menhirs, date from the Neolithic period. They are not as well known as their celebrated neighbors at Stonehenge, but their historical significance in France is on par with that of their British counterparts. How the heavy stones, each of which weighs tons, got there is an unsolved mystery—but the historical consensus is that they were arranged here by the early Celts, who settled in France beginning as early as 8000 BC. Debate continues about the stones' original purpose, but it was most likely related to astrological forecasting or religious worship.

Mysterious origins aside, modern France has embraced its ancient Celtic roots through music festivals, literature, and efforts to keep the Breton language alive. Even the fictional character Obélix, from the beloved comic book series *Asterix,* is a menhir sculptor by trade, often depicted lugging around one of the giant stones on his enormous back.

Skip forward a few millennia from the Neolithic period to the 1st century BC, when Julius Caesar and his massive army of 65,000 men marched into France with an eye on transforming the country into the newest corner of the Roman empire. In 49 BC, after nine years of near-constant battle, their conquest was complete. Their legacy was sealed with the introduction of a newly revamped centralized political system, the introduction of the Latin language, and an art-and-architecture overhaul that gave France a distinctly Roman aesthetic. In the southern city of Nimes, the "Rome of France," a well-preserved amphitheater hosts gladiator reenactments for enthralled crowds of tourists, and other relics—aqueducts, arches, forums—remind the contemporary population of the lasting influence of the Roman reign.

STORMING OF THE BASTILLE AND THE REVOLUTION

Long before a mob of angry men marched toward the Bastille prison on the infamous gray and dreary afternoon of July 14, 1789, discontent had been brewing among the French common classes. While the First Estate (nobility) and Second Estate (clergy) were essentially exempted from taxation, the Third Estate—the bulk of the population, made up of middle-class merchants and farming peasants—was left to pay the price for an overindulgent parade of kings, beginning with Louis XIV and ending with Louis XVI and his queen, Marie Antoinette.

As the country sank into bankruptcy, the commoners of the Third Estate felt the sting the sharpest. The price of bread, their primary food staple, had risen so high that the average family spent 80 percent of its income just to feed itself. Unemployment had reached frightening highs of nearly 50 percent, and the burden of heavy taxation showed no signs of ebbing. Meanwhile, Madame Deficit, as the spendthrift queen was nicknamed, continued to indulge in her excessive shopping habits while her king struggled to keep all the segments of French society in a state of relative calm.

When the alienated public learned that they would be denied voting privileges at a representational meeting of the Estates General, social discontent reached a fever pitch. Instead of sulking, the people formed a new national assembly and, when the king saw he had no hope of wielding his absolute power against the growing legions of disgruntled citizens, he struck a deal: We'll make it formal, he suggested, with a newly established National Assembly, wherein each Estate will have equal representation. Sovereignty of the people in, absolute monarchy out. This was the first revolutionary act. The storming of the part-prison, part-munitions warehouse known as the Bastille was next.

While the events of July 14 were more symbolic than truly revolutionary—there were only seven prisoners being held at the Bastille at the time, and the amount of arms collected was negligible—it is recognized as such because it returned power to the people after a long spell of rather tyrannical rule. Not long afterward, King Louis XVI relinquished his governing power, though he was left with the honorary title of King of the French. He held this new post until being tried and convicted of treason, then guillotined in front of a public audience in Paris's Place de la Révolution (now Place de la Concorde) in January 1793. His wife of 23 years, the reviled Marie Antoinette, was beheaded on the same spot nine months later.

Less than a month after the Bastille drama unfolded, a 17-point blueprint for a new constitution was drafted. The Declaration of the Rights of Man—a pastiche of ideas borrowed from the Declaration of Independence and the English Bill of Rights—proclaimed that the law exists to support and carry out the idea that every French citizen is born equal and with inalienable rights; that man is entitled to freedom of speech and freedom of religion; and that he is innocent until proven guilty. The 10-year revolutionary period was marked by brief changes in control, juggled in turns by the middle-class liberals, the radical revolutionaries, and the counterrevolutionaries whose champion, Napoléon Bonaparte, helped cement France's future as a global powerhouse. On September 21, 1792, the French royalty was abolished and, amid much celebration by the people, the First Republic, founded on the principles of *liberté, égalité,* and *fraternité,* was born.

© AURELIA D'ANDREA

Public châteaux abound in France, giving visitors a glimpse into the country's fascinating past.

NAPOLÉON BONAPARTE AND THE FIRST REPUBLIC

Even before he became emperor of France, in 1804, Napoléon Bonaparte reigned as a well-respected military leader in the French Revolution whose ambition for power matched his skill at war. Throughout his adventurous life, he earned a reputation as both a misogynist and a genius, but there's no debating the petite corporal's legacy as a reformer in the areas of education, religion, and government.

Before the monarchy was dissolved, education was a privilege extended primarily to the wealthy. Napoléon believed that developing a strong, unified population began with education—for boys in particular—and under his leadership, a uniform system of post-elementary schools called *lycées* was established. Through these education hubs, which most closely resemble North American high schools, a unified body of thought could be transmitted to generations of moldable minds. This is still the basis for today's highly centralized French public school system, which continues to preach loyalty to the republic and dictates which path a young student will follow later in life.

Subverting the dominant role of the Catholic church became an obsession for Napoléon I, who kickstarted this project at his coronation, which was completely devoid of any religious pomp and circumstance. He bucked tradition by denying Pope Pius VII the honor of crowning him the new emperor, but he wasn't anti-church. Napoléon saw the power that religion wielded in the lives of French citizens, and he merely wanted to seize control of that. With the signing of the Concordat, Napoléon got his wish, gaining the right to choose bishops and control land once belonging to the church.

Not long after being crowned emperor, Napoléon made one major restructuring move: The constitution, known as the Rights of Man, was transformed into the Napoleonic Code. For some, this presented a distinct advantage: Special privileges for the wealthy were effectively abolished, which was good for the 99 percent of the population that fell into the common class. Religious freedom was also guaranteed, as was the right to a trial before being sentenced for a crime. At the same time, the changes weakened status for others. Women and children were essentially deemed the property of their husbands and fathers, and women were stripped of the right to buy or sell property. The freedom of the press suffered, too, with Napoléon famously proclaiming that "if the press is not controlled, I shall not remain in power three days." But it's probably safe to say that Napoléon's good deeds outweighed the bad. The public works projects he commissioned—wide boulevards, shipping canals, and the famous Arc de Triomphe—are the modern-day symbolic reminders of the diminutive leader's vision of France.

FIRST AND SECOND WORLD WARS

When Archduke Franz Ferdinand was shot and killed by a Serbian assassin in Sarajevo on June 28, 1914, the Austro-Hungarian government didn't waste any time before declaring war on Serbia. Soon, one country after another was at war with its enemy, but World War I wasn't *officially* called until Austria's strongest ally, Germany, declared war on Russia.

As a Serbian ally, France was pulled into the fray, but there was no widespread public support for this war. Speaking on behalf of the pacifist community, French Socialist Party leader and lefty newspaper publisher Jean Jaurès called for peace, but he was silenced by a bullet fired by an overzealous pro-war French nationalist on July 31, just a month after war was declared. Four years later, on November 11, 1918, the signing of an armistice agreement put an end to the long, catastrophic conflict.

The final tally of France's dead reached nearly 1.4 million, and the number of wounded a staggering three million. Birthrates dropped, the national debt exploded, and a third French Republic was declared. It took years for France to recover, and when it did, it didn't get much of a breather before being thrust back into the cold embrace of another devastating world war.

No event in modern history has had as profound an effect on the French national psyche as World War II, especially in the way it has shaped French identity and solidified the necessity of social unity. In 1939, after Germany invaded Poland, France (a Polish ally) and Great Britain jointly declared war on Germany. By 1940, France had surrendered to the Germans, who began a humiliating occupation of France lasting four years.

On October 24, 1940, after the French had already surrendered to German forces, a new regime took control of the country, collaborating with the Nazis but still retaining some small level of autonomy. The Vichy Government, led by Marshall Philippe Pétain, was merely a French extension of the Nazi establishment, and the effects of this collaboration spawned its own post-traumatic stress disorder: the Vichy Syndrome.

Through the hardship of occupation and war, a sense of solidarity grew among the greater French community. Thousands of men and women joined together to form the French Resistance, and volunteer armies from North and West Africa sprang up to fight alongside the French army. Mini-armies began to sprout, too. The most significant of these independent brigades were the maquis, small groups of men and women who worked in concert with the resistance movement against German forces. Rather than be conscripted into the German workforce, they took to the hills with their guns and ammunition, battling long and hard in their signature Basque berets.

© ELISSA V. SHAW/WWW.THETRAVELINGPEAR.COM

Symbols of France's greatness, like the Arc de Triomphe, greet you at every turn in the capital.

In 1944—the same year French women earned the right to vote—the Allied Forces liberated France from Germany's iron grip. After a triumphant promenade down the Champs-Élysées, General Charles de Gaulle addressed his fellow citizens in a celebrated speech thanking them for their concerted efforts, closing with a fervent *"Vive la France!"*

The memory of occupation is never far from the modern French person's consciousness, yet there isn't a palpable sense of melancholy rooted in those memories either. *C'est la vie,* say the French, but let us not forget completely *les années noires.*

MODERN FRANCE

The Fourth Republic sprung up on the heels of World War II, with de Gaulle,

France's trusted and revered wartime chief, serving a brief stint as head of the provisional postwar government. He stepped down not long after his appointment but was elected president of France more than 10 years later, in 1958, marking the beginning of the fifth and current republic.

After a successful first term, he was reelected to the country's top post, which he served until retiring from politics in 1968, when his viewpoints were falling out of favor with the young postwar generation. The end of his political career was punctuated by a wave of social unrest throughout France, beginning at the universities and ending at the heart of the industrial sector: the factory.

In the spring of 1968, what started as a couple of small student protests against comingling of the sexes in student housing at the University of Nanterre and Paris's Sorbonne quickly morphed into something out of a fictional police drama: students and armed riot police going toe-to-toe on the streets; hundreds of young men and women being thrown to the ground and arrested; tear gas shot from cannons, the air so thick with haze that it felt like a battlefield in winter. Three days later, on May 6, more than 20,000 students, professors, and supporters marched through the streets of the capital to call attention to an overzealous police response to a simple, nonviolent campus protest—and again were met with baton-wielding riot police, tear gas, and aggressive arrests.

The great *manifestations* (political demonstrations) lasted for days, virtually halting all normal activity in Paris and its close suburbs. Brick throwing and Molotov cocktail tossing brought the city to a standstill. Students, borrowing ideas from anarchist ideology and using language tinged with Marxist rhetoric, demanded social change to benefit the people rather than the powers in charge.

Events took a turn for the worse when a 17-year-old high school student was killed by

Political activism takes many forms in France, including the ever-popular *manifestation*.

© AURELIA D'ANDREA

riot police in Paris's Latin Quarter on June 10; reverberations were felt acutely during the following weeks. Simultaneously, discontent that had been percolating in France's automobile factories reached a boiling point, prompting a frustrated labor force to engage in both sit-ins and walkouts. Workers at Renault, Citroën, and Peugeot voiced their own demands for a set minimum wage, salary increases, and reduced work hours. At one Peugeot factory, two workers were killed by police, prompting another wave of dissatisfaction to ripple through the country. Walkouts at banks, public transportation centers, department stores, and even hospitals paralyzed France. An estimated 10 million *grévists* (strikers) from Toulouse to Saint-Nazaire took to the streets in protest throughout May 1968, and made their thoughts about France's old-school, outdated political direction known in their cry: *"Adieu,* de Gaulle!"

The government reacted with tough-guy posturing, threatening an official state of emergency if things didn't simmer down. They finally did. The government met the demands of the automobile unions, offering a shorter work week, increased salaries, and an increased minimum wage, which the unions accepted, and students returned to their university lecture halls. Yet as daily life settled back into a state of normalcy, the days were numbered for de Gaulle's government. The aftereffects on French society were still being registered decades later, with political analysts referring to the period as "a revolution" with many of the same attributes of revolutions past. A body of rebel artwork—graffiti, protest posters—produced during the era survives in archival galleries as testament to the social upheaval.

In the decades that followed, France underwent several presidential shifts: Georges Pompidou ('69-'74), Valéry Giscard-d'Estaing ('74-'81), socialist François Mitterrand ('81-'95), and former prime minister and Paris mayor Jacques Chirac ('95-'07). Mitterrand's presidency marked the first time a leader on the political left had taken

© AURELIA D'ANDREA

The French president calls the Palais de l'Élysée home.

that office, and during his tenure he abolished the death penalty and initiated a moratorium on nuclear testing.

Chirac, who founded the center-right RPR (Rally for the Republic) party, led France with a more conservative vision, but he will probably always be remembered in North America for taking an active stand against the U.S. invasion of Iraq. (Remember "freedom fries"?) The French supported his opposition to the war, but his domestic policies left much to be desired among French voters, who ranked him the least popular president of the Fifth Republic in 2007.

Chirac's successor, former minister of the interior Nicolas Sarkozy, was voted in as the sixth president of the Fifth Republic on May 7, 2007. The son of a Greek-Jewish mother and a French-Hungarian father, the former lawyer promised to give France a good kick in the pants to bolster the economy, get tough on immigration, and reform the social welfare system. Part of his reform agenda included tightening access to foreign student visas, which he saw as an easy ticket for potential ne'er-do-wells to obtain residency status. At the end of his first and final term, faced with dismal popularity figures and an underperforming economy, Sarkozy was still able to count a handful of accomplishments, including passing a referendum that whittled down presidential term limits from a limitless quantity to two, easing taxation to encourage entrepreneurship, and extending the imposed 35-hour workweek to allow workers to put in as many as 48 hours each week without employers having to pay overtime benefits.

François Hollande, a member of the Parti Socialiste, was sworn in as the 24th president of the Republic on May 15, 2012. More than three years into his first (and, mostly likely, his last) term, Hollande has heard the deafening roar of enthusiasm that ushered him into the Palais de l'Élysée dwindle to a chirp, with just 19 percent of the population who voted for him happy with his performance after his first year in office. His approval rating more than doubled to 40 percent in the aftermath of the *Charlie Hebdo* tragedy, with the French public and political analysts applauding his swift solidarity-building actions, including his appearance alongside other world leaders at a rally drawing millions to Paris's Place de la République. There's no question that the ability to pull the country together in times of domestic strife is a quality the French value in their leaders, but the president's approval rating is likely to tumble back down to pre-crisis levels once emotions settle.

During his campaign, Hollande promised to bring "normalcy" to the country's highest post after five years of the arrogance and flash displayed by President Bling-Bling, as former President Nicolas Sarkozy was known. If he was derailed by the tabloid drama that plagued him midway through his first term, he hasn't let the public see it, plodding on with his ever-changing ideas on economic reform.

Government

As a representative democracy, the Republic of France is ruled by a president who is elected by the public and eligible for a maximum of two five-year terms. The president appoints a prime minister and a cabinet to help run the show, but there's no question who holds the top spot—and with it the larger burden of responsibility for ruling the country. In addition to ensuring that the constitution is upheld, the president enacts French laws, oversees the military, and has the ability to dissolve the French parliament. The president must also solicit and acquire the signature of his prime minister—Manuel Valls has held this position since 2014—for every official document he signs, with the exception of dissolving parliament.

On the legislative end, parliament is made up of a 577-member lower house called the National Assembly, whose representatives, called deputies, are elected directly by the public to five-year terms. The 321-member upper parliament, or senate, is voted in by an electoral college representing each of the 92 departments, overseas territories, and French citizens living abroad; each member serves six-year terms. Together, the two houses meet for nine-month sessions that begin in October and end in June, voting on issues as varied and contentious as whether to increase French military presence in Iraq to fight Islamic extremists (approved in January 2015) and reshape the boundaries of French departments and territories.

France has a multiparty system that spans the spectrum from the extreme right to the extreme left, but a few parties dominate, including former president Nicolas Sarkozy's UMP (Union pour un Mouvement Populaire); the left-leaning Socialists, the

© VILLE DE TOULOUSE, PATRICE NIN

Place du Capitole is the historic center of government in Toulouse.

Trierweiler's Titillating Tell-All

French president François Hollande's relationship with journalist Valérie Trierweiler was messy in private *long* before it got messy in public. Each has a history of marital infidelity, she having left her husband for Hollande, and Hollande having left *his* ex and mother of their four children, fellow politician Ségolène Royal, for Trierweiler. For many political observers, then, it was no surprise when Hollande's affair with the actress Julie Gayet came to light (this is France, after all), but not everyone saw Trierweiler's vengeful tell-all book coming.

Published in late 2014, mere months after the scandal broke, **Thank You For This Moment** has been described as a scorned woman's woe-is-me rant and an obsessive cry for help—which might explain why the French public pushed it straight to the top of the best-seller list.

Both Trierweiler and Hollande appear to have recovered from their respective traumas, and Trierweiler, at least, has come out on top, financially speaking. Besides the reported $1.5 million she's earned so far in book royalties, a film adaptation of her tell-all tale is now in the works.

far-right Front National, and communists and greens pick up the remaining seats in parliament. Regional elections are held every four years; departmental representatives and city council members are elected every six. Elections are always held on Sundays, which helps ensure a solid voter turnout. The French take the voting process quite seriously, and the rules governing campaign advertising and the prognostication of results on the day of the election are tightly controlled. If no candidate wins more than 50 percent of the vote in a presidential election, a runoff election is held.

Though President Hollande is eligible for reelection, a bid for a second term would likely end in failure. With record-low approval ratings plaguing his first term and a reputation for being wishy-washy on big topics dogging him, the public isn't likely to usher him in for another five years, and Hollande himself has gone on the record saying he won't run if he isn't successful in his attempts to lower unemployment figures.

Economy

After World War II, France boomeranged back into shape with unrivaled optimism and vitality. Those three fruitful decades even earned a special moniker: *Les Trente Glorieuses,* or the Glorious Thirty. Under de Gaulle's leadership, an initial five-year plan was instituted, launching public-works projects and creating a climate ripe for new industries. French factories were overhauled, churning out products for a postwar population that skyrocketed to numbers not seen for more than 100 years. This baby boom sparked a cycle of production and consumption that helped keep the economy moving. New motorways were built to keep up with the number of new cars on the roads, and by 1960, the French owned more automobiles than refrigerators.

The big shift from rural to urban that took place in the 1960s and '70s translated to overcrowding in the major cities. To meet the needs of this expanding population, giant housing developments mushroomed outside the clogged metropolises, and the *banlieue* was born. The sense of France in transition was palpable from Paris to Perpignan.

With the establishment of the European Union and the introduction of a single currency, trade barriers were torn down and competition increased, generating new revenue streams that flowed throughout Europe. But the latest global economic crisis has done a lot to destabilize the French economy and the faith of the French people with regard to their future economic security. The Sarkozy government passed a number of stimulus packages, but at the time of writing, France still faced high unemployment (10 percent), public debt (for which the government is trying to compensate by curtailing politicians' wine-fueled, expenses-paid lunches), and stagnant economic growth.

Since he was elected in 2012, François Hollande has made quite a few ripples in the political pool, mostly in the area of taxation; during his presidential campaign he earned notoriety for proposing 75 percent taxation on Paris's wealthiest citizens. Those whose feathers were most visibly ruffled by the idea included actor Gérard Depardieu, who vowed to quit France for good if this promise was made real. It wasn't long before the stocky thespian was offered Russian citizenship directly from Vladimir Putin, who delivered on his proposal. (Depardieu currently holds a Russian passport even though he's chosen to live in Belgium.) But reaction to the tax increase hasn't been so dramatic across the board. Everyday citizens understand that putting the tax burden on the rich to support needier citizens is a core Socialist value, and one of the reasons the disenfranchised masses elected Hollande in the first place. His promises to increase corporate taxes, lower the retirement age for those who've paid taxes for a minimum of 41 years, and introduce thousands of new jobs into the French fold are still a work in progress.

PEOPLE AND CULTURE

France is fertile ground for cultural stereotyping. Those tenacious mental renderings of a beret-clad, baguette-hugging, bicycle-riding population have been etched into our collective unconscious via film, fashion magazines, and yes, even holiday snapshots. More than anything, perhaps, the French are known 'round the world for their way of life, which focuses on maximizing sensual pleasures. The truth is, they do love their wining, dining, and song, but surprisingly, not a whole lot more than their European neighbors. Over the years, the French have abandoned some of their legendary habits (like smoking, which is being supplanted by "vaping," or electronic cigarette smoking) in favor of newer, healthier ones (gyms, yoga, and *le jogging*, among others).

Per capita wine consumption has plummeted by more than 50 percent since 1970, when the average Jacques quaffed 103.6 liters all on his own each year. The French do guzzle more booze than the Poles, the Dutch, or even tipplers in the UK, but Jacques still throws back fewer drinks than his Irish counterpart. The amount of bread consumed per day by the French has steadily dwindled over the last century (though you'd hardly know it by the ubiquity of the *boulangerie*), but the consumption of yogurt, brie, and crème fraîche has nearly doubled since the 1970s. Stroll down the dairy aisle at the nearest *hypermarché,* and you'll see just how dependent the French are upon products. But an entire culture can't be distilled into a food-and-wine caricature.

Like the country they inhabit, the French are complex, idiosyncratic, and a tad mysterious, which makes them all the more interesting. "French" has come to mean something different in the 21st century than in previous eras: it now means Algerian, Tunisian, Malian, Moroccan, Senegalese, and even American. Each of these immigrant populations has left its mark on the established culture, producing something of a multicultural patchwork that gives France its special flavor.

Ethnicity and Class

One of the ideas propelling the French Revolution was that the social playing field could—and should—be leveled. The revolution gave birth to a new constitution, the cornerstone of which was the Declaration of the Rights of Man. This critical rulebook defined the future of the Republic, setting forth the novel idea that all men are created equal. In subsequent decades, the leadership grappled with the inconsistencies of that basic assertion, particularly in light of the fact that slave ownership was alive and well in the French colonies and the role of women remained subordinate to that of men. The Declaration has been rewritten over the years (and renamed the Constitution), but its fundamental assertion remains a critical component of what it means to be French.

Today, the issue of national identity remains a hot topic throughout France, especially in this post-*Charlie Hebdo*, pre-election period. The right-wing, anti-immigrant political party, Front National (FN), is led by Marine Le Pen. Le Pen inherited her father and FN founder Jean-Marie's passion for a very, well, "French" version of France, and she has put the issue at the front and center of her party's platform ever since assuming leadership in 2011. The FN promulgates the idea that a more homogenous France can be restored with measures that include expulsion of certain populations—primarily Arab Muslims—and shoring up immigration laws to prevent what the party believes to be unbridled waves of unworthy immigrants destined to burden the state welfare system. The Front National motto "France for the French!" says it all.

In the 2014 European Parliament elections, the Front National won 25 percent of the French vote, and captured a grand total of 24 Parliamentary seats, suggesting a nationwide shift in political consciousness toward the far-right. However, the right-wing, anti-immigration sentiments actually have the largest stronghold in two specific regions, notably, along the eastern Riviera and the far northern reaches of France—areas that correspond with higher-than-average unemployment rates. In major cities where ethnic diversity is visible on the urban landscape, voting trends swayed toward the moderate, including Paris, Bordeaux, Rennes, and Toulouse.

In France, ethnicity and class aren't dinner-table conversation topics, but they are a palpable component of life in the bigger cities, and especially so in the capital. In Paris, for example, the arrondissement in which you live—and, more specifically, the Métro stop you're closest to—gives others a preliminary indication of your socioeconomic status and hint at your level of hipness. Tell someone, for example, that you live near Métro stop Victor Hugo in the 16th, and they might assume you're a work transfer from a multinational pharmaceutical company and your children attend private

Expat Experience: In Living Color

Name: Asia Chantal Aniwanou
Age: 29
Occupation: English language instructor, freelance strategic management consultant, and fashion designer
Hometown: San Bernardino, California
Current city: Paris, 8th

Asia Chantal Aniwanou moved to Paris in 2003. Her move was initiated by her father, originally from Benin (a French-speaking country), who wanted her to come to France to learn French. She loved it, and, more than a decade later, she's still here. Here, Asia shares her experience as an African American woman in Paris.

Describe the experience of coming to France to live for the first time.
I remember my first year in Paris going very well, meeting friends from all over who are still my friends today. However, growing up in a Seventh-Day Adventist Church–a religion characterized by its vegetarianism, and going to church on Saturday, among other things–I remember telling my mom about how France seemed like a country full of heathens who don't eat vegetables. Ha ha. Shortly after my arrival I became acquainted with the term *"laïcité"*–the separation of state and religion, and well, regarding food, it's become a big trend to eat organic.

Do you identify as a "person of color"?
Most definitely. I identify myself as a black American woman, or an African American woman, in every sense of the term as my dad is from Benin, born and bred, and my mom is American. Each one of these three "identities"–black, American, and woman–have eclipsed the other two at some point in time; however, these "identities" I'd like to think are only really identifying factors among people who don't know me. I do, however, re-member feeling "black" for the first time when I first arrived in Paris, in the sense that that was and is how I am perceived by others, before anything else.

Has your experience with identity changed with your move to France?
Yes, I have more or less grown up in Paris. I'd like to think of myself as a hybrid of an American and French upbringing, hopefully coalescing the strengths of the two.
    What is different following my move to France is the way that I approach identity. It is personal of course, but my identity is also representative of a whole–the black community.

school. Mention you live in Belleville, however, and you earn a bit of street cred, possibly coupled with the question, "So, do you work in the arts?"

If you're an American working in Strasbourg, the seat of European Parliament, people might assume you work in politics, and if you divulge that you live in Cannes, you might be mistaken for an independently wealthy entrepreneur (and lucky you if they guessed correctly!). Generally, where you live doesn't make or break your ability to integrate, though if you live in a neighborhood that's too edgy or cutting edge, your new friends may suggest a more neutral, *plus bourgeois* meeting place than the local café in your *quartier*.

So now a sense of responsibility has been incorporated into my way of being, in the sense that there is a duty to be a good example for those who have little to no interaction with black people, to defy negative stereotypes of black women or maybe even Americans.

You have visited many countries. When examining your experiences through the prism of race and ethnicity, how does France compare?
I just returned from Madrid. It felt like a breath of fresh air, and not only because the weather was amazing. For example, I felt like when I asked a question it was just me as a person asking the question. Perhaps it was the setting, but I went to a museum with a Spanish-speaking black friend who is currently living in Madrid. When he asked the security guard a question the interaction seemed like a simple interaction between two people. I know Paris is reputed for its bad customer service, so a black person and a white person might experience the same bad service, but a black person might interpret it as racism.

In Paris, the diversity is horizontal, whereas in London it is vertical. Horizontal diversity is described as "letting people in," while vertical diversity is about "letting people up." At the top of the social ladder in Paris there is very little racial diversity.

What do you love most about your life in France?
The thing I love the most about my life in France is that it's home. I always pronounce that phrase "I'm going home," referring to Paris. I love that it's the center of Europe, making so many other places accessible, and that so many people pass through Paris. You never get bored. Although at times it feels like you can hold Paris in the palm of your hand, there will always be something to discover. I also love that Paris feels like it has so much potential, that there are things that even I might be able to change, that it will change, for the better.

Describe a typical day in your life.
I work with French people on a daily basis. I give business English lessons in a very relaxed and fun environment, but it's fast-paced as I'm always running from one lesson to another. My days include a lot of reading and texting, and organizing of my days and evenings. I often get to meet up with friends for lunch or dinner because I'm working near or sometimes even for their companies. There is always some random event, a new restaurant to try, or new project to work on. After work, if I'm not out catching up with friends, then you can find me doing my second job, designing clothing (www.asiaanou. carbonmade.com).

Customs and Etiquette

One of the first things you'll notice about life in France is the formal politesse that pervades daily interactions. Neighbors greet each other with a cordial *bonjour* and *au revoir*, sales clerks will always refer to you as *madame, mademoiselle*, or *monsieur*, and most of the time, drivers will actually slow their Citroëns and Renaults down to a stop at crosswalks for pedestrians—which may or may not be a direct result of the Ministry of Transportation's efforts to establish a Day of Courtesy. More important than mimicking the French version of Miss Manners is to simply treat everyone you encounter with respect. Do as the locals do and be liberal with your pleases and thank-yous.

Remember to call out *"Bonjour!"* when entering boutiques, *boulangeries,* and mom-and-pop shops, and when boarding public transportation, step aside from the doorway to allow others to exit first. Offer your seat to the elderly, pregnant women, and parents juggling one or more children. The warm smile and gratitude you'll get in return are worth it, and you'll feel good about contributing to the social order.

LINE JUMPING

One annoying exception to the standard trend toward politeness is line jumping. It happens each and every day at Disneyland Paris, the local post office, and the *hyper-marché:* A silver-haired granny or twentysomething hipster will glide ahead of you, occasionally with cash in hand as if to announce that the transaction will be a swift one. Fussing about this is rarely worth the effort—and many young transgressors sport headphones, making communication practically impossible—though many expats dare to speak up once they've mastered the language, and find the act of defending one's territory to be a confidence builder!

PDAS (PUBLIC DISPLAYS OF ANGER)

The French are quirky, so it follows they would have quirky customs, many of which foreigners find simultaneously befuddling and charming. The tradition of the *bisou*—kissing on each cheek as a form of greeting—is so ingrained that kids in diapers are practically pros by the time they reach the Terrible Twos. The French are not entirely immune to the urge to blow a figurative gasket in horn-honking traffic—as you'll discover any day during rush hour in Paris—but road rage isn't practiced here the way it is in other countries. If you want to react in a manner befitting the locals, you'll learn to puff out your cheeks, throw up your hands, and say *"Oh là là là là"* like the rest, while leaving the shouting and aggressive driving maneuvers to the uncivilized world.

TIPPING

Many North Americans are pleased to discover that tipping is not mandatory nor even expected in France. Taxes are built into your bill, making anything extra you want to add purely icing on the cake for your server. Restaurant work is a profession with a modicum of respectability attached to it, and because waitstaff earn a living wage and are entitled to full benefits, they aren't motivated to perform any better in expectation of a monetary bonus. However, at cafés, it's customary to leave any small coins floating around in your pocket on the table or counter, and many diners—if they feel like it—will leave a euro or two after a restaurant or brasserie meal. These little acts of generosity are entirely voluntary, and you shouldn't feel obligated to leave anything beyond what's tallied up on your *addition.*

INVITATION ETIQUETTE

There are a few key rules of thumb to commit to memory, just in case you are lucky enough to earn a coveted invitation to a French person's home. Many expats report never having received a party invitation, let alone a dinner invite, even after years of working with someone or decades of daily chats with the next-door neighbor. This is less about you and more about the separation of public and private life—a cultural idiosyncrasy that is sacrosanct among the French. But when that elusive invitation comes, arrive at your host's home 15 minutes late, bring flowers instead of wine (they've already selected the wine to drink that evening), and don't be afraid of "awkward" silences; think of them as food-enjoyment pauses instead.

Food

Some tourists come to France almost exclusively for the food, and no wonder: They really know what they're doing here when it comes to creating culinary magic. Standard, everyday French fare tends to fall into the "honest" category—what you see is what you get, with the unique selling point of being exceptionally well-prepared and made with good-quality ingredients. Fancy, no; delicious, yes. From humble brasseries to revered Michelin-starred restaurants, menus tend to reflect seasonal produce while adhering to a perennial list of *plats principals* (main courses): *poulet rôti* (roast chicken), *steak frites* (steak and french fries), *steak tartare* (raw minced beef, sometimes mixed with egg and onion), *porc rôti* (pork roast), *salade de chèvre chaud* (green salad with slices of warm goat cheese), and a variety of pasta (*pâte*) dishes.

Many of the meats served in France fall into categories many North Americans would file under politically incorrect. If eating baby animals is your thing, you're going to love dining in France. Veal is a popular meat, as is lamb. Foie gras, which translates as "fatty liver," is a specialty of the southwestern region; it's created by forcing a tube down a duck's or a goose's throat and pumping in an excessive quantity of grain. This causes the liver to inflate at an artificially induced rate. Expect to see lots of foie gras around the winter holidays, when it is marketed as a celebratory treat. Horse meat can still be found on restaurant menus, and butchers who sell it can be identified by the horse head mounted above the door, but its overall appeal is waning, particularly in light of the 2013 horse meat scandal, which revealed that horses from research labs who'd been dosed with experimental drugs were later sold for human consumption to unsuspecting French consumers. That old culinary cliché, *escargots*, is alive and well, but oysters and mussels are more popular among French diners.

French fast food resembles its North American counterpart, though McDonald's offers wireless Internet, table service, and made-to-order burgers. A more traditional fast food is the crêpe.

© OFFICE DE TOURISME DE GRENOBLE

Apéro hour—that sweet spot before the evening meal that is centered on adult elixirs and light nibbles—is one of France's great pleasures.

Halles, or covered marketplaces, are a common feature in cities and towns across France.

In big cities and small towns, look for stands, both permanent and mobile, where you can order sweet crêpes topped with everything from sugar and lemon juice to a thick slather of Nutella, or savory versions topped with *oeuf* (egg), *fromage* (cheese), *jambon* (ham), or any combination thereof.

ALLERGIES AND DIETARY RESTRICTIONS

Vegetarians, vegans, and people with food allergies won't have trouble sourcing comestibles for home-cooked meals in Paris, but eating out can occasionally pose a challenge. Restaurants are still grappling to understand nonreligious dietary modifications or restrictions, and it's almost not worth explaining to them. Making food substitutions isn't part of the French dining-out style, so if you have a wheat allergy, you're better off ordering things you know to be wheat-free. That's getting much easier throughout France, where gluten sensitivities are becoming more commonplace and restaurants, *boulangeries,* and supermarkets are rising to the occasion and filling the voids with food that looks and tastes good. Look for the words *"sans gluten,"* and ask if you're feeling up for the challenge. Vegans will need to master *"sans fromage, s'il vous plaît"* (no cheese, please) when ordering pizza and sandwiches. Better still, seek out one of the hundreds of vegetarian restaurants throughout France, which range from macrobiotic to Indian and beyond. Natural-food chains such as Naturalia and La Vie Claire are worth a visit for anyone with a special diet who plans to cook at home or partake in *le pique-nique.*

Gender Roles

As quick as the leaders of the French Revolution and the authors of the Declaration of the Rights of Man were to espouse *liberté, égalité,* and *fraternité* as the founding principles of the new republic, they kind of forgot a big hunk of the population: women. Women's rights and the ideas supporting them didn't really enter mainstream French discourse until relatively recently. The country's earliest outspoken feminists and women's rights advocates—such as Olympe de Gouges, who also advocated on behalf of minorities—were simply silenced by the guillotine for their uppity ideas about equality. Those early rabble-rousers brought the idea of gender equality to the forefront in the 18th century, but women were not given the right to vote until 1944.

World War II altered the male-female dynamic in profound ways, for better and for worse. During wartime, traditional gender roles took a back seat as women and men crawled through the trenches side by side in the resistance effort, bearing arms with equal strength and commitment to both personal survival and the protection of their country. When the war ended, society fell into recovery mode, followed by a slow and steady rebuilding of the economy. The shift from rural to urban and from agriculture to industrialization fostered a new middle class. After decades of declining birthrates, the postwar message broadcast toward women from the church, the government, and the media echoed loud and clear: Stay home and have babies. Women listened; between 1943 and 1965, there were 14 million new additions to the French population. Thus began a return to the traditional family structure, with men reengaging in the burgeoning industrial workforce and women staying home, dutifully raising children, cooking meals in their shiny new kitchens, and otherwise presiding over the domestic realm.

In 1949, five years after women were given the right to vote, writer-philosopher Simone de Beauvoir penned *the* manifesto on French gender equality theory, *The Second Sex,* which is often credited for kick-starting the modern feminist movement in France. Her writing encouraged women to examine their role in society, to consider themselves as autonomous agents rather than merely inferior sidekicks to the dominant male power, and to "aspire to full membership of the human race." De Beauvoir's work heralded a new way of thinking that laid the groundwork for significant improvements for women's equality. In 1967, birth control was finally legalized in France, and the roaring baby boom slowed down considerably, beginning to rise again only in the early 21st century. This allowed women to consider their work potential outside the home.

In early 2014, France's then-Minister for Women's Rights, Najat Vallaud-Belkacem, introduced a gender-equality bill to bring parity between the sexes in the workplace and beyond. After much debate, the bill passed, giving women easier access to abortion and increasing paid family leave for those who decide to have children. Unpaid parental leave for fathers was also increased from 6 months to 12, though it is usually the mother who stays home with the newborns.

Even before the bill passed, women were entitled to up to four months of paid, federally mandated maternity leave (in contrast, employers in the U.S. are not required by law to offer paid leave) to postnatal "vaginal rejuvenation therapy." (Really.) Those

Expat Experience: Gay Paree

Name: Steve Kocheran-Letrouit
Age: 64
Occupation: History teacher at a private international high school
Hometown: San Diego, California
Current city: Paris, 3rd

In his own words: In 2004, I had reached the point where teaching was no longer fun, so I decided to take an early retirement to live my dream of residing in Paris. That same year I met my husband, Eric, which added an extra incentive to make the move. We were PACSed (joined in a state-recognized civil union) in 2008, which helped with my paperwork and allowed me to work at any kind of job in France. No limits. It also gave me access to social security. We were married in the U.S. in 2013.

I have never experienced homophobia personally, either in Paris or in the small villages we have visited throughout France. Acceptance and validation are the norm. Once same-sex marriage was approved here, the religious extremists, who came out of the woodwork, returned to their homes and have been quiet ever since. This differs from the United States because every day there is some bigoted politician or religious leader spewing hatred against the LGBT community.

Being gay is really a non-issue for me. Our friends here, as well as Eric's family, have accepted and validated our marriage. Congratulations and love arrived in abundance. It was such a great feeling. Even at my favorite café, the staff and owner know I'm gay and celebrated my marriage. I truly wish I could say the same thing about being gay in the United States.

The gay scene is pretty much the same no matter where you are. There are specific bars for whatever your interests are. There are cliques just as there are in the United States. It is just as difficult to meet someone for a long-term relationship. This is based on conversations with my single gay friends. Eric and I are not into the "gay scene," so to speak. We love to go to the Marais for dinner and drinks, but really avoid the bars. We've been there, done that.

I firmly believe that when you live your dream, the universe blesses you with abundance. I did just that. The moment I knew it was time, everything fell into place. It has been and continues to be a fulfilling, abundant life. Contentment. I love that word because is describes me and my life with my husband.

perks aside, women in France still have a long way to go before they reach true equality. Most medical school graduates are female but the majority of hospital heads are male, and women still earn 75 *centimes* for every euro a man earns. Though they invest as many hours working outside the home as men do, women carry the heavier burden in the domestic sphere. Women are still the primary caregivers for children and devote a larger chunk of time to housekeeping, grocery shopping, and other household chores.

GAY AND LESBIAN CULTURE

Paris in the early years of the 20th century attracted a wild and woolly lot of characters who defined themselves as "artists." Many of them also called themselves "gay." Even though the Assemblée Nationale didn't vote to decriminalize homosexuality until 1982, the closet door swung wide open throughout those heady Lost Generation years, and artists, intellectuals, and everyday folk resisted the urge to hide their sexuality from the judgmental eyes of the world. Gertrude Stein and her longtime partner, Alice B. Toklas, lived out and proud in Paris's Left Bank, as did Sylvia Beach, the respected proprietor of landmark bookstore Shakespeare & Company. Oscar Wilde, the great Irish writer entombed beneath a majestic headstone in Paris's touristy Père-Lachaise Cemetery, sought sanctuary in France after a horrible episode in which he was imprisoned in England for the crime of being gay. World War II was a dark era for gays and lesbians, who were shipped off with Jews, gypsies, and other "deviants" to concentration camps. Thankfully, a lot has changed since then.

In 1999, the Assemblée Nationale passed a law to protect individuals in civil unions and extended this coverage to gay men and lesbians. PACS (Pacte Civile de Solidarité) allows gays and straights alike to register their partnerships and share in some of the social benefits and protections extended to married heterosexual couples. The PACS union is so popular that it's well on its way to eclipsing traditional marriage as the bond uniting most straight couples. In 2009, more than 170,000 French couples were "PACSed." In that same year, 200,000 couples married. In theory, based on the French constitution, France only recognizes *citoyens;* special rights are not accorded to these citizens with relation to their gender, sexual orientation, and religious preference.

In May 2013, President Hollande kept one of his campaign promises and signed into a law a measure making it legal for same-sex couples not just to marry, but adopt children together, too. Believers in true *egalité* cheered the long-overdue gesture, while French conservatives did everything they could to halt the law's passage, with legal maneuvering and noisy nationwide protests. Still, polls report that 60 percent of the population stands in support of gay marriage, and in the first six months after the law was signed, more than 7,000 same-sex couples tied the knot throughout l'Hexagone.

Each June, gay pride festivals throughout France draw hundreds of thousands of participants and spectators. In Paris, former mayor Bertrand Delanoë usually makes an appearance at the rainbow-heavy funfest as it weaves through the city, blasting techno music to enthusiastic crowds, and the city's homosexual hub, the Marais, begins to resemble a gay Disneyland in all the best ways. One way to get a sense of French ideas on homosexuality is by watching films with gay themes. Some of the most interesting, entertaining, and popular among the international crowd are *Blue Is the Warmest Color, Côte d'Azur, Défense d'Aimer, Donne-moi la Main, Do Not Disturb, Drôle de Félix, Entre Nous, French Twist, Like a Brother, Ma Vie en Rose, Presque Rien, Tomboy,* and *La Vie d'Adèle.*

Religion

When the Romans conquered Gaul, in 58 BC, they claimed their territory using an age-old approach: religious conversion. The tactic worked. More than 2,000 years later, Roman Catholicism is still the most widely claimed religious group in France, though it's difficult to say for sure; in 1872, the government banned the gathering of both religion- and ethnicity-related statistics. All information collected today is via voluntary polls. Recent figures point to the not-so-surprising fact that Roman Catholics are the reigning religious group, claiming 85 percent of the population, though most are largely thought to be nonpracticing, with a mere 12 percent attending mass on a regular basis. Muslims, Protestants, and Jews split the remaining 15 percent, and for the most part, everyone coexists peacefully.

THE JEWISH COMMUNITY

France is home to the largest Jewish population in all of Europe, with more than 500,000. Nearly two-thirds of those live in Paris, while smaller Jewish communities thrive in Marseille, Lyon, Toulouse, and Strasbourg. During the 1950s and '60s, the population grew when more than 200,000 Sephardic Jews from North Africa abandoned their homes in an extended exodus kickstarted by the Six-Day War. Settling primarily in the French capital, where a solid Jewish infrastructure including synagogues, *cacher* (kosher) restaurants, and Hebrew schools was already in place, they formed new communities and assimilated into existing ones. Jewish artists Amedeo Modigliani and Marc Chagall came to France to work and live, and their creations are celebrated in art institutions nationwide, including the Musée d'Orsay and the Paris Musée d'Art Moderne.

Throughout France's larger cities, Jewish neighborhoods tend to spring up around synagogues. In Paris, there are more than a dozen; besides the well-known Jewish quarter in the Marais, where there are multiple synagogues, there are also sizeable communities around the Grande Synagogue in the 9th, Beth Yacov in the 19th, and Kehilat Gesher in the 17th. In these neighborhoods you'll find kosher restaurants, delis, bakeries, and even kosher chocolatiers. On Saturdays in Jewish quarters in cities across France, expect to see bearded men in tall black hats and starched white shirts and plenty of men of all ages sporting yarmulkes.

THE MUSLIM COMMUNITY

France also houses Europe's largest population of Muslims—more than 5 million, a full eight percent of the population. In big cities such as Paris, Marseille, and Lyon, Arabic fills the air, and street scenes are alive with women in hijabs, bustling halal butcher shops, and kebab joints. Fast-food chains—notably Quick Burger, the French equivalent of Burger King—offer halal hamburgers to observant Muslims, to the chagrin of some political groups who see expanding menus as "preferential kowtowing." This is one of the selling points used by the Front National to promote its anti-immigration platform, suggesting that specialized menus create a sort of divide that isn't in line with "French values," in particular the separation of church and state, known in France as *laïcité.* Despite these challenges, hundreds of mosques throughout the country help solidify a sense of community, and they often serve as all-in-one centers with hammams, daycare, and meals.

As with Paris's Jewish communities, Muslim communities often congregate around places of worship. More than a dozen mosques, *masjids,* and Islamic cultural centers can be found within Paris's city limits, but the most popular are the Grande Mosquée in the 5th, the Mosquée Al-Fath in the 18th, and Mosquée Abou Ayou al Ansari in the 11th. In these neighborhoods and others in cities with large Muslim populations, including Strasbourg, Lille, and Roubaix, expect to see halal restaurants, Islamic bookstores, and Arab-style *salons du thé,* as well as men and women dressed in traditional Islamic clothing.

THE ROMAN-CATHOLIC TRADITION

At major Christian holidays, such as Christmas and Easter, you'll be reminded that this country is still Roman Catholic at heart. Christmas is celebrated with an endless parade of fanfare: Town halls are kitted out with giant *sapins de Noël;* the *rues* and boulevards are strung with colorful lights; shops bust out the bows, balls, and flocking spray and go to town. Best of all, the *boulangeries* and *pâtisseries* churn out seasonal treats that people of all religious persuasions enjoy. The *bûche de Noël,* a cake baked in the shape of a log, is often decorated with tiny wintertime scenes, and the *galette des rois,* a frangipane-filled pastry eaten in celebration of Epiphany, comes with a hidden trinket and a paper crown that lets one lucky indulger be king or queen for the day.

© NITO500/123RF.COM

Sacré Coeur basilica in Paris is a symbol of France's Roman Catholic tradition.

The Arts

The earliest creative expression in France can be found in the now famous caves in the verdant river valleys of southern France. The art of the *Homo sapiens* zeroed in on the important issues of the day: food, shelter, and threats to safety. Rendered in rudimentary paints and chalks, these primitive pictures offer a glimpse of the more refined art to come. Millennia later, France has transformed into a cultural nirvana, and Paris is its artistic epicenter. Fine arts, architecture, music, sculpture, and literature are just some of the arenas in which France boasts a disarming number of highly skilled denizens. So beloved are these contributors to the artistic canon that streets, hospitals, and schools throughout the country bear their names: Voltaire, Balzac, Renoir, and even Gainsbourg among them.

To say that the French place an extremely high value on the arts would be a grave understatement. In this country of 65 million, 30,000 are registered "dramatic artists" and dancers, and an equal number are registered musicians. The country boasts 1,200 museums, 288 yearly arts-related festivals, and an annual arts-and-culture budget that tops €7 billion. This investment clearly pays off: Every year, millions of visitors come to Paris to ogle the Mona Lisa, peer up at la Tour Eiffel, and take in a feathers-and-sequins show at the Moulin Rouge, pumping in billions of dollars to the local economy. (Equally impressive numbers visit the popular museums in Antibes, Bordeaux, Lyon, Nice, Grenoble, Pau, and Strasbourg.) The government has even created a special dole just to support the new generation of artists, who are guaranteed a living wage should they find themselves unable to find work in their craft.

IMPRESSIONISM

France has given birth to numerous art movements, but none whose global impact has been as profound as Impressionism. It began with Édouard Manet. After being turned away from the great Paris salons (sponsored by the government-run École des Beaux Arts) in the late 19th century for expressing ideas on canvas that were too avant-garde and nonconformist, Manet rallied together a few other rejected painters eager to show their work to an interested audience. Together, he and his artistic consorts developed an alternative salon featuring work focused on everyday life, much as their Cro-Magnon predecessors had: on the streets, in the home, at lively cafés, at work in the fields, and at play on the *plage*. The movement began in Paris and spread south to Provence, where Auguste Renoir and Paul Cézanne lived and painted.

The work of Renoir, Camille Pissarro, Edgar Degas, and Cézanne evoke a specific vision of France, one where distinctive brushstrokes and reflected light conspire to dazzle the eye. Considering the era, the movement was very progressive—and it was also short-lived, petering out in just 10 years—paving the way for the post-Impressionists. Always in high demand, Impressionist paintings from the great French museums are often loaned to art institutions outside of France, but the Musée d'Orsay's permanent exhibit is a perennial go-to for a broad cross section of art lovers.

ARCHITECTURE

Walk down any street in France, and you'll undoubtedly encounter the past. Maybe it's one of those troglodyte houses built into a hillside in the Loire Valley, its chimney jutting out from an earthen roof; or a medieval château whose towers cast tall shadows over an empty moat now harboring a lush green lawn. In Paris, it's said, you're never more than 10 paces from a view onto that iconic monolith, la Tour Eiffel, but it's the broad avenues hemmed by manicured trees and tidy apartment buildings that your gaze will surely settle on time and again. The City of Light wasn't always the bright and airy *ville* it is today; those beautiful sand-colored buildings, with their giant, wooden double doors and ornate metal balconies festooned with potted geraniums, are the work of baron Georges-Eugène Haussmann, a 19th-century architect and urban planner commissioned by Napoléon III to revamp Paris's cramped, unsanitary alleyways and transform them into broad, beautiful boulevards.

Beginning in 1852, Haussmann took to his task of modernizing Paris and making it easier for the bourgeois class to partake in their preferred pastime: strolling. In Haussmann's distinctive style, which made great use of straight lines, the streets were widened, groomed parks were constructed, functional squares were designed and built, and those sometimes confusing star-shaped roundabouts were put in place. This regimented style was fraught with design restrictions that defined the height, width, pitch, and color of all new construction. In 1870, Haussmann completed his work of transforming the Paris of the past into the Paris of the future. Today, the architects behind the design are acknowledged for their work by an engraved stamp on the front of many private and public buildings throughout the capital.

Charles-Édouard Jeanneret, better known as Le Corbusier, is Swiss by birth, but he is easily France's second-best-known architect. Like Haussmann, he was engaged by

© ELISSA V. SHAW/WWW.THETRAVELINGPEAR.COM

The French place an extremely high value on the arts.

© BERGERAC TOURISME

The mythic Cyrano is the unofficial patron saint of Bergerac.

the government to design aesthetically pleasing urban housing that would offer function and design at once. Many of his ideas didn't make the cut—there are, for instance, no 60-story tower blocks in central Paris, as he proposed—but the structures that did come to life have stood the test of time, including the boxy, beehive-like Maison du Fada in Marseille and the Notre-Dame-du-Haut chapel in Ronchamp. Simultaneously loved and loathed for his modern, hard-edged style, Le Corbusier is credited with ushering in the prevailing aesthetic of contemporary French design.

Throughout France, architecture is taking a turn toward the modern. France especially loves Frank Gehry, whose flashy, übercontemporary glass-and-steel Fondation Louis Vuitton building made its debut in late 2014 in Paris's bois du Boulogne, though less glamourous but equally modern urban housing developments are popping up in cities throughout l'Hexagone. If you're interested in environmentally friendly design and have an eye on energy conservation, you're in luck: This combination represents the next big thing in French urban planning.

LITERATURE

Their reputations are so heady and their work so iconic they need only one name to be recognized: Balzac, Camus, Colette, Flaubert, Molière, Proust, Zola. France's premier contribution to the arts might very well be its body of literature, even if the majority of Americans have never read from it. The heyday of French literature peaked in the 19th century, when Jules Verne pumped out his sci-fi body of work and Flaubert titillated readers (and irked early censors) with *Madame Bovary.* French students begin studying the great writers in elementary school and have read many of the classics by the time they finish *lycée.*

French literature has had an interesting cultural impact on the rest of the world as well: Alexandre Dumas's stories have been made into ballets—*The Nutcracker,* for starters—and his *Trois Mousquetaires* was co-opted by Disney (and morphed into Mousketeers, if you recall), as was Victor Hugo's famous *Hunchback of Notre-Dame.* Hugo is also responsible for one of Broadway's longest-running musicals, *Les Misérables,* which was made into an Academy Award-winning feature film in 2012.

Jean-Paul Sartre won the Nobel Prize in Literature in 1964 but famously declined the honor, saying that were he to accept it, he would be in some sense beholden to the awarding institution and thus compromising his artistic integrity—a risk that he believed no writer should feel compelled to experience. Writers who have happily

Escape Artists

For more than a century, North Americans have migrated to France in search of creative freedom, heady inspiration, adventure tinged with a seductive accent, and a slice of that celebrated *joie de vivre*. It's no wonder that writers, musicians, actors, and especially painters are drawn to this country where access to the arts is seen as a right rather than a privilege, and creative types are appreciated for their ability to bring beauty and food for thought to the public table. From the Lost Generation to Gen Y, meet some of the daring dreamers who shipped off across the pond to hone their craft in l'Hexagone.

- Josephine Baker
- James Baldwin
- Art Buchwald
- Belinda Carlisle
- Sofia Coppola
- R. Crumb
- Johnny Depp
- John Dos Passos
- Feist
- F. Scott Fitzgerald
- Adam Gopnik
- Ernest Hemingway
- Langston Hughes
- Washington Irving
- Henry James
- Scarlett Johansson
- Diane Johnson

- Aline Kominsky
- Carson McCullers
- Henry Miller
- Jim Morrison
- Charlie Parker
- Cole Porter
- Natalie Portman
- Ezra Pound
- Man Ray
- Molly Ringwald
- Jean Seberg
- David Sedaris
- Nina Simone
- Gertrude Stein
- Alice B. Toklas
- Tina Turner
- Edith Wharton

accepted the award include Algeria-born Albert Camus, who won the prize in 1957 for his contributions to the field of modern literature.

Modern French writers who have also cracked the global literary scene include Faïza Guène, whose 2006 book *Kiffe Kiffe Demain* (*Kiffe Kiffe Tomorrow*), about life in a contemporary suburban housing project, has been translated into more than 20 languages, and Michel Houellebecq, whose literary offering *Soumission* tells the tale of a new France under the leadership of a Muslim president.

FASHION

For the past 100 years, France and fashion have been synonymous. Blame Gabrielle "Coco" Chanel, who began her career as a milliner; she put Paris on the fashion map with her signature tweed jacket that combined a masculine edge with a ribbon-trimmed feminine sensibility. A century later, the Chanel brand—and the cut of that jacket—is still a coveted symbol of high style. In the 1950s, Christian Dior reigned over the glamorous world of couture party dresses, ball gowns, and stylish prêt-à-porter suits, giving French women a fashion prototype to emulate (or at least to admire on the pages of fashion magazines). In the 1960s, the house of Courrèges altered the fashion landscape with an ultramod aesthetic that married bright white dress suits with shiny patent boots that hinted at fashion's space-age potential.

When revered couturier Christian Dior died in 1957, a very young Yves Saint Laurent took over as head designer at the fashion house, giving the brand a modern makeover. In the '70s, the bespectacled designer revolutionized the sartorial scene with Le Smoking—a structured, menswear-inspired jacket that became one of the harbingers of the gender-neutral fashions of later decades. Saint Laurent's designs have been showcased in popular exhibitions in both French and American museums, and several years after his death, he remains one of France's most beloved fashion icons.

Chanel, Dior, Céline, and Chloé still attract the world's deep-pocketed pretty people to high-end boutiques on Paris's avenue Montaigne and beyond. But as if the incessant television commercials don't give it away, designer perfumes are reeling in the most cash for French fashion houses, to the tune of billions of dollars each year. Also making a comeback after a long lull in inspiration is Jean Paul Gaultier, whose glam Spring 2014 couture shows sparkled with a femininity inspired by butterflies. The hottest name in contemporary French fashion, however, is Isabel Marant. Marant's chic, urban, gender-neutral garments are coveted by Parisian women of all ages, and spawn knock-offs (remember the colorful wedge-heeled sneaker?) each season.

Sports

When France lost to Germany 0-1 in the quarterfinals of the FIFA World Cup games in Brazil in the summer of 2014, the mood among French sports fans turned somber. Instead of screaming in anger at the television or sharing conciliatory slaps on the back with fellow sports fans packed inside cafés and brasseries, the French sulked in silence before the big screens, staring into their pints of Pelforth with a mixture of shame and denial.

Some analysts called the sporty comedown a metaphor for the social problems plaguing French society: Both, they say, are mired in ego, strained relations among minorities, and the refusal to accept blame for failure. To others, football—what Americans refer to as soccer—is just a game. Everyone in France, however, has some sort of opinion on the country's most popular sport. Football is played in minor and major leagues throughout the country, packing stadiums and luring multiple generations of fans. When the home team wins, packed stadiums vibrate with the stomping of feet, waving of flags, and the chanting of thousands of vociferous spectators.

© JACQUES LÉONE/LYON TOURISME ET CONGRÈS

In urban centers and small villages alike, sports are a vital component of French life.

Paris's Parc des Princes and Saint-Denis's Stade de Paris—with more than 100,000 seats between them—play host to the most international football games. If there's one place you don't want to be stuck, it's in your car anywhere near the choked arteries around these arenas, especially if the home team has lost. For an authentic local experience, regional stadiums in smaller cities and towns are the places to be to see a match. Expect up-close views of the action that allow you to see the subtle nuances of the game and to feel part of the local community every weekend, year-round (or almost year-round—like the rest of the country, football takes a two-month summer holiday).

Like football, France's cycling culture reaches back to the 1800s, when velodromes drew crowds (Ernest Hemingway was a fan) for dizzying races that sometimes lasted six days, ending for some fatigued riders in a bloody pile on the wooden racetrack. (The historic La Cipale velodrome in Paris's Bois de Vincennes is still open to the public.) It's the sexy Tour de France, though, that has earned the most international attention when it comes to the two-wheeled sport. Every July since 1903, racers from around the world have pedaled a circuit that takes them up and over some of the country's tallest peaks, down through picturesque medieval villages, and finally up the Champs-Élysées for a final lap before hundreds of thousands of whistling, cheering, clapping fans.

Other sporting events include rugby, which is big in Toulouse, and the very popular French Open tennis tournament. Everyday sports in towns across France lean toward the more relaxed sort, including *pétanque*—a favorite among the silver-hair set, who play year-round in parks everywhere—swimming in the local pool, and inline skating.

PLANNING YOUR FACT-FINDING TRIP

It's easy to fall in love with the surface image of France, but there's only one way to find out whether the French personality meshes with yours and whether there's hope for a long-term relationship, and that's to come visit and stay awhile. Besides exploring the celebrated corners of the capital and its less flashy residential neighborhoods, a trip to the suburbs and provincial corners of the country are a true scout's mustn't-miss list. How else will you be able to make an educated decision about where to settle down? Branching out enables you to attune yourself to the country's various rhythms before making a commitment.

The sedate vibe of rural France is kilometers away from the urban bustle, but each offers something special worth checking out. The most important part of your reconnaissance mission is remembering to veer off the tourist trail: Skip the hotel directly beside the Eiffel Tower and instead consider parking yourself at a private apartment rental in a neighborhood in a less touristy arrondissement. When exploring the suburbs, you'll benefit by skipping the budget chain hotels near the freeway and looking for accommodations (independent or otherwise) in the center of each town you're considering. Give yourself at least a few days to *really* get to a know a place: when and

© AURELIA D'ANDREA

where the nearest outdoor market is held, which of the cafés feels most like home and which *boulangerie* bakes the best baguettes, and who your future neighbors will be.

Bring your sense of adventure, your best manners, and your French phrasebook, and don't be afraid to ask questions—even if you don't always understand the responses. Reaching out will let the locals know you've got nothing to hide, and will give you the opportunity to see what the regional mores and attitudes are toward foreigners. Eat out, take public transport, visit the post office, explore the area on foot, and imagine what life will be like in your adopted hometown.

Preparing to Leave

France is a large country, but the (relatively) fast and efficient train system means no major hub is more than a five-hour journey away. If you'll be venturing into smaller towns not connected by rail service, it's worth booking a rental car in advance to take you off the beaten path and into those quaint pockets tucked into valleys and on hilltops. You'll find rental-car agencies at train stations—but, like much of France, they take a midday break for lunch, so try to schedule your arrival time before noon or after 2pm. Cheapie air companies have made the move into France as well, so if your time—and the amount of baggage you're carrying—is limited, consider Easy Jet, Ryanair, and other low-cost carriers. Advance bookings can turn up some pretty amazing deals, like the yes-it's-really-true €10 flights to the UK and elsewhere in mainland Europe.

Your fact-finding mission is different from a standard vacation because you're looking not just to enjoy yourself and see the sights, but to make an assessment that has the potential to alter the course of your life for the better. The important thing to remember, besides to have fun, is to carry your critical eye with you on your journey. Consider each place you visit with a dash of realism. How close are amenities? Are there parks nearby for walking the dog? What about schools and libraries? Where is the closest transportation stop, and will you mind the walk to the bus or Métro when it's January and snow blankets the cobblestones?

The Internet is a traveler's best friend and can support you on your living-abroad adventure before you've even hopped the plane for Paris. Begin by seeking out blogs written by locals to get an insider's perspective that's tailored to your situation. Are you moving with kids? With a major food allergy? With your four cats? Odds are good that someone before you has done it already, and has survived long enough to write about it. Find them online and get acquainted—you might even strike up a friendship if you take the initiative and send a note of introduction. Also use the Internet to check the pre-departure weather forecast so you know whether to pack an *imperméable* in addition to your *parapluie*. And if you're ready to practice your French, it couldn't hurt to see if any transit strikes are in the cards. The website www.francegreve.com will keep you up to date.

Guidebooks are indispensable travel companions that will point you in the direction of a dependable hotel, restaurant, or sightseeing spot without your having to weed through the never-ending possibilities that the Internet is so good at providing. If traveling light is a major concern, pack your e-reader and buy the digital version of your favorite guide. Having maps, language guides, and tourist information in one handy place can simplify the travel process and offer a sense of security.

As you narrow down the areas to explore and consider your needs, wants, and dreams, you might find it helpful to rank your wish list in terms of importance. What comes first: career, school, recreation, or family? If you're moving without a job and finding work right away is imperative, Paris proper is the obvious choice for the sheer variety and number of employment opportunities. Ditto for rental housing. Crave access to wide-open green spaces, unbridled sunshine, and cringe at the thought of tourists asking you for directions? The provinces might be more to your liking. And if you're a retiree on a limited budget, you'll want to consider areas where housing is affordable but where you'll still have access to cultural amenities—*and* a decent *boulangerie.* Be realistic as you begin your search, but don't deny your dreams. A happy medium does exist!

WHAT TO BRING
Passport

Before you book your travel plans, make sure your passport is up to date, and ideally valid for six months beyond your expected return date. Make two copies of the first few pages of your passport, then leave one with a trusted friend or relative back home and stick the other in your travel bag. If your passport is lost or stolen, you'll be able to take a copy to the American embassy in Paris and have a new passport issued, usually within 24 hours. While you need to carry your passport with you, if you're staying in France for fewer than 90 days, you won't need a long-stay visa. Keep in mind that many travelers bend the rules and stay longer than 90 days without any problems, but it's always best to err on the side of the law and play by the rules, lest you are sent home with a mysterious red mark scribbled into your passport.

Money and Credit Cards

At the time of writing, the **exchange rate** is €1 = $1.14. **Credit** and **ATM cards** are widely accepted in France; a sticker system, usually posted on the doors or windows of businesses, indicates exactly which cards you can use at a specific establishment. Some shops—most often small grocery stores and many restaurants—have minimum-purchase requirements that hover around €10 or €15, in which case a notice of some sort will be posted at the register or another easily visible spot. There is one major difference between U.S. credit cards and French ones, and that's the *puce.* Embedded inside French cards (and most European credit cards) is a tiny microchip encrypted with a variety of data. These cards are known within the banking industry as EMV (short for Europay, MasterCard, and Visa) cards and they generally require a pin code. Unlike American cards that are fitted with a magnetic strip, the EMV cards are much more fraud-proof. Some companies, including American Express and Discover, are already rolling out EMV cards in the U.S. It's worth checking with your bank to see if a *puce* card is possible; if you'll be traveling with a non-EMV credit card, you may not be able to purchase Métro tickets from every station's vending machines or rent a Vélib' bike from a kiosk (though you can still do this online before you leave). But as long as the credit card reader is equipped with a swipe feature (you may need to assist the person behind the counter with this—it's not every day they see a non-European card), your card will be readable and therefore usable. Keep in mind that *boulangeries* and small mom-and-pop shops still aren't outfitted with any kind of sophisticated apparatus, so it's wise to always carry at least €10 in change at all times for those little necessities, like your morning *café* and *pain au chocolat.*

Before you ship off, check in with the banks that issue your credit and debit cards to let them know you'll be traveling and to expect foreign transactions to appear in their computer systems. If you forget to do this, you may find your account suspended after the first foreign purchase, and undoing this damage from a continent away can be a frustrating challenge. If you forget to make the call in advance of your trip, do so the moment your memory is jogged. Some banks and credit card companies charge a commission or a one-time transaction fee for every foreign purchase or cash withdrawal. These 2- and 3-percent charges on purchases and as much as $10 in fees for each withdrawal are annoying and can add up, so your best bet is to withdraw the maximum amount of cash possible from an ATM to use for your purchases or carry cards that don't penalize you for foreign purchases. If your bank account has a per-day withdrawal limit, ask about increasing it before you leave.

ATMs (*distributeurs*) are ubiquitous throughout France in cities big and small. Cash-back on purchases isn't commonplace here, but you will nearly always find a cash machine at the post office (la Poste) when all else fails and cards aren't accepted at those rare exceptional destinations.

Driver's Permits

International driver's permits are not required by car-rental agencies in France, but it can't hurt to have one just in case you need an extra piece of ID, or if the rules suddenly change overnight (which is altogether possible), or if you're stopped by the *police routière* and want to show what a good citizen you are by having an "official" document translated into French. An International Driving Permit (IDP) is valid for one year and can be purchased by licensed drivers 18 years of age and older at AAA offices, where they cost $15. The forms are available online at www.aaa.com, and can't be purchased more than six months before your departure. Another option is to secure your permit through one of many private companies acting as intermediary agents, and that generally charge twice as much as AAA. You'll need two passport-size photos and your U.S. driver's license to complete the transaction, either way.

Communications

The value of a **French phrasebook** cannot be underestimated. If you're polite and apologetic, it is very likely that the person you're trying to communicate with will break into English (don't ruin your chances by immediately asking, "Do you speak English?"), but attempting to speak French—even if you're reading straight from a guidebook and sound like an uneducated automaton—will make the locals more inclined to help you when you need it most. Foreign phrasebook applications are available to smartphone users, so for the light traveler, this may be the way to go. Many people who aren't yet conversational in French find making telephone calls nearly impossible. Still, if you can't live without your phone for the duration of your stay, check with your carrier to see if your mobile roaming privileges extend to France. If not—or if the costs are prohibitively exorbitant—you have other options.

If you own a late-model mobile phone and it has been unlocked, you can buy a France-friendly **SIM card** to temporarily replace your American SIM card. If you want to take care of those details before you leave, purchase one online through a company such as www.lefrenchmobile.com, www.lebara.co.uk, or www.cellularabroad.com. Some *tabacs* also sell SIM cards, but this might require a bit of advanced French to navigate. A better bet would be to visit a store in Paris such as Phone House, where many of the staff are bilingual and can fit your phone with the correct card while you wait. Cell phone rentals are not necessarily cheap, but they do exist; look for kiosks at Charles de Gaulle Airport or rent one at home before you leave. You might also consider purchasing a pay-as-you-go phone once you arrive; they usually cost between €30 and €50. Recharging the phones is easy: You simply visit the nearest *tabac* and ask for *une carte recharge*. You might be asked whether you want the more cost-effective SMS (texting) option, and you'll certainly be asked how much credit you want, usually a minimum of €5 and increasing in increments of €5 or €10. Keep in mind that phone credit has an expiration date—usually one or two weeks from the date of purchase.

Electronics

The power animating all those electric hair dryers, microwave ovens, televisions, and other appliances in France courses through the wires at 220 volts—double the U.S. and Canada's 110 volts. Some machines—laptops and tablets, digital camera battery chargers, mobile phone chargers—are designed to run on both voltages, so they simply need a cheap and easy-to-find **outlet adapter.** In North America, Best Buy is a reliable place to buy these adapters. If you can't live without your iPod docking station or your electric razor, you'll need to source a **transformer.** They come in different shapes, sizes, and degrees of reliability. For a dependable experience, invest in one or two of those rather industrial-looking step-up/step-down transformers. They aren't worth the extra weight or investment for a short trip, but you'll definitely want to consider them if and when you make the big move. A good one will allow you to use your stereo, lamps, or food processor if you've shipped them from the U.S. For short trips, a small adapter will do the job.

Even if you don't see one in your room, hair dryers are available at most hotels in France. Ask about availability when you check in, or send an email inquiry in advance. Online language converters such as www.freetranslation.com and www.translate. google.com can help you get your question across in a way the recipient will understand.

Medication and Personal Items

One of the hardest things to get used to in France is learning which products are and are not available at the supermarket or drugstore. Everyday items like multipurpose contact-lens solutions and good ol' Advil are only found in pharmacies, and often they're stashed behind the counter, requiring you to practice your French yet again to get relief from that headache or dry-eye spell. Prices are comparable to those you'd find in the U.S., though some items are noticeably cheaper, including homeopathic remedies and many prescription medications. For the most part, you'll find that discount-price goods are hard to come by. Expect to pay around €10 for a bottle of multipurpose contact-lens solution, €3 for a box—yes, a box—of 20 ibuprofen or acetaminophen (which is called *paracétamol* in France) tablets, and €3 or €4 for sore-throat lozenges.

The French are among the world's leading consumers of prescription drugs, so tracking down your prescription medication at the pharmacy shouldn't pose a problem, and it will likely cost far less than what you're used to spending. But for convenience's sake, you're still better off carrying your prescriptions from home. If you must get a refill while you're here, make sure to bring the brand name, generic name, and dosage, along with your doctor's prescription.

Clothing and Accessories

If you want to look like a local, then it helps to dress like a local—and in Paris, that means black, black, and more black. Women, men, and children tend to take a formal approach to dressing, and the style is easy to mimic with a monochromatic ensemble and a few nice accessories. Parisians in particular tend to shy away from too much color, sticking to black from their berets right down to their stiletto boots. Wearing your nicest shoes might not be the most comfortable route, but you'll look less like a tourist if you choose style over comfort. The good news for those who enjoy exploring on foot is that sporty running shoes and sneakers (called *"baskets"* in France) are now *de rigueur*. What you couldn't get away with last year without garnering disapproving glares—white sneakers with a dress, for example—will earn you nods of approval from the sartorial avant-garde. Flip-flops, however, are strictly beachwear, so save them for summer on the Riviera, if you must. Men might find it difficult to trade in their baseball caps for an empty head, but if you want to blend in, leave the sportswear at home.

France is a four-season country, so you'll want to pack gloves, scarves, and hats for wintertime travel, and they'll come in handy during early spring and late fall, too. These items are easy to find at chains like Monoprix and in little shops throughout the country, but if you have them already, stuff them in your suitcase, just to be safe (and warm).

The most indispensable year-round item to carry with you is an umbrella. Showers can and do erupt without warning in any season. Umbrellas are easily acquired once you're here, but even the cheapest models aren't that inexpensive by American standards. Expect to pay €15 for a small travel umbrella at a department store or pharmacy. If you're lucky, you might bump into the clever salesmen who congregate outside some Métro stations on rainy days selling cheap Chinese models for about €5.

Until recently, the French really didn't do sunglasses. They're becoming more common with each passing year, but people still rarely wear them in winter or on overcast days. If you're a sunglasses devotee, consider bringing an extra pair,

© BORNA MIRAHMADIAN/123RF.COM

Always carry an umbrella, as it often rains without warning.

National Holidays

On certain French holidays, such as Bastille Day, the whole country is out partying.

The French celebrate a handful of national holidays, or *jours feriérs*, throughout the year (and despite the country's claim to be utterly secular, many are religious holidays). They include:

- **New Year's Day** *(Jour de l'an):* January 1

- **Easter and Easter Monday** *(Pâques* and *lundi de Pâques):* March/April, date varies

- **Labor Day** *(Fête du Travail):* May 1

- **WWII Victory Day** *(Fête de la Victoire/Commémoration de la Victoire):* May 8

- **Pentecost and Pentecost Monday** *(la Pentecôte* and *lundi de Pentecôte):* May/June, date varies

- **Bastille Day** *(Fête nationale):* July 14

- **All Saints' Day** *(La Toussaint):* November 1

- **Armistice Day** *(l'Armistice):* November 11

- **Christmas Day** *(Noël):* December 25

as they aren't as easy to find as they are in the United States and Canada. In a pinch, head to the Marché aux Puces Saint-Ouen in Paris and comb the African-run stalls outside the main market. You can find trendy designer doppelgängers for around €10. Otherwise, you're guaranteed to find a suitable pair at any Monoprix market.

WHEN TO GO

You'll find France a welcoming destination at any time, but there are seasonal idiosyncrasies to keep in mind when planning your trip. Weather can certainly impede travel, so always be prepared for delays if a serious snowstorm blows through this part of Europe. And if you plan to travel to smaller towns and villages, be warned that some virtually shut down for the entire winter season, making it a challenge to find accommodations. (In Paris, you'll be fine.) During the month of August, when the entire country goes on vacation, you will also find signs affixed to the doors and windows of many businesses announcing closures for *"congés annuels"* or *"fermé pour les vacances,"* often accompanied by a very apologetic note explaining where in the neighborhood you'll be able to find similar baguettes/chocolate/shoe repair services/haircuts, as well as the business's reopening date. During the winter and spring school breaks, you'll find that many tourist hubs—especially the ski and seaside resorts—are full of Parisians, who often grab the best deals on accommodations months in advance. If you plan to escape the Île-de-France region and head for one of the French resort towns at these peak times, it's a good idea to book in advance, too.

Aside from requiring you to bundle up to ward off the cold, winter can be a festive time of year to make your investigative visit. Paris kicks up the visual charm with yuletide displays befitting a world-class city: Christmas lights, markets, and roasted chestnuts for sale on street corners are all part of the allure. Getting a reservation at the hotel and restaurant of your choice is usually easier this time of year, too. If you're focusing your search on Paris, expect most everything to be open for business. Depending on the neighborhood, more businesses are actually open on Christmas than on New Year's Day, so you won't go hungry or thirsty just because it's a major holiday. (This is especially true in Jewish and Muslim neighborhoods.) In smaller provincial towns, however, you'll be lucky if the *boulangerie* is open for a couple of hours in the morning, if at all.

Spring and autumn offer the mildest temperatures and possibly the best glimpses of "real France," without the vacationing hordes to impede your views. (If you want the Côte d'Azur all to yourself, plan to head south in late September.) Pack layers—shirt, jacket, trench coat, scarf, hat—and be sure your umbrella makes its way inside your suitcase.

Summer has the most predictable temperatures, which tend to fall into the warm range. But it can get scorching hot, and some of us have been known to turn on the heater on oddly nippy July mornings. Remember that late July and the entire month of August are national holiday periods, as well as the standard vacation time for much of the rest of Europe, so some destinations can feel quite crowded with a mix of international and local tourists. Men: If you foresee wanting to make use of Paris's affordable and accessible public swimming pools, pack your Speedo—they're mandatory. For everyone: If you've got a swimming cap, bring it along. Otherwise, you can purchase suits and the requisite caps in special vending machines inside the lobbies of public pools throughout France.

WHAT TO DO

The French value face-to-face interactions, so you'll have more success arranging things like real-estate viewings and mortgage inquiries if you wait until you arrive in France and do it in person. After you've settled in the hotel or short-term rental apartment, set off and explore. This is Phase One of your where-to-live assessment. As you stroll, keep your eyes peeled for banks, real estate agencies (*immobiliers*), and neighborhood associations offering courses in French and other activities.

Assess Where to Live

Know thyself: Never has this maxim held more relevance than when searching for a place to live. What do you value most in a community, and what are the deal-breakers? Do you need to be near the sea? Close to schools for your children? Within walking distance of a hospital? Culture and community are at the top of my where-to-live wish-list. That translates into an ideal dwelling situated within a five-minute walk of a Métro or Vélib' station so I can get to museums, concerts, and restaurants easily; a lively neighborhood with a weekly market and *boulangerie* within a few blocks' walk; and a quiet street without the incessant honking of car horns or scream of police sirens. (I lost out on the last one, but there's always a compromise.) What does your wish-list look like? You'll need a few items at the ready to outline your dream, including the following:

* pen

* notebook

* French phrasebook

* list of deal-breakers

* digital camera or smartphone camera

* a local phone number for real estate agents and others to contact you

* an open mind

With these tools, you'll be able to communicate with locals, jot down addresses of businesses and telephone numbers printed on *à louer* (for rent) and *à vendre* (for sale) signs, and photograph any housing contenders. If you plan to enroll your child(ren) in local schools, find the nearest park and introduce yourself to *nounous* and parents, and ask questions about the quality of schools and amenities for children. A trip to the weekly outdoor market is another good method of reading a neighborhood or village and seeing who lives there.

Rendezvous with Real Estate Agents

In cities small and large across France, you'll discover real estate offices with "for sale" and "for rent" signs in the window, complete with photos and details of each property. Once you've surveyed the outside, head inside and ask to speak with a real estate agent. You'll be invited to sit (and maybe even offered un café) and explain your situation. Are you looking to rent or buy? What is your budget? Do you have a *garant?* (See more on this in the *Housing Considerations* section in the *Daily Life* chapter.) Finding a friendly, motivated agent will support your quest to make a home in France.

Suss out Financial Institutions

In some ways, it's better to set up a bank account after you've established a permanent address. The branch where you opened the account becomes your "home" bank, and it's here that you create a relationship with the bankers and handle important matters relating to your account, including picking up new cards, applying for a mortgage, or modifying your account in any way. (See more in the *Finance* section of the *Daily Life* chapter.) Still, scoping out the banking situation and inquiring about documents for

Visit the local *mairie* for information about the community.

your dossier are good first steps. Popular banks throughout l'Hexagone include BNP Paribas, Caisse d'Épargne, and Société Générale.

Mingle with Locals

This is your opportunity to meet some of the people you've established relationships with before you ever set foot on the airplane bound for France. Bloggers, friends of friends, or even host families from your high-school trip abroad—hopefully, you've sought them out in advance and are using this visit to (re)establish those connections and glean valuable insider information. Joining a local **Meetup** (www.meetup.com) group event is one of the smartest and most fun modes for connecting with locals. Events span the spectrum from running-club outings to language-exchange groups and even tarot-card reading meetups. Find one that appeals to your interests, then plan to meet and mingle.

Mosey Over to the *Mairie*

Find your local *mairie's* office and have a peek inside. This is an important hub, especially if you want to get married, have a child, or take city-subsidized French-language classes while you're here. Help yourself to the free local newspapers and cultural calendars available in the lobby; these make good reading at the café. Talk to the person behind the desk to learn about upcoming events, and to inquire about anything else with a municipal focus—schools, libraries, and public markets, for example. Armed with these resources, you'll be better informed to assess your preferred neighborhoods, villages, and towns.

Arriving in France

If you're flying to France from North America, you'll mostly likely land at Charles de Gaulle, the country's primary international airport that sits roughly 27 kilometers northeast of Paris. The airport is connected to bus, train, taxi, and private-car services that can ferry you to other destinations—including Orly Airport, south of Paris, where you can catch flights elsewhere within France and Europe.

CUSTOMS

The customs experience is generally a no-fuss exercise requiring little more than standing in line for 10 minutes, followed by a friendly *bonjour* as you hand over your passport for stamping. In France, appearances do matter, so to make sure your experience runs as smoothly as possible, trade in your comfy sweats for dark jeans and a nice jacket, tuck your green mohawk inside your beret, give your shoes a shine, and be prepared to offer a friendly *bonjour* and *merci* in French. There is always a chance you'll be pulled aside to have your luggage unceremoniously rifled through. Officials are looking for contraband items, so it's best not to pique their curiosity by smuggling in your favorite fresh fruit or your beloved Venus flytrap. If you're flying with a pet, have your travel documents ready, but don't expect anyone to actually ask to see them. (In years of back-and-forth travel with a small dog in a carrier, I've never once been asked to show officials my doggy's dossier, though it's a given that were I to travel without the proper paperwork, I'd certainly be asked to cough it up.) Once you've cleared customs, the real adventure begins.

TRANSPORTATION

There are multiple options for escaping the airport frenzy and getting to your final destination; the one you choose depends on where you're headed, your budget, and your time constraints. Want to address your jetlag by going to sleep immediately? Consider taking a shuttle bus to a nearby airport hotel and starting fresh in the morning after a little shut-eye. Shuttles are free, and there are many bargains to be found within 10 minutes of the airport, from budget-friendly chains to cushy five-star digs.

If you're headed into Paris, the possibilities abound. One of the simplest is RoissyBus (wah-see-BOOS), which runs every 15 to 20 minutes, depending upon the time of day. The extra-long bus—two cars with an accordion-style middle section—costs €11 per trip and drops you off in the heart of Paris, behind the Opéra Métro station. You can pay with cash or a credit card once you're on the bus, and there are pickup locations at every airport terminal. During rush hour, the journey can take more than an hour; on a good (no-traffic) day, the trip takes about 35 minutes.

The RER B is a regional train line that connects all three airport terminals to Paris and its suburbs. For roughly the same price and same time commitment you'd invest in RoissyBus, you can hop aboard a train and arrive at one of three central Paris train stations: Gare du Nord, Saint-Michel, and Denfert-Rochereau. If you're staying in Paris's popular Latin Quarter, the Saint-Michel station is your stop. Tickets can be purchased from the agents staffing the station kiosks (ideal if paying with a non-*puce* card), or you can use an automated vending machine (best if using cash). Tickets are €10 and the trip takes 30 minutes from the airport to Gare du Nord.

Air France offers a deluxe bus service into the city, stopping at the Porte de Maillot Métro/RER Station in northeast Paris, as well as Gare Montparnasse via Gare de Lyon. Tickets are available for purchase online (www.lescarsairfrance.com) for €17 (Porte de Maillot) or €17.50 (Montparnasse), and roughly a euro more when you purchase tickets from the driver or the airport kiosks.

Shuttle buses are a newly emerging alternative to RoissyBus, the RER, and the Air France bus, but they're slightly more expensive and offer a somewhat clunkier experience, since you have to call the company—albeit on a toll-free number accessible from an airport pay phone—to let them know you've arrived. To get the best deals, it's imperative you book your pickup in advance. Try www.bluvan.fr, www.supershuttle.fr, or www.parishuttle.com, each of which offers English-language options on its website.

If money is no object, or if you just want to get to your hotel or apartment with a minimum of hassle, taxis are the way to go. Expect to pay between €45 (early-morning or late-night light traffic) and €100 (rush-hour traffic) to ride from the airport to the front door of your Parisian abode. Though tipping isn't standard in France, there is an exception for taxis. An extra 5 percent on top of the fare is standard, or 10 percent if your driver is extra helpful with your baggage or doesn't make a fuss about your dog or cat in its carrier.

Sample Itineraries

Even if you only have a week, you can pack a lot of exploration into your fact-finding experience, thanks to France's marvelous public transportation system. Two weeks will provide you with a cursory sense of what to expect when you land permanently. If you have a month to spare, consider yourself an honorary local. Before you leave, you'll want to get familiar with the national railway website, www.sncf.com, for making online reservations for trains, cars, and flights. Once you're here, try to imagine yourself as a resident. Hit the neighborhood cafés, visit the cinema or the theater, take in a musical performance, picnic in the neighborhood parks, and above all, sample the wares at the local *boulangeries;* there's no underestimating the importance of a good baguette.

ONE WEEK: THE PARIS COMMUTER
Day 1
Once you've settled into your temporary **Paris** digs, you need to get out there and explore. Use your first day to orient yourself to the city and its major landmarks as you shake your jet lag. Pick up a free city map at a tourist office or invest in a Michelin guide of the city; it's indispensible if you're going to make Paris your home.

If you're not *trop fatigué* (too tired), today is also a good day to secure your **travel passes.** If you plan to use a combination of public transportation and walking, spend €14.10 on a *carnet* of 10 tickets good for the Métro, city buses, and tramways that will last the duration of your stay—if you limit your travel to one or two rides a day and walk the rest of the time. The Paris Visite pass is geared toward the short-stay tourist,

Finding a Temporary Rental

A short-term rental makes the ideal home base during your reconnaissance trip, because it allows you to try on the local lifestyle in an authentic French home instead of a sterile hotel room. But there are several differences between American apartments and French apartments for which most Americans are unprepared. Marie-Reine Jezequel, a native of Brittany, founded **New York Habitat** (www.nyhabitat.com) in 1989 to help people like you find the perfect temporary dwelling in Paris and the South of France. Here, she shares her tips for making your short-term rental experience stress-free and fun, no matter what corner of l'Hexagone you dream of settling in:

- Many French buildings (even seven- or eight-story ones) do not include **elevators.** The first floor in America is considered the ground floor in France. Request a **rez-de-chausée** (ground floor) option if you have bad knees or need special access.

- In many French apartments, a full **kitchen** is not included. Often, there will be a hotplate stove and a small fridge and sink, but no oven, dishwasher, or toaster. Always ask your agent if you have any questions about apartment features.

- Unlike American bathrooms, French **toilets** are often in a separate room (the *toilette*). **Showers** are also different; while most American showerheads are attached to the wall, many French apartments have bathtubs with manually held shower attachments. If you want a full shower make sure you check the apartment photos carefully before you book.

- **Heating** in French apartments is either *collectif* or *individuel.* Ask your landlord what your building has; otherwise you might get stuck with an expensive heating bill in winter.

- It's common to have exterior doors with *digicode* systems instead of **keys** in France. It relieves you of the stress of forgetting your keys at home—just don't forget your code!

- Avoid planning major outings or shopping trips on **Sundays**—all the shops will be closed! Part of the charm of France is the quality of life and the aversion to materialism. Get used to spending your evenings chatting with friends over a bottle of fine wine and leave the chores for another day.

and will give you five days of unlimited travel throughout each of the five zones for €61.25, which includes regional train (RER) trips to both Roissy and Orly airports, plus suburbs as far reaching as Versailles and Fontainebleau. If you're committed to staying in France for a month or more, the Navigo pass is a good option. For €70 per month or €770 per year (students pay half that price), you get access to buses, trams, and trains in zones one and two. The new Véligo program is an add-on to your Navigo pass, and offers commuters secure bike parking at major train stations and other transport hubs. To create your account and order a Navigo pass in advance of your trip, visit the official site at www.navigo.fr.

Besides la Tour Eiffel, the **Marais** is probably the biggest tourist magnet in all of Paris, and with good reason: It's lively, fun, and crammed with history and visual interest. Make this your home base for a week and you might not even need to rely on

© LEMBI BUCHANAN/123RF.COM

The Marais neighborhood in Paris is lively and fun.

public transport; just be sure to pack your (stylish) walking shoes, because some of Paris's most exciting neighborhoods are within a 45-minute promenade of that shopper's thoroughfare that slices through the Marais, the rue de Rivoli.

If you're not quite ready to dive into the serious business of assessing your future home, consider popping into **Berthillon** on Île Saint-Louis for a scoop or two of dark chocolate sorbet, and devour your icy treat as you walk to the **Hôtel de Ville**, where rotating art exhibits are always free and, more often than not, an extremely interesting way to spend your first jetlagged day in the capital.

Days 2 and 3

Once you've got your bearings, you'll be able to settle on a couple of neighborhoods to explore on foot. Starting on the Right Bank at place de la République—where the revamped plaza hums with the energetic buzz of skateboards, bikes, and *flâneurs*—you'll pass several neighborhood attractions, including streets lined with boutiques offering clothing in varying degrees of affordability, art galleries, and several museums. You could continue walking north toward **Belleville**, or lean left and explore **Canal Saint-Martin**. Either direction you follow will lead you to enchanting corners brimming with cafés, food shops, and street art. Wine bars like **La Verre Volé** (67, rue de Lancry, tel. 01/48 03 17 34) and hipster cafés like **Ten Belles** (10, rue de la Grange aux Belles, tel. 01/42 40 90 78) or **Holybelly** (19, rue Lucien Sampaix, tel. 09/73 60 13 64) offer great opportunities to refuel with your tipple of choice and a nibble before your exploration recommences.

Days 4 and 5

Every visitor to Paris has to give the Rive Gauche a go, if only to visit that celebrated tower that's left an indelible mark on the skyline. Once you've scaled the Tour Eiffel's heights, meander on foot toward the nearby 15th arrondissement and wander the family-friendly streets of the **Grenelle** neighborhood, stopping in at the American Library to peruse the bulletin board and learn about upcoming events.

Next, take the Métro toward the **Alésia** neighborhood in the 14th, visit the cool (and kind of creepy) Catacombs, then pick up a copy of *Particulier à Particulier* at the nearest news kiosk, tote it to an inviting terrace café, and enjoy the last rays of the sun while perusing your collection of apartment-rental listings.

You have a feel for the city now, and you've even prowled a few prime neighborhoods. It's time to brave the French-speaking sphere by making phone calls and arranging visits to some of those Parisian abodes you've been scoping out. If you don't have a phone or a phone card, pick one up. It's as easy as a visit to **Phone House** (there's one in nearly every arrondissement), where €30 will get you a *portable,* a SIM card, and calling time to make those vital connections. Don't forget to check out Craigslist (www.paris.craigslist.fr) and FUSAC (www.fusac.org) for both housing and job leads.

If you're leaning toward a specific neighborhood, this might be a good moment to explore your **banking options** and even open a French bank account. Whatever branch you select will become your "home" branch, so be thoughtful in your choice—changing banks isn't impossible, but like every other bureaucratic process, it is time-consuming and a tad draining. If you're planning to buy rather than rent, consider discussing mortgage prospects with your banker, too.

If you have any energy left, reel it in and make the walk to the Latin Quarter, where you can explore the campus of the Sorbonne, celebrated bookstore Shakespeare and Company, or perhaps visit any private language school you're considering. With a little planning, you could also hit a Meetup to get to know some of the locals before you make the big leap.

Day 6

Spend your penultimate day in Paris exploring Versailles or another city **suburb,** or maybe just get out and enjoy a spot of relaxation. To the north of the city center, past Sacré Coeur basilica and over the *périphérique,* sits the antiques oasis Marche aux Puces de St. Ouen, a must-visit for anyone who loves old furniture and hunting for treasures. After browsing and dreaming about furnishing your Paris apartment, take Métro line 4 to line 10 and get off at Porte d'Auteuil. Nearby, the newly renovated Molitor (www.mltr.fr/en) offers access to an Olympic-size swimming pool, a fashionable restaurant where you can take brunch on the terrace, and spa services. A short walk away, the beautiful Bois de Boulogne beckons. As you relax beside one of the park's two lakes, synthesize your experiences and make a mental checklist: What neighborhoods can I really imagine living in? What job prospects deserve further consideration? Do I need to make another visit?

Day 7

Spend your final day in Paris parked at a café, taking notes and logging impressions of your experience. Did any neighborhoods call out to you? Did you make any contacts you'll want to reconnect with by email or Skype when you get home? Are you able to rule out places to live and narrow the search down to a quartier or two? When you get home, log onto FUSAC (www.fusac.org) and bookmark the *les annonces* page; you'll want to check back frequently to see if any apartments have become available in your preferred neighborhoods, and whether any dream jobs in your area of experience and expertise have opened.

With all the real-estate information, business cards, email addresses, and phone numbers of new friends tucked safely into your suitcase, you can enjoy your final breakfast of a croissant, *thé,* and *Le Parisien* before heading to Charles de Gaulle for the flight home.

TWO WEEKS: THE WEST COAST JAUNT

You've done the Paris region, and now it's time to broaden your horizons westward and southward to see what life could be like outside France's largest metropolis.

Day 1

Begin with a train ride from Paris's Montparnasse station to **Rennes,** the gateway to Brittany. After checking into your hotel, mosey over to the university town's liveliest square, **place des Lices,** with its colorful half-timbered buildings, crowded cafés and brasseries, Saturday-morning market, and generally lively tempo. After you purchase your fill of fresh apples and snack on the requisite crêpe from a market stand, visit the tourist office, where the friendly staff will supply you with maps and answer all your questions about Rennes' history and its varied quartiers, and offer you tips on where to dine and sightsee. Spend the afternoon strolling along the canal and exploring the pedestrian walkways and parks before heading back to the place des Lices for dinner of pizza and wine at an outdoor eatery.

Day 2

If it's a sunny day, get yourself a day pass for the Vélo Star, Rennes' public bike-share program, and start exploring the neighborhoods of this flat, cycle-friendly city. Check out the two University of Rennes campuses—you might be working or attending classes here at some point—and pick up a copy of *France Ouest,* the local daily, to get a read on life in Western France. After a long day cruising the city, roll over to O'Connell's Irish Pub, Rennes' unofficial Anglophone hub, and just *try* not to make a new friend or two over your pint of Guinness.

Days 3, 4, and 5

A bit more than an hour away by bus, iconic **Mont St. Michel** beckons as a fun day or overnight trip. Middle Ages architecture and fairytale ambience reign in this corner of France, where awe-inspiring ocean views and Romanesque churches compete for your attention. From here, you can hire a rental car and drive south to **Vannes,** a pretty little medieval town on the Morbihan coast. Check into your hotel and then hit the streets, where a walk through the pedestrian-friendly *centre ville* works up a craving for crêpes and cider. Indulge! You'll need food to fuel your walkabout. Vannes is small enough to get to know on foot—unless you're interested in "rural" Vannes, in which case a cruise in your rental car is a great idea. Market days are Wednesdays and Saturdays, and everyone in town turns out for the shopping experience—you should, too. Meandering by foot gives you plenty of opportunity to collect real-estate brochures and pop into agencies to ask questions, and don't be shy about talking to local shop-keepers about the way of life here.

A 20-minute drive southwest brings you to **Carnac,** where stone megaliths as far as the eye can see offer visual reminders of Brittany's ancient Celtic roots. The *fleur de sel* (sea salt) produced in this region is among the most coveted by epicures, and regional treats—from buttery caramels to locally harvested sea beans—conjure up the salty flavor of the ocean. Driving back into Vannes, take in the sea air. Does this feel like a weekend-getaway destination or a dig-in-your-heels-for-the-long-haul kind of place? To take the live-like-a-local experience a step further, try a yoga class or catch a live musical or theatrical performance at the Théâtre Anne de Bretagne.

Day 6

Breathe the word "**Bordeaux**," and it's hard not to visualize that ruby-red elixir of the gods. This is indeed the gateway to one of France's most celebrated wine-growing re-gions and most vibrant urban communities. Getting here from Vannes involves a six-hour train ride, leaving you with enough time to catch up on sleep, finish that novel you've been toting, or delve into all the job- and house-seeking materials you've gathered.

Assuming you arrive in Bordeaux in the late afternoon, check into your hotel, don your walking shoes, and make a beeline for the Garonne River and its pedestrian-friendly promenade. Take in the vistas and the atmosphere, then head back across the street toward a lively shopping street, Sainte-Catherine, and settle in for a meal at one of the many nearby tapas restaurants.

Days 7, 8, and 9

You'll need at least one day in Bordeaux just to get the lay of the land. Pick up a bus pass or *carnet* (10 tickets good for the bus and tramway), and set off exploring, making sure to cross the river into the emerging neighborhood of La Bastide to visit the botanical gar-dens. Head north to Le Lac for a bit of sunbathing and people-watching if the weather is warm, and explore several centuries' worth of old churches in between. Take time to stroll on foot, and to examine the *"à louer"* (to rent) and *"à vendre"* (to buy) listings.

Weekdays are prime for scheduling home-viewing appointments; after you've vis-ited a few *immobiliers,* perused online listings, and made a few phone calls, your day should include several hours of home-scoping, leaving you enough daylight to visit the sprawling Université de Bordeaux campus and meet with potential employers. Every Thursday night, Franco-American social club Bordeaux-USA (www.bordeaux-usa.com) hosts a language exchange meet-up; don't miss out on this wonderful chance to meet local expats.

If one of your Bordeaux days is a Sunday, lucky you: It's market day, and the of-ferings range from fresh-cut flowers to oysters on the half-shell. You've earned a day of relaxation, so consider a visit to one of the city's many museums. Move from the past to the present at the Musée des Arts Décoratifs, or zoom straight into the eclectic 21st-century at the Musée d'Art Contemporain. Finish your final day in Bordeaux with a *verre de vin* at an outdoor café in the Chartrons district, overlooking the river.

Day 10

When your inner Bacchus begins to stir, pick up a rental car or catch a train at Gare St.

Jean and head east toward the beautiful wine-growing region of the **Dordogne Valley.** Independent wineries punctuate the landscape; if you're traveling by car, stop for a sip and maybe pick up a bottle to enjoy later. Pop into **St. Émilion** before heading to **Bergerac,** and if there's enough daylight left, wander the compact old town, visit an art opening, and stop for a pizza at a homey restaurant.

Day 11

If you've made arrangements with local real-estate agents to view properties for sale, book your appointments for the morning so you'll have time for an afternoon boat ride on the river before making the 60-kilometer journey to **Sarlat.** On your way, pass through the medieval villages of Milandes, Lanquais, and Montbazillac. In **Les Eyzies,** stop at the national museum of prehistory to see what the first Frenchies were up to all those millennia ago.

Days 12 and 13

After getting situated in Sarlat, explore the pretty village. Don't forget to visit the covered market (where you can pick up the local specialty, truffles) with its sky-scraping metal doors and Disneyland atmosphere. Stop for *un verre* at a café on the place de la Liberté and soak it all in. In the summer, expect music, art, and theater in the streets. The rest of the year, similar cultural activities move indoors. Take a sculpture- or jewelry-making class, and get to know some of the locals who may soon become your new neighbors.

It's a great idea to dedicate a day to exploring housing possibilities; after cruising the surrounding countryside, you may be thinking that a more rural living situation is right up your alley. Allow enough time to meet with several different agencies and explore all your options—setting aside an hour or two to visit the *mairie* and the chamber of commerce would also be wise, especially if you plan to open a business here and have questions about how to do so.

Day 14

Before heading for the airport, train station, or highway in your rental car, take one last spin through town and pick up some of the locally produced treats, including a bottle of the heavenly walnut wine. If you haven't visited the tourist office yet, pop in and pick up any brochures you may have missed, and ask any final questions about the area. Oh, and that truffled omelet? This is now-or-never time.

FOUR WEEKS: SEA, SUN, AND SNOW

With a month to amble around *la belle France,* you'll not only come away with a solid sense of the varied geography, but you'll have time to relax and absorb the unique characteristics of each region.

Weeks 1 and 2

Even with all this time on your hands, it still makes sense to begin your adventure in Paris. From here, you can move either clockwise or counter-clockwise. Following our route east, you could visit Strasbourg, Lyon, and Grenoble, or head the other way toward Rennes, Vannes, Bordeaux, and the Dordogne Valley. Alternately, you could do a bit of hopscotching to reach the areas that hold the most appeal—the Riviera, perhaps?—to allow time for in-depth exploration.

Weeks 3 and 4

The capital of France's Béarn region, **Pau,** is a lovely little castle town where the views of the Pyrenees alone are enough to lure an outdoor-loving Anglophone. From the Dordogne Valley, it's a three-hour drive through rolling countryside, and the reward for all that driving is that first glimpse of those southerly snow-capped peaks. Visit the museum at the chateau de Pau—birthplace of Henri IV—and take a stroll along the boulevard des Pyrénées, stopping for *un verre* at one of the many terrace cafés offering fresh-air views and opportunities for refueling.

A couple hundred kilometers north and east is the capital of the Languedoc region, **Toulouse,** a sprawling, sophisticated metropolis settled by the Romans way back in 120 BC. You'll also find a cosmopolitan blend of people here—Anglophones among them—drawn by the area's thriving high-tech and aerospace industries. Meander the medieval back streets of the old city; visit France's largest cathedral, the Basilique de St. Sernin (pray that the organist is in session); and relish a steaming dish of cassoulet in the local tradition.

If you want to meet friendly locals, go to the English in Toulouse Meetup that takes place every Friday evening. Walk or ride the Canal du Midi path, and spend a day or two gallivanting about town and getting to know the neighborhoods.

When you arrive in **Montpellier,** you can abandon your rental car and rely on trains to move you around the Mediterranean coast. If the sun is shining—which it most likely will be—mosey over to place de la Comédie, the city's pedestrian plaza, and find a terrace café beneath the palm trees to sip a cool glass of rosé and watch the world go by. The tourist office on the northwest edge of the *place* is a hotbed of activity and information: Stop in here to ask questions, collect brochures, and make theater reservations. You'll also find rental-housing information and brochures for Anglophone real-estate agents here.

Next, take the train or drive 130 kilometers to the quintessential Provençal college town of **Aix-en-Provence.** Make it your southerly home base for a few days to explore the region that inspired painters from Cézanne to Van Gogh. Don't forget to stop into the Book in Bar bookshop and make use of their English-language resources for newcomers. The bulletin board and friendly staff are just the beginning; the books, muffins, and tea are the icing on the cake.

Back along the coastal route, make **Antibes** your home for a day or two. Walk the cobbled city streets within the ramparts and admire the pleasure boats in the harbor; bike, walk, or drive around Cap d'Antibes; look at some of the rental possibilities for sale; and take a dip in the sea if it's between June and October. Next stop: **Nice,** where it really is nice, and a lunch of *socca* and sauvignon blanc awaits beneath bright blue skies. Get a short-term bus pass and explore Monaco, Menton, and the tidy, sun-dappled streets of Nice's diverse neighborhoods. Real-estate agencies by the boatload beckon on nearly every *rue,* so make good use of them—and don't miss the tourist office, in a dated building on the promenade des Anglais. The staff can point you toward the next ski bus headed for the Alps or book you a hotel room in the city center.

When you grow tired of the seafaring views and sunshine, head north toward

Grenoble, where the palm trees give way to pines and the snow-capped Alps come into focus. Hemmed in by mountains, Grenoble is prime outdoor-activity territory, the place to give in to your urge to commune with nature. After you've settled in to your *chambre d'hôte,* hotel, or by-the-week apartment, hit the hiking and biking trails to breathe in the delicious, conifer-scented air.

A visit to one of Grenoble's daily markets will give you a sense of the city's varied population and will introduce you to all the wonderful produce and other edibles at your disposal. If you're here on a Tuesday, visit the Open House Grenoble Meetup and talk to other expats, who'll share their wisdom and experience to help make the transition into life here easier and smoother. If you have an interview at one of the many American companies with French offices here, you'll likely meet someone at one of these events who'll be able to share information on office culture, too.

A 90-minute train ride from Grenoble puts you in **Lyon,** France's second-largest city and the country's gastronomic capital. Big but not intimidating, Lyon deserves at least a few days. Ride the funicular to the top of the hill overlooking the city and take in the broad-reaching panorama, across red-tiled roofs and two rivers. Visit the famous basilica and the beautifully preserved Roman amphitheater, then eat a meal—or two or three—at a *bouchon,* where humble Lyonnais cuisine rules.

Once you've scoped out the housing situation and investigated the local job market, you might as well dive right into the networking scene. Anglophones at Lyon's social get-togethers offer a chance to mingle with a youthful, enthusiastic group of expats who are ready to welcome you into their fold and share tips and suggestions. An exploratory visit to a few of Lyon's many French-language schools might factor into your plans, too.

From Lyon's Part-Dieux train station, a half-dozen trains depart each day toward **Strasbourg**. Tickets for the four-hour journey begin at the bargain price of €20, and if you time your departure for the morning, you'll arrive in the geranium-filled city center in time for a lunch of *flammenküche* (a thin-crust pizza that's one of the local specialties) at a canal-side restaurant. After lunch, take a guided tour of the European Parliament, and finish the day with a ride around the city on a Batorama barge.

Practicalities

ACCOMMODATIONS

One of France's best-kept secrets is its value-for-money lodgings. Who needs a fancy €2,000-per-night suite at the Plaza Athénée when, for a fraction of the price, you can relax for a night or two in a comfortable room with free Wi-Fi *and* a view of the Eiffel Tower? Bargains aren't limited to Paris nor to hotels—you'll also discover great deals on bed-and-breakfasts, *gîtes,* and short-term apartment and villa stays—from the top of the country to the bottom and from east to west—offering clean comfort for the night. France holds the distinction of having a counterintuitive cheaper-on-the-weekends hotel policy, so if you're flying in on a Friday, Saturday, or Sunday, you'll likely get your room for an even better rate than you would during the workweek.

If you're going the good old-fashioned hotel route, it's helpful to know what those stars posted at the hotel entryway mean. The French government has instituted a rating system that the majority of establishments adhere to, with the number of stars clearly visible outside, usually affixed to a blue sign on the wall adjacent to the front door. The number of stars doesn't reflect quality per se, but it does correspond to the amenities available to guests, which may act as an indicator of quality. A hotel with five stars might have a swimming pool and a refrigerator full of booze and bottled water, but that doesn't mean it's immune to the dreaded cockroach. What you *can* expect at the bottom level is a no-frills room with a bed, a TV, and a bathroom equipped with a tiny shower stall. There may or may not be an *ascenseur* (elevator) to take you to your fourth-floor room. Budget chains include Kyriad, Etap, and Formule 1, which offer a uniform aesthetic with predictable, midlevel quality and comfort. Further up the starry ladder are the Ibis, Novotel, and Mercure chains, which fall into the three- and four-star range. Only a handful of French hotels reach five-star status.

In a small village in the Dordogne Valley, you might find a family-run place situated above a café-brasserie for €45 a night. For €55, you could easily find a quaint room overlooking a castle in the Loire Valley, within walking distance of a number of restaurants and sightseeing destinations. For €65, you could rest your head on a fluffy pillow in a homey bed-and-breakfast on the Brittany coast. In Paris, you could find a chic little boutique hotel with a cut-rate room priced at €100, with a Métro stop a two-minute walk out the lobby door and a *boulangerie* on the corner where all of your brioche-for-breakfast dreams can come true. In other words, there's a lot of variety, and the prices aren't bad either. Airbnb rentals start at rock bottom (€35-a-night studios in Nice, or an entire house with a garden in Grenoble for €65) and skyrocket to the top ranges of even the most generous budgets. Similarly, private rental agencies offer great deals on simple accommodations and deluxe digs alike, with something to fit your budget if you take the time to scope out the possibilities.

If you're securing a place to stay on the spot rather than booking in advance, ask to see a room before committing. In France, you always pay at checkout and you'll be asked for your passport at check-in, at which time they might decide to hold on to your passport for the duration of your stay. While the room you get may not exactly match the description precisely, you can be sure of quality, safety, and a good night's sleep.

Paris

The French capital is loaded with options for accommodations, from short-stay apartment rentals and niche B&Bs to swanky upscale hotels and family-run one-star dives. Craigslist is a great place to start your search for a temporary apartment rental, but beware of anyone who asks you to wire money in advance (though if they accept PayPal, you're safe). Veering off the tourist path will lead you to more bargain digs than you could ever hope to find near the Champs-Élysées and will give you the chance discover neighborhoods worth considering as your new home.

On a small but lively street five minutes from the Métro, 10 minutes to the Moulin Rouge, and 20 minutes to Sacre Coeur, **Hotel Eldorado** (18, rue des Dames, tel. 01/45 22 13 42) offers bucketloads of charm and comfort at great prices. With rooms beginning at €60 per night, expect garden views, on-site café, and free wireless Internet, but don't count on television or telephones in the room. To ensure guests have a restful stay, these amenities are left off the hotel menu.

On the other side of Paris, near Bastille, the **Hi Matic Hotel** (71, rue de Charonne, tel. 01/43 67 56 56) offers über-modern décor and eco-friendly rooms that are particularly popular with young travelers. Quarters are tight, but packed with all the mod-cons, plus free tea and coffee all day. The location is ideal for exploring eastern Paris. High-season rates begin at €93 for a colorful double with Wi-Fi and satellite TV.

For something on the swanky end of the hipster spectrum, try **Hotel Le Citizen** (96, quai de Jemmapes, tel. 01/83 62 55 50), in the city's trendy Canal Saint Martin neighborhood. Rooms begin at €199 for two with breakfast, and include big fluffy pillows, flat-screen TVs, and free iPad use during your stay.

Brittany
RENNES

Beautiful, laid-back Rennes has some beautiful, laid-back hotels in the city center. One of the comfiest is **Hotel des Lices** (1, place des Lices, tel. 02/99 79 14 81) just off the busy weekend-market square, Place des Lices. This 48-room hotel offers soundproof sleeping quarters with balconies and prime access to all that the old town has to offer: restaurants, markets, parks, shopping, the Métro, and people-watching. Chic, contemporary doubles start at €70 per night.

Feeling splurge-y? The luxe and lovely **Balthazar** (19, rue de Marechal Joffre, tel. 02/99 32 32 32) is worth the extra euro. The location is perfect for exploring central Rennes, and the on-site Nuxe spa gives you something to look forward to at the end of a long day of

Finding temporary digs in France is easy and can be suprisingly affordable.

neighborhood scouting. Rooms start at €120 and include a coveted Nespresso coffee machine and flat-screen television.

VANNES

An hour away by train is Vannes, where nearly all the town's hotels are within walking distance of the *gare*. At the **Hotel Manche-Océan** (31, rue de Lieutenant Colonel Maury, tel. 02/97 47 26 46), you'll be welcomed by a convivial staff who'll make you feel at home *tout de suite* (right away). From here, you can walk to the old city in five minutes and the port in 15, and access the seashore in half an hour on a groomed walking trail. Doubles, which begin at €58, are spacious and comfortable.

Near the *mairie* and the historic ramparts of the old city, **Hotel Le Bretagne** (36, rue de Mené, tel. 02/97 47 20 21) offers cuteness and quaintness in one well-placed hotel. Double rooms begin at €46, and creep up to €60 during the high season (mid-June to mid-September). Unlike most hotels in France, dogs are *interdit* (prohibited) here, so if you're traveling with Fifi or Fido, choose the Manche-Océan instead.

Bordeaux and the Dordogne Valley
BORDEAUX

Bordeaux's beautiful and historic city center boasts a broad spectrum of hotels, and it's worth making the short tram journey into the *centre ville* and laying down your temporary roots there. If you must stay near the train station, you'll find no shortage of hotels within a two-minute walk, including chains such as Ibis and Mercure.

At the cute and quirky **Hotel Notre Dame** (36, rue Notre Dame, tel. 05/56 52 88 24) in the heart of the Chartrons antiques district, you'll find comfortable rooms and

When checking out potential places to live, look for community gardens and other neighborhood gathering spots.

© FREEPROD/123RF.COM

Bordeaux is one of France's most important wine-producing regions.

very friendly staff who'll happily dispense free maps and local information. Double rooms begin at €63. From there, it's a five-minute tram ride or a 15-minute walk past cute restaurants and shops to the city center. Warning! There isn't an elevator in this hotel, so if you've got bad knees, ask for a room on the *premier étage*.

If you prefer to stay where all the action is, the bright, modern **Hotel de la Presse** (8, rue Dijeaux, tel. 05/56 48 53 88) is ideally situated a two-minute walk from the Place de la Bourse, right in the thick of the pedestrian shopping promenade called rue Sainte-Catherine. Rooms start at €75. Don't even think about driving to your hotel; Bordeaux is a challenge to navigate by car, and the many pedestrian-only streets make parking a Herculean task.

BERGERAC

Whether you arrive in Bergerac by car or by train, you'll be able to get to the city center by following the signs to *centre ville*. If you meander to the small, quaint old quarter of town, just beyond République near the covered market, you'll discover **Hotel le Family** (3, rue du Dragon, tel. 05/53 57 80 90), a no-frills, clean, and comfy hotel attached to a traditional Périgordine restaurant. Double rooms start at just €39.

Edging closer to the Dordogne river on a pretty tree-lined street is **La Bonbonnière** (15, place de la Mirpe, tel. 05/53 61 82 04), a B&B run out of an authentic medieval abode by a friendly French couple. Simone will make you breakfast, with homemade jam to slather on your warm bread and strong coffee to get you through a day of sightseeing. Rates begin at €65.

SARLAT-LA-CANÉDA

Martine and Patrice, the proprietors of **Le Petit Mas** (22, rue Gabriel Tarde, tel. 05/53 30 34 09), offer charming rooms for rent at their comfortable home a 10-minute walk from Sarlat's Disneyesque medieval town center. Expect to pay between €35 and €60, depending on the room, season, and number of people, plus an extra €5.50 for breakfast.

If a one-minute walk to the heart of Sarlat is more to your liking, you'll appreciate **Le Couleuvrine** (1, place Bouquerie, tel. 05/53 59 27 80). The lovely old hotel is run by another husband-and-wife team who offer food, accommodations, and a cozy little bar to make yourself at home in. Rooms are hard to secure in the summer without a reservation, but if you land one, you'll pay between €43 and €90 for a comfortable, character-filled *chambre* with bathroom, wireless Internet, and television.

Pau, Toulouse, and Montpellier

PAU

If you've come to Pau by train, you'll want to take the free funicular up to the top of the hill, where the *centre ville* and all its hustle and bustle await. If you've come by car, skip the chain motels on the outskirts of town (unless you're on a really tight budget) and find your way to **Hotel Roncevaux** (25, rue Louis Barthou, tel. 05/59 00 00 40), where parking for guests is free and all that Pau has to offer is right at your doorstep. Expect a warm welcome, comfortable, quiet rooms with modern furnishings, and double rooms that start at €109 per night.

Another centrally located option a short walk away from Pau's central shopping district is the **Quality Hotel** (80, rue Emile Garet, tel. 05/59 83 58 00). Simple, tidy doubles start at €90, and there's free parking on-site, Wi-Fi in every room, and plenty of hot water when you need it.

TOULOUSE

Toulouse is a big city with oodles of hotels, hostels, and *chambres d'hôtes* in every price range. The hard part is simply deciding what part of the city you want to settle in. In the center, near Place du Capitole, you'll find **Le Grand Balcon** (8-10, rue Romiguières, tel. 05/34 25 44 09). This cushy, Art Deco hotel offers great location and heaps of style, and has the added cachet of having once hosted the author of *The Little Prince*, Antoine de Saint-Exupéry. Doubles start at €98.

Not far from Le Grand Balcon and a short walk from the train station is the three-star **Grand Hotel Raymond IV** (16, rue Raymond IV, tel. 05/61 62 89 41), where a double room will set you back €61 in the low season. If you're traveling by car, you'll be delighted to know that on-site parking is available for a small fee. Expect free Wi-Fi and toiletry products in your modern bathroom.

MONTPELLIER

Montpellier is a popular convention destination, so don't make the mistake of rolling into town and expecting a comfortable bed for the night, just to discover that the French Medical Association is holding its annual conference and every last hotel is booked solid for the week. (But if you do find yourself in this predicament, most hotels will help book you a room in a neighboring town.) With advance planning, you could stay in the heart of the city a block from the magnificent place de la Comédie and

© R. CINTAS FLORES/AIXEN PROVENCE TOURISM

Aix-en-Provence is a vibrant college town.

five minutes from the train station at the 46-room **Royal Hotel Montpellier** (8, rue Maguelone, tel. 04/67 92 13 36). Chic, comfortable rooms start at €72, and the location couldn't be more central.

Deeper into the city's ancient center on a narrow little street near both the lovely Parc de Peyrou and the botanical gardens is **Hotel Le Guilhem** (18, rue Jean-Jacques Rousseau, tel. 04/67 52 90 90), part of the Best Western chain. Doubles at this comfortable hotel, which is housed in a 16th-century building brimming with old-world character, start €80 per night. This is a great spot for exploring the old pedestrian area of the city.

Provence and the Côte d'Azur

AIX-EN-PROVENCE

In Aix-en-Provence, you might find yourself so charmed by the terra-cotta-colored Provençal architecture and plane tree-shaded boulevards that you forget to take note of the hotel situation. If it's easier for you, the nice people at the rather dated-looking tourist office will happily book you a place to stay. Or you can BYOR (book your own room) at the quaint little **Les Quatre Dauphins** (54, rue Roux Alphéran, tel. 04/42 38 16 39), on a side street in the center of old Aix. It's within walking distance of the *gare* and all the terrace cafés, bookstores, and picturesque squares your heart could fancy. Doubles start at €80, and you'll pay slightly more in the high season.

Five minutes from the *gare* sits the chic **Hotel Cezanne** (40, ave Victor Hugo, tel. 01/57 32 38 29), where modern design meets comfort. An on-site bar and free fitness facilities will tug you in two different directions, but the big draw is the ease with which you can access all of Aix on foot from the hotel's front door. Pets are welcome and parking is available, and doubles start at €100.

ANTIBES

Antibes has a small-town feel about it, and the limited number of hotels in the *centre ville* lend credence to that notion. Visit in the off-season and you'll feel like you have the place to yourself, but not so much in the summer. Close to the port at **Relais du Postillon** (8, rue Championnet, tel. 04/93 34 20 77), you'll find fair prices and a friendly welcome in the cozy, fireplace-lit reception room and bar. During the low season (October 1-April 30), spacious rooms—some overlooking the park across the street—range from €69-99 per night, and slightly more in the high season.

A few blocks farther inland in the pedestrian quarter is the simple but comfortable **Modern Hotel** (1, rue Fourmilière, tel. 04/92 90 59 05), with double rooms with

Wi-Fi, television, and local taxes included that start at €58 per night in the low season, €82 in high season.

NICE

You'll have a lot to choose from in Nice, and you can even find charming little hotels for less than €100 across the street from that turquoise wonder, the Mediterranean. The trick to landing the perfect accommodations in the heart of town is booking in advance—way in advance—if you plan to stay in town during the busy summer months. Off-season, you can walk into most hotels and secure a room on the spot.

Just two blocks from the sparkling sea sits **Hotel Felix** (41, rue Massena, tel. 04/93 88 66 73), perfectly positioned on the main pedestrian promenade in the Carré d'Or (Golden Square). You'll get a decent-size room with a small balcony, wireless Internet, and that French hotel-room rarity, the hot-water kettle for morning tea and coffee, for between €63 and €83 per night, depending on the season.

Down the street and around the corner is the two-star **Little Palace** (9, ave Baquis, tel. 04/97 03 00 00). Simple but comfortable, this affordable spot offers great proximity to the beach, museums, and the city's famous pedestrian zones, including the Promenade des Anglais. In the off-season, rooms can be had for the rock-bottom price of €37, but you'll pay more than twice that in high season. Note: Unlike the Hotel Felix, Little Palace isn't pet-friendly.

Lyon and Grenoble

LYON

Lyon is a pretty city with a fitting number of pretty hotels to choose from. If you haven't made reservations, visit the tourism office on place Bellecour, where the staff will book you a room in your price range for no extra charge. Easy access to all the action in Lyon can be found in that sliver of the city sandwiched between the Saône and Rhône Rivers, where tramlines, the Métro, and bus service crisscross, taking passengers in different directions. Within walking distance of Gare Perrache (with direct trains to Paris) is chain hotel **Kyriad** (24, quai Perrache, tel. 04/78 37 16 64). Standard rooms fall into the affordable category at €49, including nice amenities like bath gel, hair dryers, and complimentary coffee, tea, and biscuits in your room.

At the foot of Fourvière, in the überadorable St. Paul neighborhood, **Hotel Saint Paul** (6, rue Lainerie, tel. 04/78 28 13 29) offers a cozy welcome to travelers in its purple lobby. Rooms are painted with equally colorful panache, with doubles beginning at €79. The Renaissance-period building is equipped with modern conveniences, including free wireless Internet and cable television.

GRENOBLE

Grenoble is one of many potential home bases for snow enthusiasts who've come to this corner of the country to tackle a mountain or two. The tourism infrastructure is well established, and there are many accommodations to choose from as you scope out the city and its neighborhoods. Smack in the middle of town is Grenoble's oldest hotel, **Hotel de l'Europe** (22, place Grenette, tel. 04/76 46 16 94), where cheerfully decorated, modern double rooms—some with fireplaces—range from €64 to €81 per night. After pounding the pavement looking for that perfect apartment, you'll appreciate the hotel's sauna and fitness room.

A 10-minute walk from the train station is **Apparthotel Privilodges** (1, rue Guy Alard, tel. 04/76 12 98 98), which is a great option if you're going to stay a few days and want to save money by shopping at the *marché* and cooking meals at home. These studio and one-, two-, and three-bedroom apartments are set in a lovely old mansion, and prices are competitive with hotels: Studios start at €70 per night, with discounts for longer stays. The usuals—Wi-Fi, toiletries, flat-screen televisions—are included in the price.

Strasbourg

You'll find scads of accommodation possibilities in Strasbourg, including an enormous selection directly across from the train station. The neighborhood isn't the prettiest, but it's convenient and a short walk to the center of town. For something easy, clean, and a good value, consider the trendy **Hotel Graffalgar** (17, rue Déserte, tel. 03/88 24 98 40), where each of the 19 rooms are designed by different local artists. Bikes are available to guests, and an on-site café makes getting your afternoon pick-me-up easy as pie. Rates start at €90 for two people.

A more traditional hotel experience can be found at **Hotel Cathedral** (12-13, place de la Cathédrale, tel. 03/88 22 12 12) directly across from the towering, rose-colored cathedral that Strasbourg is famous for. Rates begin at €69 for a double in low season, and with that price you'll get a friendly reception and superior access to Strasbourg's best sights.

FOOD
Paris

If Parisians aren't the dining-out champions of the world, then who could it possibly be? In even the quietest neighborhood, every street seems to have at least two restaurants, one of which is guaranteed to be hopping with happy patrons. Do like 62 percent of Parisians do, and eat in the quartier you call home—if only temporarily. Don't know where to look? Start with this short list, but know that you really can't go wrong at any of the city's thousands of brasseries and cafés.

Not far from the infamous Bastille neighborhood is the festive, traditional **Baron Rouge** (1, rue Théophile Roussel, tel. 01/43 43 14 32), a perpetually popular wine bar and caféthat's a year-round favorite with locals and tourists alike. The cheese and charcuterie plates are popular, and in months ending with "r," you'll also find oysters on the menu.

For something a little less rustic, head a few blocks north to **Clamato** (80, rue de Charonne, tel. 01/43 72 74 53), a trendy spot next to even trendier (and more exclusive) sister restaurant Septime. The wine list alone is worth the trip, and omnivores rave about the seafood-heavy menu and local celebrity sightings

On the Right Bank, a 10-minute walk down the hill from Montparnasse station is possibly the best pizza spot in town. **Pizza Chic** (13, rue Mézières, tel. 01/40 45 30 38) is indeed chic, with gorgeous pies and a waitstaff that really know what they're doing. The artichoke pizza and a glass of the house Chardonnay borders on perfection.

In an unassuming neighborhood in Paris's far northwest corner, the scent of roasting coffee beans signals your proximity to **Menelik** (4, rue Sauffroy, tel. 01/46 27 00 82). At this lively Ethiopian eatery, every guest is greeted with a complimentary glass of *kir,* and everyone leaves utterly sated and happy.

Brittany
RENNES

Once you've settled into your hotel, it's time to mosey over to the **place des Lices** for a slice of the weekend-market action. In between the market's two covered *halles*, fast-food vendors dole out hearty crêpes, roast chickens, and Thai noodles from mobile carts. Get in the longest line and you can be assured whatever you order will be delicious.

If meandering through the market with food in hand isn't your cup of tea, work your way through the vegetable stalls and the flower vendors and over to **place Rallier du Baty,** where a bustling terrace hums with diners from three different restaurants on the square. Grab one of **La Luppa's** (10, place Rallier du Baty, tel. 02/99 79 31 15) tables and order a thin-crust, wood-fired pizza and a *pichet du vin,* and you'll have all the fuel you need to explore the city afterward.

Breton crêpes are a must in this neck of France, and at **La Saint-Georges** (11, rue Chapitre, tel. 02/ 99 38 87 04) every number on the menu is named after a famous George, from Sand (smoked salmon and potatoes) to Clooney (spinach and goat cheese, served with a side of cucumber sorbet). Service is solid and the atmosphere is at once cozy and modern.

VANNES

In Vannes, you'll have to resign yourself to the fact that this really is crêpe country. Give in to it, and soon you'll be addicted. Some of the best examples are at **Crêperie Saint-Exupéry** (8, rue Orfèvres, tel. 02/97 47 28 18), on a cobbled corner of a medieval street in the old town. The buckwheat galettes (savory crêpes) are thin and tasty, and if you want fries with that, they've got you covered.

For comparison's sake, take a stroll down to the water's edge approximately half an hour from the city center, where you'll find three crêperies on the little harbor at **Conleau.** Whichever one you choose, you can be sure of a cheap and tasty lunch, accompanied by a *bolée de cidre,* and a lovely, sunshiny view across the sea.

Bordeaux and the Dordogne Valley
BORDEAUX

In Bordeaux, it's all about the tapas. And the couscous. And the kebabs. And the curry. You won't go hungry in this town, no matter your food preferences—and if you happen to be vegetarian, vegan, or gluten-free, you'll be glad to know about **Rest'o** (6, quai de Bacalan, tel. 05/32 08 01 93). Located on the waterfront in the northern reaches of the Chartrons district, you'll get a very warm welcome and colorful, flavorful food ranging from lasagne to lemon tarte.

Vegetables not your thing? Perhaps you're better off hitting one of the many tapas bars in town. One of the tastiest, **Meson La Venta** (17, place Meynard, tel. 05/56 91 59 80), sits smack across from the daily *marché aux puces* on place Meynard. Sit inside or out and dig into a buffet of small plates, including a Spanish tortilla, cheese-stuffed peppers, and potatoes with aioli, and wash it all down with glasses of tangy sangria.

BERGERAC

Bergerac is a humble little town with a nice community feel that's reflected in the food offerings about town. Sure, there are the handful of Michelin-star-type restaurants, but if you want to eat like a local, skip the fancy places and head straight for the **River Side** (12, quai Salvette, 05/53 73 86 94), the place to bring your appetite on a sunny day. Sit on the terrace and sip a glass of rosé with your hearty pasta dish or charcuterie plate. During football season, the inside dining room doubles as an afternoon sports bar. You've been forewarned!

If you're in the mood for a more refined dining experience try **Restaurant le St. Jacques** (30, rue St. James, tel. 05/53 23 38 08). The proprietors, who are originally from Holland, serve traditional French food based on what's in season—which, if you're lucky, will be some sort of mushroom. Eat in the cozy main dining room if it's raining, or choose the pleasant outdoor courtyard in summer.

SARLAT-LA-CANÉDA

In Sarlat, you can always get a croque monsieur or a slice of quiche Lorraine for a few euros at a *boulangerie,* but this is truffle country, so let yourself be seduced by the myriad menus proffering these treats. Truffled omelets seem to be the perpetual *plat du jour;* if you feel like having breakfast for lunch (or dinner), you'll have no trouble finding a restaurant serving the local specialty.

Some say the only Sarlat dining address you need to remember is that of **l'Adress** (8, rue de 8 Mai 1945, tel. 05/53 30 56 19). Menus are centered on local, in-season produce, and the staff is attentive without being intrusive. Classics like risotto, burgers, and even Caesar salad get a modern makeover, and desserts are house-made. Pop in for a three-course lunch (€21), then wander the romantic city center in a happily sated state.

Burgermania hasn't just swept through Paris; it's also hit Sarlat, and **Les Tontons Burgers** (4, rue Lakanal, tel. 06/26 24 45 23) is the local hotspot. Sure, this is fast food, but the loyal following will tell you that the burgers, fries, crêpes, and shakes served up with a smile are anything but pedestrian. Good news for homebodies: they deliver!

Pau, Toulouse, and Montpellier
PAU

Food options in Pau run the gamut from Indian to Mexican and beyond, but sometimes, the traditional *cave à manger* is the best bet. At **Les Papilles Insolites** (5, rue Alexander Taylor, tel. 05/59 71 43 79), the house specialty is natural wine, and your server will help you pair the right plate of food to accompany your glass(es). Expect lots of meat with sides of locally grown, in-season vegetables, and broad strokes of visual appeal on every plate. Reservations advised.

Another popular dining spot worth fumbling through your French to book a table at is **La Fiancée du Desert** (21, rue Tran, tel. 05/59 27 27 58). Cheap and downright delicious, you can expect traditional Lebanese dishes with a heavy Greek influence. Moussaka, tzatziki, chiche kebab, and salads galore compete for your mealtime attention, and vegetarians will sup like royals right alongside their omnivorous dining companions.

TOULOUSE

If you aren't tempted to try the cassoulet in Toulouse, the locals might wonder what's wrong with you. To taste this regional specialty, bring your empty stomach to **Le Bibent** (5, Place du Capitole, tel. 05/34 30 18 37), right on the central square. The people-watching from the terrace is just one of the restaurant's many virtues; the menu, which brims with traditional French fare heavily influenced by Basque cuisine, is the main draw.

Neo Asian cuisine is the current culinary fashion in Toulouse, and a great spot to take a taste of the trend is **Chez Pham** (1, rue Mage, tel. 05/62 19 12 36), south of the city center near the Parc Royal. With communal tables and a cantine-like atmosphere, you'll be energized as much by the atmosphere as you will be by the food. The *pho* is a Friday favorite, and the salads are not to be missed.

MONTPELLIER

Montpellier is student central, and where there are students, there are cheap and fill-ing restaurants. At the little family-run restaurant **Les Saveurs de Liban** (7, Faubourg Figuerolles, tel. 04/30 10 83 36) off the busy boulevard Gambetta, you'll stuff yourself for less than a tenner on perfectly prepared falafel, fatayer (small pastries stuffed with spinach), creamy house-made hummus, and not-too-sweet pastries for dessert. The mint tea, spiced with cardamom and served in tiny glasses, is a must-try.

For something with a bit more ambiance, head to **Pizzeria du Palais** (22, rue du Palais des Guilhem, tel. 04/67 60 67 97), Montpellier's oldest pizzeria. For 50 years, this Sicilian-owned spot has been firing up the oven and baking some of the best pizza pies this side of Palermo. Fresh pasta, salads, wine, and tiramisu round out the menu.

Provence and the Côte d'Azur
AIX-EN-PROVENCE

Aix is another student's paradise: coffee shops, bookstores, and affordable eateries abound in the old town and beyond. At the fast-casual locavore haven **Maison Nosh** (42-44 Cours Sextius, tel. 04/52 86 22 39), you can choose between fresh and afford-able English-muffin sandwiches, hotdogs (including a tofu-based version), and warm-ing soups. Juices, shakes, and smoothies are a few thirst-quenching options.

For foodies interested in exploring the Aix-style *bistronomie* scene, the quest starts at **Le Mille Feuille** (8, rue Rifle-Rafle, tel. 04/42 96 55 17). The daily menu is de-termined by what's fresh and in season at the local markets, and diners are typically offered a choice of four entrées, three or four plats, and an equal number of desserts. Think risotto with squash blossoms, salmon tartare, and luscious desserts that are as enticing to look at as they are to taste.

ANTIBES

In pretty little Antibes, tucked into the old town behind a salmon-colored façade, sits **Chez Helen** (35, rue des Revennes, tel. 04/92 93 88 52), a certified organic restaurant specializing in vegetarian cuisine. Helen, a native of England, serves up homey, filling fare such as lasagna, cordon bleu, and creamy soups. The restaurant is closed evenings, but long lunch hours make an early dinner possible. Tea, beer, and wine are also on tap.

A block from the beach on the Juan Les Pins side of the city, **Ti Toques** (9 avenue Louis Gallet, tel. 04/92 90 25 12) welcomes diners with friendly service and an inter-esting, somewhat eclectic menu that moves from French onion soup to paella to chili con tofu. Belgian beers, Provençal wines, and George Clooney-certified Nespresso coffee keep spirits high and thirst at bay.

NICE

Nice is famous for *socca,* and there are scads of opportunities to try the delicious chickpea crepe, including the Chez Thérèsa, the very casual socca stand (think plastic chairs and wine cups) at the Cours Saleya market in old Nice. For something a little more refined but still casual, head over to **Rene Socca** (1 rue Pairoliere, tel. 04/93 92 05 73). Besides the namesake dish, the busy little spot serves up other local specialties, including *pissaladière* (caramelized onion pizza with olives and anchovies) and tapenade.

If you want to see what kind of a life an expat can carve out for herself in Nice, book a table at **Le Speakeasy** (7 rue Lamartine, tel. 04/93 85 59 50). The owner of this charming vegan restaurant is American, and she has a passion for both France and for plant-based cuisine. Expect simple, rustic fare that's mostly organic. A three-course dining experience will set you back less than €20.

Lyon and Grenoble

LYON

Ask gourmets which city is the food capital of France, and they'll inevitably say Lyon. If you want a taste of no-frills French food cooked to perfection and served in a homey atmosphere, get thee to the old town, spin yourself around, and walk into the first *bouchon* you bump into. These traditional Lyonnais restaurants serve food like Grandma used to make, if Grandma happened to live in the Rhône-Alpes region and wasn't a vegetarian. Meaty dishes like goose-liver terrine, duck cooked in cognac, and chubby pork sausages take center stage at *bouchons,* so remember to bring your heart meds.

For something on the lighter end of the spectrum, **Wasabi** (76 rue d'Anvers, tel. 04/37 28 08 77), on the other side of the Rhône River in the university district, serves Japanese fare that will leave you sated but not belly-ache full. Sushi, miso soup, and Korean-style *bulgogi* are on the menu, as are special *formules* for children and vegetarians.

Arsenic (132, rue Pierre Corneille, tel. 9/62 39 85 55) is a rather questionable choice for a restaurant name, but the food at this néobistro is worth the gamble. Each chic and artistic plate coming out of the kitchen is based on a traditional French recipe, but given a modern twist. Unexpected flavor combinations—smoked trout with cabbage, for example, or beets and bacon—win converts on a daily basis, including Sundays and Mondays, when many restaurants are closed.

GRENOBLE

The mist-shrouded, mountainous landscape around Grenoble brings to mind Alpine resort foods, like fondue and cheesy raclette. You actually will find those dishes here, but that's so predictable. How about going for southeast Asian instead? Grenoble has a sizeable Vietnamese community, with bountiful authentic restaurants catering to those locals. Near the Tuesday-Sunday *marché l'Estacade,* **Saveurs d'Asie** (3, boulevard Gambetta, tel. 04/76 84 41 32) serves up traditional Vietnamese favorites like *pho,* rice-paper rolls, and *bahn xeo.* When you're full, you can shop for condiments at the nearby Asian grocery stores.

For something a little more traditional, there's the gastronomic heaven of **Le Mas Boterro** (168, Cours Berriat, tel. 04/76 21 95 33). You'll walk away with a much lighter wallet, but the quality of food and service is worth the price of admission. In truffle season, a glorious menu dedicated to the prized fungi will set you back about €100, and include such delicacies as ravioli with pear, vanilla, and truffles, and smoked potato soup with truffles and leeks.

Strasbourg

In this corner of eastern France, the German influence is palpable, and nowhere more so than in the local cuisine. Think *choucroute* (sauerkraut), hearty *spaetzle* (potatoes), and plenty of meat to keep the carnivores happy. **Au Pont Corbeau** (21, quai Saint-Nicolas, tel. 03/88 35 60 68) is a hot spot for trying Alsatian specialties, including the delicious white wines produced in the area. The atmosphere is convivial and occasionally very, very crowded, so make a reservation. A post-meal stroll along the canal will help revitalize you.

For an afternoon pick-me-up that packs a sugary wallop, visit the bright and cheerful **Salon de The Grande'Rue** (80, Grand'Rue, tel. 03/88 32 12 70) where huge slices of cake and warming cups of tea and coffee await you. The decor screams "every day is Christmas" and the food—which also includes hearty breakfasts and Alsatian-inspired lunch plates—is equally festive. Locals swear they make the best cheesecake in town, and in summer, you can enjoy a berry tarte in the backyard terrace.

DAILY LIFE

MAKING THE MOVE

Congratulations! You've decided to make the leap and live the dream, integrating baguettes, berets, and cafés into your everyday life. *C'est super!* By now, you've already made a reconnaissance trip or two, decided where you want to live, and have begun researching the area for schools, employment opportunities, and housing. Now comes the tricky part: Synthesizing everything you've learned and making it all happen. Visas, *cartes de séjour,* residency permits—what do they all mean, and what exactly do you need to make this big step a success? There's a lot to consider, but with a bit more planning and a lot of moxie, the transition can be practically pain-free. Stumbling blocks are bound to appear, but don't let the bureaucratic sludge drag you down. Follow the rules and somehow, thankfully, it all comes together. Excited? You ought to be! Just a few more hurdles and you're on your way.

Immigration and Visas

As a citizen of Canada or the United States, you don't need a visa for stays of fewer than 90 days. France is a signatory of the Schengen Agreement, which means it shares a flexible internal border-control system with fellow Schengen countries and a stronger border-crossing process with non-Schengen countries, such as the United Kingdom. Passport checks are rare between, say, France and Belgium, but they're a given if you're traveling to the UK. Your free 90-day visa is valid throughout the Schengen zone, but don't mistakenly believe that to extend your stay you just need to Chunnel on over to England, get your passport stamped, and resume another 90-day sojourn in France. Unfortunately, it doesn't work like that. If you want to stay legal, you can make only one 90-day visit within any six-month period. When in doubt, apply for a long-stay visa or accept the risks involved in overstaying your welcome.

TYPES OF VISAS

To determine what kind of visa to apply for, ask yourself the following questions:

How long do you plan to be in France? If you're subletting your flat back in Minneapolis and just want to try a three-month trial run, that's considered a "short stay"—as is any stay shorter than 90 days—and a valid passport is all you need. But if you're planning on a year (a school year or an actual calendar year), you'll need to begin the visa application process *tout de suite* (right away). Even though it probably won't take this long, give yourself a good two months to make it all come together.

What are you going to do once you arrive? This information will help you zero in on which long-stay visa to apply for. Maybe you've always fantasized about living in France and just want an extended vacation to relax, study independently, or meet a handsome Frenchman or -woman and see where the relationship takes you. If so, you'll need money in the bank to show you can support yourself for the duration of your stay. Do you have a brilliant idea for a new business that *has* to be launched in France? There's a visa for that. It also requires evidence of your means of support, plus detailed information on how you plan to carry out the project, and you must prove that the idea itself fills a void in France to be eligible for approval. Maybe you're a college student who wants to study abroad for the semester or a nanny (or manny) who just landed an au pair job through an agency. Whether you're an artist, an entrepreneur, an intern, or a student, there's a long-stay visa with your name on it. Now, getting that visa will take a bit of elbow grease and perseverance, but armed with willpower and solid resolve, you can make it happen.

WHERE AND HOW TO APPLY

Submitting your visa application must be done in person at a French consulate since you'll be sized up by consular officials and have your fingerprints indelibly inked into an inter-governmental database, but not every state or province in the United States and Canada has a French consulate. If your region does not, you'll have to make the trip for a scheduled appointment. One appointment is all you need: Follow-up requests for documentation can be mailed or faxed in, and your passport—with or without a shiny

Dossier or Die

Dossier. OK, let's try saying that out loud the French way: "dohs-YAY." You'll want to practice this a few times to get the hang of it, because you're going to use it a lot. You'll need a dossier every step of the way on your move to France, beginning at the consulate, and ending with—well, it never ends in France. You'll create a dossier for the *préfecture*, the bank, the real-estate company, the movers, your university, your children's school, the gas company, the veterinarian, the doctor, and just about everything else you can think of.

The dossier is simply a file containing documents relating to whatever business is at hand. The foundation of nearly every dossier includes the following:

- a copy of your passport, *carte de séjour*, or other ID

Your various dossiers will require several passport-size photos, which you can take at France's ubiquitous photo booths.

- your EDF (electricity) bill or another proof of residence (often an *attestation* written by the person hosting you, including *her* gas bill and copy of her *carte d'identité*)

- two or three passport-sized photos, which you're expected to have taken in the automated photo booths found in administrative buildings and train stations, among other places

Then, like a bureaucratic buffet, each agency adds on a series of extra must-haves that give your dossier its special flavor. Though most expats find the dossier system tiresome, each pile of paperwork you create makes building the next one that much easier.

new visa inside—can be mailed back to you in the pre-stamped express-mail envelope you provide at the time of your appointment. To find the consulate closest to you, visit www.ambafrance-us.org (United States) or www.ambafrance-ca.org (Canada).

LONG-STAY VISA

Visa laws have relaxed in the past few years, so most long-stay visa holders don't need to visit the *préfecture* on arrival, as had long been standard protocol. (An exception to this rule is the *carte compétences et talents*, which still necessitates a visit to your local *préfecture*.) Instead of schlepping yourself and your dossier full of paperwork to endless appointments, the streamlined system allows you to register with the French Office of Immigration and Integration (OFII) by mail within three months of your arrival.

Registration involves submitting copies of your passport pages that show your photo and expiration date; the entry stamp for your arrival in France; and the visa issued to you by the French Consulate. You'll also need to include a completed Demande d'Attestation OFII form, which you'll receive from consular officials when your passport is returned to you with your new visa. (If you don't automatically receive this form, ask for one or visit the OFII website to download a copy: www.ofii.fr.)

These items must be sent via *lettre recommandé,* which is essentially a registered letter that the recipient must sign for. Once your documents are received, you'll receive a notice of receipt from the OFII, which serves as temporary proof of your legal right to reside in France. Within three months, you'll be called in for the requisite medical exam, which includes lung X-rays and blood-sugar analysis, at which time you'll also pay for your *timbres* (tax stamps)—which, depending on your residency status, will vary between €77 and €260. Once this process has been completed, you'll receive the final passport stamp in the visa-acquisition process: a *vignette* stamp alongside your French visa.

STUDENT VISA

Probably the most popular of all move-to-France visas is the student visa. French universities are open to anyone of any age who has earned his or her high school diploma or equivalent. Because it's a relatively straightforward point of entry into France that also gives the holder the right to work part-time, this is an attractive option for getting your foot through the French front door.

Students used to have to apply for a visa even if they intended to stay for fewer than 90 days, but that's no longer the case: Your American or Canadian passport is sufficient if you'll be living and studying in France for less than three months—say, a summer study-abroad course. However, because students who hold a *carte de séjour* are entitled to work part-time during their residency, you might consider jumping through those more challenging hoops to get the long-stay visa even if you don't plan to reside in France for the entire duration, just for the added perk of being allowed to work legally.

If you'll be studying for more than three months, you'll need to apply for a long-stay student visa, which first requires you to register online with Campus France, an intermediary agency that handles the initial phase of your visa formalities. Here, you'll create the first of many dossiers, so consider it a necessary evil. Whether you're a Canadian or an American citizen, you will be expected to have your Campus France ID number at the time of your appointment at the consulate, as well as a long-stay visa application, travel itinerary, and proof of financial means of support while you're away. You may also be asked for several other documents, making for a multi-visit experience before you've even left the country. (If you live out of state or out of the area, you'll be allowed to fax or send in supplemental documents.) You'll need several passport-size photos throughout the process, so have a set made and carry them with you to each appointment in your home country as well as in France.

With most types of visa, once you arrive in France you'll need to follow the OFII registration procedure outlined in the long-stay visa section above. If, after your first year in France, you'd like to renew your residency permit, you'll have to do so at the prefecture two months before your current residency permit expires.

WORK VISA

If you're one of the lucky ones who has already received a job offer in France, you'll have to apply for a visa before you can receive your work permit. But before *that* happens, the company sponsoring you must file all the necessary paperwork on its end with the French labor department (DDTEFP). (The exception to this is the work contract for

90 days or fewer; no visa is needed for short-term workers, but your employer must still file paperwork on your behalf to make the arrangement legal.) Once it's approved, you can start cultivating your own paper trail.

Don't have a job offer yet? Start scouring the employment opportunities on sites like FUSAC (www.fusac.org), Craigslist, the UN, OECD, and UNESCO. A wise idea is to investigate all the American-owned companies in Paris, of which there are scads, including restaurants, boutiques, hotels, and tourism-related enterprises. Note that high-level, well-paid positions are in high demand among future expats, and the pool of qualified applicants will be full and competition stiff. Be honest with yourself when submitting your résumé: If you don't have a college degree, the likelihood you'll land one of the coveted positions with an international NGO or multinational with offices in Paris or the La Défense business district is slim. The odds aren't impossible, but they're not great. The more advanced your educational qualifications, the better your chances of getting a sponsored gig. Ditto for your language skills. If you aren't equipped with at least conversational French, you may have a tough time securing your dream job with a company that will sponsor your visa. (See more about working in France in the *Employment* chapter.)

If you work at a company in the United States or Canada with offices in France, explore transfer opportunities. Many banks, high-tech companies, and fashion-related organizations have set up shop here and offer first-consideration privileges to those who have been on their employment rosters for at least three months. As a final option, you can hit up your French friends to "hire" you to work for them. If a good friend or family member is willing to climb the bureaucratic Mont Blanc on your behalf, this could be your ticket. As with any endeavor that attempts to skirt the standard procedure, there are inherent risks involved; still, this sort of creative problem-solving is not unheard of. Approached with a modicum of professionalism, it can be a successful way to move to France and secure legal permission to work.

CARTE DE SÉJOUR COMPÉTENCES ET TALENTS

In theory, this "skill and talents" card is a dream come true for independent, creative types who want to live in France but don't fit into any of the other visa categories. The idea is that you come up with a project you'd like to work on in France that fits within your professional and educational experience. The tricky part is that it must in some way function as a means of bridging the cultural relationship between France and your home country. Perhaps you own a bicycle shop in Portland and teach mountain-biking clinics on the weekend; you may want to parlay your experience into a business that teaches children how to ride downhill in the Alps. Or maybe you're finishing up your PhD in 20th-century American literature and want to start a tourism business that takes travelers on a journey along the path of the Lost Generation in Paris and beyond. There are countless ideas, but this visa is still in the experimental phase. There are no exact parameters on what the powers-that-be are looking for, and therefore no guarantees that they'll accept your proposal. To boost your chances of getting the green light, invest time in creating a solid business plan before presenting it to French consular officials. Get creative with your powers of persuasion, pull out all your credentials (letters of recommendation, diplomas, and certificates), and really sell yourself and the lasting contribution your project will have on the French public.

Expat Experience: Use Your Talents

Name: Kaori Tomaru
Age: 37
Occupation: Education Specialist
Hometown: New York City
Current city: Paris, 13th

Kaori Tomaru moved to France in 2007 under the *Assistant des Langues Étrangers* program, with the intention of staying nine months to a year—just long enough to improve her French. Nearly a decade later, she is happily ensconced in the French capital, where she lives with her rescue dog, Ralph. Here, the former New Yorker shares her experience acquiring one of the most interesting visas for Americans who want to spend up to three years in France: the *Carte Compétence et Talents.*

DAILY LIFE

How did you determine which visa/*carte de séjour* to apply for?
I was simply in the right place at the right time. I was working with the Académie de Créteil and already had a project that qualified. The *Compétence et Talents* visa was introduced at exactly the moment I needed a visa to continue my work with the Académie.

Where did you apply for your *carte de séjour*, and what was the project you proposed?
I went back to the States and applied through the Washington DC embassy. My project was based on integrating technology/multimedia and social media in order to structure language lesson planning around video and multimedia/communication projects. They not only accepted my application, but I got to meet the consul general, who was quite interested in what I was doing. This really helped down the road with the *préfecture* in Paris.

Once you arrived in Paris, how long did it take for you to receive your actual *carte*?
I had a great official letter to present to the *préfecture* to get my actual residence card (*Titre de Séjour*). It had a very short list of what I was to bring to complete the process. I got there and they asked for the entire dossier I had submitted for application. I explained that I had been told I only needed xyz, and they sent me off and said they would get the materials from the embassy. A few months later, I received a phone call telling me to come in, at which time I was told that I had been rejected. It wasn't explained why. I protested and was shuffled off to apply for another visa. I knew I was totally in over my head, so I brought reinforcement when I went back: a friend who was also a civil servant. Civil servants, or *fonctionnaires*, speak their own code. We finally learned that I was rejected because my dossier was virtually empty because they had lost almost everything. After a few hours of polite insistence and refusal to leave, we managed to get them to accept the copies of all the missing papers I luckily had with me. I filed it back to them with a letter asking them to review it again and reconsider. I also sent a letter to the consul general, who liked my project, asking to intervene. I think something worked, because it only took a year to get my card at the end of it all.

Have you renewed your *carte* since you've lived in France?
Yes. I used a lawyer to prepare the paperwork, but I was less stressed, because my project has really grown and I had great letters of reference. I got it just under a year after application, which seems to be par for the course.

When applying for a *carte de séjour compétences et talents,* you'll need to prepare yourself for the number of trees that will be sacrificed to meet the demands of consular officials: long-stay visa forms, letters from your bank, a police record release or FBI clearance form, résumé, proof of insurance, proof that you have a place to live in France, flight itineraries—all in duplicate. (You might as well make it triplicate, because if you don't, you'll surely be asked for a third copy of whatever it is you don't have a third copy of.)

If you are granted this visa, you are entitled—again, in theory—to a renewable three-year *carte de séjour* that allows you to work in your chosen profession. If you are married, your spouse will receive a *vie privée et familiale* card that entitles him or her to work as well. But don't get too excited just yet. Even if you're granted this visa, you can still expect to jump through a lot of hoops to get your *carte* once you arrive in France. Expect to spend many hours over several days, weeks, and even months at the *préfecture.* You will be asked to produce supplemental material—notarized translations of specific documents, French-language copies of your rental agreement, proof of address, copies of your passport, photographs—and even then you may be told that they're only going to give you a one-year *carte* "to see how it goes" before allowing you to renew.

FOREIGN TRADER'S CARD

Some people are born with an entrepreneurial spirit. If you want to start a business in France, it will help to be equipped with both that spirit *and* the patience of a saint. You've heard a bit about the "special" nature of French bureaucracy by now, and, well, it hits its zenith at the business-launching phase. The good news is that tax laws have been relaxed in the last few years, making it easier for startups than ever before. But before you start thinking about applying for this special *carte,* be sure to do your research and have a solid business plan ready. In addition to your long-stay visa application, you'll be asked to provide budgets, proof of funding, and other documents that support your assertion that you know what you're doing and have the backing to carry out the project. Pull out all the stops: Got an aunt in Brittany you haven't seen in 20 years? Call her up and ask if she'll act as a *garante* (financial guarantor). If you have a bank account established in France already, ask the bank to write a letter attesting to your solid financial history and line of credit. Most of all, pitch your idea by touting all the wonderful ways in which it will benefit France, fill a major void, and better serve the community. Your education, experience, connections within France, and ability to communicate in French will all be taken into consideration by consular officials.

VISAS FOR ACCOMPANYING SPOUSES AND CHILDREN

Depending on the type of visa you've applied for, your children and spouse will likely be authorized to join you, provided you've all filled out the necessary forms and provided the required paperwork. Before you begin the process, make sure you have copies of your marriage license, spouse's birth certificate, and birth certificates of your children. If you or your spouse have children from a previous relationship, a notarized letter from the other parent granting permission to move to France will also be required.

For holders of the *carte de séjour compétences et talents,* your spouse also receives permission to work—one of the many reasons this *carte* is such an alluring possibility. Workers who are sponsored by an employer and want to bring their families with them to France need to ensure that the "accompanying family member" paperwork is being managed by said employer. Be sure to follow up to thwart unwelcome surprises.

OTHER VISAS

Visas for nannies, researchers, interns, and retirees also exist, and the steps for applying for each are similar to the aforementioned visa application processes. And if you've met a French national and want to marry and move to France, there's a visa for you, too. If the visa you are applying for is likely to be denied for some reason, you will probably be notified of this at the time of your consular appointment. There's a chance that your visa request will be outright refused, in which case you have the right to reapply. If you don't hear back from the consulate within two months, this means the rejection is firm.

BEYOND THE VISA

When asked to sign formal documents at the *préfecture,* you will often be required to ink your John Hancock into a little rectangular box. Note that this box has very specific boundaries, and if your signature extends beyond any of the four sides of said box, you have effectively ruined the entire document and will have to start over from scratch. So remember to write between the lines. (Seriously.)

Before you are granted any kind of official *carte,* you will be given a temporary *Récépissé de Demande de Carte de Séjour,* a small, light-blue rectangle of paper with your photo attached and an official seal and expiration date stamped on it. Before you trade in the interim paper for the official pink laminated version, you'll be required to undergo a quick health screening at a public clinic. The government foots the bill for this—which seems appropriate considering that you'll have the un-fun task of getting naked from the waist up while a stranger photographs your lungs to ensure they're free of tuberculosis.

Depending on where you settle, your experience can vary vastly. Expats report shorter waits at *préfectures* outside Paris city limits, and less muss and fuss in general when it comes to the bureaucratic processes. You can expect long lines—sometimes to the tune of a five-hour wait—and even then, you might not get in the building before they close for lunch or, worse, for the day. Inside, you'll need to pull a numbered ticket from the little machine and wait your turn. Expect line-jumping—lots of it. It's annoying, and you can choose whether or not to pitch a fit. But whatever you do, do not lose your cool with a staff member. Even if you feel as if your brain will explode with frustration after a daylong wait and ruthless line-jumpers, you must keep a calm and composed demeanor when face to face with the people behind the desk if you want a successful experience.

Though it may seem superficial, it helps to take extra care with your personal appearance on the day of your *préfecture* visit. Wearing chic, stylish clothing—don't forget to polish your shoes and groom your hair—and having your dossier neatly organized in a professional-looking attaché case will convey to the authorities that you've got your act together, even if that's the furthest thing from the truth. Some people report getting to bypass certain steps, such as providing proof of funds, and credit the fact that they dressed the part of the professional, upstanding citizen.

RESIDENCY

Visas and *cartes de séjour* have temporary residency periods built into them. Your visa buys you a finite amount of time, and your *carte* gives specific time parameters with renewable options. After three continuous years of residency, holders of the *visiteur, salarié, étudiant, vie privée, commerçante, scientifique,* or *artistique carte* visas are eligible to apply for a 10-year residency permit, which gives you the luxury of returning to the *préfecture* only once per decade. Everyone else must have established five years of residency before they can apply for the 10-year *carte.*

French immigration laws are prone to change with disarming regularity. Keep reviewing the consular websites for new updates and changes, and keep a flexible attitude whenever possible.

Moving with Children

Getting your children to France with you is fairly straightforward, and once you're settled, you'll discover that France is an extraordinarily kid-friendly country—hardly surprising, considering the central role that the family plays here. The first stop in your children's move-abroad adventure is securing your own visa; if you're in, they're in. Like you, they'll need specific documents for the consular appointment: two passport-size photos, a long-stay visa application, a copy of their birth certificate, and their passport. If you are a single father or mother traveling without your child's second parent, you'll also need to bring a notarized letter of authorization to travel signed by him or her.

SCHOOL-AGE CHILDREN

Parents of school-age children will need to begin thinking about enrolling them in some sort of academic institution, and your options are contingent in large part on where you live. **Écoles privées** (private schools)—from Montessori and Waldorf to good old-fashioned Catholic schools—exist throughout the Île-de-France, and like elsewhere, you'll have to pay tuition. The cost varies from school to school, but it's generally less expensive than American private schools. **International schools,** which are basically American in concept and function, also exist, and provide a familiar academic structure at a premium price. Unlike other countries, where "state-run" anything has negative connotations, French **écoles publiques** (public schools) are of uniformly high quality and are a good way to integrate your child into French culture. Just like back home, schools want to see a child's academic records and inoculation history, so remember to pad your dossier with copies of those.

CHILDCARE

If your child is younger and you want to consider daycare, it's helpful to register with your local *crèche* or *halte garderie* (state-run daycare centers). These agencies follow the standard academic cycle and generally accept new wards only in September and occasionally in January, and the registration process begins months in advance, so it pays to plan ahead if you want to guarantee your child a spot. Children as young as three months are welcome, and the staff are highly trained and qualified. In public parks throughout Paris and other large French metropolises, you will see brigades of nannies, often from former French colonies in West Africa, pushing prams full of infants. You too can find a nanny via word of mouth, Craigslist, FUSAC, an agency, or a referral from your local *mairie* (city hall).

RESOURCES FOR FAMILIES

As with any major life change, there is bound to be an adjustment period for your child. Kids are often more adaptable than adults when it comes to new situations—and definitely have an edge up on older family members when it comes to the ability to learn new languages—French culture is different from North American culture, and all the unfamiliarity can be unsettling. Fortunately, there is a lot of support here for you and your family.

Families in the Paris area will want to check out **Message** (www.messageparis. org), a support network of fellow Anglophone parents and parents-to-be whose aim is to help you and your family integrate, adapt, and adjust to life in the City of Light. They produce a quarterly magazine with information about regional child- and family-friendly events and activities, host social events, and offer a slew of parenting resources. They charge annual membership dues, but you can find valuable information on their website without having to officially join, and if you want to join but find it economically unfeasible, the organization does offer subsidized memberships to those in need. Another website worth frequenting for information, forums, and articles on a wide range of topics is www.expatica.com, which is particularly comprehensive when it comes to children and family issues. Any question not answered on the site can be posed to the helpful audience in their various forums, and chances are you'll be received warmly and given plenty of helpful information from people who've been through it all already.

Moving with Pets

One of the most common complaints among expats who move to France with their companion animals is how they were allowed to just breeze right in with their pet after going through all the trouble and expense to secure health certificates and other travel documents. "But don't you want to see my paperwork?" is the common newcomer's cry, and "Not at all, madame! Welcome to France!" seems to be the official response.

This doesn't mean you should skip the pre-departure health check; your airline might request documentation confirming that your cat or dog is healthy and disease-free. For dogs and cats, a microchip is required, as well as current rabies vaccinations. Your vet back home will have the necessary animal-export forms to be stamped by the USDA, the agency that oversees domestic-animal import and export. France does not have an open-door policy for some breeds of dog categorized as "dangerous": pit bulls, Rottweilers, and dogs in the mastiff family. If your dog falls into any one of these categories, you'll have to check with the consulate to confirm the import legalities.

FLYING WITH YOUR PET

Some airlines—United and Air France are just two—allow cats and dogs who meet certain weight restrictions to fly in the cabin with you, in the seat in front of you. This does not apply to flights coming in and out of the UK, where stringent anti-rabies policies are in place (complete with quarantine) and all animals must be flown in the plane's cargo hold. If you're traveling with your dog or cat, do your best to book a direct flight. The shorter the trip, the less stressful it'll be for your pet—and therefore for you.

It's not generally recommended to sedate your pet because the risks outweigh the benefits. If your four-footed friend reacts badly and looks sick on arrival, customs officials can hold the animal for observation and evaluation by a state-sanctioned veterinarian. Better to time your flight for the evening (or your pet's normal downtime), and if he or she

© AURELIA D'ANDREA

A pet passport is easy to acquire at a French veterinary office. While not required, it will streamline travel.

is particularly prone to travel stress, consider a milder approach, such as Bach Flower Remedies' Rescue Remedy, which many pet people swear by. (It reportedly works for stressed-out humans, too.)

CARING FOR YOUR PET

Once you're here, you'll have many veterinarians to choose from, and it wouldn't be a bad idea to visit one and establish a dossier for your pet. This way, you can keep up on necessary vaccinations and have a place to go if your pet should ever fall sick. Don't be surprised if your vet writes you a prescription for Fluffy's antibiotics and then directs you to the nearest human pharmacy to pick it up; many pharmacies throughout France do double duty, vending both veterinary and human medical supplies. Pet food is easy to find in France through a number of sources, including at grocery stores, natural-food stores, dedicated pet-supply stores, veterinarians' offices, and online. Depending on the type of food your pet eats, you may want to shop around to see who offers what and at what price. You'll find premium brands such as Science Diet and Eukanuba at veterinary offices, and if your pet happens to be a vegetarian, chains like Naturalia sell plant-based dry and canned food.

Though France is home to more than 18 million dogs and cats, suggesting a country of animal lovers, some antiquated attitudes toward their care still exist here. It's not uncommon to see dogs out "walking themselves," even in big cities like Paris, and when you find a lost or injured animal on the street, it can be a challenge finding an agency willing to accept responsibility for its care. In theory, you should be able to take the animal to the local *commissariat,* which acts as an intermediary between the

© AURELIA D'ANDREA

Finding your local vet clinic will help keep you and your pets prepared in case of an emergency.

public and the SPA (Société Protectrice des Animaux); but in practice, you'll most likely find yourself shouldering the responsibility of taking a found animal to the nearest animal protection agency, which might be in a distant suburb or out in the provincial boondocks.

What to Bring

The three most stressful events in a person's life are said to be death, divorce, and moving. To take some of the stress out of the already stressful shift from there to here, it's a good idea to begin planning at least six months in advance. This gives you enough time to decide whether to ship your stuff, store it, sell it, or leave it for your subletters. It also gives you enough time to decide what you really need, what you really want, and how to reconcile the two.

HOUSEHOLD ITEMS

With a few minor exceptions, everything you could hope to procure in North America is equally procurable here: Furniture, clothing, knick-knacks and tchotchkes, appliances, automobiles, bicycles, jewelry and watches, houseplants, garden furniture, lawnmowers. While most of us don't want to add to the landfill problem by needlessly throwing away things we already have just to turn around and replace them, that's definitely one option. (And if you have a garage sale or sell your stuff on Craigslist, you might even earn enough money to cover the cost of replacement or the cost of shipping what's left.)

Many items for sale in French stores seem a lot pricier than they do back home, but often they're made better and therefore worth the investment. Tools, for example, can be very expensive, so pack your wrenches, hammers, and screwdrivers if you can't live without them. Your teenager might be disappointed to learn that video games tend to cost about twice as much as they do in the U.S., so if you're a grade-A vidiot, pack your games.

If you settle in Paris, Lyon, Toulouse, or Strasbourg, among other places, you'll be within driving distance of (or a train-bus combo trip to) an IKEA, whose goods seem to fill half of all French homes these days. It's no wonder: The Swedish chain offers handsome, modern design at bargain-basement prices. In Paris, a city where people come and go like the seasons, you'll find Craigslist and FUSAC full of ads posted by folks looking to unload their things at great prices. You can easily furnish your entire apartment or *maison* with quality secondhand goods.

For small household items, like washcloths, dish drainers, kitchen towels, and sewing supplies, try the Chinese and South Asian-owned markets found in most major cities. They're treasure troves for all those little knick-knacks you forgot to pack. At *marchés aux puces* (flea markets), you'll also find stalls selling new items—cutting boards, bars of soap—and wallet-friendly buys can be had if you keep your eyes open.

ELECTRONICS

When packing, consider whether or not to replace your electronic items. If you choose to bring them with you, you'll need a series of transformers and adapters to make them work in France, and you'll always run the risk of overloading your appliances' electrical circuits. As many of us have learned the hard way, all transformers are not created equally.

Electricity in Europe comes through the wires at 220 volts, double the amount of power that surges through standard U.S. and Canadian lines. In order to whittle the energy down to something your appliances can handle, you'll need a heavy-duty step-up/step-down transformer. This is not the kind you'll find in most travel shops—those are designed for appliances like electric razors and coffee makers—and should not be confused with the little adapters you'll be able to use to plug in your laptop, cell-phone charger, and camera-battery charger. A transformer is a solid, square, brick-size metal box that converts those 220 volts into 120. This is generally considered safe for things like televisions, DVD players, and small kitchen appliances.

Regional standards may also affect your decision on whether or not to pack your U.S.-configured electronics. For instance, you won't be able to play French DVDs in your American DVD player; you'll need a PAL (Phase Alternating Line)-compatible DVD player, which costs less than €50 new at electronics specialty stores like Darty, to watch all those straight-to-video releases.

Most new laptops come equipped with a DVD drive, making it easy to watch any old video, provided you've switched the region settings to the European standard. The only tricky part is that most computers have restrictions on how many times you can make this regional switch; five is the norm.

If you've packed your PlayStation to play games and run Blu-ray Discs, be aware that there are three disc-playing zones—A, B, and C—and the European standard is

IKEA or Bust

From posh Parisian apartments to the bourgeois villas on the Côte d'Azur, there's one striking similarity to be found in all manner of French dwellings: IKEA. The Swedish brand has definitely made its mark on the French interior design scene, and it's easy to see why. Stylish, affordable, *and* they deliver—what's not to like? For expats, in particular, IKEA makes a smart, affordable alternative to shipping your furniture from home, which can cost between $5,000 and $10,000 each way. For many making the move to *l'Hexagone*, it makes more sense to sell or store the contents of your home, especially because most housing geared toward the expat market is furnished—likely with IKEA. Those rare empty apartments, should you land one, can be filled on the cheap with the help of an IKEA catalog and a computer to place your order. There are IKEAs to be found in most major Métro regions throughout France, and if and when you decide to repatriate, you can do like the locals do and sell your furniture on Craigslist, Le Bon Coin (www.leboncoin.fr), or FUSAC. Here is some vital terminology to help you navigate the IKEA experience:

Canapé	Couch
Coussins	Cushions
Fauteuil	Armchair
Lit	Bed
Matelas	Mattress
Oreillers	Pillows
Rangements	Storage units
Rideaux	Curtains
Tapis	Rugs
Canapé	Couch

Zone B. When renting or buying Blu-ray Discs, look for Zone A on the back of the box; changing the region settings on your machine isn't possible, so anything other than Zone A discs will be unreadable.

Considering that you'll need one of those bulky, expensive transformers to run most American electronic gadgets, on top of having to futz with regional codes and standards, it really makes more sense to sell your electronic goods before you leave and replace them with European versions once you get here, especially if you plan to live here for any length of time.

If you are particularly attached to your lamps, it is possible to convert them to the French standard by purchasing a European standard plug (and 220-volt light bulb to match), available at just about every *quincaillerie* (hardware store) in the country. If you're feeling DIY-ish, you can easily splice this new plug onto your existing electrical cord and, if you end up returning stateside, repeat the conversion process by splicing a 110-volt plug on the end when you get back home.

SHIPPING OPTIONS

If all this talk of electrical currents and step-up/step-down transformers hasn't scared you away from packing your life up and shipping it across the ocean, then it's time to consider your transport options. If you've decided to start fresh and just pack your clothes, toothbrush, and passport, good for you! You'll be more mobile that way and will have a lot more flexibility in terms of where you live. For most of us, paring life down is not so simple. It's hard to let go. If you're taking everything with you, your best bet is to send it by sea in a shipping container. Prices vary depending on where you're shipping from and to, how much space you'll need in a container (measured in cubic feet or meters), and whether or not you share your container with someone else. But the first step is finding a company with availability to help you make it all happen.

To find a qualified moving company, start with FIDI (www.fidi.org), the international nonprofit agency representing moving companies worldwide. Shipping companies who are part of the FIDI alliance have met a series of quality standards that put them in a league above the rest, but that doesn't mean that if you choose a non-FIDI mover, you'll have a lesser experience. Another place to look for moving-company references is at the consulate, which should be able to provide you with a handout with some good leads. Do your research, ask for testimonials or reviews, and give yourself enough time to shop around so you're not stuck with the only company that's available when you need to move.

Peak moving season in the northern hemisphere begins in mid-May and ends in

© AURELIA D'ANDREA

If you have an adapter, you can use your computer and phone charger as soon as you land.

September. It might not be possible for you to arrange your move at any other time, but you'll have more options if you can be flexible with the date. Though you'll want to start your research six months in advance, if you're trying to budget your move with care, you'll want to book your moving reservation no sooner than one month before departure. Why? Freight charges fluctuate—sometimes drastically—from month to month, based on a number of factors including the value of the dollar and the price of oil. So the figure you're quoted could change significantly, usually in the direction you don't want.

Moving companies offer a range of services, from we'll-do-it-all-for-you to we-just-ship-and-that's-it and everything in between. There are a couple of approaches you can take to sort out all of the details.

If you're lucky enough to be transferred by your company, chances are they'll be handling (read: paying for) all the details of your move, in which case you can just kick up your heels and start plotting the adventures you hope to see unfold in your new French life. For the rest of us, there's a bit of decision-making involved. Do you want to go the cheapest route possible? Then get a shared "groupage" container, but expect it to take anywhere from one to four months for your goods to arrive. The shipping company sends movers to pick up your stuff in a truck, deliver it to the loading docks, and either put it in a container that already has someone else's (or several someone else's) belongings in it—or put it in a container and wait around for another shared load to arrive to fill the container space. This costs about half—sometimes less than half—of what you'll pay for an exclusive container. To bring the cost down further, you can deliver the stuff to the container yourself.

The next cheapest option is direct shipping, meaning your stuff goes inside your own dedicated shipping container; no shared space. The shipping company will either send movers over to pick up your packed goods and deliver them to the shipping port, or they might actually bring your shipping container right to your front door and load it there, sealing the doors afterward with a plastic security band that you will later snip open when your container is delivered to you in France.

Armed with the basics, you'll want to visit FIDI online or use *bouche-à-oreille* (word-of-mouth) references and make a few calls. Shipping containers come in two sizes, 20-foot and 40-foot, so expect to be asked how many cubic meters' worth of goods you have. The shipping company should send a representative over to make an assessment. Once you've been given an estimate that works for you—and it's definitely worth shopping around, since prices can vary by thousands of dollars—you'll be asked to submit a down payment, with the rest payable upon delivery.

CUSTOMS

Customs is a relatively straightforward process, but you won't necessarily know that if your shipping company contact isn't well informed. You'll have to fill out a customs form that your shipping company will submit to the *douane* (customs) agents at the port of entry, but unless your cargo is made up of brand-new electric items that look like they might be ready for immediate resale in France, you won't have to pay an import fee. You will be asked to attest on paper to the fact that you have lived in your country of residence for the last 12 months and that the items you are shipping are older than six months. (Items purchased less than six months before your ship date are subject to import fees.) If you can solemnly swear that this is true, you won't need to pay any fees.

One important consideration is the storage fee. If your shipping dossier is not in order at the customs agency at the port of entry in France—this usually happens when you do your paperwork yourself or use an underqualified moving agency with little overseas shipping experience—your container may have to be "stored," with daily fees in the realm of €250. To avoid getting saddled with hefty fees, confirm with your shipping company that your paperwork is in order, and that there will be no hidden and unwarranted customs fees. You or your shipping agent should have collected in your dossier the following papers:

- a copy of your passport

- pay stubs or other proof that you have lived in the U.S. or Canada for at least six months

- a copy of your rental agreement and/or proof of current residence in France (an electricity bill works)

- a French customs inventory form

- a signed letter attesting that the purpose of importing your goods is not to resell them upon arrival

- a Représentation en Douanes form

HOUSING CONSIDERATIONS

From chic Parisian flats furnished in fancy Louis XIV fashion to old stone barns with earthen floors converted into modern dwellings in the verdant countryside, housing really runs the gamut in France. Exactly where you decide to live is surely contingent on work, school, and budget. Once you've sorted out those fundamentals, you'll be ready to embark on your hunt for the perfect home. Finding a place to live is best reserved for when you actually arrive; as alluring as online ads can be, making a decision from afar isn't really practical. If you'll be spending more than six months in your new abode, you'll want to ensure that the neighborhood meets your standards, that the advertisement in square meters matches the spatial picture you had in mind (and that your antique dining-room table will fit in the *salle à manger*), and that you'll have access to transportation and other amenities. It's hard to judge this accurately without a visit. Once you're here, there's a lot to see, so bring your phrasebook, comfy walking shoes (but not the sporty white ones), and your sense of humor.

The Housing Market

After a temporary rebound in 2014 after a multiyear slump, the French housing market is going through a rough patch again, which makes it a good time for buyers to invest in real estate and a not-so-good time to sell. Paris is the one exception, having remained virtually untouched by market fluctuations in other parts of the country, and while deals can be found in the French capital, it's nothing like the provinces, where it's actually possible to find something habitable—with a garden—for the same price you'd pay for a late-model Mercedes sedan.

France has long been a popular destination for foreign investors and second-home buyers; the British especially have done a number on the real-estate industry here, snapping up properties to fix up and rent out or fix up and live in, if only for part of the year. (In some pockets of France—particularly where access to the UK by ferry, Chunnel, and plane is quick and easy—anglophones outnumber francophones.) The economic parity that is now settling in between the two countries means there isn't a feverish race to the realty finish line, and there are more options for those interested in buying now.

With the dollar gaining strength against the euro, Americans can find some incredible bargains in France, both within and outside of the capital. On one end of the spectrum are the million-dollar Parisian apartments and modern garden villas in the *bobo* suburbs, on the other are options for those with more modest budgets. Fancy a homey little cottage in the rolling green countryside of the Dordogne, or perhaps a 17th-century farmhouse in Brittany with windowsills begging to be decorated with big pots of geraniums? For less than €200,000, these options can be yours with patience, flexibility, and a little help from your banking institution.

Renting

Renting has its advantages over buying, the most obvious being a much lighter initial investment. For the French, housing laws that favor the tenant over the landlord make renting a safe and secure option. Even if you don't pay your rent, a landlord can't give you the heave-ho in the thick of winter, for instance. But as a foreigner entering the rental market, you won't necessarily have all the same advantages extended to you—one reason why French homeowners seek out foreign tenants.

Paris rental laws are particularly strict, and it's technically illegal for owners to rent to anyone—foreign or not—for periods of less than one year. To do so legally would require owners to change the status of their property from private to commercial, and securing the coveted commercial status is next to impossible. Theoretically, the law was intended to ease Paris's shortage of affordable housing; you'll often hear the story of the lifelong Parisian sent packing to the suburbs because he can no longer afford the city's astronomical rents. The law is easy to skirt, however, as evidenced by the number of ads offering short-term "furnished" accommodations. "Furnished" is a loose term that can mean anything from a bare room save a single chair or bed to a

You'll find country living in the Dordogne Valley.

decked-out space with all the mod-cons in place: microwave, television, sofa, etc. Short-term rentals bring in far more income for owners than long-term rentals, so flying under the radar and hoping not to get caught is a risk many landlords are willing to take.

French bureaucracy doesn't end at the front door of your new house or apartment, which can make finding a place to live a challenge, particularly if you are short on time or funds. If possible, rent a short-term place for a month while you look for your permanent housing, which will buy you enough time to find something that will feel like a true home and not force you into something less—or more—than you'd hoped for. You can find more affordable options for short-term and long-term rentals on PAP, Craigslist, and FUSAC. More expensive possibilities are also available via dozens of short-term rental agencies (again, check out FUSAC at www.fusac.org), but they will charge higher rents and also include a supplemental fee for finding you a place to live that could either be a percentage of the overall rental period or the equivalent of one month's rent. If you want to avoid the hassles of combing the want ads altogether, this is a viable option even for the long term, but note that nearly all rentals will come in varying degrees of "furnished." So if you're expecting a cargo container to arrive with all of your belongings, you'll need to make sure you have the room for it or risk paying hefty storage fees.

NECESSARY DOCUMENTS

You're already familiar with the dossier, and you'll be needing one to rent a house or apartment from either an agency or a private party. Your dossier should contain the following:

- copies of your passport

- your last three bank statements

- your last three pay stubs (French or otherwise)

- proof of insurance (if you have it)

- an *attestation* from a *garant* or *cautionnaire* saying you'll be covered if you can't pay your rent

- personal letters of recommendation (translated into French, if possible)

Without these, it's unlikely you'll find any standard real-estate agency that will rent to you long-term. Even familiar North America-based companies like Century 21 have rigid policies that will exclude you based on missing documents in your dossier. The tricky part is that this rule doesn't always hold. If you have time and tenacity, 1 out of 20 agencies you visit or speak with by phone (or email) might be willing to look the other way on missing documents if they like you, or more likely, like your bank statement. If you make a breakthrough and actually get someone to show you an apartment (be forewarned that some agents won't even consider showing you a place until they've seen your paperwork), and you fall in love with the place, work those negotiating skills and see what happens. Some expats have reported that homemade brownies work as a form of bribery, but simply being personable and connecting genuinely with the person you're hoping to impress is probably the best route to take. Their bottom line is, "Will she be able to pay the rent?" If you can convey a sense of trust and reliability, you're halfway there.

FINDING THE RIGHT PLACE

When you launch your home search, it helps to put *all* your feelers out—all of them! This is not the time to be a wallflower. Check the bulletin board at your local chapter of the Alliance Française back home for possibilities, scour **Craigslist, Rent a Place in France** (www.rentaplaceinfrance. com), and **FUSAC** to get a sense of the rental climate in the town you're moving to, ask everyone you know if they have friends-of-friends-of-friends who might have a place to rent in France, and visit sites like **Se Loger** (www.seloger.com) and **Particulier à Particulier** (www.pap.fr) to get a feel for French-language rental ads. The more familiar you are with the lingo and the more questions you formulate before you leave, the better prepared you'll be for your next challenge.

When you get here, get out and about and start networking. Join expat groups (see the *Resources* section for ideas), venture out to **Meetups** (www.meetup.com), and

On the Riviera, the Italian influence on architecture is palpable.

© AURELIA D'ANDREA

Why You Might Need a *Garant(e)*

In France, it may take a bit more effort to land that perfect apartment than you are used to. If you don't have a job contract and three months of pay stubs to demonstrate your fiscal stability, you can kiss that cute 18th-century walkup *au revoir*. Even a loaded bank account won't help you here. Rules are rules, and what the folks renting to you require are those pay stubs, showing earnings equal to three times your monthly rent—or, if you can't pull that off, a *garant's attestation. Garant? Attestation?* What's all this, you ask?

A **garant** is someone with income or assets greater than your own who acts as a financial guarantor in case you default on your rent. This person is expected to provide a dossier full of documents similar to those you're unable to provide: proof of residence, proof of monthly income equal to three times the amount of your rent, and copies of her own rental agreement or real-estate tax forms. Employers occasionally extend this perk to staff, but not always. If you're lucky enough to have a wealthy aunt in France who's willing to put three years' worth of rent into a "hold" at the bank, rental agencies will consider that in place of a *garant*.

Recently, public *garant* agencies have sprouted up, offering their services to desperate would-be renters, but not all rental agencies will accept this sort of arrangement. If all other options fail, there's still hope: Enroll in a university (students are usually exempt from the *garant* rule) or rent straight from the owner (try Craigslist and Particulier à Particulier), which usually allows for a more flexible negotiation process.

read every bulletin board you pass. As much as you want to integrate into French society, your best bet for finding a place to live is through word-of-mouth within the Anglophone community, so cast your net as wide as it will go.

It takes many North Americans some time to get used to the size of French dwellings. Unless you're looking at a château or a modern apartment, you'll find traditional French rooms to be a little on the small side (and often plastered with outdated wallpaper, which can make a room feel even smaller). And that oversize sofa you packed? Good luck squeezing it into an elevator (which most building *syndicats* don't allow you to do anyway) or wrangling it around the twisty stairwell. You'll need to hire a special moving *elévateur* to lift it up and through the window.

Short-Term Rentals

If you don't have someone with very strong ties to France arranging your move for you, you're probably going to need to give up on the notion of finding an unfurnished rental. They do exist, but they're *very* hard to get your hands on as a solo-flying expat on a non-corporate executive's budget. For the short term, it's usually preferable to settle into a furnished place anyway, since you'll just need something in the interim until your cargo container arrives or while you investigate a permanent place to live. And if you're only staying for a brief period, a furnished rental unit makes a lot of sense.

Your options for short-term rentals are vast and varied. You can go through a big agency that will likely charge you a big fee or a mom-and-pop business offering the same service but charging less, or you can bypass surcharges altogether by working directly with a landlord, who might himself be a subtenant to another landlord. There is a bit of risk involved in the latter option on both the landlord's and the tenant's sides; you are being entrusted with someone else's property, and you're handing over your hard-earned

Classified Information

Scouring the want ads for the perfect place to call home can be a fun pastime that helps you better imagine yourself living your French dream. If your language skills aren't up to snuff, though, it can become frustrating drudgery. Don't know your *cuisine* from your *cave?* Bone up on the essential real-estate lingo before you hit the *immobilizer's* (real-estate agency) to know exactly what you'll be investing those hard-earned euros in.

à louer/location - for rent	**immeuble ancien/neuf** - old/new building
ascenseur - elevator	**jardin** - garden
à vendre - for sale	**loué** - already rented
bail à ceder - for lease	**meublée** - furnished
cave - cellar	**mezzanine** - elevated area, often a DIY loft space for sleeping that frees up floor space
chambre - room, usually referring to a bedroom or main room in a studio	**pièce** - room
charges - supplemental charges for water, garbage, maintenance, and sometimes electricity	**une pièce/studio** - studio
chauffage - heating	**pierre/pierre de taille** - stone

cash to someone you hope is on the up and up. Odds are they will be, but always trust your instincts—if something doesn't feel right, don't feel obligated to follow through. In any situation, it is advisable to always leave a paper trail and to draft a lease, even if the person renting to you doesn't think it's necessary or, more likely, didn't think of it.

Within the law, short-term rentals of a year or less that don't come with a lease are supposed to be rented only to tenants who have a primary residence other than the one being rented. This would be a challenge for anyone to disprove, and rarely is it an issue in terms of the law cracking down on you, but the person renting to you may ask you to sign a paper stating as much to cover his or her tail.

For a nice cross section of short-term rentals throughout Paris, try www.perfectlyp-aris.com. The friendly Canadian owner, Gail Boisclair, is fluent in English and happy to use her years of expertise to help you find a place to call home, if only for a short while. If you plan to spend a month or more in France and are considering places outside Paris, it would be smart to connect with Scotland native Ross Husband at **Rent a Place in France** (www.rentaplaceinfrance.com). Craigslist and Airbnb both offer a plethora of possibilities, and don't forget to check out the ads at fusac.org for referrals to other rental agencies eager for your business.

colocation - shared rental unit	**placard** - closet
couloir - hallway	**rénové** - renovated
cuisine - kitchen	**rez de chaussée** - ground floor
dépot de garantie - security deposit	**salle d'eau** - washroom
2ème étage - second floor	**salle de bain** - bathroom with tub or shower
deux pièces - standard one-bedroom	**sans vis à vis** - an unobstructed view
disponible - available	**séjour** - living room
équipée - furnished (usually describes a kitchen with refrigerator and stove)	**toilette** - toilet
escalier - staircase	**T1/T2** - studio/one-bedroom apartment
gardien(ne) - onsite manager	**tout compris, cc, or ttc** - all-inclusive
honoraire - finder's fee to the real estate agency	**vendeur/vendeuse** - seller
hors charges - not including charges	**vendu** - already sold
immeuble - building	**vide** - empty

If you're looking for a temporary sublet, summer is a great time to check out Paris and its suburbs while the locals flee to the sea and countryside for their multiweek escapes. You will have lots of room to negotiate, since people don't want to get stuck paying all their rent while they're away, and you'll get to experience what it could be like to live in a real French home (versus a sterile short-term rental unit). For a short-term rental on the Côte d'Azur and other popular vacation spots, it's best to begin your search six months or more in advance.

Long-Term Rentals

A long-term rental has lots of advantages: It allows you to get to know a place before buying, lets you feel more integrated in a community knowing you won't have to pick up and leave in three months, and often is a lot less expensive than a short-term arrangement. The only problem is *finding* a long-term rental, though that isn't necessarily a problem if you have the luxury of time.

As with short-term rentals, it's possible to go through an agency whose specialty is expatriate rental services, but you will pay a premium, usually in the form of a "finder's fee" surcharge amounting to the equivalent of one month's rent or a percentage

Expat Experience: Settling for Success

Name: Ross Husband
Age: 55
Occupation: Realtor
Hometown: Aberdeen, Scotland
Current City: Malvezie

When Scotsman Ross Husband moved to France in 2005, he had a hard time finding a long-term rental for his family. The process proved so frustrating and time-consuming that he and his wife, Karin, decided to launch their own business to help people find rental housing. More than a decade later, Ross, Karin, and their daughter, Anna, live in the Pyrénées and continue helping others find their little swath of *la belle France* through their company, **Rent a Place in France** (www.rentaplaceinfrance.com). Here, Ross shares his advice for finding long-term housing success.

What are some of the most popular regions expats are settling in, and why do you think these places are popular with newcomers?
The southern regions attract the majority of expats. The combination of warm sunshine, medieval villages, and outside café life can prove irresistible. Languedoc-Roussillon is probably the most popular region, with its sunny climate and rental prices that are generally more affordable than in its more pricey neighbor, Provence.

What are some advantages of a long-term rental over a short-term rental?
The difference between visiting as a holiday maker and the much fuller, richer, and rounded experience of actually living in the country. You can begin to get under the skin of a place and make friends with the locals. It can also works wonders on your French language skills!

What are some common mistakes newcomers make when looking for housing in France, and what could they do to avoid them?
The main mistake is a lack of preparation and research on the accommodation and surrounding area. The climate in France can vary considerably, and the winter climate can be quite different to summer. A bustling, lively village in summer can appear quite different in the middle of winter, perhaps with some cafés and restaurants even closed. Be sure you know what temperatures to expect for your stay and find out what facilities will be available locally. Satisfy yourself that the accommodation will suit your needs. The property advertiser will normally be able to provide a wealth of information not only on their own property but also on the surrounding area.

What advice would you offer to someone who dreams of moving to France but isn't sure where to settle?
Do exactly what we did: Take on a few rental properties in different areas. We rented three properties for two months each. The third one did the trick and we have been living happily in the area ever since!

of the rent you'll pay over the months (or years) you'll be staying. It's also possible to go through an *immobilier,* a real estate agent who often deals in rental units as well as selling homes. The tricky part will always be to meet the dossier demands, which generally require three months' worth of French pay stubs proving that you earn several times the amount of the rent, a *garant's attestation,* and more.

It's no secret that French landlords like renting to North Americans. They know you'll be leaving Paris to return to your "real" home at some point, and therefore won't be taking advantage of the tenant-friendly laws that essentially guarantee you can't be forcibly evicted. This also allows many landlords to get around the law that says empty units must be rented with three-year leases; many North Americans are staying only for a year or two, so the landlord won't be locked into long-term situations. You're also generally considered more financially stable than your French counterparts, making you prime tenant material.

Renting directly from the owner gives you a lot of flexibility; you can negotiate the removal of existing furniture, open a discussion about filling voids—for example, if your "furnished" apartment doesn't come with a TV or washing machine, you may be able to persuade the *propriétaire* that these are necessities. (As always, ask nicely and be prepared to make a convincing argument if necessary.) Sometimes you can negotiate both the rent and the length of your stay. So there's a lot to be said for finding your home this way. Even though it's not as popular in France as in North America, Craigslist is a good place to start your housing search, especially if you'll be settling in Paris. Many real-estate agents use this online venue to showcase their available dwellings. You'll find a broad variety of possibilities for rent by individuals, and the people advertising are almost always Anglophones. One thing to be wary of is any deal that seems too good to be true. They almost always are! Warning signs include 1) impossibly cheap rent (such as a luxury apartment for €750 per month) and 2) a request for money transfers or wires before you've even seen the place. Don't sign anything, and *don't* hand over a euro until you've seen the place—and the person renting it—in person.

Particulier à Particulier (www.pap.fr) advertises apartments and houses directly from the owner, so if your French skills are up to snuff, you can probably circumvent the challenges inherent in working with an agency—namely, a rigid set of dossier requirements. Brush up on your French and be prepared to pick up the phone to get the best deals. If your French isn't that good but you have a friend who's fluent, have her make the call for you.

Shared Rentals

Finding a *colocation* (shared rental) situation in France is relatively simple, particularly in university towns with large student populations. The site to visit to find your next roommate situation is www.colocation.fr, but it will benefit you greatly if you speak French. You *do* want that €100 living situation, *don't* you? The downside to this otherwise wonderful site is that to access the contact information of your potential new roommate, you have to pay for the access number; usually the fee is less than €2, but if you're calling more than a handful of people, it adds up. A no-cost option is www.recherche-colocation.com—also in French, but at least membership is *gratuit* (free). If you're still most comfortable with an English-language publication, head straight for the old tried-and-true FUSAC and Craigslist.

LEASES

Before signing on the dotted line, you'll want to have some sort of contract in place, even if it's just a simple form you downloaded off the Internet 10 minutes before your hand-over-the-keys meeting. (You and your landlord wouldn't be the first.) What you sign and what kind of information it contains hinges on what you're renting and the landlord's level of professionalism. Let's say you're renting a furnished apartment directly from an owner who takes the matter rather seriously and has taken steps to keep the transaction on the up and up. In this case, you can expect to be presented with a lease or rental contract (*contrat de location*) containing the following information:

- name of the owner, contact information, and rental address

- a description of the rental: floor, door, dimension in square meters

- a mention of communal access and services: a courtyard, bike parking, elevator

- a definition of purpose: whether the space is for living or working

- the length of the contract and whether it's renewable or not

- an outline of the charges—rent, *taxe d'habitation*, electricity—and when they are made payable

- the amount of your security deposit

- an outline of any proposed work to be done on the dwelling, including dates and whether less or more rent will be charged as a result

- a statement indicating that the renter will leave the space in the same state it was rented out in to guarantee you get your deposit back

A short outline of the owner's obligations to the renter and the renter's obligation to the owner is also part of the contract, and often a *clause pénale* will be inserted declaring what will happen if the renter fails to pay his rent. But it's almost guaranteed that the contract you sign will be much simpler than the one outlined above, if you're actually offered a contact at all.

In keeping with the up-and-up theme: Even if you're not asked to provide a full-fledged dossier, you may be asked to provide proof of renter's insurance and income. Paying your last month's rent up front is not legally mandated, but landlords *are* legally entitled to ask for a deposit equal to one month's rent. They have two months to return it to you once you've moved out. You, on the other hand, can ask your landlord-to-be for a *certificat de ramonage*, which certifies they've had the chimney swept so you can have a cozy little fire roaring in the fireplace.

Buying

If you've never visited a real-estate website, consider yourself warned: They're deliciously addictive. There's nothing quite as tantalizing as poking around cyberspace and popping in and out of other people's *maisons*—homes that might soon be your own (if only in your fantasies). From a rural 17th-century cottage perched on the edge of a grassy glen in the Loire Valley to a Niçoise pied-à-terre equipped with a sunlit balcony built for two, a version of your French dream awaits you in the wonderful world of virtual real estate.

It takes a village to buy a home in France, and you can expect all kinds of seemingly superfluous individuals to become part of the transaction: *Notaires,* the mayor, insurance agents, and even doctors. For some mortgages, you'll need to ensure that you'll live long enough to pay for your little piece of France—this is solved with the addition of a life-insurance policy, which you can't purchase until you've had a blood test and possibly an electrocardiogram, the results of which are supposed to indicate a life span beyond the terms of your mortgage. No, this is not a joke. If you want to bypass all that, you can always pay cash. (And plenty of people do—especially for those bargain properties.)

You're bound to find yourself looking at one or two "fixer uppers" throughout the process, and one thing you'll notice right away is that no two are alike. Some "fixer uppers" are veritable shells with sloping walls and a resident family of pigeons. If the ad describes the dwelling as *à rénover* (to renovate), be prepared for the worst, and maybe, just maybe, it won't be that bad. The "to renovate" could simply mean they haven't yet installed the sunken bathtub in the master bath.

FINDING THE RIGHT PLACE

Where should you begin cultivating your French roots? Before sorting that out, you'll need to be firm about what sort of use you have planned for your place. Will it be strictly somewhere for you to live, or are you envisioning an income-generating rental property? Maybe you just want to let it sit empty until you come for your two months of vacation each summer, and let friends borrow it when you're not there. Buying into a retirement home where you can spend your golden years isn't a bad idea, what with the high quality of life here and the top-notch healthcare system. But don't make the mistake that many of your predecessors have: buy a place and plan to rent it out without considering how many others have done the same thing. You will have a much more challenging time finding short-term tenants for your "vacation rental" if it doesn't stand out in a sea of similar offers. Proximity to restaurants, shops, and transportation are usually what people seek in a Paris-area vacation home—not a one-room cottage in a distant suburb where the only thing open on Sundays is the village church. Hold on to the dream, but don't let practicality fall by the wayside.

REAL-ESTATE AGENTS

The most cursory Internet search points to an overwhelming reality: There are scads and scads of French real estate sites. The good news is that many of them cater to

© AURELIA D'ANDREA

Living in an urban environment usually means living in an apartment.

English-speaking shoppers. If your French is solid, even better. You'll be able to pop into any *immobilier* office during your information-gathering trip and inquire about that stately Haussmann-era apartment with the geranium-covered balcony and *à vendre* sign that caught your eye.

In the French real estate world, it's all about who you know. Ask around for references before settling on an agent. Some are nicer than others, and some charge heftier fees. You'll also need to engage the services of a *notaire* and a mortgage company. If you've got the resources, you can hire someone to see you through every step of the process and make the arrangements with notaries and bankers on your behalf. If you're flying solo—which is entirely possible to do, and definitely a money saver—and your language skills still aren't up to snuff, bring a friend who speaks French to all your official rendezvous to help translate.

You'll need a **French bank account,** since most mortgage companies are going to want to debit the mortgage payments directly from that account. (To learn more about opening a bank account, see the *Finance* chapter.)

The French home-buying system is fraught with bureaucratic peculiarities, but the oddest of all is that bit about the **blood test.** If your mortgage is approved and you'll be borrowing more than €200,000, you'll be required to take out a life-insurance policy that will cover the remaining cost of your mortgage if you're, say, suddenly swept away by a tsunami while sunbathing on the Côte d'Azur. To qualify for that policy, you'll need a blood test and possibly a urine test. Oh, and we mustn't forget about the electrocardiogram.

PURCHASE FEES AND TAXES

One person you'll get to know well during the property-purchasing process is the *notaire*. This is an independent contractor who acts as the official hand representing the state in your home-buying transaction. The stamps, seals, and signatures the *notaire* applies to your *contrats* make a document official, and the buy/sell transaction cannot be completed without this authorizing signature. The *notaire*'s fees are not low, but they don't all go into her pocket. The bulk of what you pay to the *notaire* is actually local and national taxes, with the remaining fraction divided between the *notaire*'s actual employment fees (a fixed rate determined by the government) and expenditures for things like paperwork and travel. In terms of real estate transactions, *notaires* are responsible for making sure you pay your departmental land registration tax (4.5 percent in 2015), local tax (1.20 percent), and state taxes (2.37 percent) on your real estate purchases, which adds up to more than 5 percent on top of the purchase price. If your dream home is a new-build property, your notaire will also ask you to cough up the Value Added Tax of 20 percent. (Ouch.) Real estate transactions can be complicated, so it's wise to consult with a pro and budget in that extra expense as you determine what you can afford to spend in France. To find a *notaire,* try the word-of-mouth route or visit www.notaires.fr to search an online directory in English.

Once you've found a place you love and are ready to commit, you can set the process in motion by following these steps:

- Find a *notaire* and secure her services.

- Sign the *compromis de vente* that binds the seller to the transaction and pay a deposit of 10 percent of the purchase price.

DAILY LIFE

Vendu means that the property has already sold.

- Mull it over and decide whether or not you have buyer's remorse within seven days (you can pull out without penalty before then).

- Apply for a mortgage. If you are rejected, try again and save the rejection notice. If you are unable to secure a mortgage, you can pull out of the agreement without penalty.

- Contact your *notaire* to say your mortgage has gone through and the transaction can be completed.

From start to finish, count on a good three months or more for the transaction to be completed.

If your adorable old abode has a *fosse septique,* you may be required by your local *mairie* to convert to *mains drainage,* otherwise known as the municipal sewer system. This comes at a price, so be sure to factor that in before you buy. Electricity is not a given either; if you're not already hooked up, you'll have to put a call in to state-owned Électricité de France (EDF) to see what kind of magic they can make down on the farm. To get started, you'll need proof of sale of your home, called an *attestation;* ask your *notaire* for a copy.

French inheritance laws favor children over spouses, so if you want to ensure that any greedy offspring don't snatch up and sell your property after you die, leaving Pa or Ma out in the cold, bring this up to your *notaire,* who can use the right paperwork to help ensure that doesn't happen.

BUILDING AND RESTORING

As you know by now, no transaction involving the French bureaucracy is ever a cake walk. This holds true when it comes to rebuilding, renovation, and starting a housing project from scratch. Expect a long, dossier-encumbered process—but one that might be very much worth the effort if it means getting the house you've always wanted.

Deciding between modernity and Old World charm is a common home-buyer's conundrum.

When scouring the real-estate ads, you'll often stumble upon land for sale. If there is a "permission to build" clause built into the sale deed, you're in luck: One major hurdle has been cleared. Otherwise you'll need to solicit permission to build on your own, starting at the *mairie* with a *certificat d'urbanisme.* This should be done *before* you make your land purchase. With permission to build in hand, you'll need to start beefing up that dossier with some more paperwork: architectural drawings from an officially recognized architect, building estimates, and construction contracts.

Your local *mairie* can help you along the way by directing you to free services that will ease the burden of DIY. The Conseil d'Architecture d'Urbanisme et de l'Environnement (CAUE) is one such valuable resource. To find a builder, good ol' word of mouth works best, but you can also ask for recommendations at the *mairie* or visit the website of the builder's union, Union Nationale des Constructeurs de Maisons Individuelles (UNCMI), for direction (www.uniondesmaisonsfrancaises.org).

French contractors do things at their own pace, so it helps to know who you're hiring before you hire them. You can expect long lunch breaks, regular vacations (just like everyone else), and a "What's the big rush?" attitude on the job, but it'll eventually get done. If you're a Mr. or Ms. Bricolage (handyperson), you might consider taking on some of the work yourself.

Household Expenses

Once your new title of French resident is etched in *pierre* (stone), you'll want to start gussying up your new place and making it feel homey. But not so fast. First, you need to make sure there's running water, electricity, and—if you're way out in the suburban boondocks—a *fosse septique* (septic tank). Many houses are sold in deplorable states of as-is, and it's up to you to know what you've gotten yourself into before you take the plunge.

HOMEOWNERS' TAXES

There are three taxes you will be responsible for as a new French homeowner: *taxe d'habitation, taxe foncière,* and the TV tax called *redevance audiovisuelle.*

If you lived in your home on January 1 of the given year, then you are responsible for **taxe d'habitation** (residence tax). If someone else lived there, they are responsible for paying it—so if you moved in on January 2, you're off the hook. Landlords can also pass this fee on to their long-term tenants, but this should be outlined in a rental agreement first. The tax is determined by the powers-that-be in your community and varies from city to city. You will receive a *facture* (bill) in the mail from the local government when tax time draws near. If you are over 60, lucky you! You don't have to pay this one. Families with children are taxed at a reduced rate. You'll receive your €136 bill for the **redevance audiovisuelle** (TV tax) at the same time (and yes, you're off scot-free if you don't have a TV).

The value of your **taxe foncière** (property owner's tax) is also set by local authorities and relates to the value of your home as a rental property on the open market, minus cost-of-living fees. Like the other taxes, it hinges on a January 1 ownership date. Many types of properties are exempted from this tax, including homes remodeled for energy efficiency, and new construction. Check with your local government to see if your property is exempted.

UTILITIES

If you're a homeowner or plan to invest in real estate, it's worth looking into the government-sponsored rebates for using **alternative energy methods.** Going solar has its perks; if you generate surplus energy, it could mean you get a check *back* from EDF instead of having to send one. Other energy-saving efforts homeowners make to increase efficiency are rewarded by way of tax deductions and write-offs.

Electricity

The primary supplier of electricity, **Électricité de France** (EDF, http://residential. edf.com), offers notoriously expensive power for those who live on the grid. North Americans by the droves have stood slack-jawed over their first wintertime electricity bill, expecting a two-digit number like the ones they used to see back home.

The good news is that you can choose the kilowatt supply that comes to your home and effectively reduce the figure you write on that check every three months. First, though, you have to open an account at the EDF, which can be done in person or online at www.bleuciel.edf.com. As with most French bills, you can arrange to go paperless on this one and have the money debited directly from your bank account.

The actual cost of your quarterly *facture* (bill) will vary according to the size of your home and how well it is insulated, where you live (local taxes are applied), and other factors, but annual base subscription rates begin at about €50 for smaller dwellings and reach up to €700 for larger dwellings, followed by a kilowatt hour (kWh) rate of €.15 per hour. EDF's English-language site offers more information than you'd probably ever hope to know about how electricity works in France, and is worth at least a cursory gander for anyone who'll be paying their own electricity bills in France.

Americans and others moving to France from abroad are often surprised to receive those quarterly knocks on the door from the meter reader, who is known to appear at odd hours expecting to enter your home to do his job. (And it is nearly always a man who'll turn up *chez vous*, by the way.) You'll receive advance warning from EDF before the meter-reader arrives (in apartment buildings, your *gardien(ne)* will post this notice in a common area), and if you'll be unavailable to greet him at the appointed hour—usually a general timeframe of several hours—you'll be asked to have someone else stand in for you. If all else fails, the EDF representative will tuck a slip of paper beneath your door, which you'll be expected to fill out with the meter reading before mailing in by a certain date.

Water

If the previous tenant had water services engaged, you can have the billing information transferred to your name. If you're starting from scratch, you'll need to visit your local government to find out who your water supplier is before making contact. In Paris, the agency to contact is **Eau de Paris** (www.eaudeparis.fr), along the Côte d'Azur and Brittany, it's **Veolia** (www.eau-services.com).

Like your electricity bill, the amount you'll pay for your water will depend on multiple factors, including whether your town is heavily touristed (you'll pay more to cover all the water those interlopers drink), and whether you live in a single-family dwelling or an apartment. If your home is a 19th-century apartment in the city, your bill might go directly to the building's *syndicat* (homeowner's association) and get passed on to you in the form of monthly "charges" that are bundled with the cost of standard building maintenance. If you live in a single-family home in Strasbourg, for example, you'll pay roughly €30 for your annual *abonnement* (subscription) and a further €3 per cubic meter for your water. Similar rates are found throughout France.

You can't help but notice the quality of water throughout France; though quite potable, it is loaded with lime, with telltale white flecks often visible in your glass after drinking. This may or may not explain the French love affair with bottled water, but it's perfectly OK to consume, though you might be interested in a filter system. The *calcaire* build-up will affect the look of your water kettle, your dishwasher, and your coffee maker, but anti-*calcaire* tablets that will dissolve the substance are readily available in supermarkets and hardware stores for a few euros.

Telephone, Internet, and Cable

Telephone landline options are many and a veritable bargain, thanks to deregulation in the telecommunications sector. (Deregulation has not been good for everyone— restructuring and layoffs are said to be the culprit behind France Télécom's high rate of employee suicide: a frightening total of 35 between 2008 and 2009 alone.) Usually your phone fees are bundled together with your Internet and cable television fees. Companies including **SFR** (www.sfr.fr), **Bouygues** (www.bouyguestelecom.fr), and **Orange** (www.orange.fr) offer packages starting as low as €20 per month, and you can make all the arrangements for hookup online.

Garbage and Recycling

In cities throughout France, there is an unofficial wake-up call: the garbage workers who begin their jobs at the break of dawn, dragging the giant green bins off the sidewalk and emptying them with much noisy fanfare into their trucks. This service is built into your local taxes, so you needn't anticipate yet another bill for waste collection. Ditto for recycling. Depending on where you live, you may need to recycle everything yourself in municipal bins positioned around town, or you may have services directly in your building to handle paper, plastic, and cans. Glass is almost always recycled in public bins; in Paris, you'll be able to see which neighborhoods have the most boozers by the number of bottles piled up outside the large plastic glass-recycling pods. (A sure sign that the inside is already packed to the gills.)

If you have larger items to dispose of, such as a washing machine or a sofa, check in with your *mairie* about what services they offer to help rid you of these unwanted belongings. Likewise, you might check with the charity **Emmaüs** (www.emmaus-france. org), who will happily arrange a pick-up of used items in good condition that will sell in one of their many boutiques around the country. Proceeds support services to employ mentally and physically disabled adults, and help others in need.

DAILY LIFE

LANGUAGE AND EDUCATION

It's a little-known fact that approximately 99.9 percent of all French people know at least a word or two of English, and many are darn near fluent. You'd hardly know it, though, given the way you're often left struggling to puzzle together the simplest request (*Où est les toilettes, s'il vous plaît?*), only to be met with a remarkably accent-free response (The bathroom? In fact, it's right over there.).

It's certainly possible to get by in France without speaking French—many an expat before you has done it, sometimes getting by for years on end—but language restrictions will resign you to life in a bubble that only floats on the surface of a genuine French experience. At least part of what brought you here was your fondness for the rich culture, right? Language is the biggest cultural marker you'll find, so it makes sense to give it a shot and break free of the insular and—let's face it—superficial Anglophone-only experience. Plus, there's nothing quite as satisfying as ordering your meal at a restaurant in clearly enunciated French and having your request processed *without* quizzical looks and excessive head-scratching on the part of your waiter. Even more wonderful is the (relative) ease with which you'll glide through your *carte de séjour* experience and other official processes when armed with working French.

Regional dialects abound, but getting a grasp on the mother tongue—plain old French—is all you really need to assimilate into your new community and boost your own confidence along the way.

Learning the Language

If you were clever enough to have studied French in high school or college, lucky you! That foundation will give you the confidence you need to get started. One of the most difficult things for non-French speakers to get used to is the feeling of vulnerability that comes with not being able to communicate effectively. For some, those insecurities are compounded by the genuinely-trying-to-be-helpful French person who corrects your grammar (I promise they're not doing it to make you feel bad), often in public and loudly enough for others to hear. It's a challenge for us control freaks, but now is the time to let go and embrace the linguistic fumbling and stumbling. Relaxing a little will help you—and that ego of yours—move on to the experimental chatting phase that will ultimately benefit you immensely.

If you've seen the film *Paris, je t'aime,* you'll probably remember the vignette featuring Carol, an American postal clerk who takes her dream trip to the City of Light, narrating her experience in heavily American-accented French. She charms us with her earnestness—and an extraordinarily flat delivery where rolling *R*s ought to reside. When you start out, go the postal-clerk method and focus on just speaking, rather than speaking with a perfect accent. You'll have time for that later. Besides, when you have a good accent, people assume you speak fluently or at least conversationally and will begin yakking at you in rapid-fire French that you're not equipped to handle—yet.

BEFORE YOU LEAVE

Whether or not you've studied French before, as soon as you even begin *thinking* of moving, you should also start thinking of enrolling in a language class. You'd be surprised how many resources exist. There really *is* something for everyone, no matter your budget or lack thereof. From Alabama to Winnipeg and everywhere in between, the nonprofit **Alliance Française** (AF) awaits your enrollment in one of its many classes, from structured beginner courses to more relaxed conversation groups. This isn't the most affordable option, but it might be the most fun: The AF also hosts events—art shows, film screenings, speaking engagements, mixers—with a French twist. One of the benefits of membership is access to the library of books, DVDs, and CDs, making for an all-in-one cultural immersion program minus mandatory exams and pesky report cards.

If you live near a **community college,** this is an excellent, budget-friendly option. For the cost of lunch at a French restaurant, you can take a semester's worth of classes in a structured environment with fellow beginners. The downside to college classes is that they tend to be heavily grammar-focused, and it often takes several semesters for you to work up to anything resembling a conversation level.

Private classes are another possibility. Look at the bulletin board at your local AF, troll the halls of the nearest university and look for the language department there, or ask the consulate for a list of references. Look for one-on-one lessons offered by

French students at American universities or by Francophone expats looking to earn a bit of pocket money on the side. These personal sessions tend to emphasize conversation rather than grammar, and this approach can be a really great introduction to the colloquialisms and idioms you'll likely begin hearing as soon as you land.

Many people swear by the pricey audiovisual experiences offered by **Rosetta Stone** and **Fluenz.** For between $200 and $400, you can pick up one of these programs at the bookstore or online and study in the comfort of your own living room. The philosophy and approach to teaching languages differs significantly between the two (the former applies an immersion approach, while the latter feeds you morsels of the language one bite at a time), but both allow you to go to school whenever and as often as you like. For couples studying together or for those who don't have time to attend conventional classes, this option makes a lot of sense.

The most affordable of all your language-learning possibilities is the **Meetup** (www. meetup.com). While technically not classes, Meetups are social-networking groups that share a common interest, which, in this case, is the French language. Expect culture-oriented get-togethers—museum outings, gatherings at wine bars, French cinema rendezvous, cheese tastings—that all serve as fun vehicles for ameliorating your language skills *ensemble* (together). These sessions are often great networking zones where you'll meet not only other Anglophones but also honest-to-goodness French people. The casual ambience of most Meetups will relax you enough to loosen your chat mechanism and help fuel enthusiasm for your upcoming move.

In cities and small towns alike you'll be able to find a center where you can take language classes and find affordable childcare and other services.

LEARNING IN FRANCE

France is a hotbed of language-learning possibilities, so even if you arrive with French skills in the negative values, you'll be okay. A learning institution that meets your budget and experience will be available in your newly adopted country. Always begin by word of mouth—your friends, colleagues, and even the people standing in line at the *préfecture* will be able to weigh in on their experiences learning the language in France. In Paris, visit your local *mairie,* where the staff will gladly offer you a list of references for municipally run classes in your quartier. To find a public or private course near you, log on to the French-as-a-foreign-language website **Français Langue Étrangère** (FLE) site at www.www.fle.fr. The directory is fairly comprehensive and points students toward a variety of courses in every price point and learning style, and in every corner of France, you'll find public institutions as well as courses offered by nonprofits, such as the Alliance Française. Prices can vary dramatically from organization to organization; at the Sorbonne in 2015, you could expect to pay €440 for 40 hours of summer-school French classes, plus a €50 dossier fee. Private schools in Paris are comparable in price. For example, l'Atelier 9 offers a four-week, 80-hour session for €840, but there are never more than nine students in your class, which means plenty of attention from your professor.

At the end of July, each office of the *mairie* in Paris offers the latest **livret de Cours Municipaux d'Adultes,** which lists all the courses available through the city at great prices, in multiple subjects. Expect a diverse student body, lots of structure, and a thorough introduction to the language. Throughout France, one of the best-kept language-learning secrets is that wonderful thing called the **association.** These are simply volunteer-run organizations that receive state funding for promoting the French language to the local non-French-speaking community. Year-long courses are ridiculously inexpensive—€40 was the average in 2014, and that includes workbooks—and the student-teacher ratio is low. Associations even subsidize the application fees for taking the standardized French exam known as DELF. (Having a DELF diploma in your dossier will likely impress the team surveying your file, so it's a good thing to acquire.) The nearest *association* may not be in your arrondissement; in Paris, check www.w35-associations.apps.paris.fr, and elsewhere in France, visit the *mairie* and ask for information on local *associations.*

One of the best and perhaps most obvious ways to learn French is by getting out there, interacting with the locals, and trying your best to speak in their native tongue. At the supermarket, post office, and *bibliothèque* (library), you will find

© AURELIA D'ANDREA

Your local *mairie* is a good place to start your hunt for French-language classes.

a surprisingly patient audience who will hear you out as you stumble along in elementary French, gently correcting you as you go. Don't miss these valuable learning opportunities by insisting that everyone speak English; you'll make friends and win hearts with a bit of earnest effort. Slightly more formal opportunities for interaction with francophones can be found at local language-exchange groups, some of them cleverly disguised as English conversation groups. Don't be fooled: It's almost always a 50-50 French-English exchange, often over drinks with an eclectic international crowd. In Paris, the **Big Ben Club** (www.bigbenclub.eu) meets up every Thursday for French-English exchange at that Left Bank bibliophile's institution, Shakespeare and Company. Nominal dues will be solicited, but they resemble pocket change more than mortgage payments. In Bordeaux, there's the **Bordeaux-USA** (www.bordeaux-usa.com) language and social club, which meets on Thursdays; in Grenoble, there's **Sweet Home Grenoble** (www.sweethomegrenoble.com), a social club that plans bilingual events and outings geared at helping anglophones learn French and francophones learn English. Every major city in France has something similar on offer, and the *mairie* is the place to go to discover what's available to you.

Education

Founded on the principles of *liberté, egalité,* and *fraternité,* the French education system is considered one of the better socialized-learning institutions in the world. Every child in France has access to a high-quality education, and between the ages of 6 and 16, they are required to attend school. Parents can choose between public, private, and home schooling. Girls not only receive an equal education but outnumber boys in the *baccalauréat* path leading to careers in economics and the arts. They also attend institutes of higher learning at higher rates than their male counterparts.

EDUCATIONAL LEVELS
On the surface, the French education system looks a little more complicated than the North American one, but once you understand the naming convention, the stages begin to look a lot more familiar.

Children are eligible for *crèche* (subsidized daycare) when they are three months old and *maternelle* (preschool) at two years old. They don't enter *école primaire* (primary school) until the age of six. *École primaire* is the French equivalent of elementary school. Kids begin at roughly seven years old, working their way up through five years of classes focused on reading, writing, math, geography, history, and occasionally a foreign language, including English.

When American kids look forward to graduating to middle school, their counterparts in France move up to *collège,* four years of pre-high school academic training that begins with level six (*sixième*) and ends with level three (*troisième*). Here, they study more of the fundamentals, plus French literature, music, and up to two languages, including English, German, Spanish, or Italian. Students are taught in the same classroom all day, with a rotation of teachers coming in to instruct. Each year, two students from each class are nominated to act as liaisons between the students and the teachers, facilitating dialogue and helping make decisions that affect their fellow students, from scrutinizing academic performance to weighing in on disciplinary action.

A child's entrance into *lycée* marks the beginning of the French high-school equivalent, which some might be glad to know lasts only three years. Counterintuitively, the first year of *lycée* is the *séconde,* and the second is the *première.* The third and final year is known as *terminale.* The last two years are spent focusing on a specific track of academic training. Kids following the science path can expect to take plenty of math, physics, and chemistry classes; humanities students will focus on foreign languages, including the classics, plus literature, philosophy, and history; economics students will study social sciences and math.

ENROLLING IN FRENCH SCHOOLS

If you are planning to enroll your child in the French school system, it's important that he has a language foundation to help him through the rough world of being the new kid in school. For high-school students in particular, the ability to assimilate, make friends, and thrive in any new environment is contingent on a basic ability to communicate; the better her language skills, the more successful your child will be at adapting. The younger the child, the more adaptable to the new language she will be. But if you throw a *lycée*-age teen into an all-French class without any preparation, the outcome could be disastrous: depression, failing grades, and worse.

Before being placed in a class, your child will be given an entrance exam to determine which school level is best. Even for the brightest students, repeating a grade to compensate for language deficiencies could be a reality. A handful of public schools throughout the Paris area offer special "international" sections for North American students entering the system without a solid foundation in the language. These unique curricula differ from the standard education model; they are designed especially to facilitate the integration of foreign students into the French system. (They also work to prepare French students for living abroad in other countries). Students can expect an extra six hours per week of French study, as well as a lot of time spent with their noses embedded firmly in books.

PRIVATE EDUCATION

As in the United States and Canada, private schools can be found throughout France, including parochial schools, Waldorf and Montessori schools, and elite international schools with annual tuitions that rival the cost of a new car. Despite the generally high standard of public education throughout France, parents opt to enroll their children in private schools for the same reasons parents everywhere do, including higher teacher-to-student ratios, safety, religious purposes, proximity, or to give children the advantage of being instructed in their native tongue.

French private schools fall into two camps: *Sous contrat* (under contract) and *hors contrat* (outside contract). Teachers at **sous contrat** schools are paid by the state, and tuition fees are generally on the low end of the spectrum. Curricula mirror those of public schools, and the academic calendar follows the same schedule. **Hors contrat** schools, because they aren't state-funded, are free to set their own curricula and tuition fees, and they run on an academic calendar of their own design.

The type of private education you choose for your children depends largely on your

Expat Experience: Smart Moves

Name: Bryan Pirolli
Age: 29
Occupation: PhD candidate, teacher, and freelance journalist
Hometown: Philadelphia
Current city: Paris, 10th

Bryan Pirolli has experienced many facets of French life since moving to l'Hexagone in 2008. He is currently working on his PhD and has worked in France within the food service industry, as a journalist, and as a university professor. Here, the Pennsylvania native shares his experiences navigating these and other realms within French society.

What drew you to Paris?
I moved here after my undergraduate education to work for my alma mater's study abroad program. After working in an academic setting, I realized that I was meant to be on the other end, so I went back to school at the University of Paris (the Sorbonne). Employment in a then-exotic place was enough to lure me to Paris; the idea of a graduate degree without any more debt kept me here.

What do you love most about your Paris life?
Chatting with the staff at my favorite café, seeing old friends or coworkers in the street, and being able to bike almost anywhere are just a few of the experiences I cherish. Paris does often feel like a village, and I get to take advantage of a quaint little-town lifestyle set inside a major global city. For example, I used to work at a pizza shop down the street from my apartment, and I still walk by almost every day and chat with my old colleagues and I give the *"bise"* to one of the owners when I see her there.

What are some of the ways, in your experience, that the French educational system differs from the American system?
From what I have seen teaching at the undergraduate level and studying at the graduate level, the French educational system is designed to let the cream rise to the top—if it wants. Unlike the expensive, supportive U.S. system, the affordable, laissez-faire French system is not designed so that everyone can win. Teachers just aren't as invested in student well-being. At least in the public university, if you don't do your work, no one will make sure you do. The result? A bad grade and not advancing to the next level. But if you are a motivated student, you can churn the cream into butter pretty easily. The idea of a grade curve isn't yet standard practice, though the system is changing little by little.

personal preferences, but your employer in France may affect your decision. Some employers offer new hires the option of enrolling their children in nearby international schools attended by the children of other international staffers. This may not provide the sort of enriching cultural exchange you'd envisaged for your child, but the assimilation process at an international *collège* or *lycée* will likely be smoother at an international school than at a French public school. To explore your options for French private schools, visit two online databases: www.enseignement-prive.info and www.fabert.com.

THE FRENCH UNIVERSITY SYSTEM

There are two tiers within the French university system: the *université* and the *grande école*. **Universités** are standard-issue universities that accept all who apply, as long as

But the teacher isn't generally out to fail or pass a certain number of people. It's almost refreshing, since the teachers don't have to worry about students reporting them to the dean, for example, because they didn't get the A+ they thought they deserved. This could all be interpreted as an all-too-passive student body, but I think it's just a lot more honest. Students know when they didn't put in the work.

Since it is so inexpensive, the public university also has less-than-desirable facilities, with none of the charming dining halls or student centers of American schools. This means there's less student life, even though they try.

Like the U.S., there are an elite set of schools (*les Grandes Écoles*) that are much harder to get into. I think the teaching and facilities at these institutions are better, but maybe not quite on par with the Ivy League or Cambridge.

Are you here on a student visa?

I am currently on a *"scientifique"* visa, since I am both a researcher and a teacher at the Sorbonne on a special scholarship/contract that is awarded to a certain number of doctoral candidates. I had two student visas before that (during my masters) and a *"jeune professionel"* before that to work at a study-abroad program that I got through the French Chamber of Commerce.

What three tips would you offer to newcomers?

· **Lower your expectations when it comes to any sort of administration or bureaucracy**–things take time but they will usually always happen. Expecting long waits for things like bank accounts and residency cards, expecting not to be understood all of the time, expecting not to get what I wanted–it all seems bleak but it's my reality as an expat. As soon as you don't expect *la vie en rose,* things start to seem a little rosier with each little triumph.

· **"C'est pas possible" is always an invitation to insist upon your initial demand.** If you think being told "That's not possible" means "NO" in France, you might as well stay home. Ask, then ask again. Then come back later and ask again.

· **Take advantage of free events, student discounts, and especially the perks of being "26 and under."** You don't need to spend a lot to enjoy France, but once you hit 27, it gets harder!

they meet the base criteria of having completed *lycée* (and survived the *baccalauréat*). Tuition fees are set annually and standardized throughout the country. In 2015, the annual tuition fees ranged from €184 to €610, depending on the academic credentials you'll be studying for. This doesn't reflect student social charges and mandatory health coverage, which tacks on an addition €215 or so.

Grandes écoles are elite schools, not unlike American Ivy League colleges, which accept only the best of the best and charge tuition fees that run higher than the national average. Expect to pay as much as €10,000 per year if you or your child is accepted into one of these institutions, and also expect to earn a well-paying job at the end of your education.

Whichever academic path you take, you can expect a long semester of

A university education in France is practically free and open to everyone who's willing to jump through the paperwork hoops.

it's-up-to-you-to-study independence, followed by a big make-it-or-break-it exam at semester's end. France has a relatively high university enrollment rate that's matched by a high dropout rate, due in large part to the stress of this virtually all-or-nothing system.

STUDY ABROAD

French universities roll out the welcome mat to 250,000 foreign university students every year, making France one of the most popular study-abroad destinations in the world. Coming into the French university system as an American college student is a significantly different experience than entering as a French *lycéen,* beginning with the fact that you won't have had to take the dreaded *baccalauréat* exam. Semester-abroad programs allow foreign university students to ease into the system; this is one of the most popular avenues for obtaining long-stay visas and *cartes de séjour,* which give students the right to work part-time. But first you must meet a few criteria.

To enroll without showing an *international baccalauréat,* you'll have to have two years of college under your belt already. Next, you'll have to decide if you want to study independently or through your university. The former is generally less expensive but requires more effort on your part.

Begin by contacting the school of your choice—a list can be found on the government-sponsored education portal www.enseignementsup-recherche.gouv.fr—then creating a dossier that you submit online directly at the university website. You will not be asked to show transcripts or grades; the onus will be on you to determine whether or not you're up to snuff, educationally speaking. Unless you are studying the French language exclusively, you will be asked to take a French-language proficiency exam or show a certificate attesting to your language skills.

Tuition at French universities is surprisingly affordable and varies slightly according to your academic goals. In 2014, students paid €183 annually for a standard undergrad diploma. For masters programs, the annual fees jumped to €254; doctoral students paid €388 per year; and students pursuing a *diplôme d'ingénieur* paid €606 per semester. Certificate programs, including those that allow you to bypass the French-language proficiency tests, cost considerably more; expect to pay as much as €3,000 per four-month semester for the luxury of being instructed in English. Private school tuition is, not surprisingly, higher still. Don't be shocked if that exclusive private business school asks you to fork over more than €10,000 a year to earn your MBA. Still, it might be cheaper than the American equivalent, so if you're seriously considering this route, invest in some French classes and start your research *tout de suite*.

One final word of caution: A unique difference students will notice between the French and American university education is the level of responsibility that falls on the student's shoulders. Don't expect surprise quizzes, weekly assignments, or even mid-terms—but do expect cumulative exams at the end of the semester that will determine your final grade. To learn more about your options as an American or Canadian student studying in France, visit www.campusfrance.org or check with your university.

DAILY LIFE

HEALTH

In the 2007 documentary *Sicko,* director Michael Moore used the French healthcare system to illustrate its American counterpart's many flaws. This cinematic tactic proved effective, earning the film an Academy Award nomination and prompting the viewing public to critically examine the issues that stirred such heated debate. But what stood out more than the U.S. healthcare system's startling deficiencies was that a humane, affordable, reliable government-run medical system is possible. In France, as it ought to be everywhere, medical treatment (and preventive care) is a right, not a privilege.

Consistently ranked the number-one healthcare system in the world, France's Assurance Maladie, part of the Sécurité Sociale system, is available to everyone who lives here legally and supports the system by paying taxes. People earning little or no income pay little or nothing. The rest of us pay according to our means. For the roughly 12 percent of the population that is self-employed, other forms of government-subsidized insurance is available. Even if you're not here legally, you won't be denied affordable healthcare: Low-cost public hospitals are at your disposal, and mobile doctors will even make house-calls to those unable to get to a hospital at any time of day or night.

If you play by the rules, you will have confirmed that you are insured before you arrive in France, since this is a required component of most visa applications. You're asked to submit proof of insurance, but experience proves that consular officials don't

always fact-check the documents you provide, and you aren't likely to be asked to provide proof again once you get here. Maybe you went ahead and purchased a traveler's policy that covers you in case of catastrophic illness or injury or reimburses you for travel expenses should you need to fly home to see your own doctor. If you're a student, it's likely that your school provides coverage for study-abroad programs. Or maybe, just maybe, you came with nothing at all, and suddenly that tooth with the wonky old filling is starting to give you grief. If that's you, you don't have to suffer in silence.

Types of Insurance

There are several types of health insurance available to expats in France, the first being the Assurance Maladie offered by the state. Supplemental insurance coverage, called *mutuelle,* is popular among the French, who use it to offset the already small (by American standards) deductibles, co-pays, and other types of care not covered by the regular system (cosmetic dentistry, for instance). Finally, there are private insurance options you can purchase in the U.S. or in France that provide different sorts of coverage—inpatient or outpatient or both, maternity, dental—at moderate prices. Which one you choose depends largely on your financial means and the kind of coverage you require for your own sense of security.

ASSURANCE MALADIE

The French public healthcare system is supported by the tax-paying public, which contributes approximately 20 percent of its income to prop up the system. It functions in a pay-as-you-can manner, which many tag as "socialist" because those who earn the most pay the most, and those with little pay less. (And those with no income pay nothing.) Even if you don't contribute taxes, you are entitled to Couverture Maladie Universelle (CMU) if you come from a country (like the U.S.) that doesn't offer universal coverage and will be residing France for more than three months, or if you are on a limited income. The system is stressed after years of seeing the contributor population dwindle. Retirees no longer contribute, and the birthrate has been low in France for decades—meaning there may not be enough new citizens to support the healthcare system in the future.

It's possible to come to France and sponge off healthcare, but this is not advisable. You don't want to be the proverbial straw that breaks the camel's back, nor the scapegoat for the failure of a generous, relatively smooth-running system. With public debt at an all-time high of nearly 96 percent of GDP at the time of writing, it can't take much more stress, an issue that political leaders are struggling to address. Paying into the system will help keep it operating, and has the added benefit of looking good on paper for those nerve-wracking visits to the *préfecture.*

After applying for your CMU, you may need to wait a few months to get approval and, ultimately, your *carte vitale.* If you have to visit a doctor or pharmacy, save your receipts; the coverage is usually retroactive to the date on which you submitted your documents. The cost of your annual premium is determined by your income—expect to pay 8 percent of whatever income you declare—and is due in quarterly installments.

Expat Experience: The *Carte Vitale*

Name: Elisabeth Lyman
Age: 39
Occupation: French-to-English translator
Hometown: Minneapolis, Minnesota
Current city: Paris, 17th

Elisabeth Lyman moved to Paris in 2009 to expand her already-thriving independent translation business and meet new clients. In the intervening years, she's morphed into a fully fledged Parisian, renting an apartment in the charming Batignolles district, establishing herself as an *auto-entrepreneur,* and developing an active social life in her new city. The transition was not without its hurdles and frustrations, however. It took Elisabeth more than two years to secure her *carte vitale,* the little green card that allows her to access the public healthcare system she's been paying into since 2011. Here, Elisabeth shares her suggestions to make the process easier for newcomers.

What documents did you include in your dossier before your first appointment at Assurance Maladie?
With my particular business type, I had to go through the RSI (Régime Social des Indépendants) to apply for my card. They asked for a *traduction assermentée* (certified translation) of my birth certificate as well as a photocopy of my residence permit, proof of residence, and copies of my business registration paperwork from URSSAF (a department within the French social security system that manages all aspects of *cotisation sociale*– otherwise known as the taxes that support the socialized medical system). I mailed all of this in a large brown envelope that would seem difficult to misplace. A couple of months later, after I had still not heard back from them, I called and was told my papers had never arrived. This could have been avoided if I had only sent them *en recommandée avec avis de réception* (by registered mail with confirmation of receipt), as the chance of mail sent this way getting lost is far lower. By the time I learned they didn't have my documents, it was too late to apply again because my residence permit had expired in the meantime. Renewing it took an entire year.

What was the most challenging aspect of the application process?
The most difficult parts were not knowing how much longer the process would take, and also the various dead-ends along the way. At one point, I received a letter from the RSI and opened it eagerly, imagining it held good news, or some information about progress made. Instead, it was a letter addressed to someone else who was also apparently trying to get the *carte vitale*. My name and address were on the envelope and in the header at the top of the page, but someone else's name was in the salutation and the body of the letter made references to a situation entirely different from mine. I sent it back with an explanation and a renewed expression of my desire to get a card with my own name on it.

What advice would you give to other independent professionals hoping to secure healthcare through Assurance Maladie?
Submit your paperwork in person and have them give you some kind of proof that you have done so. Also note the name of the person who took your documents. If you mail any papers, do this only through registered mail with confirmation of receipt. This way, you have proof of the steps you have taken. And above all, be friendly and show gratitude whenever dealing with the people responsible for getting you the card, whether over the phone or in person. A smile can go a long way.

Once you have your bright green *carte vitale* in hand, you can rendezvous with your doctor of choice and visit hospitals, clinics, pharmacies, and laboratories. Produce your card when you pay for your goods and services up front, then submit your receipts to Assurance Maladie, which reimburses you a percentage: 70-100 percent of what you paid for services and 15-65 percent of what you paid for your prescription medicines. Reimbursement takes about two weeks and is deposited directly into your French bank account. Sound complicated? It might seem so at first, but like all things French (and therefore heavy on bureaucratic ritual), it gets easier the more you do it.

MUTUELLE

By American standards, the full cost of medical treatment at a French public hospital borders on a bargain; depending on the treatment you receive, an overnight stay with regular nursing care and medications at a public hospital could set you back just €100—a whole lot less than it would at any public or private hospital in the U.S. Most drug costs are lower here, too. These two factors combined have resulted in some expats scheduling full-fare medical procedures in France. But for regular folks who simply want basic coverage, Assurance Maladie is a good start. Next, you might consider *mutuelle,* the supplemental insurance coverage that most French families and individuals opt for. It covers the cost of deductibles and all the little things that add up when you need them: ambulance costs, private hospital-room fees, and cosmetic dentistry, for instance. You can choose from a number of configurations, depending on your needs, and the price will reflect what those needs are. Want to make sure your contact lenses are paid for in full by your insurance company? Identify that concern when making your *mutuelle* purchasing decision.

In addition to all the private agencies offering *mutuelles,* the government also offers this additional coverage to families and individuals of limited means through the CMU website (www.cmu.fr). The information is in French, so if your language skills are still at the work-in-progress phase, you'll want a French friend to help you with the technical translating. Some well-known *mutuelles* in France include **France Mutuelle, MAAF,** and **Swiss Life.**

PRIVATE INSURANCE

All you need to feel totally overwhelmed by the private insurance policy process is to type in "expatriate health insurance" into your favorite search engine. You'll be met with links to dozens of companies, each offering similar but different insurance options that span a frighteningly broad financial spectrum. So which do you choose? The best bet is to go by word of mouth. Ask friends who've already made the move, post queries on expat forums, and check with the American Embassy in France, which offers a downloadable list of companies on its website (france.usembassy.gov). **HCC Medical Insurance Services** (www.hccmis.com) has earned high marks from some expats, with coverage in the US$700 to US$900 range annually. Also worth a gander are www.expat-medical-insurance.com and www.healthcareinternational.com. Another avenue to consider is your credit card company; some cards, including many issued by American Express, offer some sort of international healthcare coverage to members.

UNINSURED

Nearly everyone who's lived in France for any amount of time has one healthcare story or another; it usually ends with "I couldn't believe how inexpensive the bill was/how short the wait was/how friendly the staff was." Even if you have no health insurance coverage, you will be treated respectfully and without palpable bias or hostility. You will not be asked to show proof of insurance before you are treated, and you will not be denied care in the emergency room because of lack of funds. (You aren't even asked for a credit card or other payment during the course of your treatment; a bill will be mailed to you once your treatment is completed.) If you have no insurance and find yourself at the emergency room with a broken big toe or at the dentist's office with a faulty filling, be prepared to pay the bill when it arrives a week or two later, and expect the costs to be significantly less than if you were to have the same treatment back home. Remember to save your receipts, in case you sign up for Assurance Maladie; the program is retroactive and may cover a good portion of your out-of-pocket expenses.

Public Hospitals and Private Clinics

Only one third of all French *hôpitaux* (hospitals) are privately run; the rest are nonprofit public institutions run by the government, which sets fees for medical services rendered by any institution or individual medical professional on the government payroll. For example, on January 1, 2015, the reimbursable fee for an office visit to a family physician in France was set at €23, or €25 to visit with a specialist; to visit a mental health professional, the price is set at €39.70. Home doctor visits ring in at €33 during normal business hours, or €53 on Saturday afternoons, Sundays, and holidays. You'll pay slightly more as an uninsured patient.

Of the public institutions, many are **centres hospitaliers universitaires,** or research hospitals affiliated with a university. These are not the funky institutions that might come to mind when you hear "government-run facility." They are as warm and friendly as any hospital, and the care you'll receive is on par with private facilities. Expect the usual amenities in the rooms—toilets and televisions—and maybe even something more: Some hospitals post their menus online, so you can plan your overnight stay for a Saturday to benefit from the Sunday-morning croissants.

There are two different types of **cliniques** (private hospitals) in France—for profit and not-for-profit. In the Paris region, the American Hospital of Paris—which is actually in the well-to-do suburb of Neuilly-sur-Seine—belongs to the latter category, and its foundation is supported in part by member and public donations. You'll pay more here, and Assurance Maladie won't be able to reimburse you in the same generous way it would if you'd gone to a public hospital. The benefit of private hospitals is that some specialize in specific types of services—maternity or oncology, for instance—and some also tout a bilingual staff, which can ease the stress of an already stressful situation for some.

In France, would-be doctors don't go into the medical field because they want to get rich; they do it because they were fast-tracked on a science route during their *lycée* years (and possibly because the wanted a career in which they could help people). Because

The Doctor's Modern House-Call

It's 2am, and you haven't stopped coughing since 2pm. Your throat feels like a fiery furnace and your eyeballs are like dried raisins. Are you dying of some mysterious tropical disease, or is it a simple case of the 24-hour flu? If you don't have the strength to haul yourself to the nearest hospital, you're in luck. When you call SOS Médecins, an honest-to-goodness doctor will be knocking on your door within the hour, medical kit in hand, ready to diagnose what ails you and offer you a soothing balm—or at least an aspirin or two.

Assurance Maladie covers the cost of the home visit (€33), but even if you don't have insurance, there's no need to work up a sweat on top of your fever. You'll simply be charged the uninsured person's rate: €70 at the time of this writing. Don't have the strength to write out a check? Relax: They'll send you a bill.

SOS Médecins was founded in 1966 by a Parisian M.D. after one of his patients died on a Saturday—a day when doctors didn't regularly make house-calls. He figured that if you could get a plumber at home on a weekend, you should be able to get life-saving care, too. Today, SOS Médecins has been adopted by other Francophone countries, including Tahiti, Senegal, and Switzerland.

medical school costs next to nothing to attend in France, many choose this path despite its dearth of economic advantages. You will find that there are two types of doctors here, just to add another layer of complexity onto the process: *conventionnée* and *non-conventionnée*. **Conventionnée** doctors have contracted with the state to provide their services at a set cost that's reimbursable by Assurance Maladie; **non-conventionnée** practitioners have no contract with the state and set their own fees. You'll find this disparity especially among dermatologists and cosmetic surgeons, where fees can vary widely depending on the doctor, the location, and the services being rendered.

Pharmacies and Prescriptions

You can't miss the pharmacy; just look for the flashing green cross, and *voilà!* You've arrived. French pharmacies are different from their North American counterparts in many ways. First, a doctor is always on staff and has the authority to prescribe or recommend treatment at her discretion, without consulting your primary physician. These pharmacy doctors are also authorized to administer first aid if you need it. Next, you'll notice that some over-the-counter drugs you take for granted back home—cough syrup, pain reliever, even sore-throat lozenges—are found behind the counter at the pharmacist's, and requesting them requires some basic working French. Need multi-purpose solution for your contact lenses? Don't go looking for it at your local supermarket—you'll find it at the pharmacy, along with high-end face creams, diet pills and potions, homeopathic remedies, and multivitamins. (You'll also find contact-lens solution for sale at eyeglasses shops, where it is sometimes less expensive than at the pharmacy. It pays to compare.) Some pharmacies also vend veterinary medicines, so you can pick up Fluffy's heartworm medicine and your antibiotics in one fell swoop.

Picking up your prescription at the pharmacy works in a way you're probably familiar with: Bring your prescription to the counter, ask any questions, listen to the pharmacist explain how to take your medicine, pay for it (standard practice is to present your *carte vitale*, so you can be reimbursed), and save your receipts if you intend to seek reimbursement.

By law, every community must have a pharmacy that's open on weekends, holidays, and during off-hours; the information for the one closest to you can be found posted in the window or on the door of your neighborhood pharmacy.

Preventive Measures

No special inoculations are required to enter France, but it doesn't hurt to be in top health before your move. As part of the *carte de séjour* process, you'll have to have your lungs X-rayed for tuberculosis, but this is the only medical requirement you'll find here.

Like everywhere else, waves of viruses come crashing through the population every season, and many opt for flu vaccines as a prophylactic measure. If you didn't get that flu shot before you moved, you can still find one here. In France, the flu is called *"la grippe"* and often *"la grippe* H1N1," and pharmacies can direct you to health clinics where inoculations are administered or sell you the vaccine to take to your doctor to be injected.

ALTERNATIVE THERAPIES

The French love their medicine, whether it's the pharmaceutical kind or the kind created exclusively by Mother Nature. Homeopathy is particularly popular in France, and pharmacies everywhere sell homeopathic remedies behind the counter. Boiron, headquartered in Lyon, is the most popular brand, producing "remedies" for everything

© AURELIA D'ANDREA

Don't look for your contact lens solution at the *supermarché;* you'll find it at a pharmacy.

from bruises (arnica) to mental fatigue (nux vomica). The little blue vials run about €2 to €3, and many people swear by their efficacy. If you're one of the millions around the world who prefer to take the natural approach to healthcare, you'll find many opportunities to heal thyself in France. Flower essences, acupuncture, and massage are all on the menu. Herbal weight-loss formulations are in high demand in France, and you'll have dozens of varieties of liquids, pills, lozenges, and creams to choose from if you're looking to shed a kilo or two before bikini-and-Speedo season. Many healthcare services that fall under the "natural" umbrella are covered in part by Assurance Maladie, including homeopathy, which is reimbursed at 30 percent; be sure to inquire when seeking out your treatment.

© AURELIA D'ANDREA

Natural food stores offering healthy products exist in every corner of the country.

Environmental Factors

AIR QUALITY

Each year in France, 11 million tons of pollutants are pumped into the air from cars, factories, agriculture, and people living their day-to-day lives. This fact is particularly noticeable when you're stuck on your bicycle behind a two-stroke motorbike at a stoplight. In some ways, Paris looks like a developing nation when it comes to the color and quantities flowing out of auto exhaust pipes. Your health can be affected by all that pollution, both out in the streets and in your home. To see what the pollution levels are like in your town, visit www.airqualitynow.eu. In Paris and Bordeaux, the levels can look scary-high from time to time. Many city dwellers in France take the extra precautionary step of purchasing an air filter; try Darty (www.darty.fr) if you live on a particularly busy street or near a freeway on-ramp, where pollution levels are particularly high.

WATER QUALITY

The French are known for their love of bottled water, consuming 40 gallons of it per person per year. Stroll down the aisle at the nearest *hypermarché,* and you'll find yourself in a sea of drinking water. Do you like yours flat or still? Loaded with minerals or not? Are you on a diet? There's a bottled-water variety to help you through. Those who don't need fancy water (or who don't want to contribute more plastic to the wastestream) will be glad to know that tap water is safe throughout France, though it tends to have a very high lime content, which leaves a flaky white residue on glasses, in your

Up in e-Smoke

Smoking, that most beloved of French traditions, is on its way out. In its place? More smoking—e-smoking, that is. Touted as a harmless bridge between full-fledged addiction and absolute cessation, e-cigarettes offer the nicotine buzz without the toxic, lung-damaging smoke, according to the people selling them.

In the last two years, e-cigarette shops by the dozens have hatched in every city of any size in France, selling the hope of a life free from addiction, chronic coughs, emphysema, and worse for between €30 and €100. For France's 15 million smokers, this is a godsend. For your money, you get one battery-operated device in the color of your choice, plus a replaceable liquid-nicotine cartridge. *Vapoteuses* and *vapoteurs* throughout the capital swear by its efficacy, but French health experts are already issuing warnings about potentially detrimental long-term effects, and in more bad news, Health Minister Marisol Touraine has campaigned to get the e-cigarette classified as a drug, which would entail a "smoking" ban similar to the one instituted in New York City that makes it illegal to puff away in indoor public places. So far, only a ban to eliminate e-cigarette advertising has been successfully implemented.

sink, and in your tabletop water-filter pitcher. This necessitates the purchase of products that eliminate the funky buildup in your appliances, such as electric kettles and dishwashers. Public fountains are common throughout Paris—they're often green, and if it's a Wallace fountain, designed by 19th-century French sculptor Charles-Auguste Lebourg, it might even look like a piece of art. Potable water is available in public fountains, and numerous filter options are available for those who want to lessen the lime content in their glasses. Around the Alps and Pyrénées, it's not uncommon to see cars pulled over on the side of the road, with a line of people bearing water bottles to be filled at natural springs.

SMOKING

Though the café smoking ban went into effect way back in 2008, France's addiction to "cancer sticks" still clings like tar to an old Gitanes fan's lungs. Where else will you find a pregnant mother-to-be puffing her hand-rolled cigarette, with nary a glance of disapproval from passersby? The good news is that the rates of stroke and heart attack have plummeted since the ban; the bad news is that it's still too late for too many. Lung cancer kills more people in France than any other type of cancer. Bad habits are hard to break, and that's particularly evident in the outdoor seating section of cafés, which tend to take on the air of a smoker's convention in wintertime when the heat lamps are activated and the plastic walls go up to keep the cold out. Smoking is no longer legal in public places, including office buildings, hospitals, museums, and school campuses, but that doesn't mean everyone adheres to the law. Enforcement has been rather lax, and business owners are reluctant to ask clients to stub out their cigs if no one has lodged a complaint. If you're sensitive to cigarette smoke, avoid enclosed terraces at cafés and brasseries, and count your blessings that you didn't decide to move to France before 2008.

Disabled Access

Though disabled-access laws are now in place, France has a lot of catching up to do, beginning with ditching the word *handicappée,* which is the preferred term in France for people with any minor or major disability. This is not the most hospitable country for people with mobility issues. Despite a law passed in 2005 to make offices, businesses, and public spaces accessible to all, the changes are being implemented at an escargot's pace. The government agency that oversees laws relating to disabled citizens, the Ministère des Solidarités et de la Cohésion Sociale, launched a PR campaign to try to convince people that efforts are under way to make France more accessible, but those who have to navigate the cobbled streets, clogged sidewalks, centuries-old staircases, and other public spaces will tell you it's just not happening fast enough. The Métro is not worth the hassle: Not all stations are equipped with an elevator, and those that do have them can't ensure that they'll be functioning when you need to use them. Buses are more likely to have a wheelchair access. According to a law passed in 2005, by 2015, all public spaces were to have been made accessible to those with restricted mobility. Big projects rarely keep to schedule in France, and several months into the year, it is clear that the government has not met its target. Work to make public transportation and municipal buildings accessible to every member of society is ongoing.

Safety

There's no sugar-coating it: Crime is on the rise in France. Still, it isn't very likely you'll become a crime statistic if you live here. Strict gun-control laws do mean that you're more likely to get stabbed than shot, but the odds of either one are infinitesimally small.

PICKPOCKETING AND THEFT

If you are the victim of a crime in France, it'll most likely be a pickpocketing or other petty theft. In Paris, Métro line 1 is notorious for pickpockets, who hunt for distracted tourists on their way to the Louvre, the Musée d'Orsay, and the Champs-Élysées.

Also growing in popularity among thieves previously resigned to wallets is smartphone theft, with iPhones being of particular interest. A recent spate of phone thefts in train stations and on the streets—generally the purloined items are snatched directly from the hands of their rightful owners—warrants extra care with your electronic doodads. Also be aware that when you're traveling by car, your license plate gives away your nonlocal status, and visitors in rental cars have reported break-ins at popular tourist sites. The key is not to leave anything of value in your car, and be sure to keep all the doors locked when you're driving.

One technique being employed to curb crime in public areas is the closed-circuit TV camera. A public surveillance system, which counts nearly 1 million cameras on city streets, parking lots, and train stations throughout France, is set to increase in the coming years, with Marseille pledging to install an additional 2,000 cameras in public places before 2019, and other cities pledging to do the same on a smaller scale. If it feels like a futuristic police state, that's probably not too far off—but this system has proved effective in apprehending thieves in the Métro and otherwise identifying criminals in public places. In the community of Montereau, about 45 minutes east of Paris, closed-circuit cameras are being used to capture "criminals" of another stripe: Locals who fail to do their civic duty and pick up after their dogs. Surveillance efforts—and the €35 fine—seem to be working. A recent nationwide survey indicates that 75 percent of French citizens approve of public surveillance cameras.

POLICE

French police can help with matters as varied as finding a lost animal to giving you directions to helping you when your pocket is picked on the Paris Métro. There are several different types of police: *police nationale,* those legions of men and women who keep order and protect the public in metropolitan areas throughout France; *gendarmes,* who keep the peace in rural areas, provide military security, and stroll the welcome halls at airports; *police de la circulation,* who'll ticket you for breaking one of the rules of the road and issue you those pesky parking citations; and *douanes,* who enforce the law when it comes to customs and taxes. For basic issues, either go to the local *commissariat* of police in your arrondissement or town, or dial emergency number 17—it's the same throughout France—to speak with a law-enforcement agent equipped to help you. Note that French is the common language spoken, so be prepared to try to stumble through; if you get a nice person on the other end of the line, she may meet you halfway with some English.

mounted *gendarmes* (police) in Paris

© TOPDEQ/123RF.COM

EMERGENCIES

France is fully equipped to handle any emergency you may face, but you need to know where to call to get the care that you need. The fire department, or Sapeurs-Pompiers, is the go-to agency for most emergencies. The staff act as intermediaries to determine whether they should come to your aid themselves or send the police or a more urgent medical service. If they determine that you need a doctor at home right away, they'll direct you to **SOS Médecins** (or you can call them directly—in Paris, dial 01/47 07 77 77), who'll be at your home in less than an hour. Or they might send Urgences Médicales, who'll pay you a visit within 12 hours (tel. 01/53 94 94 94). Several times each year, cards with all the municipal emergency numbers are distributed to homes and apartments throughout France. Ask the *gardien(ne)* of your building for a card or request one at your local *mairie* if one hasn't been slipped under your front door in a while. The most common numbers you'll need in an emergency are 15 for an **ambulance** (Service d'Aide Médicale d'Urgence/SAMU), 17 for **police** (Police/Gendarmes), and 18 for the **fire department** (Sapeurs-Pompiers).

EMPLOYMENT

Back in 2011, as the nation ramped up for the presidential elections, then-president Nicolas Sarkozy reignited the heated debate over one of France's most controversial social issues by declaring, "The 35-hour workweek no longer exists." Threatening the status quo with that proclamation might be one of the reasons the French public elected François Hollande instead of re-electing Sarkozy in 2012, but Sarkozy was on to something: The 35-hour workweek is a bit of a myth; the national average is 39.5 hours of work-time each week, just behind the European average of 40.3 hours. But that's not to say there aren't perks galore for the employed populace. Americans are often left slack-jawed with a combination of disbelief and envy when they learn what their French counterparts are entitled to: free healthcare? A minimum of five weeks' paid vacation? Subsidized education? How can people gripe about a few increased work hours when they've got all that? Easy. The French work hard for their benefits and don't want to see them whittled away without a fight. Even if the 35-hour workweek works better in theory than in practice, at least the 218-day work year and five weeks of vacation are safe from the meddling hands of politicos.

For expatriates arriving in France with hopes of laying down roots and actually earning a living, there are numerous possibilities, some more feasible than others. In a perfect situation, you'll be transferred here through your current job, settle into a

cushy three-year contract complete with housing, travel, and food allowances. (This is a reality for many—your first social gathering in France with more than a handful of American expats will verify it.) American companies by the boatload—4,200 to be precise—have branched out with offices in France—including American Express, Xerox, Hewlett-Packard, IBM, and many fashion and beauty brands. If you've been employed with such a company for more than three months, you're eligible for an Employee on Assignment permit. Does your company have international offices? If so, it's worth checking with your HR department on the chances of an international transfer.

Teaching English has long been a popular way for Anglophone expats to earn a living in France, and it might be the one professional realm where Americans have an advantage over the French; employers often prefer native speakers and those with limited French because it reinforces the goal of the education process: teaching (and learning) English. Private language schools and individual private lessons are the two paths of least resistance, and opportunities are plentiful if you establish yourself as a niche teacher of children, perhaps, or of legal English to traveling attorneys.

For the lucky arrivals armed with a law degree, finding employment in France and securing that all-important work-sponsored visa will be much easier. The nonprofit sector—the International Chamber of Commerce, OECD, and UNESCO—are good places to start your hunt for a legal job in France. Not an *avocat* (lawyer) and don't plan to become one? There's still hope, especially if you're in possession of a student visa, which allows you to work up to 20 hours per week (and more during the summer semester). With a long-stay visa, you can continue your freelancing gigs abroad without worrying about breaking any employment laws—though if you plan to stay more than three months and intend to sign up for Assurance Maladie, you'll need to file an income tax return so the French government can determine how much to charge you for healthcare coverage.

The unemployment rate is high in France, currently at 10 percent, and unemployment among foreigners is even higher, at 25 percent (considerably lower than the 40 percent figure Marine Le Pen proclaimed at a 2014 anti-immigration rally). When a position opens up, a French employer will first look to the pool of French applicants to find a qualified candidate. That's some stiff competition, considering that the natives are already equipped with a solid (and predictably uniform) educational foundation and, presumably, an extremely high level of French fluency. Bundled with the fact that they are citizens and you are not, they will most likely trump your qualifications unless you have some tricks up your sleeve. (Or if the jobs you're applying for aren't desirable, meaning the qualified locals may pass and take unemployment or job offer *numéro deux* instead.)

Another option for anyone not averse to a bit of risk-taking is under-the-table work. Though it's not discussed much in the open, there is a thriving underground economy in France, supported primarily by expats here on legal visas, as well as illegal immigrants who haven't taken the steps to get their visa situations sorted out. From restaurant work to teaching English to watching children and giving tours, there are endless opportunities to earn some euros by working *dans le noir* (under the table), but keep in mind that this option is neither ideal nor legal. Unsurprisingly, the big cities have the most opportunity, with Paris being the employment mecca of France. It's possible to tap into the diverse population and exploit it, if that's your thing. But be warned that getting caught could have dire consequences not just for you—including expulsion and being banned from returning for four years—but also for the person who hires you, who'll be slapped with a hefty fine.

Taxes run extremely high for employers in France; to cover your *cotisation,* or social benefits, they must pay the state an average of nearly a third of the wages they pay you, so the temptation is always there to add an extra undeclared body or two to the payroll. Surprisingly, even long-established companies, particularly those in the tourist trade whose day-to-day workings are limited mostly to foreign visitors, fly under the radar and employ people off the books. Either they have good lawyers, know the ropes, or are genuine roulette players willing to engage in the risks. Whatever the case may be, they're here, hiring people like you and me to our mutual advantage—but not without considerable hazards.

If all this talk of deportation, fines, and other risks have you reconsidering the illegal employment minefield, making your freelance status official or even starting your own business might be the solution. Be prepared to build a fat dossier of tax forms, *cotisation* papers, and endless copies of your *carte de séjour.* If your desire to make it work in France supersedes your fear of paperwork, prepare to investigate your moneymaking options.

Self-Employment

FREELANCING

Once you've been granted your visa and have either your *carte de séjour* or *recepisée* in hand, you'll need to register as an *auto-entrepreneur* with the Centre de Formalités des Entreprises des Autoentrepreneurs (www.lautoentrepreneur.fr). This allows you to go legit by declaring your activity and subsequent income, then paying the taxes that help support that generous healthcare system you're now entitled to take advantage of. You'll create an online dossier that describes the sort of work you'll be doing and answer all the nosy questions the government wants to ask about you to make your status official. Then hit the *envoyer* (send) button. (This process can also be done in person at the **Centre de Formalités des Entreprises** (CFE), Chambre de Commerce, or Chambre des Métiers). A month or two later, you'll receive a Notification d'Affiliation au Statut Auto-Entrepreneur, the form you'll use to declare any earnings. You'll also receive a chart that will help you determine the taxes or *cotisation* that you need to remit, which will fall somewhere between 13 and 23 percent of your declared earnings, contingent on the type of work you perform. You'll do this three times a year, and you'll be glad to know that if you've earned nothing, you owe nothing. However, if you declare no earnings or income for three consecutive trimesters, you'll lose your *auto-entrepreneur* status and be required to seek an alternative tax status.

STARTING A BUSINESS

Starting a business in France is a marvelous idea—if you have a solid plan, a healthy respect for paperwork, the patience of a saint, and, perhaps most importantly, a healthy bank account balance. Recent changes in French tax law have made it more feasible (and less expensive) for Average Jacques and Jacquelines to launch their moneymaking ventures here. But to get your foot through the self-employment door, it's wise to have it all worked out on paper for the consular officials before you even get here, meaning you must possess a student visa, *carte compétences et talents,* or other work-friendly visa.

If you can afford to hire a consultant before you get started, it's not a bad idea. She can help you with all the befuddling aspects of taxation, idiosyncrasies in labor law, and other formalities. The **Agence Pour la Création d'Entreprises** (www.apce.com) is a semiprivate organization—the government funds 60 percent of its budget—that helps entrepreneurs develop and launch their businesses in France. The APCE has devised a helpful checklist for prospective *auto-entrepreneurs* to determine the viability of their ideas and help them pick which *statut juridique* they'll need to register under once they decide to give it a go.

Next, the process moves in much the same way as becoming an *auto-entrepreneur:* You create a dossier with the Centre de Formalités des Entreprises des Auto-Entrepreneurs (www.lautoentrepreneur.fr). You'll be prompted to determine which category your new business falls into: Artisan/Industriel/Commerçant or Profession Libéral. If you're a commercial agent, you'll need to register with the Registre Spécial des Agents Commerciaux (RSAC). As an artisan entrepreneur, you must follow up with the Chambre de Métiers. If you choose to start your own dog-walking business, private English school, or bicycle touring company, you will need to make your status as an Entrepreneur Individuel à Responsabilité Limitée (EIRL) formal at www.eirl.fr or www.guichet-entreprises.fr. Both of these agencies offer resources and services to aid you in your quest to become a successful entrepreneur in France.

Registering under some *statuts,* including the EIRL, allows you to defer the Contribution Foncière des Entreprises (CFE) tax for the first three years. However, if you don't report any earnings whatsoever within your first two years, your status will be reverted automatically to the not-so-budget-friendly *"entreprise individuelle"* designation, which means you'll be responsible for paying taxes on estimated revenue to the tune of €3,000 the first year. Investing in a tax accountant is a good idea if you want to avoid any potential financial surprises down the line.

If you move out of the country or decide to relinquish your self-employment status for another reason, it's important to declare the *cessation d'activité* on the URSSAF website (www.cfe.urssaf.fr).

Types of Businesses

The type of business you choose to undertake depends entirely on your skills, personal interests, demands, moneymaking potential, and location. Businesses that don't require retail space or office space are, from an economic perspective, easier than others. You might also consider buying an existing business—a *gîte,* a bed-and-breakfast, a retail shop, or perhaps a vineyard—and putting your own spin on it. But keep in mind that you'll inherit the previous owner's reputation, so if it wasn't a good one, you'll have some damage control to do. If you're a brazen risk-taker, it's a clear opportunity to take a good idea, improve on it, and integrate into your new community.

As you consider your options, make use of some of the free and very handy services that are there for the asking—as long as you're asking in French. The *maire* (mayor) of your arrondissement or town wants to see new business flourish in his or her district

Expat Experience: Recipe for Entrepreneurship

Name: Jennifer Eric
Age: 36
Occupation: Owner, My Kitch'n
Hometown: Gothenburg, Sweden
Current city: Paris, 17th

Swedish entrepreneur Jennifer Eric settled in Paris in 2001. After earning her BA in political science and MBA in international marketing, she opened My Kitch'n, a vegan restaurant in Paris's Batignolles neighborhood. The road to entrepreneurship was bumpy; along the way, she experienced sexism, ageism, and institutionalized resistance to new ideas. But with her moxie, tenacity, and above-par French skills, she made her dream a reality. Here, she offers tips for would-be business owners in the City of Light.

You launched My Kitch'n in 2013. How much time did you invest in your business plan before opening?
It took me about a year and a half to get all the paperwork in order. The business plan, financial previsions, and market study were not the hardest part; that all took me about three months, but I've had both theoretical and practical practice when it comes to that, which most certainly helped speed up the process.

What component of the process required the most time and energy?
The hardest part was getting a space, as nobody believed in my idea. This took me over a year. "People don't eat like that," I was simply told. I'm sure they were rolling their eyes behind my back and calling me crazy cat lady, too. Finally, it was the City of Paris and the Ministry of Economic Development that gave me a shot by according me a space in the Marché Couvert des Batignolles, a public covered market.

What are some of the unexpected roadblocks you encountered as you embarked on opening your own business?
I didn't realize the extent of the gender gap when it comes to entrepreneurship. This is by far the most frustrating roadblock I've encountered. When trying to get the project off the ground, in meetings, I was first greeted by, "Maybe you should get some work experience after your studies before trying to do something like this." Then, after I'd set the record straight and pointed to my industry experience in addition to my education, I

and is a wonderful resource. He or she can tell you what has worked or hasn't worked in the past, prognosticate on whether your business idea has potential for success in your chosen quartier, and direct you toward local resources to help your idea succeed. The *chambre de commerce* (www.cci-paris-idf.fr) serves a similar function; remember, it's in their interest for you to succeed, so it's worth taking advantage of the help and resources they offer.

was told, "But aren't you looking to settle down any time soon?" You have to work twice as hard as a woman, and earning respect takes much longer.

Was anything easier than expected?
Yes, actually, getting people to appreciate 100 percent plant-based cooking is less of a struggle than I thought it would be in the land of frog legs and *foie gras*. I know a lot of people who thought my project was a bit of a suicide mission, but people are adapting and adopting it quicker than I thought! And they are much less confrontational than I thought they would be, considering the traditional environment I'm in.

Did you make use of any small-business associations to assist you with your project?
Through the *Maison de l'Emploi et des Entreprises* and *Boutique de Gestion* I received technical assistance (such as lawyers and certified accountants) free of charge, validating my dossier according to French standards every step of the way. It was *Pôle-Emploi* that put me in touch with the *Maison de l'Emploi et des Entreprises*, and I was lucky to meet a woman there who was really on top of things and helped me out a lot, shortening the wait period between the stages of validation.

What tips would you offer to expats thinking of launching a business in Paris, based on your own experience?

· **Never surrender.** Everyone likes to tell you that building your dream project is impossible, here more than anywhere I've ever lived. Don't mind them.

· **Take your time to find a good accountant.** Having an accountant is mandatory here, not a choice, when you put a business structure in place. (You are not required by law to have one as an *auto-entrepreneur*.) You can be audited, so make sure to keep all your papers in order from the get-go. Scan things and file everything on an external hard drive that you keep exclusively for accounting purposes.

· **Factor in one day of paperwork-only per week.** Don't underestimate the time this will take you. France is very old-fashioned when it comes to business laws, and many things are still done the old-fashioned way. Government institutions make plenty of mistakes, so make sure you read everything thoroughly. And pay your bills and taxes on time!

The Job Hunt

The job hunt in France begins much the same way it does in the U.S. or Canada. Start by talking to everyone you know—friends of friends of friends, distant cousins, elementary-school classmates—because it really is all about who you know. Don't know anyone? That's OK. But don't even think about hitting the pavement without fluffing up your dossier first. You'll need one, and it should include copies of every spelling bee award and talent-show ribbon you've ever earned, because that stuff matters here. Include copies of your college diploma—ideally translated into French—and certificates of completion for any higher-education studies you've taken, including language courses. Have your letters of recommendation handy, too, and be prepared to tote them to your job interview along with the rest of your dossier documents.

It's easy to get discouraged scouting the want ads on Craigslist or FUSAC: "Only those with working papers need apply." Well, don't take that at face value. Many companies publish similar phrasing in their ads to keep the government looking the other way, but when it comes down to interviewing and subsequently hiring, your lack of work permit may not be an issue at all. First and foremost, you'll find that you need to establish trust with your future employer. He doesn't want to offer you a job you're not legally entitled to take, only to get fined or, worse, forcibly ejected from France. If you do decide to take the below-board route, always be discreet and be honest with your employer, who is taking a risk to hire you. But don't be afraid to apply for that job, even if you're not 100 percent qualified. There may be an opportunity for a work sponsorship, or maybe your interviewer knows of another position at another company that needs someone with your skill set.

CVS VS. RESUMES

The French résumé is one of those oddball documents that differs greatly from its North American counterpart in many ways, beginning with the word "résumé," which means something different in French than in English. From this point forward, you'll refer to your summary of skills and qualifications as your **CV.** Remember those passport-size snapshots you've been forewarned to stock up on? You'll need to attach one of those (or a high-quality copy) to each CV you submit to a French company. Here, unlike in the U.S., it's understood that looks really do matter—as do your level of language fluency, age, and marital status, although these last two points are becoming less relevant to employers with each passing year. But don't be surprised if you're asked to divulge your nationality and the number of children you have, among other things; it's totally legal for employers to ask. And it's worth reminding you that your CV needs to be written in French. Ideally, you'll have someone completely *courant* (fluent) translating for you if you're not fluent yourself, since some words and concepts don't translate directly. Always keep a current English-version copy of your French CV, since employers may ask to see both.

INTERVIEWS

You've landed a coveted interview, and now you want to charm their socks off. Start by adhering to standard interview protocol—dress sharply, show up on time, and come prepared with a bit of background knowledge and questions for the person interviewing you—and end with a thank-you note. Take great care to tout your strengths and accomplishments without sounding like a braggart, and be prepared for questions that dip into personal territory; it's not unusual to be asked about your hobbies and whether your plans include starting a family.

French employment laws make it difficult for you to be fired once you've been hired, so expect the interview process to extend the limits of thoroughness. This is so your future employer can get a full sense of what you're all about before she extends a potentially lifelong offer your way. You will be asked about your weaknesses and strengths and what you think makes you right for the job. Above all, you will be assessed for your French-speaking abilities—you must be conversational, at the very

Working at a café isn't a bad gig in France.

least, if you want to work for a French company. Don't expect special treatment as an *exotique* Anglophone, because you'll likely not get it.

LANDING THE JOB

If you've been offered a job contract in France, it will fall into one of a few categories. The *contrat à durée déterminée* (CDD), a fixed-term contract good for 18 to 36 months, might be the most popular. This is the usual "starter" agreement between an employer and an employee; if the work relationship is to be extended, the CDD is transformed into a *contrat à durée indéterminée* (CDI). The CDI is an open-ended contract that implies permanency, though it usually comes with a two-month probationary period. It is also possible to work without any sort of contract, in which case it is implied that you will be hired on an ongoing, open-ended basis. When you sign your contract—whether it's a CDI, CDD, *contrat de travail temporaire* (CTT) or *contrat jeunes en entreprise* (CJE)—make sure it clearly states your salary, as well as any monetary perks to which you've agreed or are entitled. Many employers offer staff an annual bonus known as the "13th month" check, which is, ostensibly, a holiday bonus—check your contract to see if it includes one.

BENEFITS

As with most jobs, a contract position entitles you to social benefits ranging from family healthcare to retirement pensions. The onus is on you to learn what all the perks are and to maximize your access to the ones that may take a bit of sleuthing, such as restaurant meal vouchers or commuter compensation. Like everyone else, you will earn 2.5 days of vacation for every month worked. Both women and men are entitled to leave after the birth of a child (for women, it's 16 weeks; for men, it's just two; but both parents can take additional time off at a decreased salary). A few different forms of sabbatical are also available to *salariés* (employees), including up to a year off to study in a field that will enhance your work performance.

One significant difference between the U.S. and France is the frequency of paychecks. In the U.S., getting paid every two weeks—and sometimes every week—is the norm. In France, you'll likely get one paycheck on the first of each month. And if that paycheck looks small, it might be because it is; you contribute a share of your salary—up to 40 percent in the highest income brackets—to support the social benefits you and your colleagues are entitled to. But your company is also contributing on your behalf, usually considerably more than what you pay, to offset the financial burden.

Surviving the *Grève*

Type A people, prepare yourselves: You *will* have to wait in line at the grocery story as a slow-moving octogenarian counts change (those minutes feel like hours). You will *not* get "the customer is always right" service at the department store. And, at some point during your French sojourn, you will definitely experience the infamous *grève*.

A *grève*, otherwise known as a strike, is a part of the French political process that often precedes or immediately follows a legislative act. Like flu season, the *grève* makes an appearance every year—sometimes two or more of them. The key to surviving this inconvenience lies in planning. Because most strikes are coordinated in advance, it's very possible to create a Plan B that'll get you to work or to the airport on time.

Euphemistically called "disruptions," transportation strikes rarely last more than 24 hours. For commuters, this means exploring alternative ways of getting to work: public bike-sharing, *covoiturage*, or walking are common solutions. Should you have bigger travel plans during a planned strike, check with the airline for up-to-the-minute changes; if you're traveling on the French national railway lines, chances are your ticket will be valid on any train heading in the right direction after the strike is over.

Labor Laws

WORKERS' RIGHTS

France has such strong laws in favor of the employee that getting fired is practically impossible here—but that doesn't mean you should show up an hour late for work, take two-hour lunch breaks, and leave at 3pm every day. Plenty of people do this, but some actually get fired for it, as former Paris-based secretary Catherine Sanderson did back in 2006. Sanderson, who blogged under the nom de plume "La Petite Anglaise" until 2009, got the boot when her employers—an English law firm with offices in France—discovered she was blogging about her personal and professional life while on the job. She wound up winning a wrongful termination lawsuit, but you'll want to avoid that by simply showing up on time, taking the allotted hour-long break, focusing on your work, and leaving with the rest of your colleagues at the appointed hour. If you feel like you need a bit of support, you'll be able to find a trade union to advise you; though only 8 percent of French workers actually belong to a union (mostly those employed by multinational corporations), the unions still represent the entire workforce, so you can benefit from the strides they've made on your behalf without actually paying dues or participating in *grèves* during strike season.

By law, employers with more than 50 employees on the payroll must create a *comité d'entreprise* (an employee's council), which acts as an intermediary between employees and staff on all issues affecting workers, and all companies with 11 or more employees must also have *délégués du personnel* (personnel representatives) that serve a similar function. Depending on the size of the company, there will be between one and nine elected *délégués*, each with an elected stand-in. Elections are held every two to four years, and *délégués* spend between 10 and 15 hours per month in their roles, which includes keeping employees abreast of changes in salaries, updated health and safety codes, modifications to the work code, and other changes in the workplace.

MINIMUM WAGE

In 2015, the French minimum wage added up to €1,457.52 per month, which breaks down to €9.61 per hour. This wage increases when the cost of living index rises, ordinarily by 2 percent a year. Undocumented workers are clearly not protected by employment laws, adding extra risk to working under the table. Tipping for waitstaff and other service-industry jobs is not standard practice here, but it has come to be expected in heavily touristed areas. Don't feel obligated to leave a tip, and if you happen to find yourself employed in the service industry, don't expect to be tipped (but do expect a decent quality of life, even on your minimum-wage salary).

FINANCE

Whether you're a student, a work transfer, or a business entrepreneur, moving to France means getting intimately acquainted with your finances. From the moment you embark on this journey, you'll need to provide officials with financial data to prove your solvency in France; your visa application will ask for letters from your bank and proof of means of financial support. Once you arrive in France, you'll see how your previously prodigious peck of dollars morphs into a much smaller bundle of euros, which necessitates adjusting your way of thinking about your finances and your new currency. France can feel expensive as a tourist, but as a resident, you won't have to worry about spending as much. You'll actually find some things to be a much better value for your money: food (even if you eat more of it), wine, and medical care, for example. You'll also come face-to-face with the startling realization that some products and services are much more costly, including gasoline, electricity, and even manicures (don't expect to find the $10 equivalent anywhere in France, except at the local beauty academy). Sticker shock will happen, but many a newcomer to *la belle France* is surprised to learn that the overall cost of living is less than in the United States.

© LAURENT RAVIER/OTG

VALUE ADDED TAX

VAT, or Value Added Tax, is called **TVA** in France. Conceptualized by Frenchman Maurice Laure and implemented in 1954, it has since been adopted by many European countries, where the tax rate reaches as high as 25 percent on consumable goods such as clothing, electronic equipment, and wireless Internet and phone service. In France, the VAT rate was recently increased to 20 percent on most consumer goods; a smaller VAT tax is levied on the purchase of books, air and train travel, and food and drink. The tax is one of the key financial props holding France together, bringing in 45 percent of the country's tax revenue. The good news is that it is built into your purchases, so when you see something for sale for €20, that's exactly how much it will cost you.

THE EURO

France ushered in the euro in 2002, but that wasn't the end of the franc. In some Parisian shops, you'll find prices still listed in that old relic of a currency, and bank receipts often include the franc rate, too. The little town of Le Blanc, in the Centre region, had a harder time than most letting go; 30 local businesses continued to trade in the franc right up until February 2012, when the currency was phased out for good.

Cost of Living

GROCERIES

Locally produced fruits and vegetables are sold by the kilo (2.2 pounds). Break it down and compare it to the dollar to see what a great deal you're getting. When shopping at daily or weekly outdoor markets, buying conventionally grown carrots, potatoes, and onions, expect to pay about €1.50 a kilo. For tomatoes and peaches, you'll pay about double that in peak season, and in wintertime, delicious little clementines from Spain and lychees imported from Madagascar will set you back about €3-4 per kilo. Much of the tastiest stuff (bread, wine) is subsidized or otherwise regulated by the government; a standard baguette costs about €1.20, and a perfectly quaffable bottle of Bordeaux or Côtes du Rhône can be had for less than €5.

The key to shopping and saving is to do as the locals do: patronize the outdoor markets for your produce, the *boucherie* for your meat, the *fromagerie* for your cheese, and the *caviste* for your wine. It's slightly more time intensive than hitting a *hypermarché* for an all-in-one experience, but when you factor in the potential travel time (Paris's biggest supermarkets are always situated near the *périphérique,* or outskirts of town), fuel prices, and quality, those one-stop shops begin to lose their appeal. Besides, French refrigerators and freezers are so small that it doesn't make sense to stock up; if you're lucky to have a little *balcon,* it can do double duty as a cold-storage unit in wintertime. But otherwise, you'll have some serious food shuffling to do.

If you're going to shop like a local, it's worth investing in a *chariot*—a shopping bag on wheels—or a reusable basket or bag. A ban on nonrecyclable plastic bags has been in effect for several years in France (though not everyone adheres to it), and you'll have to buy a recyclable bag on the spot if you come to the market unprepared. At outdoor markets, you'll still be given small plastic bags for your fruits and veggies, but not a bigger bag to shove the lot of them into.

Grocery stores throughout Paris and the suburbs offer two kinds of customer perks, including online shopping options and free delivery service with a minimum purchase, which is usually somewhere in the €50-75 range. Natural-food-store giant Naturalia offers delivery service, and most stores also offer free *cartes de fidélité* that you scan each time you make a purchase to receive on-the-spot discounts and coupons for future purchases.

DINING OUT

Eating out in France is a good value for your money. Wine is usually affordable; expect to pay €3-4 a glass at typical French restaurants. (Coca-Cola and that bottle of bubbly water will almost always cost you more than wine or beer.) Plats du jour at lunchtime run anywhere from €10-15 and rise to €12-20 for dinner. For a few euros more, you can order a *formule,* which consists of either an *entrée* (first course) and *plat* (main course) or *plat* and *dessert* for those prices; occasionally you'll be offered all three and a *café* or a *verre de vin* for that all-inclusive price. Meals are hearty and filling and usually include meat, a vegetable, and something starchy. Everyone in France takes advantage of these home-away-from-home-cooked meals at some point in their lives, so you might as well try it, too.

Many newcomers find that their budgets are heavily hit by the allure of French wining and dining. The food is, generally, so very tasty and lovely to look at, and the wine is so darn cheap that it's easy to make a habit of eating out—as in twice a day or more. After settling into your French life, you'll eventually strike a balance—maybe opting for dinner out twice a week instead of five times—and you'll learn to appreciate the

© AURELIA D'ANDREA

The French can't pass up the good deals at Picard, the popular frozen food store.

little pleasures, like the €3 afternoon *goûter* of a croissant and café instead of the €30 lunch washed down with a couple of cool glasses of rosé.

HOUSING

Both renters and buyers will find good housing values in France; you'll probably spend about as much putting a roof over your head as you will putting food in your mouth. Students—French and foreign alike—are entitled to special housing allowances that can cut down the cost of living considerably. In Paris and beyond, the **résidences du Crous** (www.crous-paris.fr) offer government-subsidized studios or one- and two-bedroom apartments exclusively for students, with prices ranging from €280 per month for a studio in Pau (with parking and electricity included) to €650 for a one-bedroom garden apartment in Bordeaux, Wi-Fi included. If you're here to study and are based in a university town, check with the *mairie* to find out which options may be available to you. They'll likely steer you to **Lokaviz** (www.lokaviz.fr), which is the main student-housing portal for university students outside of Paris. Within Paris, it's worth checking in with **Services d'Acceuil des Étudiants Étrangeres** (www.ciup.fr). The benefit to any student housing option is that you won't have to meet the same rigorous rental criteria that average renters must adhere to, such as providing proof of income history or engaging the services of a *garant*.

TRANSPORTATION
Cars

It's *très cher* (very expensive) to own a car in France, particularly in the big cities, where forking out €50,000 for a permanent parking spot is not unheard of—and that's in

© AURELIA D'ANDREA

addition to insurance and maintenance costs. Fuel, sold by the liter at stations attached to big *hypermarchés* and at unassuming little curbside stations throughout Paris, is seriously spendy. Expect to pay €1.30-1.60 per liter depending on the type of fuel, or as much as €100 every time you fill up your tank. For the best fuel prices, skip the big service stations off the freeways and opt for fill-up stations attached to supermarkets, where it's significantly cheaper.

Bicycles and Public Transportation

Depending on where you live in France, you'll want to budget around €70 per month for public transportation; less if you're a student purchasing a youth pass, more if you're a party-hopping Parisian who's used to the convenience of taxis.

Fuel may be pricey in France, but the guy who pumps your gas won't charge you a *centime*.

Public bike-share system **Vélib'** costs €29

per year plus any overtime fees (only the first half-hour is free), so buying your own bike will pay off over time if cycling is your primary means of transit. Beware, however, that bike theft is common in Paris, so a good lock—threaded through the rear tire for added security—is worth the added expense. The national train system, **SNCF,** offers discount cards for an annual fee of between €50 and €75 for those who travel regularly by long-distance train. The discounts—always a minimum of 25 percent off the standard fare, and as much as 65 percent off—can make the yearly investment worthwhile.

CLOTHING

Unless you shop exclusively at discount stores like H&M, Etam, or Tati (or Monoprix during the semiannual sales), you'll probably find the cost of clothing in France to be considerably higher than what you're used to. There are many reasons for this: the VAT, which tacks nearly 20 percent on top of the base price; quality (French-made *everything* is built to last and priced accordingly); and salaries, which are higher here than in most countries even for minimum-wage workers, and therefore factored into the price of goods. You'll notice that at resale shops, called *depôt-ventes,* the sticker prices aren't all that discounted from what you'd pay for the same item brand-new in a department store or boutique. Eventually, you'll get used to paying more for things you used to take for granted, but in the meantime, let's set some reasonable expectations of average clothing prices:

- **shoes** (men and women): €100

- **boots** (men and women): €150

- **dress** (department store): €60-120

- **dress** (neighborhood boutique): €40-70

- **coat** (men and women, department store): €200

- **jacket** (men and women, neighborhood boutique): €80

- **underwear** (women): €10

- **underwear** (men): €7

- **socks** (men and women): €7

ELECTRONICS

Sticker shock is bound to strike when you go computer shopping. When the time comes to invest in a new machine, you'll start asking yourself questions like, "I wonder if it's cheaper to buy a laptop on Amazon and spend $200 to have it shipped to me in France?" You'll grow accustomed to the steep prices, but if you have to get that *lave-linge* (washing machine) or *micro-onde* (microwave oven) right away, Darty, an electronics- and household-goods chain, is a good bet. From water-filter systems to American-style refrigerators, they can be found here—but it can't hurt to do a little comparison-shopping first. At www.prixmoinscher.com, you can compare goods by brand or product type and see who carries the most affordable version of the appliance you're looking for. A Sony 37-inch flat-screen television will set you back €279 (delivery included), a basic DVD player runs about €50, and you can nab your very own washing machine for around €175.

When you make an in-store purchase of a large electrical appliance such as a TV or an oven, don't expect to necessarily leave the store with your purchase in tow on that very day. Many items for sale in stores like Darty and Conforama aren't stocked on-site, but rather stored in warehouses in distant suburbs. You might have to wait as long as a week for your refrigerator to be delivered. (Sorry!)

Banking

Opening a bank account in France is another exercise in red-tape aerobics, but it's a very necessary evil. If you're planning a reconnaissance trip to scope things out before you move, pencil in a visit to a bank and open an account so you'll be ready to roll with your *carte bleue* (debit card), checkbook, and French banking history when you need them, which will be right away. You'll need a checkbook for your home hunt, setting up house, paying utilities through *prélèvement* (automatic debit), and receiving Assurance Maladie reimbursements.

Most banks across France are open from 9am to 5:30pm Tuesday through Saturday, 9am to 2:30pm on Saturdays. Don't expect to get your banking needs met by a live person on Mondays, when banks are normally closed, or during your lunch break, because that's when bankers are dining or out running errands, too. This is true even in Paris, Lyon, and other large cities, and practically a certainty in small towns. If you just need to withdraw cash, you'll be happy to know that many banks and post offices are outfitted with external *distributeurs* that function 24/7. If your local branch happens to have an enclosed *distributeur* space, you can access it off-hours by simply swiping your card in the *lecteur* (card reader) beside the door and withdraw your funds in a safe, warm space.

CHOOSING YOUR BANK

Deciding which bank to work with is the first hurdle in the dizzying adventure of finding a new home for your money. There are so many banks, and who has time to check with each and every one to find out who has the most to offer? It's not just banks, either. Even La Poste—the post office—offers banking services. When making your choice, consider the following:

- **minimum-balance requirements**

- **English-language staff services** (if you need them)

- whether you need a **savings account,** a **checking account,** or both

Banks that can offer the services you need include **Barclays France, BNP Paribas, Caisse d'Épargne, Crédit Agricole, Crédit Mutuel, HSBC France, La Banque Postale,** and **Société Générale.** Note that you may be asked to have your *carte de séjour* in hand before you open an account; if you don't possess yours already, there are other options. At BNP Paribas, for example, you can open an international account at the

© AURELIA D'ANDREA

La Poste is more than a post office; it's also a bank and a bill-pay center.

Champs-Élysées branch without proof of residency, but you will need to meet their minimum bank-balance requirements.

You will end up developing a familiar relationship with your French banker, who, along with the rest of the staff, will greet you with a friendly *bonjour* and often by name. You can expect personalized service and a warm formality at your bank, especially if you have a good chunk of money stored there.

If you're a student—and especially as a student under the age of 26—you'll be entitled to all sorts of banking perks and incentives that make it easy for you to function in French society. Your school can help you find the right bank that offers the best student benefits, the lowest *carte bleue* fees, and the most advantageous interest rates.

France is idiosyncratic in a number of ways, including its approach to personal-finance management. The bank branch where you opened your account becomes your "home" office, and any changes to your account must be made at that branch, even if it's across town. If you move to another city, you'll have to arrange with your current bank branch to have your home office changed; be prepared for the time and paperwork involved, as it could take an hour or more of your life to complete this transaction. Ditto for adding names to your account: If you opened it under your own name but want to add your husband's name, it isn't as straightforward as you'd hope. Your spouse will have to provide additional financial information, including letters from "his" bank in the U.S. testifying to his banking history, plus an *attestation d'hébergement,* copies of his ID, and possibly quite a bit more.

BANK CARDS AND BANKING PROTOCOL

Generally, you'll be charged a fee for your card, which will be debited from your account. There are many types of *cartes bancaires*—commonly called *cartes bleues*—to choose from, and they all have a different price bracket. For €40 per year, you'll get a basic card that functions like most bank cards back home: withdrawals, basic traveler's insurance coverage, and supplemental car-rental insurance. For a little more—say, €130 per year—you could get a *carte* Visa Premier, with traveler's insurance that compensates you for late trains and canceled flights, as well as hospital stays in foreign countries. For €520 per year, you could get a fancy Carte Platinum American Express that earns you purchase points, covers legal fees in another country if you fall into trouble, and covers you with a new pair of glasses if yours are lost or stolen while you travel. You can also choose special colors and designs for your card for an additional €12-24 per year.

Be warned that banks also like to charge you for things you wouldn't necessarily

ATMs are commonplace, even in smaller villages.

DAILY LIFE

consider charge-worthy, such as phone calls to your banker, paper bank statements (rather than the digital option), additional cards, and, of course, checkbooks. Ask your banker to fill you in on all those little things, because they do add up.

When you open your bank account, it will be assigned an RIB *(Relevé d'Identité Bancaire)* number, which you'll need to memorize or have on hand when you want to transfer funds from your American or Canadian account to your French one, and to set up the *prélèvement* for automatic debits. RIBs also come in handy on the first of the month, when rent is due. *Propriétaires* and *locataires* alike appreciate the easy rent-paying potential inherent in direct deposit.

Depositing checks here isn't as straightforward as it is in American and Canadian banks. In France, you can deposit cash into *guichets automatiques* (ATMs), but you'll have to deposit checks by visiting the bank, filling out a form, handing it to the person behind the counter, and taking a receipt.

Fiscal responsibility and integrity are taken very seriously here. If you bounce a check, the consequences include a check-writing ban for as long as five years. If you lose your card (or have it stolen), you are responsible for the charges unless you report the loss or theft immediately and better still, file a police report. The latter is a no-fuss process that requires a visit to the nearest *commissariat* and filling out a single-page form in duplicate. Keeping a paper trail is important in France, so take the time for this if your wallet or cards go missing.

Banks won't charge you for using another bank's *guichet automatique* or *distributeur* for the first few withdrawals per month, but after the fourth, fifth, or sometimes sixth withdrawal, depending on the bank, they can—and often do—tack on a fee in the €1 range. If you're traveling outside the euro zone with your *carte bleue,* check with your bank beforehand to see which foreign banks it's partnered with. BNP Paribas, for instance, is partnered with Bank of the West in the U.S. and Westpac in Australia, and therefore doesn't charge a withdrawal fee if you use *guichets automatiques* at those banks.

CREDIT CARDS

Credit cards aren't used in quite the same manner in France as they are in the rest of the world. People tend to live within their means, and that means paying with good old-fashioned cash, or using your *carte bleue* or checkbook to debit funds directly from your account. If this feels kind of 1950-ish to you (even if your parents weren't born then), learn to appreciate the old-timeyness of it, because it has its perks. At shops throughout Paris, proprietors may allow customers to take things home on credit. We're

Checks and Balances

It's one of those things we all take for granted: writing a check. Easy as pie, right? But in France, sending your monthly rent check to your landlord is a tad more complicated than you might imagine. First, you have to figure out what goes where.

The first blank space on a standard French check reads *"Payez contre ce chèque non endossable"* ("Pay against this nonendorsable check"). Here, you'll write out the amount of the check—in French. It might look something like *"deux-cent euros"* (€200). You have two lines available for spelling out the amount.

Next up is the space where you write the name of the person or institution to whom the check is payable. This follows *"à"* ("to"). Just to the right of this, you'll find a little rectangular box. This is where you write the figure, using standard numbers. The French don't like it when you write outside the lines, so keep everything inside that little rectangle if you can.

Next are two short lines, one reading *"à"*—which in this case means "in," as in the city in which you are writing out the check —and the second reading *"le"* ("the"), which is prompting you for today's date. If you write the date in numeric format, be sure to do it the way the French do: date/month/year.

The last thing you'll need to do to make this check valid is sign it: Often there are no written prompts, only an empty space at the bottom. Go ahead and put your John Hancock there, but keep it contained! If your signature extends off the margins of the check, it may be rendered invalid.

not talking brand-new Renaults here, but rather a baguette, newspaper, or bottle of *vin rouge* at those critical moments when you realize you've left your wallet at home.

French bank cards and credit cards are different from American ones in a very significant way: Instead of storing your information in a magnetic strip, the card houses it in a tiny embedded *puce* (literally "flea," but better known as a microchip). When inserted into an ATM, automatic ticket kiosk, or credit card reader at restaurants, the card transmits your information through radio frequencies; to complete the transaction, you need to input your PIN code. This protects you and your card from unauthorized transactions, which is the main reason Europe switched over to this credit card technology in 2004. As more and more countries switch to *puce* cards, the likelihood that North America will follow suit begins to increase.

It's important to have a card with a *puce* if you'll be spending a significant amount of time in France. For starters, many gas stations function at all hours without an attendant, and that's because you are expected to serve yourself and pay using a *puce* card. Most credit card machines can read American cards, but those cards aren't inserted into the machines the same way European *puce* cards are. If the person in charge of completing your transaction doesn't know how to do it, he is likely to tell you they don't accept those cards. (If your language skills permit, you can show him how it's done. Instead of inserting the card in the bottom of the machine, swipe it down a little trough on the right side.)

Taxes

FRENCH TAXES

It's been said that the only certain things in life are death and taxes, and that maxim doesn't lose any of its mojo just because you've moved to France. If you want to establish long-term residency, there's no way to make it more official than by declaring your earnings. For North Americans, this means double tax duty, since you'll still have to file taxes at home, too. In France, it means declaring all your income, regardless of where you earned it. Freelancers, now is the time to 'fess up, fully and completely. Don't know if you're obliged? If you've lived in France for more than 183 days out of the year, you're considered a resident in the eyes of the tax folks.

If you decide to go official with a small business and take advantage of Assurance Maladie and other perks of the social security system, you'll need to begin paying French taxes. It's a complicated process that can be made a lot less confusing by enlisting the aid of a French tax specialist. The investment may be many hundreds of dollars, but isn't peace of mind worth it? If your answer is "no," it's still possible to work things out yourself through trial and error—hopefully not too much of the latter.

As an *auto-entrepreneur,* you're responsible for paying taxes three times per year. You'll receive the paperwork in the mail; you simply have to report your earnings, calculate the amount due, and include a check if necessary when you mail it off. Those employed by French companies or independent organizations based in France will have their social charges (but not income tax) deducted from their paycheck, and the onus is on you to visit the local tax office each May to file your paperwork for the previous year's earnings (the exact cutoff date varies from year to year). Income tax is determined by the total earnings of your household, which includes your spouse and children, who are all parts of a taxable whole and subject to deductibles even if they don't work. For example, if you earned €6,011 or less in 2014, you owed nothing in 2015. Those who earned between €11,991 and €26,631 owed 14 percent, and top earners who made more than €151,000 were taxed at 45 percent.

There's no escaping death or taxes, even in fabulous France.

There are resources available online (and it's wise to check in a few times a year, since laws change with disconcerting regularity), but ultimately, the weight of figuring it all out falls on your shoulders. You can, however, share the burden with a professional tax advisor. Programs like **Click Impôts** (www.clickimpots.

Fiscal Responsibility à la Française

If you've never examined the fine print at the back of your U.S. passport, now is a good time. There, under Article D, it reads, "All U.S. citizens working and residing abroad are required to file and report on their worldwide income." So you still have to file American taxes even when you're living your dream life in France. These tips will help you survive the process with your nervous system intact.

File your taxes on time.
This is how you avoid a 10 percent penalty and stay on the government's good side. To get started, visit your arrondissement's tax office. Not sure where to find it? Plug your coordinates into the "contacts" section of the government's dedicated tax website (www. impots.gouv.fr) and get an instant referral.

Extend your extension.
It's April 14 and you haven't even downloaded your U.S. tax forms yet. It's OK! You get an automatic two-month filing extension as an American living abroad. Need even more time to get your finances in order? Take advantage of form 4868, which stretches your filing deadline until October 15.

Don't forget the FBAR.
Is your French bank account cushioned with cash? If you've got the equivalent of US$10,000 racking up interest in any foreign account, you've got to declare it to the government with the Foreign Bank Account Reports (FBAR) form. The mandatory e-filing deadline is June 30. Hurry! The form is available online at http://bsaefiling.fincen.treas.gov/main.html.

com)—the French equivalent of TurboTax software—can be very helpful *if* you understand the language. If not, find a tax specialist who speaks English until you get the hang of it on your own. The French tax year begins on January 1 and ends on December 31.

AMERICAN AND CANADIAN TAXES

Thank goodness for the Internet: Without it, we'd be cajoling our friends and family to send bulky IRS booklets to us overseas, and we'd be spending far too much time at La Poste mailing forms back when we could be relaxing beneath sunny skies at a terrace café. Because nearly everything is automated today, we get to benefit by filing taxes online from anywhere in the world. (You'll still need your W2 or 1099 forms, though, so have your employer send those to you at your French address.)

Even though you have to file your U.S. taxes as well as French taxes if you live in France, a treaty signed between the two countries means the taxes you pay in France are deductible on your U.S. tax forms. The IRS's online FreeFile program allows you to file online if your adjusted gross income (AGI) is less than $58,000. If you earned more than that, it's slightly more complicated: You'll need to purchase eFile software or go the old-fashioned paper route. Because of the potential hassles that filing at a distance can spawn, the nice folks at the IRS kindly extend a two-month filing extension to American taxpayers living abroad, so your paperwork isn't due until June 15. Tax experts will tell you that you actually have even more time—until October 15 as an American expat in France—but getting that extension requires that you fill out and include form 4868 when filing. Note that if you owe money, the IRS still wants it on or before April 15. Refunds can be direct-deposited into your existing U.S. account. Canadians can also Telefile from abroad as long as they do so before April 30, or face a 5 percent fine on whatever you owe.

Investing

France has embraced free-market economics, and with it a culture of personal investing has emerged. The best source of information for no- or low-risk investing opportunities is your banker, who will be happy to explain your options and set you up with an investment program. (Enlisting the help of an independent financial advisor is another good idea.) If you have €20,000 in the bank, that's considered a pretty hefty sum, and any banker worth her salt will offer suggestions for earning money on those funds even without a prompt from you. Forty percent of France's stock exchange value is held by foreign investors, so you'll be in good company if you decide to take this route.

If stocks, bonds, and mutual funds don't make your heart sing but you still want to invest in France, consider a business enterprise. The government-sponsored nonprofit agency **Invest in France** (www.invest-in-france.org, 01/44 87 17 27) has offices in the 14th arrondissement and offers free services and advice on setting up a corporation of 10 or more employees, tax preparation, employment laws, and all the hidden benefits of launching a large-scale business enterprise in France. With the second-largest consumer market in Europe and a very healthy tourist trade, France is ripe with opportunity for those with an entrepreneurial spirit and the extra money necessary to put an idea into action.

The one area where investing in France is still a little iffy is real estate. So many people find themselves seduced by the idea of buying a chic 19th-century pied-à-terre, decorating it with treasures unearthed from the *marché aux puces*, and earning a sustainable living from the rental income it generates, and this is where things go awry. Unless you're in a prime Paris arrondissement or another desirable city like Versailles with a year-round tourism base to pull from, you might be in for an unpleasant surprise. Furthermore, recent laws have affected the short-term residential housing market in Paris and other French cities, making it virtually illegal for owners to rent their properties for less than a year at a stretch. This doesn't affect owners of commercial property, but the taxes they pay are considerably higher. Think twice before investing in property as a moneymaking venture, and be sure to check with a tax consultant who can help you sort out the particulars if you decide to take this adventurous route.

Expat Experience: Talking Taxes

Name: Erin Quirk
Age: 36
Occupation: Editor
Hometown: Indiana, Pennsylvania
Current residence: Paris, 14th

You can get away with a lot in France–jumping ahead in lines, dodging library fines–but there's no escaping French taxes, otherwise known as *impôts fiscales*. There are many ways to fulfill this annual obligation, including hiring someone else to do the work for you, but what seems intimidating the first time becomes second nature after a couple of rounds. Here, expat Erin Quirk shares how she navigated this bureaucratic inevitability.

You'll file your taxes in France for the first time this year. Do you need to file in the U.S. as well?
As an American citizen living in France, I'll always need to file my taxes in the U.S. and in France, but because of a treaty between the two countries, I will only need to pay income tax in the country where I am working. For me, this year has been a little more complicated, since I moved here partway through the year. But the take-home point for any American living and working France is that you'll need to file in the U.S., even if you're working for a French company and paying taxes in France.

You sought out an accounting expert and looked for advice on expat tax forums. Which resources did you find most helpful?
I got the name of my tax accountant in the same way I've gotten a lot of useful information about living in France–by grilling more seasoned expats at social gatherings. Luckily, most people I've met know how bewildering French bureaucracy can be to newcomers. I also found some good information on the **Association of Americans Resident Overseas** (AARO) website (www.aaro.org), including a video of a tax seminar from 2014 for Americans living in France. And I posted questions on a forum for English-speaking parents called **Message** (www.messageparis.org). You need to pay a membership fee to get access to this members-only forum. For me, it's been well worth the money, and not just for parenting information.

What advice would you give expats who plan to declare their own revenue in France?
Every person's situation is slightly different, so I think the best advice is to talk to a tax accountant who specializes in doing taxes for Americans living in France before you even move here. The U.S. embassy in Paris has a list of accountants and firms, which may be a good place to start.

If you're planning on working in France for an American company for less than five years, you can continue to pay U.S. Social Security, but you need what's called a **"certificate of coverage"** (www.ssa.gov/international/CoC_link.html) from the Social Security Administration, which you can get with the help of your employer. This certificate is your proof that you are covered by U.S. Social Security and hence, don't need to be covered by French Social Security. Also, the fiscal year is the same in France as the U.S., but taxes are paid in May in France, and you won't get the necessary income declaration document until the beginning of May, so you'll need to file in the U.S. before you file in France.

COMMUNICATIONS

The French are fond of traditions, and cling tenaciously to some that don't always make a lot of sense. The pay phone is one of them; you'll still stumble upon them in cities and towns throughout the country, looking like the old-timey relics from another age. For the most part, however, France has joined the 21st century communications revolution. From subscription-service smartphones and surprisingly affordable Internet service to ubiquitous print-media *kiosques* brimming with domestic and international titles, staying connected to the world at large—and our work and loved ones—is easy and, unlike most things in France, practically bureaucracy-free.

France is a nation of mediaphiles, boasting one of the highest magazine reader-ships on the planet. There are more than 100 local and national newspapers to choose from, so Sunday mornings at the corner café will never be idle. Television also figures prominently in the French leisure sphere, with the average person watching 3.5 hours per day. Expect access to the outside world in unexpected places—wireless hotspots at campgrounds, for instance—and, thanks to government subsidies, count on the cost of getting connected to be within reach.

Telephone Service

There are still a couple of places in France where you're more likely to get reception using two cans and a piece of string than you are with your mobile phone, but it's not likely that you'll be stranded without access anywhere in urban France. If there's one thing most of us in France and abroad have come to depend on, it's our telephones. To meet the needs—and budgets—of a diverse population, there are numerous options: pay-as-you-go mobile phones, private pay-by-the-unit *cabines* at cybercafés, the aforementioned corner telephone booths, and numerous telecommunications companies willing to sell you all manner of packages for chatting and texting your heart out.

MAKING PHONE CALLS
Within France
When placing a call to another French phone within France, the 10-digit number will always begin with a zero. Cell phones begin with 06 or 07, and landline prefixes differ depending on the region. In Paris/Île de France, the prefix is 01; in Brest, Cherbourg, Le Havre, Nantes, Orléans, Rouen, and other cities and towns in northwest France, the prefix is 02; in the north and northeast, it's 03; in the southeast, 04; and in the southwest, 05.

When you need to find the telephone number of an individual or business, use the French version of the yellow and white pages, called *pages jaunes* and *pages blanches,* respectively. They operate the same way as back home, including online access. Hard copies are distributed by the nice people at La Poste once a year.

International Calls
When calling France from the U.S. or Canada, begin with the international access code (011) followed by the country code (33). Before you dial the rest of the number, remember to leave *off* the zero at the beginning; it's necessary to include the extra digit only when you're dialing *within* France. So if you're calling Pau from Philly, you'll dial 011 33 5 55 55 55 55.

When you want to call the States or Canada from France, dial the international access code followed by the country code, the area code, and the seven-digit number. To call San Francisco from Strasbourg, dial 00 1 415/555-5555.

LAND LINES
Back in 2009, France Telecom ended its telecommunications monopoly, breathing new life—and new deals—into every corner of the market. Where there used to be just one long-distance carrier for landlines, now there are many, each of them offering great bargains on bundled Internet-phone-cable TV packages. They nearly all work the same way: You order your service online, receive confirmation for your order, then wait for your "box" to arrive. The box is your modem/cable/fiber optic hub, and once you have it—it can take between two days and two weeks to arrive—plug it in and start calling, viewing, and surfing. For around €30 per month for high-speed fiber optic and ADSL Internet, dozens of television channels, and no-cost calls to landlines throughout the world, it's pretty much worth the wait.

© AURELIA D'ANDREA

Need to make local calls on your iPhone? Head to the nearest Orange and pick up a new SIM card.

The top companies offering this bundled service are the same ones providing cell phone service, and sometimes you can add mobile calling service onto your three-in-one "bouquet," making it a four-in-one. France Telecom owns the ubiquitous telecom company **Orange** (www.orange.fr), which seems to be leading the telecommunications race; for €36.99 a month, Orange offers a four-in-one Open Mini service that includes an hour of free mobile phone time in addition to cable TV, Internet, and landline service. **Bouygues** (www.bouyguestelecom.fr) offers a similar package, only without the mobile phone service, for €25.99 per month. If you want something simpler, **SFR** (www.sfr.com) provides landline phone-Internet packages starting at €29.99 per month. Students age 26 and younger get a 10 percent discount. **Numericable** (www.numericable.fr) is one of the newer companies to join the all-in-one game, with similar plans and less expensive monthly fees—but there's a one-time setup fee, so it makes sense only if you're looking for a long-term deal.

MOBILE PHONES

Getting set up with a "mobile" can be a tricky enterprise for Luddites and techno-wizards alike. The best solution is to carefully consider how often you'll use your phone and what you're willing to spend per month for those privileges. Quad-band smartphones, including Samsung and iPhone models, can be great for the newbie in France, especially if you make use of the scads of apps designed to help you find food, maps, train times, and more. But don't make the mistake of underestimating your American or Canadian carrier's roaming fees, which may be exorbitant. Review your contract or call your carrier to avoid becoming another telecom "victim" saddled with a bill shockingly heavy on zeros.

Buying a French Mobile Phone

If you know you're going to be here for at least 12-18 months—the average length of time for most mobile-phone contracts—you might choose to start from scratch and purchase a phone and calling plan here. At many telecom boutiques, including **Phone House** and **FNAC,** you can get an iPhone or Android for "free" if you don't mind getting locked into a 12- to 24-month contract at around €50-100 per month.

Not sure you'll use your phone enough to warrant that kind of expenditure? Then a €25 **pay-as-you-go** phone might be the best possibility. These cheapies are a good way to try out a service and see how much you use it. Phone House (www.phonehouse. fr) and FNAC (www.fnac.fr) both have big selections, and you can also find phones at *hypermarchés* like Auchan and Carrefour. This pay-as-you-go method is a little pricey when it comes to outgoing calls, but incoming calls and SMSs (texts or *textos*) are free and unlimited. You can also purchase minutes exclusively reserved for texts, which are a lot more economical and just as far-reaching. Half-phone, half-text time allotments are also available to those who want to keep their options open. The minutes you purchase for your French pay-as-you-go phone, whether for texting or calling or both, have an expiration date that's usually two weeks from the date of purchase. Keep in mind that if you don't purchase new minutes at least once every six months, you'll get a text from the SIM service provider alerting you that your account will be shut down if there's not some outgoing-call activity within a certain time frame. (You generally get a two-week warning.)

Another way to go is to invest in a second phone: Keep your North American mobile phone for when you return stateside, and purchase another cheap one to use exclusively in France. This option makes the most economic sense if you're not a phone addict or you don't rely heavily on phones for work. At special phone shops and other electronics stores throughout France, you can buy a bundled phone-and-SIM-card combo for €15-30. When the time you've purchased runs out, you can buy additional minutes in increments of €5-10, starting at €5. The time is purchased in the form of a *carte prépayée* (prepaid card), or, if you purchase it from a *tabac,* you'll be handed a small printed receipt with an access code for you to punch into your phone.

Cybercafés charge by the minute for international calls.

Using Your Own Mobile Phone

Another affordable option that's quickly becoming popular among travelers is to use your unlocked phone from home with a new France-compatible SIM card that you buy either before you depart or when you arrive in France (there are shops at the airport and in many cities and towns).

At the ubiquitous SFR, Orange, and Bouygues boutiques found throughout France, you can expect to pay €4 or so for a French phone number and an "empty" card that you refuel with prepaid cards purchased at *tabacs* and other shops for €5 or more. It's also possible to buy SIM cards that have credit built into them, beginning at about €10.

Note that in the United States and elsewhere, phones are sold "locked" by the telephone service provider to keep you roped into its service. ("Unlocking" shouldn't be confused with "unblocking" phones that have been reported stolen, which isn't kosher on any continent.) You can use online unlocking companies like **Remote Unlocks** (www.remoteunlocks.com) and **Unlock it Now** (www.unlockitnow.com) wherever you happen to be. The service isn't free, but it's cheap enough—usually less than US$50.

CYBERCAFÉS

Throughout Paris—as well as in Toulouse, Bordeaux, and Lyon—and particularly in neighborhoods with higher immigrant populations, you'll find "cybercafés," which aren't cafés in the traditional sense (you'll be lucky if they have a coffee vending machine) but often little DIY storefronts equipped with computers, printers, fax machines, and *cabines* of varying degrees of funkiness that allow you to make **international calls** for pennies. The phone's digital display lets you keep track of how much you're spending as you make the call. It's usually more affordable than you'd imagine, especially if you call during off-hours. In France, phone calling-time is sold in units, which cost more during peak calling times (weekdays) and less during off-hours (evenings and weekends). Timing your calls for off-peak periods can save you a bundle over time. Rates vary depending on where you're calling, but you can expect to pay €0.35 per minute to call the United States or Canada, and around €0.25 to €0.40 per minute to connect to other countries by phone. The website www.cybercafe.fr will point you to the nearest cybercafé near you.

SKYPE AND GOOGLE HANGOUT

By now, most people have heard about or are familiar with Skype and Google Hangout. They are the traveler's best friends when it comes to staying in touch across oceans and continents, in a very *les Jetson* sort of way. Using these forms of telecommunication is the next best thing to being there in person, since you can see the person you're chatting with in real time if your *ordinateur* (computer) or phone is equipped with a camera. If you don't already have this super communications tool at your disposal, get thee to the Internet *tout de suite* and download the free software. The only real drawback is that you need a modicum of privacy to engage this way; talking to your beloved at the *bibliothèque* or cybercafé will make everyone uncomfortable. Skype's long-distance phone calling plans are worth a gander, too. You can purchase credit beginning at US$1 per minute.

Internet and Postal Service

France, like so many other countries, depends on the Internet to connect with the rest of the world. More than 80 percent of the population uses an *ordinateur* at work, and more than 70 percent now use one at home. If you purchase a package deal from one of the big-name telecom companies, you'll get an access code that allows you to tap into your Internet service outside your home, provided your FAI (Fournisseur d'Accès à Internet) service is available in the area. This comes in handy when you're traveling, and out-of-town guests are always happy to use it, too.

You'll find plenty of places out and about, from libraries and cafés to public parks and McDonald's, offering free "wee-fee" (Wi-Fi) access. Tap in using your own code or the one given to you by the service provider. Check in at the local *mairie* or tourist office for a list of local hotspots.

POST OFFICES

La Poste (www.laposte.fr) isn't just a post office: It's a bank, a bill-pay center, an Internet hotspot, and the place where naughty Frenchies hone their line-jumping skills. Branches are open six days a week (mail is delivered Tuesday-Saturday), and hours are usually 9am-8pm Monday through Friday, with reduced hours on Saturdays and during school holiday periods. Inside, expect to find DIY *vignette* machines with English-language instructions, boxes, and padded envelopes for sale, and helpful staff to sell you dozens of different stamps and other services. Outside, you'll find cash *distributeurs* (ATMs) and *boîtes aux lettres* (mailboxes) for depositing your stamped envelopes and packages. A letter weighing less than 20 grams costs €0.76 to mail (it jumps to €1.25 when you hit the 20-gram mark), and overseas postcard stamps will set you back €1.18. A less expensive, but slower option for sending mail within France is choosing the *lettre verte,* which costs €0.68 (€1.15 if your envelope weighs more than 20 grams) when mailing an envelope weighing 20 grams or less. Don't feel like venturing out in the rain? Print your stamps at home! Go to the section marked *"Imprimez vos timbres"* at La Poste's online boutique (https://boutique.laposte.fr).

Media

NEWSPAPERS AND MAGAZINES

Want to feel like a true local? The place to begin your assimilation process is at *les kiosques,* aka the tiny green newsstands that exist in cities throughout France. Each of the country's 10 national newspapers appeals to a specific segment of the politically oriented population. On the left, there's **Libération;** in the center, **Le Monde;** and to the right, **Le Figaro.** You'll also find more than 100 other weekly or monthly journals to represent your viewpoint—and everyone else's. Don't know if your "left" is the same as your French compatriots?' Check out the online editions of each paper to see which news-delivery style resonates with you, then pick up a copy from the nearest *kiosque* and take it to the café for your afternoon coffee-and-civics lesson.

Popular free papers and journals include **A Nous, Métro, Direct Matin, Stylist,** and **Direct Soir.** Look for them in Métro stations and *gares* (train stations); occasionally you'll find them being distributed by real live humans in busy pedestrian areas.

France is a magazine-loving culture. News agents vend dozens of titles, from the standard fashion fare to a range of subgenres, such as detective tales, boating, video games, and gay culture. Unlike in the United States and Canada, you won't find much of a selection of reading material at most supermarkets or gas stations. But you will often find them at *librairies* (bookstores) in some *tabacs,* and any shop that has a sign reading "La Presse" on the outside. In Paris, English-language bookstore **WHSmith** (248, rue de Rivoli, www.whsmith.fr) offers an enormous selection of magazines in multiple languages. If you're desperate for a fix, head to the nearest train station; the Relay boutiques found at most big *gares* are a reliable source of reading material for people on the go and anyone else seeking a little mental stimulation.

Numericable is a popular high-speed internet and cable provider.

TELEVISION

The French consider television their number-one pastime, watching an average of 3.5 hours per day. This may seem a little high when you consider what seems to be on: game shows, game shows, and the occasional game show. The truth is, there's a vast and varied world of television in France, from cooking shows and cartoons (*Les Simpson,* anyone?) to music videos and home-improvement programs. Expect lots of dubbed-into-French versions of American programs and films, plus a healthy smattering of police dramas. Documentaries are also popular. Basically, anything you'd want to watch at home is available here, only in French, without subtitles.

The major cable television providers will happily offer you English-language channel add-ons for a price, but experience says skip 'em. If you're committed to learning French, relying on Anglophone television channels for your news and amusement will only handicap your efforts in the long run. Instead, use French TV to your educational advantage. Tuning in will help you adjust to the colloquialisms and idioms of modern French and keep you in the pop-culture loop. There are several national public television channels to flip through—France 2, 3, 5, and Arte on channel 7, among others—plus dozens of private and pay-TV channels at your disposal.

For small-screen addicts who can't quit *House of Cards* or *Orange Is the New Black,* there's good news: **Netflix** (www.netflix.com/fr) has finally landed in France after literally years of negotiations. For between €7.99 and €11.99 per month, you can access all the TV and films you crave, 24/7. Joining online is easy, and the first month is free for new users.

RADIO AND MUSIC STREAMING SITES

If you're one of the holdouts in the dwindling universe of radio listeners, there's no reason to stop tuning in just because the music is sung in a language other than your own. (At least 40 percent of the songs will be in French—that's a state mandate.) Whether you turn the dial over to hipster channel **Le Mouv'**, the always fun and always jazzy **TSF Jazz,** or überpopular mainstream station **RTL,** you'll be able to keep up on current events, discover the hot pop act du jour, and, perhaps most importantly, attune your ear to the language. Radio, like television, is a great tool for helping you learn local dialects and colloquialisms, and with plenty of public and private options to choose from, all your listening needs will easily be met.

Some streaming music stations you might be used to listening to, such as Pandora, are restricted by international licenses that prohibit them from broadcasting in France, but that doesn't mean a personalized audio experience can't still be yours. North America-based **Jango** (www.jango.com), **NPR Radio** (www.npr.org/music/radio), and **Live 365** (www.live365.com) offer similar DIY programming options. The French site of Sweden-based **Spotify** (www.spotify.fr) is yet another possibility.

TRAVEL AND TRANSPORTATION

One of the best quality-of-life boosters in France is the thorough, efficient, far-reaching transportation system. In most cities, you can choose between trains, buses, public bicycles, cars, trams, taxis, funiculars, and even human-powered pedal rickshaws to get you where you need to be. To reach rural destinations, there are even more trains, plus rental cars, public ride-share programs, buses, ferries, and, of course, regional airlines.

If there's one arena the French have perfected, it's rail travel. The world-renowned TGV (*train à grande vitesse,* or high-speed train) is legend for a reason: It propels you to your destination at 300 kilometers per hour, meaning you can leave Paris after breakfast and arrive in sun-drenched Nice in time to enjoy lunch at a terrace café. But the TGV isn't all France has to offer in terms of train travel. There are also normal long-distance trains, affordable regional trains, and—in Lyon, Lille, Marseille, Toulouse, and Paris—the Métro. Using any combination thereof, you could be skiing the Alps, biking along a canal in Amsterdam, or shopping in London within just a few hours of leaving Paris.

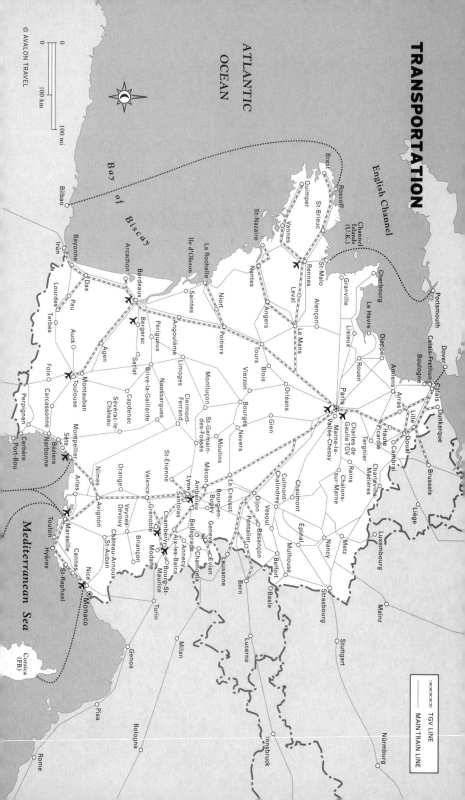

Air

Nearly everyone arriving in France from North America lands at Paris's **Charles de Gaulle airport** (CDG, known locally as Roissy, or, phonetically, "WAH-see"), 25 kilometers northeast of the city. With 62 million passengers moving through its three terminals each year, CDG is the second-busiest airport in Europe and the seventh-busiest in the world. It primarily handles international flights; most domestic flights run out of Orly, which also serves routes to Africa, the Middle East, the Caribbean (including Cuba), and other points throughout Europe. A nonstop flight to San Francisco or Los Angeles from Paris CDG is roughly 11 hours long, and to New York the trip takes 8 hours.

Orly (ORY) to the south and **Beauvais-Tillé** (BVA) to the north are the two primary Paris-region airports serviced by smaller, budget air carriers that sell almost-too-good-to-be-true cheap flights—EasyJet, Ryanair, and Wizz Air are the leaders. More often than not, however, you end up paying just as much in transport fees getting to those distant airports as you do for budget flights to Marrakesh and Malaga. (You'll also have to obey strict baggage limits, and it's wise to expect delays.)

For flights within France, **Air France** (www.airfrance.fr) dominates with the most options, but there are plenty of others worth a look, including newcomer **Hop!** (www.hop.fr), a French regional airline company that's a subsidiary of the Air France group. Hop! offers budget-friendly flights to several points throughout l'Hexagone including Pau, Rennes, and Strasbourg, plus a few other European destinations, including Amsterdam, Prague, and Venice. An Air France or Hop! flight from Lille in the far north to sunny Nice on the Côte d'Azur takes an hour and a half, and costs around €350 round trip. Passengers younger than 26 will pay about half that. On EasyJet, which has a growing presence at French airports, you could make the one-hour flight from Toulouse to Lyon for just €35, but the flight will be no-frills, and you'll pay extra for checked baggage.

One of the great advantages to living in the heart of Europe is easy access to so many different countries and cultures. To find the best travel bargains, try websites such as **Opodo** (www.opodo.fr), which offers flights and affordable weekend package deals to destinations all over Europe, North Africa, and the rest of the world. Railway site **SNCF** (www.sncf.com) is another good spot to shop for flights, trains, and hotel packages and **Promo Vacances** (www.promovacances.com) for flights, hotels, and rental cars. Each of these sites allows you to compare prices and choose dates and flights that best suit your schedule and budget.

Train

There's something romantic about train travel. It has a sense of adventure built into it that air travel lacks, and in France, it can even be a relaxing experience: No shoe-removal routines or liquid-toting restrictions apply (though if you're Chunneling over to London on the Eurostar, you'll need to go through a passport check). Between the roomyish bathrooms, generous legroom, and the café car—where a sandwich and a glass of wine are always within reach—train travel feels practically luxurious, even if it's designed for the proletariat.

The national railway line, **SNCF** (la Société Nationale des Chemins de Fer), links Paris to more than 7,000 stations all over the country. The **TGV** and other *grande ligne* trains take you on long-haul trips to major cities, and the **TER** (Train Express Régional) takes you to the smaller stations in between. Long-distance and local trains depart from the same stations, and there are several trains per day for most destinations, so if you miss the first one, you'll likely be able to find a seat on the next.

French trains are nearly always on schedule, unless there's a *grève* (strike), in which case local, regional, and long-distance trains may be delayed or cancelled altogether. Usually, *some* trains will be cancelled or delayed, but not all of them—for instance, there may be two trains running to Grenoble instead of six. This is uncommon, but when it does happen, you usually have plenty of forewarning from both the news media and the transportation officials. Remember that France uses a 24-hour clock, so a train that leaves at 3pm will read as 15h00 on your ticket.

© AURELIA D'ANDREA

France's wonderful rail system makes it easy to live well without a car.

BUYING TICKETS

Train tickets can be purchased up to six months in advance (though most are available only three months in advance) and can be secured in person at the station, at SNCF boutiques throughout Paris and the suburbs, or bought through the SNCF website (www.sncf.com). Online, you can choose the English-language option, and peruse all the options for the best deals and best amenities. Not all trains are bicycle friendly, for instance, but those that are will display a small bike icon next to the train details. You'll also be able to see which cars have wheelchair access and whether there's a café car. Using your credit card to pay online is a pretty straightforward process, and you can choose to print out your ticket at home, use your credit card to retrieve it from a kiosk at the station (but only with *puce* cards), or, with enough time, have it mailed to you. If you decide to use the phone to make your reservation, you'll be charged a premium rate of €1.35 plus €0.34 for each minute (as is common with many public services including banking, telecommunications, and electricity/gas).

Train ticket prices fluctuate according to a number of criteria: time of day, whether or not you'll be traveling during a school holiday period, what age group you fall into, whether you have an SNCF membership card, whether you're traveling in first or second class, whether the ticket is refundable, and how far in advance you're buying. Spur-of-the-moment tickets are more expensive, so buying a week or two (or more) ahead of time will generally result in a price reduction. If you foresee doing a lot of train travel, forking over a few extra euros to get an SNCF "Weekend" membership card will pay for itself over time. The 12-27 age-group membership card costs €50 per year and gives young adults up to 60 percent off ticket prices. Voyagers 60 and older are eligible for the €60 Senior card, good for reductions of up to 50 percent. Everyone else is eligible for the age 28-and-older €75 card, which gives up to 40 percent discounts. Families with one or two children are eligible for discount train-travel cards valid for three years, but you have to apply for it, and it isn't necessarily a given that you'll be awarded one. To learn whether you qualify for the *Carte Enfant Famille,* you must first create an online dossier and pay a nonrefundable €19 filing fee. Two outside social services agencies make the ultimate decision, which will be rendered within a week or two after you submit your dossier. Sample one-way, low-end fares for everyday travelers sans discount card include Paris-Lyon: €30; Paris-Pau: €35; Paris-Turin, Italy: €47. In 2013, the TGV rolled out a new high-speed train to Barcelona, Spain. The trip takes about 6.5 hours and requires a train change in Toulouse. Ticket prices begin at €93.80 each way from Paris.

Prem's is a discount ticket company that's part of the SNCF system. Tickets don't offer flexibility in terms of cancellation or changing dates, and you won't find nearly as many destinations as you would with a regular-fare ticket, but the prices are dirt cheap and worth it if you're tight on funds. You can travel from Paris to Strasbourg for as little as €20, or Annecy for €25.

On long-distance trains, a conductor will come through each car to stamp passengers' tickets, but on TER trains, you'll need to validate the *billet* (ticket) yourself. Most French train tickets are valid for two months and not just for the date you're scheduled to travel, which is an invitation for some to try to cheat the system by using their tickets twice. To avoid getting slapped with a fee for riding on a nonvalidated *billet,* you'll need to run your ticket through one of the *composteurs* found on the *quai* (platform). If you forget to do it, the onus is on you to seek out the conductor as soon as you board the train, so she can stamp your ticket for you.

Paris Métro

Even at its packed-in-like-sardines worst, the Paris Métro is still a life enhancer for commuters in the City of Light. Extensive, fast, relatively affordable, and generally safe, it gets you where you want to go—and you just feel so *Parisian* getting there. For visitors, the best Métro ticketing option is the €14.10 *carnet* of 10 tickets. They have no expiration date and are also valid for bus travel, so it's good to stock up (prices increase every year). Other options include the Mobilis card, which looks like a standard Métro ticket, but is valid for a day's worth of Métro and RER train journeys. Prices vary according to the travel zones you choose; a single-day ticket in Zones 1 and 2 costs €7, and if you want to navigate all five zones, that'll set you back €16.60. The Paris Visite Pass is similar; choose whether you want a one-, two-, three-, or five-day pass for Zones 1 through 3 or 5, and the price varies accordingly. A five-day pass valid in all five zones—which means access to Orly and Charles de Gaulle-Roissy airports, Versailles, and Disneyland—costs €61.25. Many train station Relay boutiques sell the Paris Visite pass, so if you're in there buying the latest gossip rag for your next voyage, you might as well ask for a transport pass while you're at it.

For those staying longer than a few weeks who expect to use the system regularly, a Navigo pass is a more cost-effective option. It looks sort of like a credit card, only with your photo on it. Register online (www.navigo.fr), wait for your card to arrive in the mail, then add money to it using automated kiosks inside the station. Cards are also issued on the spot for a €5 fee at Le Club RATP offices at some stations, including Gare du Nord and Gare de Lyon. Navigo rates vary depending on whether you want weekly or monthly service. A week's worth of travel in Zones 1 and 2 can be had for €21.25, or €70 for the month. Always purchase your weekly tickets on a Monday and your monthly tickets on the first of the month to maximize the value of your card.

Navigating the Métro is easy once you've done it a few times. After entering the station by sliding your pass over the sensor or inserting your ticket into the little slot, you follow the signs pointing to the final destination on your line. For instance, if you're traveling from the Louvre to Gare de Lyon, you'll take the train marked "Château de Vincennes," since Château de Vincennes is the last stop in that direction on that line. Hop on a train going the wrong direction? No problem. Disembark at the next station and cross over to the opposite platform to redirect yourself without having to purchase another ticket or exit the station.

When your train pulls up to the platform, stand clear of the doors to allow passengers to exit. You'll often see people exiting the train and standing near the doors; they're just getting out of the way temporarily to make the disembarking process easier for others. Once everyone is off, it's your turn to pile in. A buzzer will sound when the doors are about to close, usually giving you about five seconds to get moving. Once you're on the train, assess the situation. If your car is packed, don't try to sit on the pull-down folding seats near the door. Instead, stand like everyone else. Though it's not mandatory, it's always nice to give up your seat to pregnant women, parents with small children, and the elderly, for which you'll be rewarded with that rare treasure: a smile from a French stranger.

Bus and Tramway

PARIS

Traveling in Paris by bus has its merits, though it can be slower and even more crowded than the Métro. For parents traveling with children and those with mobility issues, the bus is definitely the preferred choice. Night owls will be happy to know that the Noctilien bus line offers longer running hours than the Métro, and you get the added benefit of being able to see the sights while you move about town. To access one of the dozens of bus lines zigging and zagging across the city, start by plotting your journey on the RATP website (www.ratp.fr), which has an English-language option. Once you know which bus to take and from exactly where, you'll need a ticket. Your Navigo pass or t+ tickets (the standard Métro-bus-tram-RER train tickets) will work here. You can also buy a ticket directly from the bus driver; as a courtesy, try to use coins (large bills are refused). To get off at your stop, push the red button to signal the driver. To transfer between buses you must use a second ticket. The night bus (www.noctilien.fr) runs 12:30am-5:30am with stops at big transport hubs, including Montparnasse and Châtelet, as well as suburban destinations. One bus on each Noctilien line departs every hour.

The T3 tramway that will circle the city is nearly complete; the last stretch of track is slated for completion by the end of 2017, but for now, you'll only be able to circumnavigate three-quarters of the journey around the city by tram. Use your Navigo or standard t+ tickets to board at any tram stop.

OUTSIDE PARIS

Long-distance buses also leave from Paris, heading out to points across the country and throughout Europe. UK-based **Eurolines** (www.eurolines.fr) services most of Europe with uniformly comfortable coaches that run from multiple cities in France to the UK, Spain, Portugal, and beyond. Sample fares include €29 from Paris to London (which includes the ferry ride) and €49 from Lyon to Amsterdam. **Busabout** (www.busabout.com) is one of the newer bus companies geared toward young, carefree types who want to see the sights and have the flexibility of stopping and staying a while. For around €500, you can get a nine-day Flexitrip pass that allows you to get off and on buses traversing the European continent. Unlike Eurail passes, they aren't limited to non-European citizens.

To travel long distances within France, you're better off making use of the efficient train system, but in rural areas, buses will become your best friend. Just don't expect them to take you great distances. To learn more about the buses in your *département,* check in at the *hôtel de ville,* where you'll be able to get a timetable and a bus-route map.

Boats are a popular form of transportation in France, whether for sightseeing or commuting.

Boat

If the plane, train, bike, Métro, and bus options don't meet your needs, you'll be relieved to know that France operates a few different ferry services heading to points south (Corsica and Spain), northwest (the UK), and even farther west (Ireland). Individual passengers or passengers with motorbikes, cars, and bicycles are welcome aboard, and some carriers allow companion animals. **Sea France** (www.seafrance. com) offers round-trips between Calais and Dover for €34; Société National Maritime Corse Méditerranée (SNCM) sails to Corsica, Algeria, Sardinia, and Tunisia. A round-trip ferry ride from Marseille to Scandola, Corsica, in a private cabin with two beds will cost you €110 or so, depending on the day of the week. More fares are available on SNCM's website (www.sncm.fr). **Brittany Ferries** (www.brittany-ferries.fr) is yet another company servicing France with big boats setting sail to Ireland, England, and Spain. Getting to Bilbao, Spain, from the port town of Roscoff, in Brittany, will surely be a seafaring adventure, but it doesn't come cheap: For the 23-hour voyage, expect to pay €200 each way for two passengers (but you can bring a car with you at that price).

Bicycle

When Paris mayor Bertrand Delanoë rolled out the Vélib' bike-share program in 2007, the global media went gaga. What novelty! How very modern and innovative! What had gone overlooked, apparently, was that bike-share programs had already been established in other cities throughout France for years. Maverick transport system or not, Vélib' has spawned copycat programs throughout the world, and with good reason: It's a convenient way to get around, get your exercise, and help relieve the car congestion on busy city streets. Lyon, Grenoble, Nice, Bordeaux, Toulouse, and many other cities have their own versions of Vélib', but if you want to make use of them, you'll need to get yourself set up with a *carte bleue* (only those with a *puce* will work) or look into whether the local transportation pass—like Paris's Navigo—will give you access. The transport passes can be purchased using regular old *puce*-free credit cards from vendors at *gares* and Métro stations. Helmets aren't included in your community bike rental (but are recommended), but baskets and locks are part of the nominal fee.

Car

COVOITURAGE (CAR-SHARING)

One well-kept secret among locals who want to get from here to there on the cheap is *covoiturage* (www.covoiturage.fr), which translates to "car-sharing." Once you've registered online for free, you can plug in your trip starting point and desired end point, hit the *"rechercher"* button, and see if you'll be matched up with someone who has a car who's also making that trip and wants passengers to help pay for gas. If you get a match (or two or three or more), you can read the driver reviews from other passengers, find out whether they allow dogs, music, or smoking in their cars, and see how much they're charging per passenger for the trip. Between Bordeaux and Bergerac, prices range €5-8 each way; from Pau to Toulouse, expect to pay around €10-15.

The newest public transportation system to be unveiled in the City of Light is the car-share program **Autolib'** (www.autolib.eu). Subscribing online for periods of a day, week, month, or year gives you

Bikes make a lot of sense in a country with high fuel prices.

access to a fleet of four-seat electric "Bluecars" stationed throughout Paris and the Île-de-France region. A valid driver's license and international permit are required for non-EU drivers, and charges average €11-14 per hour. They are best for short, one-way trips.

DRIVER'S LICENSES

It's possible to acquire a French driver's license, but not necessarily simple and easy. The first confusing hurdle you'll have to jump over to get closer to your *permis de conduire* (driver's license) is determining whether your state (or province, for Canadians) is one of the dozens that have a reciprocal driver's license agreement with France—British Columbia and California do not, but Pennsylvania and Prince Edward Island do. If your state is on the list, just make for the *préfecture,* show your U.S. driver's license, fill out a form, and wait two weeks for your valid-forever French license to arrive. If your home state is not on the lucky list, then you'll have to take the figurative long route to be able to take the literal long route by *voiture* (car). That means finding a school, or *auto-école.* They're everywhere: Type in *"auto-école"* and the name of your city into your favorite search engine and see what comes up. Prices vary somewhat, but you can expect to pay between €700 and €1,800 for an extensive driver's education course that includes classes in theory and driving codes, plus 20 hours of actual driving time. Don't expect to be immediately accepted into the first school you approach; there is generally a waiting time of up to several months for these in-demand academies. You can see how popular they are by looking around the streets of your town and counting the cars with the illuminated *"école"* sign on top. Classes, as you might expect, are taught in French. Don't think your language skills are up to snuff? English-language classes do exist, but you'll pay a premium for that privilege or enlist the services of a translator for the written test.

Driving indefinitely on your valid U.S. driver's license—which is only valid in France for the first year you're here—might be a gamble worth taking if the thought of dealing with another layer of bureaucracy is just too much to bear. Some drivers interviewed for this book claim to never have had a problem related to driving with their non-French licenses, even after racking up countless speeding tickets. (Tickets are generally issued by mail, after a radar trap catches you exceeding the speed limit.) Still, there's nothing like the peace of mind that comes with living life above board, so drive safely, with caution.

BUYING A CAR

Cars can be purchased in France at used-car lots and new-car lots, and through private parties on websites like ParuVendu (www.paruvendu.fr) and La Centrale (www.lacentrale.fr). You'll also see handwritten *"à vendre"* signs tacked to car windows. But you'll not likely see much in the way of junker *voitures* since the government offers financial incentives to people to trade in their environmentally hostile gas guzzlers for more modern, fuel-efficient Renaults, Peugeots, and Citroëns. Even then, the old, gross polluters tend to retain their value, which makes purchasing a new car in France look pretty wise from a fiscal perspective. Whatever path you take to buy a car, you'll need to get it registered immediately afterward.

How you secure your *carte grise,* or automobile registration card, depends on whether you bought a new or used vehicle. If you bought your car new from a dealer, the dealer will submit the paperwork to the *préfecture* on your behalf. When you buy a second-hand car, you can choose to fill out the registration forms in person at the *préfecture* and sometimes at the *mairie's* office, or you can register online (www.cartegriseminute.fr) to get your *plaques d'immatriculation* (license plates) and *carte grise*.

Like the annual smog checks that are mandatory in some U.S. states, all cars on the road for four years or more in France are subject to a *contrôle technique* every two years. You bring your car to an authorized service station, where everything from your shock absorbers to your seatbelts will be tested for wear and functionality. Expect to pay around €40 for the service, plus any necessary fix-it fees that result from the diagnostic testing. Cars older than five years are also subjected to annual smog checks.

Fuel for your French wheels costs a bit more than what you're used to paying at the pump in North America. Prices have dropped, but you can still count on spending €1.30-1.60 per liter (and it takes about four liters to make a gallon) for your unleaded gas *(essence sans plomb)* or diesel *(gazole)*.

RULES OF THE ROAD
City Driving

When traveling by car in Paris, you'll notice a distinct peculiarity: There are no stop signs. Navigating the streets by car, bicycle, or even on foot without those familiar red octagons can be tricky, and it helps to know some basics before getting behind the wheel. In general, the car(s) to your right have the right-of-way—except in roundabouts, where the cars inside the roundabout to your left take priority. Right turns on red lights are strictly prohibited. If you're on a bike, you may be exempt from this rule if you see a small red triangle with a yellow arrow. Pedestrians walk blindly into the streets both in and outside of crosswalks with disarming regularity, so be forewarned.

Before you do any driving, familiarize yourself with French road signs.

Parking in Paris, Bordeaux, and Lyon can be exhausting work, both finding a spot to squeeze into and then actually squeezing into it. In the French capital, parking spaces are generally of the *payant* variety, €2.40-4 per hour, depending on what part of the city you're in. Most of these pay-to-park spots morph into free-to-park spots on weekends, holidays, and the month of August. Purchase your ticket from the green kiosks marked with a bright blue "P," and put the little receipt face-up on the driver's side of your dashboard. (It's also possible to buy prepaid cards at *tabacs* and some newspaper stands.) Parking garages are also scattered throughout Paris, and vary in price. Visit www.parkingsdeparis.com to learn more. In major cities elsewhere in France, you'll find pay-to-park prices slightly less pricey. In Bordeaux, you'll pay €1.70-2.20 per hour, and in Rennes, you'll be charged €1-2 per hour.

Highway Driving

Outside Paris, roads vary from fast-moving toll highways to smaller, slower highways and snail-strength surface roads. They'll all get you to your destination, but it's the toll (*péage*) roads that are most efficient and therefore worth the extra cost. Toll roads, or *autoroutes,* usually begin with an A (A1 through A89) but may begin with an E. Tolls vary depending on the road and the distance traveled, so expect to pay anywhere from €1.10 to €35.60. Payments can be made in cash or using a credit card, and some toll booths are staffed by humans who can make change and direct you on what to do if you don't have cash or cards. One thing you'll learn pretty quickly after driving on French highways is that the left lane is reserved exclusively for passing; it isn't meant to be a high-speed cruising lane. Use it to pass slower cars, then move back into the right lane until you exit the highway or need to pass another car.

Routes nationales ("N" roads) and *routes départementales* ("D" roads) will also get you where you need to go, albeit much more slowly. One feature of the smaller roads that hinders speed and efficiency is the roundabout. For the uninitiated, France's ubiquitous *ronds-points* can be dizzying. Drivers to the left always have the right-of-way, which means you may have to stop and wait for several cars to pass before you can enter. Only enter the roundabout when there are no cars to your left.

Traffic Laws

To avoid the radar-enforced speed traps, it's helpful to know the **speed limits.** On toll roads, the maximum speed is 130 kilometers per hour (km/h). In wet conditions, you must slow down to either 90 km/h or 110 km/h, depending on the road. On main roads, the limit is 90 km/h; when driving through towns, reduce your speed to 50 km/h.

It is now mandatory to carry a **reflective warning triangle** and **neon safety vest** (*gilet*) for each passenger. Failing to do so could cost you €137—or worse, your life, if no one can see you changing the tire on the side of the road. You can buy the safety duo for about €20 at auto body shops, some gas stations, and the French equivalent of AAA, called **Automobile Club** (www.automobileclub.org). The Day-Glo reflective vests are also a common sight on the racks at French thrift stores.

In recent years, the government has launched a series of anti-drinking-and-driving campaigns to curb a growing problem in France. The legal **blood alcohol limit** is 0.5 grams per liter, or 0.25 milligrams in a breathalyzer, which is how you'll be tested. This is equivalent to two standard glasses of wine (10 cl) or beer (25 cl). If you're pulled

Driving Me Crazy

Circulation: Do you know what it means? In France, it has less to do with your cardiovascular system and more to do with driving. (It means "traffic.") Before you get behind the wheel of your *voiture* and become part of the *circulation*, you'd best brush up on your roadway lingo.

accident - accident	**péage** - toll road/booth
autoroute - highway	**piéton(ne)** - pedestrian
bande d'arrêt d'urgence - emergency lane	**pont** - bridge
chaîs - snow chains	**ralentir** - slow down
conducteur/conductrice - driver	**rond-point** - roundabout
dépasser - to pass	**route** - road
embouteillage - traffic jam	**sens interdit** - no entry
feu de signalisation - traffic light	**sens unique** - one way
limitation de vitesse - speed limit	**tomber en panne** - break down
passage piétons - crosswalk	

over on suspicion of driving under the influence, you could receive a fine and lose six points off your 12-point driving record, lose your license for as many as three years, or end up in prison for up to two years, depending upon your level of intoxication. More information about driving laws can be found on the government's road-safety website, www.securite-routiere.gouv.fr.

Insurance

Car insurance is mandatory and generally more affordable than in the United States or Canada, since personal health insurance is also mandatory and therefore an unnecessary component of your auto insurance. How much you pay depends on many factors, including the type of vehicle you're driving (motorcycle, caravan), how long you've been driving, and your driving record. Automobile Club offers free quotes, but you can also walk into any storefront offering *"assurances automobile"* and ask for a *devis* (quote).

PRIME LIVING
LOCATIONS

OVERVIEW

From the Right Bank Haussmann apartment with the sweeping view of the Seine to the vine-covered *longère* in rural Brittany, France has an idyllic housing option for whatever the foreign heart fancies. But what exactly will you do with yourself once you find your dream home? The best places for expats to settle in France aren't just those where jobs can be found (or created), but those with a solid social infrastructure that ensures you'll never feel alienated or isolated. If it's solitude you crave, there are plentiful opportunities for it here, but most people come to France with the aim of steeping themselves in the local culture, meeting the natives, and indulging in a daily croissant (or two) washed down with a thimble-size *café express*.

The French are mobile bunch: The waiter at your favorite café in Paris, Marseille, or Lyon is likely from the *provinces*, as the rest of the country is called; when asked, he'll tell you, with a wistful, faraway look in his eyes, what a beautiful, special, warm, and inviting place his hometown is. He's migrated to the big city for the same reasons people everywhere do: for work opportunities, education, culture. That doesn't mean the love of home has faded in any fashion.

At some point, you too will wax poetic about your adopted hometown. Before you know it, you'll be spouting facts about its long and illustrious history, defending it against any disparaging remarks, and otherwise behaving in the prideful manner

PRIME LIVING LOCATIONS

Isle of Man (U.K.)

North Sea

West Frisian Islands

UNITED KINGDOM

Amsterdam

NETHERLANDS

GERMANY

Thames River

London

BELGIUM

Lille

Brussels

Rhine River

LUXEMBOURG

Luxembourg

Nord-Pas-de-Calais

English Channel

Channel Islands (U.K.)

Caen

Haute-Normandie

Basse-Normandie

Seine River

Picardie

PARIS

Versailles

Île-de-France

Champagne-Ardennes

STRASBOURG

Strasbourg

St. Malo

Chartres

Lorraine

Alsace

Brittany

Rennes

BRITTANY

Vannes

Carnac

Pays de la Loire

Orléans

Centre

Loire River

FRANCE

Burgundy

Dijon

Franche-Comté

Bern

SWITZERLAND

Nantes

Nantes

Poitou Charles

Auvergne

Limousin

LYON AND GRENOBLE

Lake Geneva

Île d'Oléron

Lyon

Geneva

Rhône Alpes

ITALY

ATLANTIC OCEAN

Gironde Estuary

BORDEAUX AND THE DORDOGNE VALLEY

Bergerac

St. Etienne

Grenoble

Po River

Bordeaux

Sarlat

Garonne River

Aquitaine

Languedoc Roussillon

Rhône River

Provence-Alpes-Côte-d'Azur

Bay of Biscay

Biarritz

Pibriac

Blagnac

Colomiers

Toulouse

Avignon

Aix-en-Provence

Nice

Antibes

Monaco

Monaco

Pau

Midi-Pyrénées

Montpellier

Cannes

MONACO

Lourdes

PAU, TOULOUSE, AND MONTPELLIER

Gulf of Lyon

Marseille

PROVENCE AND THE CÔTE D'AZUR

Pyrénées

ANDORRA

SPAIN

Mediterranean Sea

Barcelona

0   100 mi

0   100 km

© AVALON TRAVEL

befitting a local. "Oh, Sarlat has the area's most colorful Saturday morning market," you'll say. "And in truffle season—bah! It's absolute heaven!" or *"Oh là là!* Aix in the springtime, *c'est magnifique!* The chestnut trees and cherry blossoms are blooming, and we still have two months before the tourist glut!" You'll be boasting about your town's big cinema festival/specialty liqueur/locally produced cheese quicker than you can say *"Vive la France!"*

But you have to find before you flaunt, and where you settle can make or break your experience. The life you carve out in rural France will not be the same one you make for yourself in a big city. Regional idiosyncrasies abound, and so do attitudes. The most successful transitions result from careful planning and research. The possibilities outlined here were selected for their overall livability, including opportunities to establish a working life, and proximity to educational opportunities. If settling into a thriving community with access to transportation, good food, culture, and friendly locals is on your agenda, here are some options you should get to know.

PARIS

Paris is a city of émigrés. We come from all over—North and West Africa, South East Asia, North America, the Middle East, Eastern Europe, and beyond. By far the country's most cosmopolitan locale, Paris boasts more foreigners than any other city in France. Anything you want, including burritos, can now be had here (something that makes us California transplants terribly happy), and employment and housing opportunities trump those of anywhere else you could settle. Many nonnative Parisians say Paris does not represent "true France." Why? Because so many other dreamers have moseyed over from afar that it no longer looks "French." But trust me: It does, and it is. Even so, there's no denying the international flavor that the capital exudes. In each

Parisians are multi-ethnic, multi-cultural, and always up for a celebration.

of the 20 arrondissements, you'll notice distinct differences: Some are more congested, others more verdant; some, like the 16th, have a quiet and residential air, while the 18th hums with a more active, lively vibe. Wherever you are in Paris, expect French to be spoken (along with Arabic, Swahili, English, Hebrew, Italian, Portuguese, and Spanish), polite formality to reign, and nonstop opportunities for cultural diversion, plus educational opportunities, and the chance to macerate in a history-rich marinade.

BRITTANY

Affordable property and easy access to the United Kingdom and Northern Europe have long attracted foreigners to this temperate western outpost. With a rich history punctuated by Viking invasions, a strong Celtic influence, and Roman conquests, this green and pleasant land has retained its seafaring tradition without shying away from modernity. Rennes, the regional capital, welcomes an international student community that spins past the city's 16th-century half-timbered buildings on definitively modern Le Vélo Star bicycles, one of the low-cost public transport options the city has to offer. With a socialist mayor governing a population of 210,000, Rennes has established itself as a modern city with a progressive outlook, which might explain the relatively recent influx of high-tech businesses to this former car-manufacturing region. Further west and south, Vannes perches above a conifer-hemmed seashore overlooking a handful of tiny, picturesque islands. In the *centre ville,* there's an open invitation to everyone who happens by to venture in and explore the ancient cobbled streets and step into a stone-built brasserie for an afternoon glass of the local cider. The newly revamped harbor has injected the city with a bit of seafaring sophistication, with its terrace restaurants and clusters of colorful sailboats hinting at a leisure-loving local population. Tucked in among the area's bigger towns are pretty little villages where farming and fishing are still the dominant livelihoods. Throughout Brittany, you'll find small-town community and big-city conveniences, from theater to concerts and five-star dining. Because of the affordability of real estate in this corner of France, Brittany is popular with those on a tight housing budget.

BORDEAUX AND THE DORDOGNE VALLEY

This picturesque corner of France has so much going for it. It's a pretty, cosmopolitan regional capital with small-town ambience and a big heart, close proximity to the world's most famous wine-growing region (and all that it yields), and a *trés charmant* river valley crammed with more castles than you could ever hope for. For centuries, this area has welcomed foreigners, from 16th-century Jews escaping religious persecution in Spain to 21st-century Englishmen and -women looking for an easy escape from London. Expect to hear English spoken in unexpected places—small-town brasseries, waiting areas outside elementary schools—and expect to be smitten by the fairytale feel. If you've come to France to evade your fellow Anglophones, this may not be the place to settle down: For years, the English have been ferrying over and snapping up land, which has, historically, been a great bargain. The recent global mortgage crisis put a slight damper on the house-buying spree, but the English-speaking community has put down roots and won't be going anywhere soon. If truffles, wine, and rolling green countryside are your cup of tea, this corner of France has your name on it.

Charming villages abound in the Dordogne Valley.

PAU, TOULOUSE, AND MONTPELLIER

Wedged between sea and mountains in the Midi-Pyrénées region is the little jewel of Pau, population 80,000, with its front-row-center views of the snowcapped Pyrénées and easy access to outdoor adventure. For sporty types, a veritable buffet of fun awaits, from skiing and cycling to kayaking on the Gave de Pau River. The local university is a magnet for both domestic and foreign students, and expats are also lured by jobs offered at the local research campus for Total, the French energy company, which employs vast numbers of Anglophones. With a fine balance of urban and rural, nature and cosmopolitan perks, Pau is an ideal place to consider laying down roots.

From the gateway city of Toulouse to the university hub of Montpellier, the Languedoc region signals your proximity to the dazzling Mediterranean with palm trees and sunny skies. A decidedly non-French influence can be felt here, and decidedly non-French shopping bargains are within easy driving distance (there's no sales tax in nearby Andorra). Toulouse's international flavor is enhanced by the aerospace industry that has set up shop here, attracting skilled workers from around the world. Advancing toward the Mediterranean, past the medieval fortress town of Carcassonne and over the sand-colored hillsides specked with wind turbines sits the sunny, student-heavy city of Montpellier. In its giant main square, Place de la Comédie, locals young and old stroll around, sit by the fountain, and stop to listen to a guitarist playing flamenco tunes with understated perfection.

Compared to Paris, Pau, Toulouse, and Montpellier are bargains in the housing department, and there's no need to sacrifice cultural amenities to secure your place in the sun. Year-round art, theater, and workshops are on the to-do list, and within a one-hour train ride, you can be out the door of your city apartment and sitting on a beach chair facing the sparkling sea.

PROVENCE AND THE CÔTE D'AZUR

Even for experienced urbanites, France's second-largest city, Marseille, can feel overwhelming: Its crowded, graffiti-filled, labyrinthine streets seethe with a gritty energy that only intensifies with the summer heat. It's worth a visit, but Marseille can't really stake a claim as a "prime" living location. However, 30 miles north is the much calmer, quieter oasis of Aix-en-Provence. Best known as the birthplace of painter Paul Cézanne, the capital city of Provence occupies a strategic location between the sea and the rugged mountains and is blessed with that coveted Mediterranean climate. The Romans first settled here more than two millennia ago, and remnants of their civilization—bridges, arenas, fountains—still stand as reminders of that rich past. Today, this town of 150,000 attracts a diverse student population, as well as artists, actors, and others who find the soft terra-cotta palette an alluring invitation to relax and stay awhile. Expect picture-perfect pedestrian promenades, colorful markets, and quaint shops vending everything from fresh-pressed juices to €300 shoes. But beauty has its price—Aix is not the cheapest place to settle in France.

A two-hour train ride east will bring you in the little seaside oasis of Antibes. This charming town, population 75,000 (bundled with Juan-les-Pins), has a summer-holiday atmosphere yet functions as any nontourist destination would, with a busy year-round marketplace, plenty of restaurants, and friendly locals. The neighboring high-tech hub of Sophia Antipolis (known as the Silicon Valley of France), boasts a melting pot of expatriates, with international workers staffing its software companies and pharmaceutical labs. In the summer, the locals head out of town and rent their homes for astronomical sums that sometimes supply the owners with enough income to live for the rest of the year. Just a 15-minute ride up the coast is the center of Nice, where broad boulevards, a sweeping seaside promenade, and a charming old town await. A truly livable city, Nice has historically attracted the silver-haired set, but its nearly idyllic position on the Côte d'Azur, a short hop from Monaco and Italy and the ski resorts of the Alpes-Maritimes, mean that the younger generation is catching on. More affordable than neighboring Antibes, Nice has a lot to offer the expat, including 300 days of sunshine per year on top of better-than-average employment and outdoor-recreation opportunities.

LYON AND GRENOBLE

The first thing you'll notice about Grenoble is its stunning landscape. Tucked into a flat valley high in the hills amid the snow-capped alpine peaks of three mountain chains, the city attracts sporty types in droves. The city is diverse on many levels: It has thriving Vietnamese and Sri Lankan populations and also throws out the welcome mat to the gay and lesbian community. Students come here to learn, skiers to shoot the *pistes,* and high-tech professionals to work their magic at Hewlett-Packard, Schneider Electric, and the numerous biotech companies that have made Grenoble the scientific capital of France. An hour up the road is beautiful Lyon, where medieval meets modern with an enchanting style. Though tourism is one of the city's official moneymakers, Lyon is a livable place where students, shop workers, and entrepreneurial types can build a rich and fulfilling life among the ancient Roman ruins, medieval churches, and Renaissance-era townhouses. The student population hovers around 100,000—second only to Paris—and with all that youth comes a certain vibrancy that helps keep Lyon feeling current. Throughout the city, chic boutiques sidle up to quotidian *épiceries;* on any given day in the giant main square, you'll find all ages promenading about, dancers dancing, and tourists gawking at the mishmash of architectural eye candy. This town likes to have fun, too: Nightclubs and wine bars flourish here, and judging by the number of Irish pubs dotting Vieux Lyon's charming back alleyways, you might think you've accidentally stumbled into a James Joyce novel. Multicultural, food-oriented, and progressive, Lyon is an interesting, vibrant city in which to put down roots.

STRASBOURG

Famous across Western Europe for hosting the liveliest and most colorful of all French Christmas markets, Strasbourg ought to get more play as a year-round destination. Maybe, though, mum's the word to keep this gem of a city small, safe, and livable. With 275,000 inhabitants and a thriving student population of 40,000, Strasbourg feels young, even if its roots stretch back more than 500 years. Rule over the region has changed hands over the centuries, with both Germany, France, and the Holy Roman Empire laying claim to the Alsatian capital. Today, the German influence is palpable in the local cuisine, the architecture, and on the city streets—where people wear bright clothing of the sort you don't see too often in Paris.

As the seat of the European Parliament, Strasbourg is home—at least part of the year—to a thriving international community that gives the city its cosmopolitan flair. At its heart, though, Strasbourg is small-town France writ large, with a strong sense of community that is attractive to anyone looking for a place in France to call home.

PARIS

For centuries, daring dreamers have flocked to this beautiful, history-rich city on the Seine in pursuit of education, to develop their art, and to simply be able to say, "I used to live in Paris." There's a lot to love about this city, and many a writer—from Ernest Hemingway to David Sedaris—has taken pains to describe Paris in all its glory, the good and the bad. The good is easy to measure: You'll find it in the postage-stamp-size squares that mark every neighborhood; in the endless dining options that will take your taste buds on a journey from Alsace to Sri Lanka; in the corner *boulangeries,* where still-warm *viennoiserie* call out to you from inside a gleaming glass case; and in the dozens of museums offering up centuries of world-class art to overwhelm your senses. Paris is beautiful beyond belief, and even in the grittiest neighborhoods in the northern section of the city, you need only look up at a building's façade to revel in a moment of aesthetic pleasure. Ornate curlicued balconies decorated with geraniums in full bloom, carved wooden doors hemmed by art nouveau sculpture, and 100-year-old advertisements peeking out from a faded brick wall never fail to tantalize the eyes.

Paris is certainly not without its flaws. Petty crime is common. It's not unusual to see the torched remains of an unfortunate Vespa lying in the street, and graffiti is cropping up on edifices of even *maisons particulaires* in the bourgeois 16th. Traffic, particularly on Thursdays and Fridays at rush hour, when Parisians head for their weekend

© AURELIA D'ANDREA

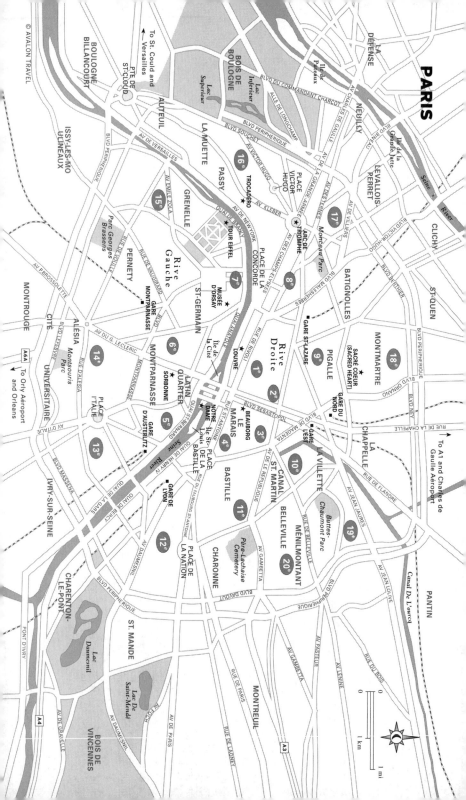

PARIS

© AVALON TRAVEL

homes in the provinces, can be brutal. The pollution is so pervasive that it stains the sand-colored buildings a dirty gray, prompting a municipally mandated cleaning at least once a decade. And let's not forget the Métro, which resembles a human-packed sardine can during peak commute times. If you're driving, good luck finding a parking space. But even if you're crazy enough to hit the streets of Paris in a car, you'll find that the trade-off is worth all the hassle.

The Lay of the Land

ARRONDISSEMENTS

Paris is carved into 20 distinct regions called arrondissements, each an administrative unit with its own mayor and town hall. These districts spiral out clockwise from the geographic center of the city, ending in the northwestern quadrant. The Tour Eiffel and Musée d'Orsay can be found in the 7th; the Louvre is just across the river in the 1st. Sacré Coeur is in the 18th, and Notre Dame is in the 4th. Studying a map of the city—or, better still, picking up the very handy pocket-size Michelin map atlas of Paris—will facilitate your orientation within each of the various districts.

Wherever you settle, you'll be within 45 minutes of anywhere else in the city. The thorough and efficient Métro system makes the distances less daunting, though one of the benefits of Paris life is the bounty that your quartier offers (making it unnecessary to leave if you don't want to). With the exception of the 16th arrondissement, every neighborhood in Paris has, within a two-block radius of your apartment, a *boulangerie,* a butcher shop, an *épicerie* for buying vegetables and fruit, and a Métro or bus stop.

view from the top of the Arc de Triomphe

RIVE GAUCHE AND RIVE DROITE

Each of the two sides of Paris, *la rive gauche* and *la rive droite,* has its own special flavor, and locals feel passionate about the benefits of their side of the Seine. The **Left Bank,** or *la rive gauche,* is where you'll find the Sorbonne, the Eiffel Tower, the Catacombs, and those cafés and brasseries made famous by centuries of writers and philosophers: Brasserie Lipp, Les Deux Magots, Café de Flore. Today, more tourists than locals pull up a chair on the sidewalk terraces, but if you move just south of St. Germain des Prés, you'll discover homey neighborhoods and a safe, child-friendly atmosphere. The Left Bank feels more sedate, more residential, and slightly less *populaire,* or working-class crowded.

On the **Right Bank,** on other side of the river, you'll find the Champs-Elysées, Place de la République, the Bastille, and Sacré Coeur. *La rive droite* feels hipper, younger, and edgier, particularly in quartiers like the Northern Marais and Canal Saint Martin. Paris's gay hub is on this side of town, in the old streets of the Marais, where art galleries and great shopping are just two of the many neighborhood draws. Culturally, a lot is happening here, too. The 19th arrondissement, especially, has seen a boost in art and music, as evidenced by the opening of Le Centre Cent-Quatre and, in early 2015, a brand-spanking-new, €386 million concert hall, la Philharmonie de Paris, in La Villette.

DOWNTOWN

Paris doesn't have a typical "downtown" in the way that, say, New York City has Lower Manhattan or San Francisco has its financial district. But what it does have is **La Défense,** a cluster of skyscrapers on the northwest edge of the city where more than 150,000 workers migrate seven days a week. Besides being home to high-tech corporations, government offices, and state-run businesses, La Défense also houses the region's largest shopping mall, Les Quatre Temps (open on Sundays), and a handful of residential complexes.

One of Paris's unique features is its truly livable, well-integrated neighborhoods. Each quartier in the city's 20 arrondissements is a self-contained village, with all the amenities you'd find in a big city compressed into a single neighborhood. While there are legions of commuters who live outside the city and drive or take public transport in each day, many more Parisians live and work within a short distance of their homes. For those who do traverse the city for *travail* (work), the efficient, relatively fast public transportation network means no point within the *périphérique* is more than 45 minutes away.

Daily Life

CLIMATE

When this four-season city turns chilly and gray, around mid-November, people simply dress more warmly and continue their everyday outdoor activities: biking, trips to the market, Sunday strolls, and walks to the park. Outdoor cafés erect plastic walls and roll out the heat lamps, and life continues as usual. Then, in spring—especially after a rough winter with snow and freezing temperatures—the city springs to life with an unrivaled vibrancy that makes winter, even with all its holiday fanfare, look like a pretty dormant season. In summer, when the weather turns muggy and hot, Parisians make weekend escapes to their country abodes, leaving the city to the tourists during August, the standard vacation month.

The expat who stays citybound in the summer will find Paris perfectly pleasant, between Paris Plages—the temporary beaches erected along the Seine and the Canal de l'Ourcq—and the outdoor concerts such as those that erupt across the city at the annual Fête de la Musique, plus film festivals and other events sponsored by Anglophone organizations like the **American Church in Paris** (www.acparis.org), **Shakespeare**

Grappling with Gray Skies

Paris, for all its beauty and charm, cannot be called a city with a sunny disposition. When the sky is dark and broody, Parisians and others living in the north of France tend to parade the streets with mouths pursed in perpetual non-smiles, a visual reminder to each other that this is *definitely* not the sun-splashed Riviera. So what can we do to keep the blues at bay until clear skies reappear? Cynthia Davis, an American psychotherapist who lives and works in the French capital, says it's possible to survive the gray gloom and thrive if armed with a few coping strategies.

"Seasonal Affective Disorder (SAD) is a factor in mental health in Paris, and people do tend to bring it up the longer they have been living here," says Davis, who moved to Paris from Seattle in 2008.

"People manage the effects better when they make a point to include more exercise, healthy foods, and plans to get outdoors to enjoy the city and friends. These aspects create better living all times of year, but the dark and rainy winters in Paris create a hibernation mode in people that can quickly spiral into a depression."

Davis says that some people affected by SAD find extra relief when adding light therapy and Vitamin D supplements to their wellness routines—especially during the autumn time-change, when days become shorter and darker. But the key, says Davis, is staying connected and creating community. "Being proactive in that regard helps," she says.

To stay sunny on the inside even when it's gray outside, remember to practice Davis's strategies on a regular basis. It's also smart to avoid excessive alcohol consumption, and seek help when needed.

and Company bookstore (www.shakespeareandcompany.com), and **WICE** (www. wice-paris.org).

EMPLOYMENT

"Métro, boulot, dodo." It's the 9-to-5 worker's lament: commute, work, sleep. Rinse and repeat. We'd all rather be on permanent vacation, but if you must participate in the daily grind, Paris is the place to be. After you've been in town a while, you'll discover that a lot of people really are here just for work—after university, the upwardly mobile move to Paris to earn enough money for all those vacations, and especially for retirement back in the village or city where they were raised. There's a sense of transience in this metropolis, made more palpable by the tourists who help shore up the city's financial infrastructure and by the international working community here on short- and long-term (but rarely permanent) work contracts.

The standard workweek is 35 hours, but Parisians are notorious for working long, American-style hours. To compensate, they invest a comparable amount of time in urban leisure activities: eating and drinking; going to the cinema, concerts, and theater; and haunting the countless green spaces that have become a communal backyard for apartment dwellers whose personal habitats aren't equipped with one (most aren't).

PARIS TIME

Historically, on Sundays and often on Mondays, huge chunks of the city have felt like a ghost town, with iron gates pulled down over shop doorways, paper shades drawn across *boulangerie* displays, and supermarkets sitting dark, forlorn, and empty.

Living in Paris means being surrounded by tourists every day of the year.

Legally, big business such as chain stores and supermarkets are only allowed to open their doors on five Sundays per calendar year, but a movement to increase that figure to 12 is gaining support from merchants and politicians who believe the "American" open-every-day model will stimulate the French economy. (Naysayers believe it will hurt small businesses that can't compete with their jumbo-sized counterparts.) In neighborhoods with sizable Arab populations—the 18th, 19th, and the 20th, in particular—shops are closed on Fridays instead of Sundays, and the same neighborhoods are alive and open for business on Christmas Day. In Jewish districts, particularly the 4th, 11th, and 19th, many businesses are closed on Saturdays. If you happen to find yourself near rue des Rosiers and have a hankering for a world-famous l'As du Fallafel sandwich, don't bother; they're not open on the Sabbath.

PARKS AND GREEN SPACES

In the southwest and northeast sections of the city sit two gloriously verdant areas that also happen to be among the few green spaces in Paris where dogs are free to roam off leash. Both parks, **Bois de Boulogne** to the west and **Bois de Vincennes** to the east, are accessible by Métro, car, bike, or bus and are open 365 days a year. In the summer, paddle boats and canoes can be rented at each park's picturesque lake, and there are plenty of picnic tables, cafés, and other amenities available to help maximize your outdoor pleasure.

In Bois de Boulogne, prostitution has become a 24-hour phenomenon, so it's not uncommon to see women—and some men—teetering around in the woods wearing little more than high heels and underwear in the middle of the day. This practice becomes especially acute in the evening and during rush hour, and it seems to be relegated to the areas of the park with the most road traffic. Prostitution aside, both *bois* (woods) are a city slicker's oasis, as well as wonderful places to spend a spring, summer, or autumn afternoon.

Where to Live

Outside of work, what your daily Parisian life looks like will depend on where you choose to settle. In Paris's trendier right-bank arrondissements—the 11th, 10th, and 4th—you'll find that the hipsters have hogged up all the affordable places and sent the rent sky-high for what's left. Still, you may want to try your luck in these vibrant neighborhoods. If you lay down roots in the perpetually popular, thick-of-it all Marais, where museums, bars, shopping, and nightlife are right outside your door, your leisure-time commute will be shortened to mere footsteps. The sleepier corners of the 14th, 15th and 16th, on the other hand, offer the sedate sense of suburban calm—which certainly has its own appeal, especially for families with children—and more sidewalk room for pushing strollers and wrangling wee ones. If you prefer a sedate atmosphere with an aura of security, you'll love the 16th, which has a calm, homogenous ambience with a dash of Americana thrown in. (Step into the Starbucks on Victor Hugo, and you'll see what I mean.) Back across the Seine in the Alésia neighborhood in the 14th and the Grenelle quartier in the 15th, it's practically suburban, though you're never far from critical amenities, including transportation, markets, and restaurants. Even these more placid neighborhoods aren't lacking in the perks that nearly everyone who comes to Paris expects—corner cafés, boulangeries, and outdoor markets—but access to the city's nightclubs and cabarets will likely require a taxi trip or Métro ride.

During your housing hunt, you'll start to get used to diminutive dimensions of Parisian living spaces. That 20-square-meter apartment in the 11th for €900 per month that looked so good on paper might take on a different hue when you realize the entire place is just 215 square feet, which is probably the size of your (very small) living room back home. It's wise to sample a few different places before signing on the dotted line—you'll also notice that prices will drop if the place is on the market for more than a month. If you're renting directly from the owner, don't be afraid to negotiate. That doesn't mean trying to get your 60-square-meter flat with *un ascenseur* (an elevator) down from €2,000 to €1,000, but if the apartment needs work or is missing amenities, you have a bit of haggling room.

Unless you have a money's-no-object budget, finding a place to call home in Paris isn't as simple as choosing a neighborhood. Many other factors come into play, including the local housing supply and the time of year. A move in winter shrinks your options, because really, who wants to move house when there's snow on the ground? This big a transition is challenging enough in the warm months, so skip the winter move and plan for May, June, or July. Toward August, you begin to compete with college students and *rentrées* coming back from long summer holidays who also need to get down to the important task of finding accommodations.

Saint-Sulpice, on the Left Bank, is a functioning church as well as a tourist attraction.

LE MARAIS

The Marais neighborhood encompasses most of the **3rd** and **4th arrondissements.** Its border stretches from the Seine on the south to the Place de la République on the north. To the west is the shopper's paradise of Les Halles, currently undergoing a multi-year facelift; and to the east, the Place de la Bastille and its gold-statue-topped Colonne de Juillet rise above the traffic of the frenetic *rond-point.*

As the **oldest neighborhood in Paris,** the Marais is, not surprisingly, one of the most stereotypically French in character, with crooked cobbled streets, half-timbered buildings, charming squares, and loads and loads of tourists. If you want to live in the **heart of the city,** with direct access to bars, restaurants, museums, and shopping, the Marais is your place. It helps if you're OK with crowds (narrow streets coupled with a never-ending tourist stream can make the claustrophobic feel edgy), and don't plan on driving a car. Access to parking is not a selling point in the Marais, which is **best navigated on foot or by bicycle.**

Though not as ethnically diverse as some other Parisian quartiers, the Marais does offer more than just croissants and coffee as its metaphorical neighborhood composition. This is the **old Jewish quarter,** with nearby synagogues, Holocaust memorials and museums, and Jewish delicatessens galore where you can have your rugelach and eat it, too. Every day except the Saturday sabbath, tourists and locals in droves queue up for the famous Israeli falafel at **L'As du Fallafel** (32-34 rue des Rosiers), considered by many (including famous patron Lenny Kravitz) to be the best in town. But wander the skinny streets within spitting distance of L'As and you'll discover dozens of copycats eager for your business.

The hub of Parisian **gay life** is in the Marais, which is the equivalent of San Francisco's Castro or Montreal's le Village. To immerse yourself in this aspect of

Marais culture, attend the next Gay Pride parade, held each June, which starts on rue des Archives.

Housing

The Marais's housing opportunities vary wildly. Tucked into unassuming alleyways (and protected by enormous and imposing wood doors) are magnificent *maisons particulières* that fetch small fortunes on the real estate market, and equally, there are oodles of ancient walk-ups with beamed ceilings and bucketfuls of more accessible Medieval charm. The most expensive areas (surprise!) sidle up to the area's prettiest green spaces, so if you want to live near the stately Place des Vosges (and who doesn't?), expect to pay upwards of €13,000 per square meter if you're buying. The best deals for **homebuyers** can be had in the Les Halles shopping district north and west of the Georges Pompidou center. Once the site of the city's main wholesale food market and then a haven for all manner of illicit activities, the area is now undergoing a revamp that will be completed in 2018. Part of the overhaul includes creating more green spaces and pedestrian zones, adding new housing developments, and cutting down crime.

If this area holds any appeal, don't dilly-dally; get in while the getting is good and affordable! It won't be cheap for long. As of 2015, it was still possible to buy something deep in the heart of the Marais for the reasonable price of €7,500-8,500 per square meter. You might get lucky and find a 55-square-meter, one-bedroom flat on rue de Temple, constructed in 1700, with a spic-and-span courtyard and friendly *gardienne* for €650,000. For the slightly more affordable price of €390,000 you could land yourself a smaller version a block from Place des Vosges with beamed ceilings and an entirely refinished and modernized interior.

Renting is another ball of wax. Prices per square meter average around €36, which translates to a one-bedroom apartment with those high-in-demand beamed ceilings and views over a pedestrian promenade for €1,300 per month. With a bigger budget, you could find a two-bedroom corner apartment for €1,450 in the Saint-Paul neighborhood (in the southern Marais), known for its plethora of antiques shops and Old World ambiance. Hopefully you like exposed-beam ceilings, because most every apartment in this area is equipped with them.

© AURELIA D'ANDREA

If you've ever harbored a romantic vision of living on a riverboat, the Seine welcomes you with opportunities aplenty.

Schools and Community Centers

The Marais isn't Paris's most family-friendly neighborhood (some sidewalks are barely big enough for two feet, let alone a stroller), but kid-oriented amenities including nurseries and playgrounds, and elementary-, middle-, and high-schools are scattered throughout its narrow streets. If you settle in the 3rd, it would behoove you to visit the **Relais Informations Familles** on the ground floor of the *mairie* (RIF, 2, rue Eugène Spuller, tel. 01/53 01 75 90). Here, friendly staff people will answer all of your questions about enrolling your child in local educational institutions and childcare centers. The 4th arrondissement is home to three different university campuses, including the **Sorbonne's Malher center for historical and legal research** (www.univ-paris1.fr). To learn more about the educational opportunities available to you in the 4th, no matter your age, pay an actual or virtual visit to the *mairie* and investigate the *vie scolaire* section (2, place Baudoyer, www.mairie.04.paris.fr).

Getting Around

Finding secure parking here takes serious effort—even with a Smart Car— and car ownership will limit the fun you can have on your Parisian adventure. Better to invest in a Navigo pass or buy a *carnet* of public transport tickets and leave the driving to someone else. The Marais is well served by an efficient network of underground trains (especially **Métro lines 1, 8,** and **11**) and above-ground buses. **Bus line 69,** which is almost as good as a sightseeing bus, is a stellar option. You can hop on the bus on rue de Rivoli and hop off at the Louvre, la Tour Eiffel, and even Père-Lachaise Cemetery.

For trips further afield, Marais locals head to the Châtelet-Les Halles station, where regional trains whisk travelers to destinations throughout the Île-de-France region.

Hundreds of **Velib'** stations pepper the Marais, and are the ideal way to navigate the tiny back streets, most of which are outfitted with bike lanes. On clear days, there can be traffic jams at certain times of the day around Velib' stations positioned in popular café areas, so plan accordingly. You may end up having to race another rider to the next open parking space a few blocks away. (It happens to all of us at least once!)

16TH ARRONDISSEMENT

The only bad thing you'll ever hear about the 16th arrondissement is that it's "too bourgeois." What does that mean? Well, the implication is that the **streets are so tidy,** the **crime rates so low,** and the **parking so manageable** that it borders on, well, boring. But if that is its only detriment, you'd have to call that a win for this upscale district on Paris's southwest end.

To reach the 16th, simply follow the Seine downstream to the Pont de l'Alma. On the left bank, you'll spot a familiar landmark—la Tour Eiffel—and to the right, the splashy Trocadéro esplanade. Getting here by boat is just one of the many ways you can reach the 16th, but most people choose the Métro, the bus, or, as is more common in this neck of the woods, a car. The 16th is **roomy and expansive,** and far enough from central Paris to allow you to exhale and leave the sound of honking horns and police sirens behind you.

The 16th arrondissement has long been a magnet for moneyed expatriates and wealthy French families attracted by the proximity to the forest, the deluxe housing opportunities, and the open, airy feel of the oh-so-safe streets. Diplomats and NGO leaders feel right at home here amid the many **embassies** and **international think-tanks,** and the dozen or so **private schools** makes it convenient for parents who want their kids educated nearby.

English is spoken more widely here than in most other arrondissements, which can make the transition process a lot smoother for native Anglophones. Enter the popular Starbucks on pretty shopping street rue de Passy, close your eyes, and tune in to the background noise. You could be in New York or San Francisco, based on the accents of the teenage clientele.

The Trocadéro and La Muette neighborhoods are popular choices for expats, and are especially favored by single women who can afford the serenity and sense of security that the areas offer. The 16th is also a hospitable place for **seniors;** expect to see lots of ladies in fur coats roaming the *rues,* shopping bags and fluffy dogs in tow. Mostly though, the 16th is known as a **bourgeois family district,** and it becomes clear after a few hours spent roaming the tidy neighborhoods that there are a lot of children here. If you want easy access to beautiful parks and gardens, **great schools** (many of them private), and room to park your his-and-hers Citroëns or your family-style French minivan, the 16th is a really good bet.

Housing

The 16th is Paris's largest arrondissement. While it is well-served by public transportation, there aren't Métro stations on every other block the way there are in other parts of the city. The areas around the main transport hubs such as RER station Henri Martin and the busy Trocadéro center command higher real-estate prices in part because of their proximity to trains, buses, and taxi stands. If you're shopping for deals, you might want to choose a different arrondissement, or at least focus your search on the far southern fringes near the Métro Exelmans. **Foncia Real Estate** (www.fr.foncia.com) offers a broad selection of housing options, including a 44-square-meter Trocadéro studio built in 1930 going for €390,000 (it's on the ground floor, which might help explain its "cheap" price), and a 100-square-meter Passy area flat with ornate moldings and a decorative fireplace for €1.2 million.

Renting affords some slightly more accessible options. For €1,700, you could curl up every night in a Passy apartment and watch the Eiffel Tower lights twinkling right outside your living room window. Spending €3,000 per month will land you a two-bedroom apartment in a 1930s Trocadéro unit equipped with a dishwasher (*mon dieu!*) and private deck. **Paris Stay** (www.paristay.com) offers a slew of options and takes the fuss out of the rental process—for a price.

Schools and Community Centers

The *mairie* of the 16th (71, avenue Henri Martin, www.mairie16.paris.fr) offers a free booklet listing all of the neighborhood associations. Seniors will find plenty to keep them busy here, but because of the family-friendly nature of the area, activities geared toward children dominate. The 20-page *Guide Jeunes 16ème* lists every public and private school in the area, job-search resources, and student-housing contacts. The 16th might very well be the only arrondissement where private schools outnumber public institutions; for every public *collège,* there are two private schools to choose from. Among them is the **International School of Paris** (www.isparis.edu), which counts Princess Caroline of Monaco's son, Andrea, as one if its alumni. A popular choice among expats with younger children is **l'École Bilingue les Moineaux** (www.

Expat Experience: Living in the 16th

Name: Christopher Horton
Age: 38
Occupation: Software developer
Hometown: Los Angeles, California
Current city: Paris, 16th

How did you find your current home?
I rent a large studio with my girlfriend. We found our apartment via the well-known site **Particulier à Particulier** (www.pap.fr). We tried www.Century21.fr, but the requirements for people just starting their jobs in the trial period were a bit much.

What are some of the factors you considered before moving to this location?
My girlfriend and I didn't have a lot of choices. The owners were looking for a responsible couple and we fit the bill. Our strong references helped a great deal as well. The agencies that we visited required that we have a *garant* to ensure rent payments. We find that the cost of having an apartment is about what you would expect. The area is quite safe and getting into the center is relatively easy via the Métro or by walking. I can get to my job in about 20 minutes door to door.

Describe your quartier to someone who's never been there before.
We live in the lower part of the 16th near the Porte de Saint-Cloud Métro station. Our quartier is extremely diverse. You will find people from all walks of life here thanks to various restaurants, a large and diverse street market, bars, bistros, le Parc des Princes, at least two schools, the wonderful Métro system, and la Seine. The proximity of la Tour Eiffel is also a nice aspect of living here. The neighborhood's character and vibe can be described as typically French. The large street market, which begins every morning until midday, allows everyone to get together and talk. It really does help to allow people from all walks of life to connect.

Is the quality of life in your arrondissement what you expected it to be?
We didn't think much about moving to the 16th at first due to the average cost of rents here, along with the famous posh reputation of the people. Living here for just a few months changed our view for at least part of the 16th. I thought I'd find the people rather reserved given the posh history of the 16th. Perhaps that is still the case in the northern parts of the 16th, like in Passy.

What do you like least about where you live?
I find that l'Administration Français is still the main hindrance to any sort of progress. For example, simply changing the address on your identity card will take months via their registration system, a system put into place to make things *easier*. Administrative tasks seem to take more time here in Paris than in Toulouse, where I have also lived. I guess that is due to the larger population.

What do you like most?
The transportation system, the supermarkets, and the many top-notch restaurants.

ecolebilingueslesmoineaux.com), a bilingual elementary school that accepts children as young as two years old.

Resources
The little-known **Mona Bismarck American Center for the Arts** (34, avenue de New York, www.monabismarck.org) was founded in 2011 and is dedicated to expanding the American art influence in Parisian circles. Volunteering at this museum and education institution is a creative way to make contacts within the formidable expat American community in west Paris.

Getting Around
Car enthusiasts, gather round: The 16th arrondissement is practically **parking paradise.** In addition to street parking, you'll be happy to know there are several secure short- and long-term parking garages scattered throughout the district. If you register with the city and apply for a parking permit, you'll be eligible for a discount of up to 40 percent off the proletariat price for both garage *and* street parking. For more information, visit the city of Paris website (www.paris.fr) and enter "*stationnement*" into the keyword box.

The 16th is served by **Métro lines 6, 9,** and **10,** and by the **RER line C.** Between these four options, you'll be able to reach most of the arrondissement's neighborhoods with a minimum of walking. The RER is a comfortable option, with stops at the sleepy Henri Martin station and the avenue du President Kennedy station, just before the train crosses the bridge over to la rive gauche. Another speedy option is the **PC1,** which plies the inner ring road from Porte de Champerret all the way down to the deep southwest of Paris, stopping at rue de Longchamp, Porte de la Muette, and Porte de Saint-Cloud along the way.

GRENELLE
The **family-friendly** Grenelle neighborhood is in the **15th arrondissement,** south of la Tour Eiffel. The Pont de Bir-Hakeim acts as the gateway from the Right Bank to this quartier and the Métro tracks overhead are your tour guide. Follow them past *boulangeries*, corner cafés, and shops and into the pleasant neighborhoods that comprise the area.

This neighborhood isn't as polished and scrubbed on the outside as the nearby 16th, but it holds a lot of the same appeal, with **community safety** at the top of the list. Because of its proximity to various American institutions including the **American Library, American Cathedral,** and **American University,** the Grenelle neighborhood is popular with (yep, you guessed it) Americans and other **English-speakers.** If you've landed a job or are pursuing academics at one of the Anglophone institutions, the Grenelle neighborhood makes a lot of sense. Plus, it's one of a few neighborhoods where you'll find a celebrated **Poilâne bakery** (49, blvd de Grenelle), known for its delicate sourdough loaves. Buying and devouring fresh-from-the-oven croissants is a neighborhood tradition.

Housing
You'll have **stiff competition** while out combing the cobblestone streets for your ideal Grenelle-area home. Networking your way into a river-view apartment is a smart idea

and it would behoove you to enlist the aid of an agency if you are set on living in this desirable neighborhood.

Vingt Paris (www.vingtparis.com) specializes in executive housing and offers a nice selection of homes for sale and for rent in the Grenelle area. How about a modern, penthouse apartment with its own celebrity-designed rooftop garden overflowing with jungle-like greenery? All 130 square meters can be yours—sweeping views included— for a cool €1.9 million. Working with a more modest budget? The same agency just sold a darling studio apartment for the more-down-to-earth price of €145,000, and with luck, there could be something else like it with your name on it when you're ready to take the real estate plunge.

For students at the American University, there's an entire housing division dedicated to helping you find a place to lay your head for the duration of your study-abroad experience. The university has partnered with a local real estate agency to get you settled in an apartment that meets your needs, whether that's a solo situation or *co-location* arrangement. And, of course, every living space on offer is equipped with that all-important high-speed Internet service. Send your queries to the English-speaking staff at housing@AUP.edu, or call 01/40 62 05 99 to speak directly to someone armed and ready with resources to assist you.

Schools and Community Centers

This corner of Paris brims with American academics, political analysts, and even librarians who serve both the Francophone and Anglophone communities at various American-based institutions, including the **American University of Paris** (31, avenue Bosquet, www.aup.edu) with its nine campus outposts scattered throughout the area.

Resources

The **American Library** (10, rue du Général Camou, www.americanlibraryinparis.org) is noteworthy for its fun, informative, and free monthly events where wine and snacks are always part of the program. The library's old-school bulletin board is a good place to look for leads on housing and jobs, and the speaker events offer some of the best networking opportunities this side of the Seine.

Another networking hotspot is **WICE** (10, rue Tiphaine, www.wice-paris.org), an American-run nonprofit organization offering classes, workshops, and friendly community. At their teeny-tiny headquarters a few paces away from the La Motte-Picquet-Grenelle Métro stop, you can attend art openings, volunteer your time, or just pop in to learn more about the programs and services offered by the dynamic group of expat women and men.

UNESCO (www.en.unesco.org), known as the intellectual arm of the United Nations, has its headquarters here, and is a major employer in the Grenelle area. The UNESCO website should be one of the first stops for job-seekers with global nonprofit experience, and the site also lists leads and resources for apartment seekers.

Getting Around

Public transportation is a big plus, with **RER line C** passing through at the Champ-de-Mars station, as well as **Métro lines 6, 8,** and **10.** The Métro is easy to spot; it's that noisy thing clanging as it charges through on the elevated platforms looming over boulevards de Grenelle and Garibaldi. A dedicated bike lane studded with **Vélib'** stations following the path of the Métro tracks encourages the local populous to get out of their cars and turn-of-the-century sardine cans and enjoy a pleasant commute to the local Monoprix, university campus, or UNESCO office job.

ALÉSIA AND PLACE D'ITALIE

Walking distance from Montparnasse are the pleasant, **family-friendly** Alésia and Place d'Italie neighborhoods. Slightly **off the beaten path,** their out-of-the-way distinction contributes to each district's "authentic" Paris vibe. In both quartiers, you'll find independent butcher shops, *boulangeries*, and stinky cheese stores that further propel that old-timey ambiance, yet each neighborhood is outfitted with all the modern conventions you'd expect in a world-class city like Paris, including department stores, supermarkets, transport links, and tidy, user-friendly green spaces.

Students—and those who appreciate peace and **quiet**—discovered Alésia (in the **13th arrondissement**) and neighboring Place d'Italie (in the **14th arrondissement**) long ago, but these two Left Bank neighborhoods are still mostly unknown to tourists and Parisian outsiders. This is good news for anyone considering settling here, because when the **competition is low,** the odds of scoring the perfect apartment increase.

You'll find these neighborhoods tucked behind—but still within easy proximity of—some of Paris's best features, including Luxembourg Gardens, Parc Montsouris, and the Jardin des Plantes. This so-close, yet-so-far-away feel is what makes these areas so appealing. Alésia sits between Porte d'Orléans on the southern *périphérique* and the Montparnasse Cemetery to the north. To the east is Place d'Italie, the portal to Paris's Chinatown, and beyond, the Porte de Choisy and the A6 motorway leading to the famous forest and château at Fountainebleau.

The Place d'Italie roundabout in the 13th arrondissement gets its name from the road that originates here and stretches all the way to the land of pizza and linguini. For decades, **immigrants from China and other Asian countries** have settled here, subsequently building infrastructure to meet the needs of their community. It's a slightly unexpected yet recommended location for expats. Look past the tall office complexes and thundering roundabout traffic and give this neighborhood a chance to work its charms on you.

Housing

Alésia is a quartier rich with housing possibilities *à la ancienne*—in other words, vintage construction to match the pace of the neighborhood's demographic, which leans a little older. **Subsidized student housing,** in particular, abounds here, partly due to spillover from the nearby 5th arrondissement and its many university campuses. If you're a student looking for roommate situations, check the listings at www.parisetudiant.com.

Graduates will find housing opportunities aplenty on Alésia's staid streets. Stop in and visit a local real estate agent (there are several to choose from on the main commercial drag, avenue du Général LeClerc), or call the numbers listed on the *à louer* and *à vendre* signs affixed to the windows of available dwellings. The price per square meter for buyers is less expensive than in the nearby Quartier Latin, and it's not entirely out of the realm of possibility to find a stand-alone house to call your own here.

The average price per square meter in this neck of the woods is €8,800. Prices creep slightly higher on either side of the adorable rue Châtillon, where old and new

Expat Experience: Living in the 14th

Name: Dan Smith
Age: 62
Occupation: Currently a bon vivant, but previously worked in the pharmaceutical industry.
Hometown: Idaho, followed by New York state and Philadelphia
Current city: Paris, 14th

When and why did you move to Paris?
I moved to Paris in 2004 as a temporary expatriate for my global pharmaceutical company. We are supposed to say "global" but it is really a French company.

In which arrondissement do you currently reside?
In the 14th between Alésia and Pernety.

How did you find your current home?
I found my current apartment, which I rent, on **SeLoger** (www.seloger.com). I made the application myself with the many required documents.

What are some of the factors you considered before moving to this location?
I selected this area because of the proximity to my company's shuttle bus to my place of work in the southern Paris suburbs. Since moving here, I have grown to know and love this area.

Describe your quartier to someone who's never been there.
The 14th arrondissement is what I would call a French middle-class area, not as diversified as other Paris areas but not as "prosperous" as others. It's a working-class area even though the apartments are fairly expensive. The area around Alésia has a wide range of services: *boulangeries, bouchers, fromageries,* supermarkets, cinemas, boutiques, and

construction sit side by side, giving the neighborhood a contemporary flavor. A two-bedroom, 70-square-meter flat built in 1990 and overlooking a public garden will set you back €490,000. Better deals can be found nearer boulevard Brune, otherwise known as the inner ring road. Here, it's possible to find a spacious one-bedroom dating back to the belle époque and oozing period charm (fireplace, wrought-iron balcony) for as little as €275,000. Renting something similar would ring in at the more affordable price of around €800 per month, while something a bit larger and more modern—like a brand-spanking-new 100-square-meter flat currently on the market overlooking Parc Montsouris—will cost you closer to three times as much.

Schools and Community Centers

Throughout the 13th, there are roughly 75 public and private schools open to children ages two and older; a nice cross section of those institutions fall within the Place d'Italie neighborhood. The combination **Collège-Lycée Claude Monet** (1, rue Docteur Magnan) promises a solid education on traditional subjects, only with an extra emphasis on the arts, including music, theater, and classic languages. The private **Group Scholaire de Saint-Vincent-de-Paul** (49, rue Bobillot, www.gs-svp.com) provides a Catholic education to children from elementary school through high school. The more. It's more diverse than my former residence on rue de Vaugirard in the 6th. Everyone establishes relationships and often goes to the same store for daily needs. There is a market Wednesdays and Sundays that I attend. The vendors recognize me and know what I bought before.

Is the quality of life in your arrondissement what you expected it to be?
The quality of life is very good here. I know vendors in the area and have discovered many special boutiques and restaurants that are out of the mainstream of tourists in Paris. There is only one touristic place in the 14th, the Catacombs, where I take guests to view a special macabre experience of ancient Paris.

Describe your experience making friends with neighbors or others in your community.
I have met many people and experienced many one-on-one relationships with vendors, my *gardienne*, and people on the streets. The closeness of living in a city requires a certain level of mutual understanding. Interaction with others, even strangers, makes life special here. At the same time, proximity with others brings conflict. I am often frustrated when tourists, casual shoppers, and families who walk hand-in-hand with toddlers block us fast walkers who know exactly where we are going. Even these negatives seem trivial compared with the benefits.

Have you made any unexpected discoveries in your neighborhood?
Some of the streets and buildings in the 14th have not changed in the last 100 years. I feel like a piece of history living in an apartment where people have lived for 120 years, walking the streets where people have walked for centuries. All I see now will exist a century after I leave. I will become like the others before me, a ghost of the past, a habitant of this quartier forever.

mairie of the 13th (1, place d'Italie) is the best resource for detailed information on the full buffet of academic choices in this part of Paris.

Getting Around

If you really want to own a car, you could do so here without too much trouble. Public parking lots are easy to find, and street parking opportunities are generous. Of course, the smaller your car, the better your chances of finding an on-street parking space. Online portal **Neoparking** (www.neoparking.com) can help find a place to park and even offers the opportunity of pre-booking your spot. Better still, subscribe to **Autolib'** (www.autolib.eu) for a reasonable annual fee and minus all the parking hassles.

Métro lines 4, 5, 6, and **7** serve the Alésia and Place d'Italie neighborhoods. The **RER line B** also whizzes through the area, stopping at Denfort-Rochereau before continuing toward Sceaux and other southern suburbs. The closest long-haul train stations are **Montparnasse** (closer to Alésia), and **Gare d'Austerlitz** (closer to Place d'Italie).

PRIME LIVING LOCATIONS

Transportation

One of Paris's finest features is its **public transportation** system. There is an option for everyone: Métro, bus, bike, boat, taxi, public car share. It's helpful to know that the Île de France is divided into six transportation zones, the most critical to the average Parisian being zones 1, 2, and 3. Zone 1 is Paris, and Zone 2 includes the nearby suburbs. Zone 3 includes the suburb of St. Cloud, while Versailles and Orly Airport are in Zone 4, and Charles de Gaulle Airport and Disneyland Paris are in Zone 5. Way out in Zone 6, you'll find plenty of rolling green farmland and small commuter towns.

On New Year's Eve, all public transportation is free. For access to all the information you could ever hope for, you'll want to visit www.translilien.com. And hooray! It's all available in English. Transportation maps are free from ticket booths in the stations, and wall-mounted maps are plentiful too.

Of course, there's always the tried-and-true mode that nearly everyone can use to navigate the city: **on foot.** Sure, Paris is a big city, but it's also compact. It's possible to walk from top to bottom if you've got several hours to devote to the task, and walking allows you to experience the city in a way you'll never find underground or from the seat on a bus.

TICKETS AND PASSES

The standard Métro tickets are known as the Ticket t+ and cost €1.70 at time of writing. They are valid on trains, buses, and tramways in Zones 1, 2, and 3. If you buy a *carnet* of 10 tickets, you save 20 percent; this is a good deal if you'll be in Paris for just a day or two, and they never expire (though the prices always increase), so buying a bunch and saving them for future travel is a smart idea. Children younger than four travel for free, and those age nine and younger are entitled to *tarif réduit* tickets, which cost half as much as the adult fare. Adults 26 and younger are also entitled to reductions with *jeunes* tickets. If you're going to stay awhile, consider investing in the handy Navigo Pass. This laminated card that you purchase at human-staffed kiosks in Métro and other train stations allows unlimited weekly access on buses, Vélib' bikes, and Métro trains. The tricky aspect of this pass is that once you purchase it, it's only valid between Monday and Sunday. So, if you buy your weekly pass on a Saturday, you get two days of travel. Better to buy your card on Friday, Saturday, or Sunday for the following week. Once you have a card—you'll need to attach a passport-size photo—you can renew it weekly in automated machines in the station (provided you have a credit card with a *puce*).

HOURS

During the week, Métro service begins at 5:30am and ends at 1:15am; on weekends, hours are extended to 2:15am. From 12:30am to 5:30am, the Noctilien bus system's 42 different bus lines will get you most places you want to go in the city. You'll need to time your journey right, however—the buses come every 60 minutes or so, sometimes more frequently on weekends.

BRITTANY

Book a seat on the TGV from Paris heading in the direction of Quimper—that final outpost on the windswept wedge of western France jutting out into the Atlantic—and ride for two hours, and you'll find yourself in the middle of rolling green countryside, thick with conifers, chestnuts, and plane trees, rivers and streams, and beautifully preserved architecture dating back to the Middle Ages. There's so much to love about this section of l'Hexagone, beginning with (but certainly not limited to) the relaxed atmosphere of the region's big cities, including Nantes, Vannes, and Rennes, which l'Express magazine named France's most livable city in 2012. Though Brittany is a short hop away from the French capital in terms of distance, it is worlds away in terms of urban ambience. Where Paris is go-go-go, this corner of France seems to simply say "take it easy." You feel the difference at the local train station, at the *mairie,* and especially in the parks, which aren't pocked with signs reading "No dogs allowed" or "Don't sit on the grass." This area is primarily agricultural in its economic output (10 percent of the French population is employed in Brittany's agricultural sector), but some manufacturing—automobiles and electronics—happens here, as does a whole lot of tourism. The academic community also helps shore up the local economy.

Rennes

Most of France's most livable cities are equipped with a college campus or two, and Rennes is no different. This city of 210,000 supports more than 60,000 students on its many campuses, including a prestigious university dedicated to the study of politics (Sciences Po), with roughly 27,000 of them working toward a degree or diploma at the University of Rennes 1 and 22,000 at the University of Rennes 2. Of that population, 6,000 are foreign students. Each UR campus is dedicated to a different sector within the academic spectrum: UR1 falls under the "sciences" rubric—life medicine, math, and life sciences—and UR2 focuses on the arts, humanities, and social sciences. While this is a city full of young people, their presence is subtle. The urban panorama encompasses the old, young, and middle-aged, all sharing the same dialed-down pace of the Breton capital without eclipsing each other.

Rennes has an interesting history, remnants of which are still very visible in the old city center. In the 9th century, Brittany became an autonomous kingdom, complete with its own language, dress, cuisine, and social customs, and it remained independent until integrating into the rest of France in the 16th century. Today, it still holds firm to its unique cultural roots, which are celebrated through several annual music, art, and theater festivals, including the street theater festival Les Tombées de la Nuit in July and the modern bagpipes-and-beatbox Breton music festival called Yaouank in November.

Rennes is equally compelling from an architectural perspective, with its 18th-century *hôtel de ville,* its renowned 16th-century cathedral, and its 14th-century half-timbered houses, called *colombages.* It's a wonder any of the latter are still standing: In 1720, a devastating fire swept through the streets, burning long and hard for six nights. The fire, which started two days before Christmas, ravaged more than 900 homes on 33 streets in the center of town, leaving thousands homeless.

Today, the *centre ville* is a blend of old and older. Most of the newer architecture has been relegated to the periphery, where the growth holds steady, with new commerce and industry being created to accommodate the needs of an expanding community of students and families. Rennes is very much a city for walking; pedestrian zones dot the city center and a multi-use path along the canal invites strollers, cyclists, and skaters. A solid public transportation system combined with a moderate-size downtown area means having a car isn't a must.

There are lots of tiny details to discover while walking the old streets of Rennes.

THE LAY OF THE LAND

Rennes sits 320 kilometers southwest of Paris, a three-and-a-half-hour drive or two-hour train ride away. In 2016, the rail journey will be whittled down to 90 minutes from Paris, when the new BPL Brittany-Loire Valley high-speed train line between Rennes and Le Mons is completed. The gateway to Brittany is surrounded by sea and countryside, making it an ideal position for weekend getaways. Fifty-five kilometers to the north is that much-visited, often waterless bay that holds Mont St. Michel. To the south, the Golfe du Morbihan, where ancient Celtic megaliths, sailboats, and buckwheat *galettes* washed down with *bolées* of cider reign, is approximately 100 kilometers away by car, or an hour by train. Smack in the middle of rolling green farmland where cows, sheep, and donkeys graze, Rennes also boasts thick forests of sycamore, conifer, chestnut, and apple. Though not all of Brittany sidles up to the sea, a maritime flavor does permeate the region, which you're sure to notice at even the most landlocked *marchés,* where all manner of sea life (lobster, oysters, snails) is up for sale.

Rennes sits at the confluence of the Ille and the Vilaine rivers, in the *départment* of Ille-et-Vilaine. These two waterways are part of an important natural ecosystem and an important tourism infrastructure; the preservation of one supports the other. More than 5,000 kilometers of walking trails, bridle paths, and cycling trails encourage outdoor pursuits here, and the diverse flora and fauna—think egrets, otters, and wild boar—keep the terrain diverse and add to the area's natural allure. Accessing the city by car, you'll enter through one of the 15 *portes* that dot the ring road circumnavigating the city. Porte de Beaulieu (coming from Paris) and Porte de St. Nazaire (arriving from Nantes) are two of the most common entry points.

Throughout the past few decades, Brittany has developed into a favorite expat

© AURELIA D'ANDREA

Central Rennes has the usual amenities—cafes, bars, restaurants, and shops—plus plenty of students, giving the city a youthful vibe.

destination for Britons, who cite a high standard of living, a slowed-down pace, and affordable real estate as the main attractions. Proximity and ease of travel to the UK are another draw; ferries, planes, and trains are all possibilities for getting across the Channel. But even without ties to the UK, Brittany's central location has a particular appeal, especially for history buffs with a thing for the sea. The D-Day beaches are near, dozens of Breton châteaux welcome visitors, and noteworthy lighthouses provide even more grist for the sightseer's mill.

DAILY LIFE

It's hard to describe the pace of a city as relaxed as Rennes. In this college town, you can expect the usual helping of culture: music, art, theater, themed festivals. You'll also find an easy-to-navigate public transit system and a user-friendly urban environment that feels very livable.

Rennes is the 10th-largest city in France, which is to say it's not really all that big, and that's a huge part of its appeal. You can get to know your neighbors here, though be warned: They often head to Paris and elsewhere once their education is out of the way. You'll also learn to invest in a lifestyle that's heavy on urban pleasures (markets, restaurants, art) and light on the bad stuff (Rennes has lower-than-the-national-average crime rates).

One of the city's few drawbacks is that supermarkets are hard to come by; most are on the outskirts of the city center, though there are several Carrefour City markets and Super U stores in the middle of town. The dearth of *hypermarchés* makes getting acquainted with the many daily (except Mondays) outdoor markets and covered *halles* mandatory.

All public signs in Rennes are displayed in both French and the Breton language.

Employment and Education

Rennes' **University 1** (sciences) and **University 2** (arts) are the two important axes of higher learning around which the city's student life revolves. These institutions are the main employers in Rennes, too. Outside the city, **car-manufacturing plants** and **animal-agricultural factories** employ thousands of Rennois. After Paris and Île-de-France, Brittany (and its capital) is the **second most touristed region in France,** which brings money into the community and adds to the cosmopolitan feel. It's not hard to see what people are coming in droves for: Between the tidy, attractive, walkable city center and the great green outdoors beyond the city limits, there's a bit of something for everyone.

Resources

The expat Anglophone community in Rennes is composed primarily of students, so you'll find it skewed slightly younger than its counterparts in other cities throughout France. That's not to say that you won't meet middle-aged men and women from England, Canada, North America and beyond here, because you will—especially if you become a member of the **Institut Franco-Américain** (www.ifa-rennes.org). This cultural organization was established more than a half-century ago to foster intellectual exchange between Americans and Rennois. The nonprofit hosts a variety of entertaining events, from art openings and film screenings to lectures and musical performances, and the membership community is diverse and welcoming. IFA's Facebook page is updated regularly and newcomers are encouraged to attend an informal event to network and make new friends. Because IFA acts as a hub for many local Anglophone events, you're bound to meet others like you—and others who want to get to know anglophones like you.

If you're the type to benefit from a bit of liquid courage before going out and meeting new people, **O'Connell's Irish Pub** (www.oconnellspub.fr) has your name written all over it. While Rennes seems to have an Irish pub on every corner, this hot spot right on the square in front of the Parlement de Bretagne has an edge over the others, thanks to its weekly events—Monday night language-exchange Meetup, concerts, and festive football match screenings—and friendly staff. Pop in for a pint and without fail, you'll leave with a new acquaintance or two.

WHERE TO LIVE

The city is carved into nearly a dozen different districts, some of which are popular with students, others with families, and others with the *bobos* ("bourgeois bohemians," also known as the yuppies of France). Where you settle is contingent on your lifestyle and budget.

Villejean-Université and Pontchaillou

In the northwest quartiers of Villejean-Université and Pontchaillou, **students** will find easy access to student-oriented activities and amenities: *bibliothèques* (libraries), municipal swimming pools, a fully equipped sporting complex, a research hospital, and, of course, a university campus (**University of Rennes 2**). This area is undergoing a long-term urban-renewal overhaul that includes the creation of new apartment communities, expansion of transportation services, and the development of commercial

Tongue-Tied

Language is an important component of every culture, and it's no different in Brittany. The ancient local language, Breton, is alive and well here, as evidenced by road signs, regional television and radio (more than 10 shows are broadcast in Breton), and particularly in the streets in Brittany's villages and urban centers, where 200,000 people speak the language fluently.

Breton's roots are Celtic. Looking at a map, you can see how proximity shaped the local tongue: Breizh (Brittany) sits just beneath western England, and in the 7th century, thousands of Britons—especially from Cornwall—migrated south across the sea to settle in France, bringing their language and customs with them.

At the turn of the 20th century, Breton was banned from schools and French was officially positioned as the dominant language by constitutional decree. Half a century later, the laws relaxed a little, allowing Breton culture and language to be taught once again in public schools and spawning the development of private language institutions throughout the region.

You won't need to understand Breton to get by in Brittany—by law, public signs must now be written in both French and Breton—but still, it can't hurt to learn two important words imbued with deep cultural significance: *krampouez* (crêpe) and *chistr* (cider).

zones. If you want room to breathe in a place that melds modernity and a young sensibility, the northwest is worth considering.

This quartier is more of a **renter's zone** than a buyer's oasis. When an apartment hits the market, it's usually a modern build and lacking that quintessential French charm that so many newcomers are seeking. Still, you can just about bet that the price will be right; the average cost per square meter is €2,500, which might translates to a two-bedroom apartment with balcony and views for around €140,000. Renting here will yield better housing options. A light-filled studio apartment within walking distance of campus costs €400; a bright and cheerful, newly built 60-square-meter, two-bedroom apartment complete with its own parking space could also be yours for €550 per month.

Sacré Coeur and Ste. Thérèse

Directly south of the city center, just beyond the *gare,* you'll find the quartiers of Sacré Coeur and Ste. Thérèse, both of which are highly sought-after neighborhoods for people with a little more money to spend on accommodations. Here, **single-family houses** hide behind green exteriors, sheltering little gardens that make coming home feel like you've entered an urban retreat. Rue des Omeaux is the hot place to buy right now, and the price tags match the demand. Expect to pay around €2,800 per square meter for a house here, half that to invest in an apartment. If you want to (or must) go the economical route, become a *locataire* (renter) and expect to fork out approximately €550 per month for a 40-square-meter apartment.

Thabor

Just north of the city center sits the lovely, English-style garden-park called Thabor, and around it, a comely neighborhood has blossomed, with **upper middle class family**

homes and a few mid-century **apartment complexes** in between them. Thabor is an especially attractive option for **families with children** moving to Rennes, but the nearby University of Rennes school of law means the neighborhood is also welcoming to **students** and other academic types. You'll need to budget a bit more to live here than you would for other neighborhoods, but the proximity to commerce and the low-key suburban feel are worth the price of admission if you like a bit of peace and quiet with your urban lifestyle. Single-family homes begin at about €200,000 and skyrocket straight up to the limits of even a millionaire's budget from there. For €218,000, you could have a tiny stone house that comes with a diminutive backyard and two parking spots. Add a million euros to your budget and you could have yourself a 280-square-meter modern dwelling with a backyard pool and a chic wood terrace. For a better sense of prices in your preferred neighborhoods, visit local newspaper *Ouest France*'s real estate site at www.ouestfrance-immo.com.

GETTING AROUND
Bus and Métro

Even though Rennes is a walkable city with well-maintained *trottoirs* (sidewalks) and a compact city center, the Métro and bus system, known as **Star,** comes in handy when you need to traverse the city quickly. Tickets cost €1.50 and are valid for unlimited journeys within an hour of validation. *Carnets* of 10 tickets cost €13.70, and with a rechargeable KorriGo card, you can choose from a generous handful of travel *formules* that take the hassle out of the local travel experience. Students, seniors, and *invalides* receive discounts as high as 80 percent, so it's worth exploring the Star website (www. star.fr) to peruse your options. If you want to take the leap with a local transport card, you can download the application form online.

The neighborhoods surrounding Thabor park are full of single-family dwellings.

© AURELIA D'ANDREA

Tickets can be purchased from bus conductors, at kiosks in Métro stations, or at businesses marked with a blue sign reading "Star Pointe de Vente." As you access the handicap-friendly Métro, you'll pass small, yellow validation machines; it's imperative that you validate your ticket before entering by inserting it into the small reader. Otherwise, the transit authorities standing sentinel over the exit at your stop will slap you with a fine. Métro hours are 5:10am-12:45am on weekdays (7:30am on Sundays), and until 1:45am on weekends. A new Métro line, Ligne B, is in construction and slated for completion in 2019, which will take passengers from southwest Rennes to the northeast of the city, with 13 stops along 12 kilometers of railway.

Bicycle

The fleet of 900 royal-blue public **VéloStar** bicycles are available at 83 stations around the city, and they work the same way all the other bike-share programs do: by short- or long-term *abonnement*. As always, the first half-hour is free, and €2 an hour for each subsequent hour. If you have a rechargeable KarriGo pass, you can use it to access these bikes 24/7, too. Not every bike kiosk is outfitted with a credit card reader, so if you're planning to pay as you go instead of buying a transport pass, look online (www.levelostar.fr) to find out which of the 10 stations that accept credit cards is near you. You'll find bikes outside the main *gare,* most Métro stations, and at other popular hubs around Rennes and its suburbs.

Train

The glass-paneled, *très* modern main train station, **la Gare de Rennes,** is on the south side of the city center, where it's connected to the Métro and several bus lines. The *guichet* (ticket office) is open Monday through Thursday from 5:40am to 9:05pm (9:15pm on Fridays), with slightly reduced hours on the weekends. From here, you can take the TGV or regional trains to destinations across France and northern Europe. To get to the compact Rennes airport situated 10 kilometers southwest, take bus number 57, which runs to and from the République stop near the *mairie* every 10 to 30 minutes, seven days a week. It'll drop you off at the St. Jacques de la Lande stop, 300 meters or a five-minute walk to the airport.

Vannes

If Vannes were a North American city, it would be Hyannis, Massachusetts (on Cape Cod); or maybe Providence, Rhode Island; or Halifax, Nova Scotia, only without the skyscrapers. Clean, compact, and pretty in a seafaring way, Vannes is surrounded by a lovely body of water bobbing with sailboats and seagulls. With a population of 55,000, this little refuge from France's big-city hubbub has a definite charm. Maybe it's the cute harbor that brings the sea practically to the center of town, or the half-timbered houses pitched at odd angles and painted in candy colors. Whatever it is, you'll get a sense of it as soon as you arrive here. Life in Vannes feels manageable; traffic congestion is nil, drivers stop for pedestrians at crosswalks, and the old town isn't so labyrinthine that you'll get lost trying to find the *boulangerie.* Come for a visit, sit down for a meal of the local specialty—a buckwheat *galette* with a *bolée* of cider—peruse the "*à louer*" ads, and prepare yourself for a shock: Studios for €300? One-bedrooms for €450? Rental accommodations fall on the right side of affordable here, and with the Golfe du Morbihan staring you right in the face, just watch as Vannes's allure increases the deeper you dig into the classifieds.

THE LAY OF THE LAND

With 2,000 years of history and a fortified castle at its core, Vannes stares down at the sea from a thicket of medieval half-timbered townhouses that hem the old cobblestoned streets. This town is small, but you won't find it lacking in much—beyond the theater, cinema, and cafés, tucked in and among the pedestrian-friendly streets, there's even a Monoprix to fool you into thinking you're in a more

Vannes's city center sits on a slight hill brimming with colorful old buildings.

© ERIC D'HEROUVILLE/OFFICE DE TOURISME VANNES

populous metropolis. But no: This bright, orderly little town with a University of Bretagne-Sud (UBS) campus right in the *centre ville* (a second UBS campus is in Lorient, 60 kilometers west), a wealth of restaurants and shops, daily markets, and outgoing neighbors packs the best of France into 71 hectares.

The town, in the *département* of Morbihan, has its own *gare* a 10-minute walk from the *centre ville,* which offers daily trains to Paris and beyond. To the south of the city, accessible by road, paved bike trail, or pebbly walking path, is the Golfe du Morbihan. As you look out to sea, a series of small islands come into focus, beckoning you to pay a visit. This is entirely possible by either ferry or private boat, giving you access to campgrounds, castles, dolmens, and megaliths, all of which are worth building a weekend getaway around. Footpaths for exploring the beautiful countryside abound, and you'll discover unexpected amenities, like cafés, hidden among the seaside greenery. North of the city lies the N165, a small highway that skirts the southern coast, connecting you with the many picturesque villages (including nearby Arradon and Carnac) that make this corner of the country a tourist mecca year-round. The city government oversees and administers the Rives du Vincin, a coastal nature preserve that attracts more than 12,000 visitors each month. They come to walk the groomed footpaths, amble over the rocky seashore, and explore the tidepools dotting the shore. Bird-watching is a popular pastime, too, and the nearby bird-protection zones are a feast for eyes, especially when aided by binoculars.

If you really must leave this little oasis by the sea, Nantes and Rennes are both an hour away by train, and Paris is reachable in three hours by train or in four hours by toll highway. From Vannes, you can also easily access the Loire Valley and its beautiful châteaux, as well as Normandy, with its D-Day beaches and pretty seaside villages.

DAILY LIFE

Even though it is home to a university campus, hotel-industry training school, and several *lycées, collèges,* and elementary-level *écoles,* Vannes doesn't possess the overtly youthful vibe of nearby Rennes. You will notice the local population spans the age spectrum, and that there seems to be a healthy gay and lesbian community, but there's not a lot of cultural diversity here. (It does exist within Brittany, but not so much in Vannes.) What is most palpable is the influence of the Breton culture, which has Celtic roots and is proudly distinct from French culture. Road signs and street signs generally display both the French and Breton languages, and the number of shops vending Breton-specific products (salt, biscuits, edible seaweed) exhibit a pride in these locally produced, culturally significant goods.

Like Rennes, Vannes isn't exactly brimming over with supermarkets, but all your fresh produce can be found at the local covered and open-air markets. At the Place des Lices, in the heart of the medieval city, jousting matches used to be a common spectacle—but now locals jockey for fruits and vegetables at the twice weekly (Wednesdays and Saturdays) market.

Climate

The sun doesn't shine nearly as often here as it does in Nice, but Vannes still gets 2,000 hours of sunshine each year and counts itself among the few French regions with a true temperate climate, meaning it's never extremely hot or cold (though it did dip down to -11 degrees Celcius in 1963!). Summers are particularly glorious, when the afternoon warmth is tempered by cool sea breezes.

Employment

Considering its proximity to the sea, it's not a shocker that Vannes's economy relies on this strategic location to provide locals with their livelihoods. Some of the world's top boating-industry design teams and builders are here—you'll see their headquarters clustered in modern low-rise office complexes along the waterway leading to the bay as you go for your morning jog. **Multiplast** (www.multiplast.eu), the biggest name in the manufacturing of yacht bits and bobs, is located here, and a good place to start your job search if you have seafaring tendencies. They offer a training program to get you started on a nautically inspired career. **Fishing, sea-salt harvesting,** and **sea-vegetable harvesting** also provide jobs within the community. **Tourism** is another major employer, and the **service industry** is a reliable source of jobs as well.

As you meander the old town munching the ripe cherries you just bought at the *marché,* you might notice a selection of empty storefronts that, on the surface, seems to indicate a less-than-thriving economy. But the city's chamber of commerce wants you to **launch your business** there and enables local startups through several programs that offer support, financial and otherwise, to would-be entrepreneurs. If becoming a retail business owner in France is something you've dreamed about, this might be a good place to let your dream set sail.

Resources

The rest of Brittany is loaded with Anglophones, but somehow Vannes escaped the English invasion. If you're desperate for a conversation in your native tongue, take a day trip to Redon or Josselin, where English Meetups are regularly held. Better still, consider starting a language-exchange group to give your skills a workout and meet your new neighbors at the same time.

The three local *mediathèques,* in addition to providing the community with reading material, music, and DVDs, also serve as a center for cultural events, including book readings and live performances of the literary variety. At the Anne de Bretagne theater, invest in a membership to take advantage of year-round performances ranging from classical music to modern dance. A four-show *Le Breizh Pass* subscription costs €48, giving you access to one performance per season. Not-to-be-missed outdoor events include an annual book festival, a jazz festival, and numerous art festivals. At the time of writing, a new Maison des Associations was scheduled to open at the site of a former police academy to serve as a sports center and meeting place for local nonprofit organizations. Keep up with the latest cultural information on the city's Facebook page.

WHERE TO LIVE

It's no secret among would-be home buyers in France that older homes are less expensive than new construction. New homes are more energy efficient, and in a country where electricity rates border on astronomical, this really means something. Herein lies the conundrum for the house hunter: buy an affordable-right-now oldie or a newly constructed, affordable-over-the-long-term place? In Vannes, the choices seem limited to these two options, and nearly all the new buildings in town are houses (versus the older apartments).

Centre Ville

In the **most expensive part of town,** the *centre ville,* finding a charming apartment

Houses with character, like these half-timbered dwellings near the port, abound in Vannes.

with *colombages* will take some work. A better bet would be to settle for something newer—say, constructed within the last 200 years. Limiting your options to "modern" living opens up the possibility for more space, more light, and more energy efficiency. In the **St. Patern** district, a five-minute walk to the *gare* in one direction and five minutes to the medieval center going the opposite way, you could buy yourself an authentic 19th-century, two-bedroom apartment with southern exposure for less than €100,000. Renting that same apartment will cost you approximately €500 per month.

Vannes Ouest

In Vannes Ouest, **modern apartment complexes**—many constructed within the past five years—offer a bevy of living options for those who want more space and more modernity than the city center offers. Some of these places barely register on the appeal chart, but if it's both indoor and outdoor space you're after, this is your neighborhood. A 100-square-meter house with a spacious yard will cost around €300,000, while an apartment of the same size can be rented for €600 per month.

Tohannic

On the other side of town, near the university district, the Tohannic *quartier* is another option for accommodations near enough to the city center to be utterly convenient but far enough away so you don't feel claustrophobic in peak tourist season. The modern look of the **apartment complexes** here aren't to everyone's taste, but for **students,** proximity to the university and the lower prices hold a lot of appeal. A two-bedroom apartment with wood floors and a little balcony in a verdant, 12-unit complex costs €160,000. To rent, you'll need to budget approximately €400 for a contemporary one-bedroom place with a balcony and parking.

GETTING AROUND

Vannes doesn't have a Métro, but it does have **Vélocéa,** a solar-powered public bike-share system with 26 stations that make it easy to access the area's 50 kilometers of cycling paths with a daily (€1, and the first four hours are free), weekly (€5), or annual membership (€28). To travel greater distances, you'll want to familiarize yourself with **TPV,** the 10-line bus system. A mini-*carnet* of four voyages costs €5, and the standard 10-ticket *carnet* costs €11. Tickets are good for an hour's worth of travel after validation in a *composteur*. Monthly and annual Tango passes cost €36.50 and €365, respectively. Discounted student cards cost €26 per month or €234 per year, and senior passes are also available for €110 per year. If you foresee traveling regularly on the train, you'll want to investigate the Uzuël+ pass, which offers steep discounts (75 percent off) to those who travel regularly throughout Brittany by train.

BORDEAUX AND THE DORDOGNE VALLEY

Perfectly positioned between the picturesque Atlantic coast and the rolling green hills of France's most renowned wine-growing region, Bordeaux has a lot to offer expats in terms of leisure activities—but there's more to this area than just fun in the sun with a glass of St. Émilion in hand. With seven universities, an international airport, and a revamped waterfront area that's attracting new businesses, Bordeaux feels young, hip, and alive in every language. This city also has proximity going for it: Just 80 kilometers east—an easy one-hour train ride away—sits Bergerac, a sweet old city with a 21st-century sensibility. The population of 29,000 feels about right, and you'll find all the cultural amenities—movie theaters, restaurants, museums—and an unintimidating small-town feel. Another hour east by train or car is the charming medieval village of Sarlat. Smaller than Bergerac, with a hint more than 10,000 inhabitants, this little oasis smack in the middle of Dordogne castle country has old-world charm and modern-day functionality. This region is particularly well suited to gastronomes who care about such things as fine wine, traditional cuisine (foie gras and truffles are big business around here), and the natural beauty of a riverine environment. The region has long held special appeal to the Brits, lured by cheap flights between the UK

© JOFFREY REVOY

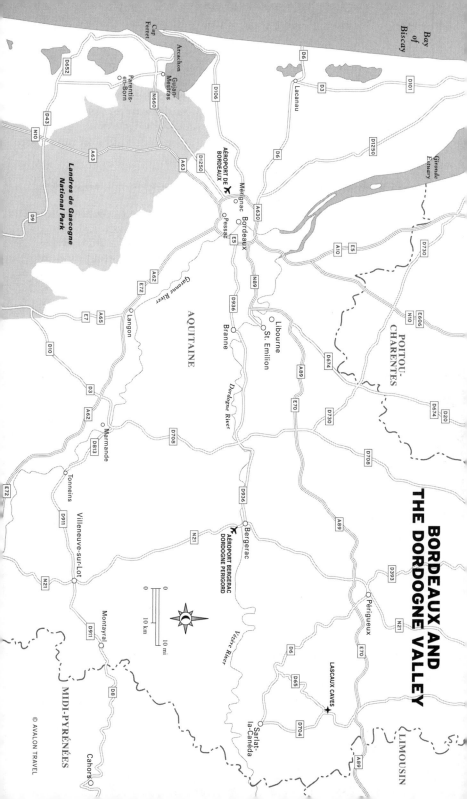

and the local airport in Bergerac, affordable land and housing, and abundant entrepreneurial opportunities. Thinking of opening a bed-and-breakfast? Great idea! Ditto for anything related to the seasonal tourist industry. But think year-round when you're hatching your business plan—tourism slows to a trickle in the wintertime.

Bordeaux

For more than 500 years, Bordeaux has been a magnet for foreign-born émigrés. In the late 15th century, Marranos—Jews who were forced to convert to Christianity but retained their culture and religious practice in private—migrated northward after being expelled from Spain and Portugal. They settled here and started businesses, built synagogues (including France's largest), and otherwise assimilated into the local community. Beginning in the 1600s, wine merchants from northern Europe—the Netherlands, England, and Ireland, in particular—came here to export that magic elixir back to their homelands. Maybe it was the climate, the work opportunities, or the potable potion itself, but these immigrant populations stayed and thrived (take one look at the number of Irish pubs, and you'll know this to be true). In another immigration boom in the '50s and '60s, waves of North Africans came by invitation from the French government to staff the automobile factories and take part in the great postwar economic revival, many staying long after the factories closed to open *épiceries* and other small businesses.

Today, the economy has slowed somewhat, but the city's sparkle hasn't dimmed a bit. Bordeaux is in the throes of an urban rejuvenation that has given it an injection of vitality. You see it when you first arrive at the Gare St. Jean: Step outside, and you'll take in the backdrop of old and new buildings, with a brand-spanking-new tram in the foreground. Pile in with a mixed crowd of locals and out-of-town visitors, heading north toward the city center and its bars, restaurants, museums, and pedestrian shopping districts.

Medieval architecture continues to meet modernity at the photo-worthy riverside promenade, where joggers, cyclists, and *flâneurs* busy themselves as far as the eye can see; and contemporary gardens contrast with the magnificent and massive 18th-century architectural marvel, the Palais de la Bourse. With all the architectural glory mixed with 21st century functionality, it's no wonder Bordeaux was designated a UNESCO world heritage site in 2007. Today, this city of 242,000 is coming down from the high of that honorable designation and doing its best to live up to its revamped image as a truly livable, lovable city.

Diversity is Bordeaux's middle name, and nowhere is this more evident than in the dining scene. From Spanish tapas to Indian biryanis, Brazilian *feijoadas* and even savory vegan plats du jour, there's a culinary destination to fit your craving. Bars—tapas bars, wine bars, and the ubiquitous Irish bars—welcome a hip college crowd and even let the old folks feel OK about hanging out for *un verre* and a morsel or two. Bordeaux has its own special nightlife, and it feels a tad more laid-back than Paris's amped-up version. Relax, sip your elixir of choice, and enjoy the friendly ambience in one of the city's many café-hemmed squares.

Bordeaux resembles the French capital, which is why it's sometimes referred to as "Little Paris."

THE LAY OF THE LAND

Bordeaux hugs both sides of the Garonne River, which spills out into a brackish estuary before it reaches the windswept Atlantic 100 kilometers northwest. Less than 50 kilometers west as the crow flies, sandy and swimmable beaches await, reachable by car and train. Wine country begins as soon as you reach Bordeaux's eastern border and continues for hundreds of square kilometers to the north, east, and south.

Bordeaux is divided into eight quartiers, each with its own flavor: Centre, the administrative heart of the city; St. Michel, an up-and-coming residential district not far from the train station; Bordeaux Maritime, a giant swath of the city to the far north that encompasses the trendy Chartrons neighborhood; Grand Parc, near—you guessed it—the city's largest park; La Bastide, a neighborhood in transition from industrial to residential, which sits across the river from the rest of the city; Victor Hugo, a lively section with cafés and gay-friendly establishments; and Caudéron, north and west of the city center. It's worth spending a day or two wandering each neighborhood to get a reading on what makes it special: Try the cafés, visit the local greengrocer, and, if you're brave enough, talk to the locals about what they like best about their quartier.

DAILY LIFE

Roughly 50 percent of Bordeaux's population is younger than 30, which isn't surprising when you consider there are a dozen universities and other institutions of higher learning in and around the city, and an equal number of primary and secondary schools. Young people have a real stake in this community, and the city has developed programs to ensure that all voices are heard. Yearly municipal campaigns encourage civic engagement by soliciting opinions on local projects and keeping residents abreast of proposed

Popular with students from around the world, Bordeaux offers city-center educational opportunities.

changes that would affect the community before, during, and after implementation. Each year for the last decade, the #JeReleveLeDefi (I Accept the Challenge) program has solicited the opinions of local 13- to 25-year-olds to discover what changes should be made to make their lives better as Bordelais, and to help bring their ideas to fruition with funding and other types of support. Some recent projects born out of the initiative include the creation of an online job board for teens, a public venue where youth could meet to socialize indoors, and activities and events for those young people who don't leave town in August.

For the over-30 segment of the population, life in Bordeaux has the potential to be equally as rich and interesting as it is for the young ones. Besides all the adult pleasures that abound here—especially wine and gastronomy—there are niche opportunities for enjoyment at every turn. Love the outdoors? Bordeaux is within easy reach of forests, lakes, and the seashore, and there are nearly 1,000 kilometers of bike paths in and around the city. Mountains and rivers with all manner of sporty activities are within easy reach, too, and the Spanish border is just two hours away. The temperate climate makes year-round outdoor activities a very real possibility. Whether it's kayaking the Garonne, jogging along the riverside path, or swimming in one of the municipal pools, there's something for everyone. In the culture department, you can choose among film festivals, music festivals, oyster festivals, wine festivals—if you can make a festival out of it, there probably is one in Bordeaux. Can all this fun possibly be part of everyday life? Around here, it can indeed.

Climate

In addition to its UNESCO-designated architecture and rich wine history, Bordeaux has a moderate climate that adds to its overall appeal. It's never too hot nor too cold; snowfall is rare but sunshine is not. Expect rainfall in the summertime, above-freezing days in winter, and a pleasant humidity, thanks to the city's proximity to the Atlantic. The temperate climate resembles that of the San Francisco Bay Area (but with more sunshine and less fog).

Employment

The Bordelais are a happy, welcoming bunch, and why shouldn't they be? Unemployment in the region hovers around the national average of 10 percent, but new jobs are being created, and a new campaign to develop 75,000 jobs in the greater metropolitan area by 2030 is high on the local government's agenda. When you do land that new position, odds are that your workplace will be within a 10-kilometer journey of your front door, as is the case for 75 percent of the people who live here.

The fact that job prospects in Bordeaux look good is no accident. A big "Invest in Bordeaux" (www.invest-in-bordeaux.com) campaign has put the city on the map as a destination for new industry, and it is currently a national leader in **biotechnology** (especially R&D), **high-tech development, education,** and, of course, agriculture—more specifically, **viticulture.** More than 400 **international businesses** are located here, a third of them American-owned, which opens up possibilities for work transfers if you're already employed by **McKesson, IBM,** or **Sanofi-Aventis.** The **international student** population is significant, and if you arrive as a student, you'll automatically be granted work privileges; whether you choose to sling beer in a pub, teach English, or invent a cure for cancer is up to you.

The climate is ripe for entrepreneurship in Bordeaux, and both city and regional government agencies offer plenty of information and resources for locals interested in **launching a business** here. If you have an idea for a start-up, visit the *mairie* for help bringing your project to life with the possibility of grant money and other financial support.

Healthcare

Bordeaux wouldn't be such a livable city without top-notch medical facilities. If you ever get sick or require medical attention here, you'll see what really great healthcare looks like. The local public healthcare network has won Best French Hospital awards, and Hôpital Saint-André is celebrated for its cancer-treatment facilities.

Resources

To help Anglophone newcomers ease into life here, groups such as the **Bordeaux Women's Club** (www.bordeauxwomensclub.com), the very friendly **Association Bordeaux-USA** (www.bordeaux-usa.com), and the **Bordeaux British Community** (www.bordeauxbritish.com) host more potlucks, pub crawls, book clubs, and countryside excursions than you could ever hope to attend. Three times a year, the *mairie*'s office hosts a newcomer's salon to acquaint new arrivals with all that's available. To register for the next *réception des nouveaux arrivants* event, fill out a form online at www.bordeaux.fr.

PRIME LIVING LOCATIONS

Expat Experience: Bordeaux for Beginners

Name: Concetta Lapeyre
Occupation: English teacher
Hometown: Atlanta
Current city: Ambès

American Concetta Lapeyre moved to the Bordeaux area from the United States in 2006. Today, she is the president of the fun and welcoming expat social club, **Association Bordeaux-USA** (www.bordeaux-usa.com). Here, Concetta shares her experience of living in southwest France's cultural capital.

How did you find community in Bordeaux?
In my experience, it takes longer here in the Bordeaux area to establish friendships. I think you will hear that from French people as well; even if the Southwest region attracts people, it does take more time to be accepted. I am fortunate to have married a Frenchman with family and friends in this area, plus he has had another American wife, which meant he knew about some resources already. When I came in 2006, Association Bordeaux-USA was my first choice, because it included a mix of Franco-Americans, Franco-Anglophones, and many other expats. I was anxious to learn more about living in France and French customs and culture while also being able to interact with other Anglophones, not to mention learning the language. I also took French classes at **DEFLE** (the department for French as a foreign language studies, or Département d'Etude du Français Langue Étrangère), which helped me feel more integrated, and I joined **Bordeaux Women's Club.** Also, now we have the **International Club of Bordeaux** (ICB), which started in 2013. All three offer memberships and opportunities to become involved in running the club or its events and activities.

In the years you've lived in Bordeaux, what discoveries have you made?
There's history everywhere! I just have to look out my front window to see a historic château. We live in Ambès, a tiny village north of Bordeaux, on my husband's family's land. They used to live in the Château Lansac, which is more than 300 years old. Also, vineyards, vineyards, vineyards! Both for the obvious reason—wine—and the being able to spend time in nature. I also appreciate the convenience of living one hour from the Atlantic coast and two hours from the Pyrénées...not to mention being just six hours from the Mediterranean coast!

What can newcomers expect when they join the Bordeaux-USA community?
We are a French association promoting Franco-American friendship. Our main objective is to share Franco-American culture and language with residents of La Gironde. Our membership is 70 percent French and 30 percent American, British, and other nationalities. We encourage people to come to a couple of meetings before they actually join. The most striking aspect about this association is that it's a friendly environment to learn and practice both French and English while learning something about a variety of subjects that are pertinent to French and Anglophones alike. We offer conversation groups four times a week, weekly presentations in English on a variety of topics, a monthly potluck dinner, a book group, film discussions, a Thanksgiving dinner and 4th of July picnic. In addition, the association has a library of over 4,000 English books and DVDs, which members can borrow free of charge. For more information about events and schedules, you can find us at www.bordeaux-usa.com and on our Facebook page.

WHERE TO LIVE

You can expect to pay a lot less for more living space here than you would in Paris: a one-bedroom (*deux-pièces*) a 5-minute walk from the train station and a 15-minute walk to the center of town costs about €600 per month. A two-bedroom in the shadow of that gothic looker, Cathédrale Saint-André, will set you back about €900. Looking to buy? In the heart of the city, in the antiques district of Chartrons north of the city center, one-bedroom flats start at about €150,000, but you could also buy a house here for upwards of half a million euros. Prices drop as you move out of the city center and away from the three primary tramlines.

Bordeaux's population is expected to increase by 30,000 by 2019. To meet the housing needs of this expanding population, city planners have set a goal of building 50,000 new dwellings in and around Bordeaux. The city also offers financial aid to first-time homebuyers who want to make Bordeaux their primary place of residence through **Passeport 1er Logement** (a program that offers tax breaks and other financial incentives to new homeowners that's worth investigating wherever you choose to settle). But before you sign up, get to know a sampling of the city's diverse residential neighborhoods—you'll find a mélange of housing, from single-family dwellings to modern, energy-efficient lofts and everything in between.

Chartrons

Northeast of the city center sits Chartrons, the city's onetime industrial hub, transformed today into a **pleasant neighborhood** with lots of antiques shops, cafés, and residential housing. For centuries, the wine trade lived and breathed here. Ships from England, Ireland, and the far reaches of Northern Europe would sail up the Garonne, park in the docks, and load up with that locally grown elixir of the gods, *vin,* before setting sail back down the river toward home. The edifices of local buildings are decorated with wine motifs—clusters of grapes, curlicued vines—and locals and visitors alike relish walking around to ogle the architecture. Residents of this quartier have the benefit of being positioned between tramlines B and C and close to several museums, a skate park for kids, and a popular covered market. On Thursdays along the quay, an open-air organic market welcomes shoppers to pick out plums, tomatoes, and grapes.

Laying down roots here is a smart idea. At least 60 percent of the Bordeaux population thinks so: That's the percentage of residents who own their own homes, several points above the national average. In Chartrons, **housing prices are slightly higher** than in bordering neighborhoods, but then, this is prime Bordeaux. Price per square meter for buyers is approximately €2,300. For €205,000, you could buy a modern two-bedroom apartment with a huge terrace and a dedicated parking place. For €400,000, you'll be able to afford a mid-20th-century, four-bedroom house with a fountain in the backyard and that urban rarity, a garage. If you'll be renting, count on spending between €400 and €500 for a studio, and €550 and €700 for a one-bedroom with all kinds of old-world charm.

Victor Hugo-St. Michel

Since medieval times, this quartier has housed the bulk of Bordeaux's **small specialty businesses.** Bordered by the Stade Chaban-Delmas to the west and the Garonne to the east, this neighborhood has a strong **Spanish influence** that you'll feel in the streets from shops and restaurants, the chatter that fills the air, and the cosmopolitan vibe. Try smoking a hookah in a Moroccan tea salon, sipping mint tea in a Turkish café, and shopping at North African markets. Six days a week, in front of the St. Michel church at the Place de Cantaloup, there's a funky flea market where clothes, books, records, chandeliers, garden tools, and just about anything else you might want is on sale and ready to be bargained for. Surrounded by cafés, this cute square has several eating and drinking spots where you can sit outside and watch the parade of people as you dine on tapas and sip a cool rosé.

Finding a place to settle in this neighborhood is easier than in Chartrons. It's slightly **younger,** and slightly rough around the edges, but that's bound to change with the gentrification that hits most neighborhoods at some point. Living spaces here are older and haven't been renovated to the same extent as those in Chartrons. This means they're smaller, but the **prices are considerably lower.** You could rent a light-filled, 40-square-meter one-bedroom apartment for around €550 or buy a similar-size space for around €170,000.

La Bastide

La Bastide could be called the Park Slope, Brooklyn, of Bordeaux, only much less expensive and with a smaller, prettier waterfront view. La Bastide wasn't incorporated into the city of Bordeaux until the 19th century. In its earlier incarnation, this section of town was looked down upon by the inhabitants of the other side of the river; for a long time, it was a factory-clogged quartier with a raucous reputation for shady cabarets and prostitution. Today, the *rive droite* neighborhood is a lot less disorderly and a lot more tame. Newcomers will find La Bastide making a name for itself as a pleasant—and

© AURELIA D'ANDREA

Chartrons, one of the most charming neighborhoods in Bordeaux, is north of the center, hugging the river.

some might say sleepy—**residential oasis.** Just a 10-minute walk, five-minute bike ride, or two-minute tram trip across the pedestrian- and cycle-friendly Pont de Pierre, this former warehouse neighborhood is now home to cute bistros, little boutiques, and a beautifully landscaped botanical garden full of modern sculpture. For **families,** La Bastide is a welcoming place with schools for children of every age; the riverside Parc des Berges, with plenty of room for play and family picnics; and enough shops and services to keep you on your side of the river for weeks on end.

If you want **a lot of space for not a lot of money,** this is the place to launch your search. For €300,000, you could have yourself a 100-square-meters, three-bedroom house built in 1900 with a remodeled kitchen, parquet floors, and fireplaces. An old three-bedroom house with a big garden loaded with flowering trees and bushes will set you back about €830 per month; a new build of the same size near the tramline will cost a couple hundred more per month.

GETTING AROUND

A major component of Bordeaux's urban renewal project was the installation of a modern **tram system,** inaugurated in back in 2003. The tramway crisscrosses the city from north to south and east to west in three simple lines: A, B, and C. Line C is currently undergoing a major extension project to better serve the communities north and south of the city center. Trains run as early as 4:20am until as late as 1am, and single tickets (€1.50) can be purchased from manual kiosks at the tram stops and directly from the driver if you have cash. Daily, weekly, and bulk-journey passes called Tickartes can be purchased at automated kiosks, at *tabacs,* or by mail directly from the local transport system, TBC (Tram et Bus de la CUB). A seven-consecutive-day pass will cost you

A standard bus or tram ticket will also buy you access to the little boats that ferry you across the Garonne River.

€12, the same price as a *carnet* of tickets good for 10 trips. A yearly pass costs €420. Discounted passes are available to job seekers, senior citizens 60 and older, people age 26 and younger, and *familles nombreuses* (families with multiple children).

A **bus system** with nearly 90 different lines—connected to the tram system—is another option for getting around. You can travel on the same tickets as you use for the tramline, and the buses go farther afield. Transportation maps are available on the TBC website, www.infotbc.com. Don't forget to validate your card when you get on the tram. Like a lot of things in France, the transportation network is run on the honor system, so do the right thing! The penalty for riding ticketless or for not validating your ticket is only €5, but you don't want to have to go there—or pay that—if you don't have to. If you want a free ride, hop one of the little boats, or *"navettes fluviales"* that take you across the river. You pay nothing for that journey with a valid transport ticket.

If you're feeling spunky, you might want to try out **VCub,** Bordeaux's public bicycle system, with 155 stations positioned near tram and bus stops and at the train station. Like Paris's Vélib', VCub is both convenient and affordable: A one-day membership costs €1.50, or get a whole year for €30. The first 30 minutes of each trip are free, then you pay €2 per hour for each subsequent hour.

Bergerac

Hop on one of the 8 daily trains that depart Bordeaux's Gare St. Jean east into the Dordogne Valley, and €17.70 and an hour and 15 minutes later, you'll be in Bergerac, a hospitable little town of 29,000 on the banks of the Dordogne River. While not the prettiest town in the Dordogne, Bergerac does have its charm, and because of its wealth of amenities, it has established itself as an important hub in this picturesque and highly touristed river valley.

THE LAY OF THE LAND

Bergerac, the gateway to the beautiful châteaux country of the Dordogne Valley, is surrounded by tobacco farms and vineyards. It straddles two sides of the Dordogne, but the city's heart rests on the north side of the river, where you'll find the train station, *mairie,* tourism office, and oodles of restaurants and cafés. Venturing outside the city limits, you'll find yourself in verdant countryside dotted with lakes, streams, and farmland. In town, there are friendly neighbors and plenty of diversions to keep you occupied all year round.

You will definitely *not* be the first Anglophone to make your mark in this corner of France. Expect to find a surprising degree of multiculturalism and cosmopolitanism, but with an alluring small-town feel. Winding little backstreets with half-timbered medieval houses will make you feel like you're wandering around Disneyland France, but the skateboarding teenagers remind you that this is no fantasyland. The British invasion that peaked here in the '90s has calmed down quite a bit, though you'll likely hear English spoken in unexpected places, like the tailor shop, on the bus, or in a quiet bistro. The town movie theater is popular but, sadly, plays dubbed versions of English blockbusters more often that it does VOs (*versions originales,* i.e., English-language

© JOFFREY REVOY

Bergerac comes alive in the summer, with festivals spanning the spectrum from music and wine to food and dance.

films) with subtitles. This might be just the impetus you need to get serious about your French lessons once and for all.

Bergerac's twice-weekly (Wednesday and Saturday) outdoor organic markets aren't only for picking up fresh flowers, fruit, vegetables, cheeses, and other edibles, but also for community socializing. It's here that you'll learn who your new neighbors are, what their current preoccupations are, and be caught up on all the local gossip. If your new hometown ever starts to feel too small, hop a train to Bordeaux or Toulouse to get your city fix, then return with a newfound appreciation for your little village in the valley.

DAILY LIFE
Climate

Never mind truffles, wine, and natural beauty: The Dordogne Valley's weather is really something to get excited about. One of four distinct seasons rises up to greet you every three months, and each seems nicer than the next. Summers are bright and warm, with breezy afternoons and beautiful sunsets. The occasional thunderstorm brings a cool blast of meteorological excitement to a typically balmy summer day, but they're generally short-lived, blowing in and out before your picnic is completely ruined. Snow isn't common, but frosty winter mornings are. Pack your gloves and your caps; you'll learn to cherish them come January.

Employment and Education

As in any small town, employment opportunities aren't as plentiful here as they are in the big cities. Still, finding work is possible. There are **seasonal jobs** in **tourism,** as well as in **agriculture.** A job board outside the Centre Information Jeunesse, at Place de la République, has listings for all kinds of employment, and you can visit the center's website for more leads: www.info-jeune.net. **Construction workers** and **skilled laborers** in that arena are in luck—that is one stable area of employment for the entire region. **Independent professionals** whose office consists of a laptop and a cell phone will be happy to know that Bergerac has a reliable telecommunications system to help you and the rest of the region's mobile workforce get the job done.

From sliding-scale *crèches* to private music lessons, all of your children's educational needs will be met in Bergerac. Of the 18 elementary schools, two are private; two of the five *lycées* is also private, as is one of the four *collèges*. Yoga, painting, swimming, and horseback riding are just a few of the other educational possibilities. The one exception here is higher education: To start—or finish—your university degree, you'll have to commute to Bordeaux.

Healthcare

You'll never be too far from a medical professional in Bergerac. The city has three hospitals and countless dentists, opthamologists, kinesiologists, and ear, nose, and throat specialists. At the Clinique Pasteur in the *centre ville,* surgery is the specialty, particularly orthopedics. For more pedestrian maladies, the public Centre Hospitalier Samuel Pozzi is the place to go. Babies are birthed here, X-rays are administered and examined, and laboratory tests are analyzed. Long-term care is also offered.

Resources

The best resources for expats settling in Bergerac can be found at the *mairie,* where the staff can tell you about home-buying tax breaks and other incentives, provide you with printed information about the city's services, and answer all of your questions about relocating here.

The Dordogne section of **French Entrée** (www.frenchentree.com) is packed with interesting and informative articles on life in this area, including information on local real estate, putting your kids in local schools, adapting to the region as an Anglophone, and how to find the best local services.

WHERE TO LIVE

One of the nice things about this patch of France is that even in the city center, you can still *tell* you're surrounded by countryside. It's practically guaranteed you won't feel that suffocating "Get me out of here!" panic that some Parisians are prone to after a long workweek. Life in this region has a perpetual vacation feel, partly due to the green and pleasant surroundings, and partly due to all that wine. Settling in the heart of the city rather than in the rather suburban-feeling outskirts frees you of dependence on automobiles—the local bus system and SNCF train can take you all the places you need to go. You become more integrated with your community when you view it on two feet rather than from the inside of your *voiture* (car). The most quaint and interesting part of town is the *centre ville,* northwest of the river. The medieval backstreets lean into each other over quiet pedestrian walkways, and neighbors greet each other with a familiar *"Bonjour!"* on their way to and from the *boulangerie.* You'll learn to appreciate the ancient architecture—the arched doorways, the solid stone edifices, the fountains—and feel at home. If you want to make friends and feel part of a cozy community, restrict your home search to the center of town rather than the outskirts. When you want more breathing room, bring the dog out for a run along the green stretches at the river's edge. Perhaps you'll even take up kayaking and make use of the famous river.

The cost of living in the center of town borders on affordable. For around €400, per month, you could live in a generously proportioned, modern one-bedroom in a newly built complex with a communal pool. Don't forget, though: You've got to find a job that will *pay* that bargain-basement rent once you're here. If you're in the market to buy a home, the choices are immense, with something possible to fit nearly every imaginable budget. We're talking houses starting at €30,000 (but don't get your hopes up too high, this is a tiny two-bedroom in need of work) on the low end, moving all the way up to five-bedroom villas for 10 times that much (or more). Deciding whether or not you want to depend on a car should factor highly into your house-hunting decision. The bus system is OK here, but it's not the Paris Métro.

GETTING AROUND

The local *gare* (train station) is a 10-minute walk from the *mairie* in the town center. From here, trains running west to Bordeaux depart nearly every hour, with the final train leaving at 7pm. Heading east toward Sarlat, trains leave every three hours. Taxis and rental cars can also be hired at the station. **Aeroport Bergerac** is four kilometers outside of town and offers direct flights to London and Paris. Footloose and car-free? Bergerac has three **Les Transports Urbains Bergeracois** (TUB) lines to get you where you need to go. Tickets cost €1 individually or €6.50 for a *carnet* of 10. Students and underemployed folks get a steep discount, and weekends, beginning Saturday at 1:30pm, is free for all. Weekly, monthly, and annual passes are also available. Single tickets can be purchased on the bus, and you can buy your pass at the tourist office, *mairie,* or youth center.

Sarlat-la-Canéda

Sarlat-la-Canéda, commonly referred to simply as Sarlat, is positively mobbed with tourists in the summertime, and it's no wonder: This town of 10,500, founded in the 9th century, is charm central. Its earliest community was anchored to the Benedictine monastery, but populations dwindled during the Hundred Years' War, followed by the Black Plague. In the 1960s, Sarlat got a major makeover to bring back its shine after years of neglect, and after 25 years of ongoing structural revamps, the town grew into a major tourist hub.

THE LAY OF THE LAND

Two hours north of Toulouse and two-and-a-half hours from Bordeaux, Sarlat is well positioned for those who like the feeling of living in a rural small town but like to have big-city conveniences within reach. Just outside town, you'll find yourself surrounded by lots of greenery, full of walking paths suited to every fitness level. The Dordogne River is a good 10-kilometer drive south, and that other picturesque river, the Vézère, is equidistant to the north. The terrain rolls gently in these parts, making it superb cycling territory.

Sarlat is small. *Really* small. There aren't neighborhoods as such, simply "in town" and "outside of town." Living *in* town affords you all the benefits this beautiful part of France has to offer: delicious, locally grown food; arts and entertainment; cafés and shops; and the quintessential outdoor market experience. Why live outside of town when you can hop on your bike and get your nature fix anytime you want it? One of the joys of living here is getting to know your neighbors and involving yourself in civic life, but if Green Acres is what you want, that can be found here, too.

Sarlat's city center is compact and oh-so-charming. What's not to love about medieval cobblestone squares hemmed in by umbrella-shaded café chairs, occupied in turn by happy locals sipping an afternoon *bière pression*? The town may be diminutive, but there's a subtle sophistication here, and a friendliness among locals that hasn't been diminished by the swarms of summer tourists who invade each year. The farther you move away from the *centre ville,* the more modern the architecture becomes, losing a bit (but by no means all) of its allure. If you want a slice of vintage, postcard-perfect Sarlat, confine your house hunt to the center of town, moving out if you must—but not too far.

The area north and west of Sarlat is equally beautiful, with castles, adorable restaurants, and touristy little shops wedged in among the more utilitarian butcher shops and *fromageries.* Exploring the rich historical heritage of the surrounding communities is a weekend activity that never turns mundane or boring.

DAILY LIFE

With 500-year-old cobblestones paving the streets and modern suburban convenience on the periphery, Sarlat has everything you need—plus wine and truffles, a festive Saturday morning market, and a Thursday afternoon organic market that lures shoppers from kilometers around. In the summertime, the place crawls with tourists who come to ogle the medieval architecture, sit and sip a foamy beer in one of the many quintessentially French cafés erected on the ancient squares, and luxuriate in the heady ambience of this pleasing village. If you live here, you'll find that the tourists are a mixed blessing. On the bad side, it can feel suffocatingly crowded; but on the good side, if you happen to run a tourism-related business, your income can multiply many times over throughout June, July, and August.

Employment

To make a go of living in Sarlat, you'll have to add a dash of realism into your dreamy, castles-and-cobblestones dream. **Jobs are not plentiful** here the way that they are in Bordeaux to the west or Toulouse to the south. If you're coming here without a mobile income stream or retirement funds, you'll want to examine the options that are left, which primarily include **seasonal jobs** in the **hospitality** industry. From May through September, the town hums with tourist activity, and local business—gift shops, hotels, bars—bring in extra hands to get through the season. Once the visiting masses head home from their summer vacations, Sarlat morphs once again into a sleepy—but still utterly delightful—little fairytale village, and some shops shut down entirely.

So, you're not a home-based entrepreneur nor a retiree who doesn't need to rely on

Mushroom Madness

Every now and again, you hear a cautionary tale: The hapless mushroom gatherer—or was he a stealthy bandit?—in search of the gold nugget of the fungi family, the truffle, meanders a little too far over on property that doesn't belong to him. The next thing he knows, an angry, occasionally firearm-wielding neighbor is standing before him, ready to take it to the next level. (The latest incident, in 2010, resulted in the death of one such truffle hunter.)

The business of truffles and other fancy fungi is big in the southwest of France. Each winter in the Dordogne Valley town of Sarlat, a truffle festival launches the seasonal truffle market, where the "black diamonds" can fetch as much as €1,000 a kilo. The region has its own *trufficulteurs* union, and it depends on truffles and other mushrooms to keep the local economy afloat. Trespassers who've been caught foraging on land that does not belong to them have had to answer to the local authorities—something you definitely don't want to do, whether you're on vacation or living in your new hometown.

If you haven't been frightened away from the idea of hunting for your own wild 'shrooms, follow these rules for drama-free foraging.

- **Seek permission.** If you're unsure whom the property where you'd like to forage belongs to, go to the *mairie* and ask.

- **Make sure your mushrooms are mature.** In order to reproduce, fungi have to release their spores, which they can't do if they're picked prematurely.

- **Pack a knife.** You'll need it to cut your 'shrooms. (Pulling is not allowed.) Tools other than knives are *interdit* (forbidden) by the mushroom-hunting rulebook.

- **Carry a basket.** Putting your freshly foraged gems in a basket allows the spores to escape and reseed the earth for future generations of fungi.

regular outside income? One option for you to consider—and mind you, you will not be the first to do this—is opening a *gîte* or B&B. You could also **start a business**—a café, a tourism company—and you'd be extra welcome to lay down those money-generating roots if it meant hiring locals to help you out. Some who settle here take **domestic jobs,** such as au pairs, gardeners, pool maintenance people, or a combination thereof. Check in with the local **Pôle Emploi** (employment agency, 89, ave. de Selves) for leads and support.

WHERE TO LIVE

If you've come up with the brilliant idea of buying an old stone cottage, fixing it up, and opening a quaint little B&B in this corner of the Dordogne, you wouldn't be the first. That doesn't mean there isn't room for one more, but choosing where you settle should—as always—be done with great care; after all, how can you welcome guests at your abode if they can't find it out there in the countryside? Choosing to live in the center of town opens up the possibility of integrating with the local community, making friends you'll see on a daily basis, and feeling, well, more French. Settling farther afield in this lush and fertile area is tempting; who wouldn't want a place with a big garden, swimming pool, and barbecue for summer grilling? If you decide to chuck village life in favor of Green Acres, you'll need a car, and investing in a bike for short trips to the *boulangerie* isn't a bad idea either.

In Sarlat's historic *centre ville,* properties tend to be a little more expensive than in some neighboring areas, probably because there's only so much to choose from. You'll pay about the same for a four-bedroom home inside the city's old fortified walls as you would for a house with a pool and huge yard in the surrounding countryside. For a two-bedroom apartment, expect to plunk down €150,000, and throw in additional €50,000 for a small house with a yard. With a bigger budget, your options increase, as do opportunities to acquire something with a bit of regional character. It's still possible to find fixer-uppers for less than €50,000, but make sure you're fully aware of what you're getting into before you throw down your hard-earned euros, or you may end up spending double that to make your newly acquired abode habitable. If you go the city-center route rather than the more rural one, you'll have excellent renting potential in July and August, when tourist accommodations are at a premium and weekly rents are as high as you'd pay per month the rest of the year. Renters lucky enough to find a long-term rental in the medieval city center can expect to pay between €500 and €600 per month for a one-bedroom apartment.

GETTING AROUND

If you move to Sarlat, you'll want a bicycle, motorbike, or car to explore the lovely areas outside city limits: Lascaux and its famous prehistoric cave; the Dordogne and Vézère Rivers for swimming, canoeing, and picnicking; nearby castle towns Beynac, La Roque-Gageac, and Domme for cobblestone rambling. If you're a homebody, you can rely on the local Transperigord's 10-line bus system to ferry you around. Buses leave from the Place Pasteur and a few other spots in town, heading north toward Perigueux (1 hour) and Souillac (40 minutes) to the west, stopping at towns and hamlets along the way. Tickets cost €2 per trip, €1 for those 25 and younger. You can buy a *carnet* of 10 trips for €14, or opt for the monthly pass for €40.

PAU, TOULOUSE, AND MONTPELLIER

One of the most alluring prospects of moving to an urban environment in France is finding a villagelike community atmosphere that gives you the best of both small town and big city France in one neighborhood. At least three cities in the southwest of the country offer opportunities for laying down roots and carving out a life enhanced by good neighbors, fresh food, efficient public transportation, and that small-town-within-a-city feel: Pau, Toulouse, and Montpellier.

The smallest of the bunch is Pau, a sweet little city of 80,000 perched on the edge of the meringue-peaked Pyrénées. With its fresh air, sparkling views, and mild climate, it gives off an outdoorsy vibe all year round and holds the promise of an activity-filled future for anyone who settles here. With its fine museums, thriving local food-and-wine scene, and rich history harkening back to bygone royal eras (Henry IV was born at the chateau here in 1553), there's plenty to keep history-loving intellectual types engaged here, too. Families are attracted to the region for its plethora of opportunities for school-age kids, and the local university has long been a draw for international students torn between getting an education in Spain or in France; in Pau, you feel both

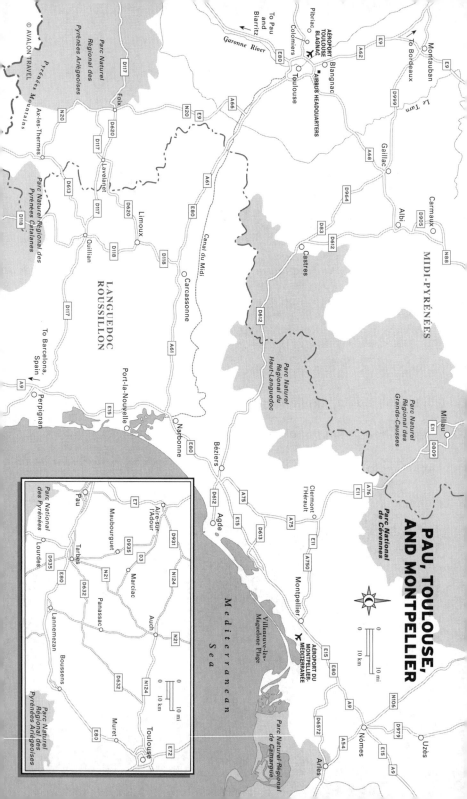

the Basque and Spanish cultural influences, which isn't surprising when you consider that Spain is just 35 kilometers away.

In the eastern edge of the Midi-Pyrénées region, in the *département* of Haute-Garonne, bigger, busier Toulouse awaits. Sandwiched between giant expanses of undeveloped wilderness and the craggy peaks of the Pyrénées, this regional capital city boasts a population of 450,000 (a fifth of whom are students at Toulouse's many higher-education institutions) and hosts an enormous expat population. Many of these newer arrivals are employed in the aeronautics industry, especially at Airbus, which has its headquarters just outside the city in the northwest suburb of Blagnac. Weekly language Meetups in town draw droves of Anglophones and their French friends in the high-tech community, plus students and others who like the international flavor of the group gabfest. If you must live among fellow English speakers, you'll find yourself surrounded and content here.

Cross into the Languedoc-Roussillon region into the *département* of Herault, and inch over in the direction of the Mediterranean, where Montpellier welcomes with its bright, cheerful, youthful energy. This isn't the postcard-perfect Mediterranean (the coastline is interrupted by kilometers of brackish ponds and the occasional power plant), but never mind. It's still gorgeous, sunny, and not too hilly, which makes it perfect for rambling, ambling, and exploring. For cyclists, students, and wine aficionados, Montpellier is an ideal base for the short or long term.

Pau

In 2014, *Forbes* magazine featured Pau in an article on the best places to retire, based on its low crime rates and mild climate. Even without the money magazine's seal of approval, you'd probably agree that Pau is a pretty pleasant place, for a day, a year, or a lifetime.

Since the turn of the 19th century, Pau has welcomed expatriate anglophones, who virtually colonized this corner of France, turning it into a mini-UK outpost in the heart of the Pyrénées Atlantique. The English in particular—but also Welsh and Irish—arrived here in droves by boat and then by train to take the "water cures" from nearby thermal springs and to take a literal breather from life in what has been considered by many the "ideal" climate. With four distinct seasons boasting temperatures that rarely dip to freezing in winter nor climb beyond 80 degrees Fahrenheit in summer, and with crisp, unpolluted air blowing in off the mountains, it's easy to see how the area's reputation as a health retreat was born.

THE LAY OF THE LAND

Pau sits at the very bottom of France, butted up against the mountains without actually being in them. While Pau has its share of hills, you'd be pressed to refer to the area as "foothills." From a park bench or terrace café on the boulevard des Pyrenees, you get a sweeping panorama that puts Pau's place into perspective; from here, one is close enough for great hiking and mountain biking, but not so close that you'll need to dress like an Inuit to survive the winters.

Heading west from Pau along the A4 toll (*péage*) road is the bright, sunshiny coast and the popular summer vacation towns of Biarritz and Bayonne. The trip to the sea is 125 kilometers and takes an hour and a half by car or by train. If you plan to drive, you can find up-to-minute information on toll fees and auto route advice at www.autoroutes.fr. A 40-minute ride southeast brings you to Lourdes, the celebrated pilgrimage place for followers of the Catholic faith. It's worth at least one visit here, if only to marvel at the parade of pilgrims marching (and often rolling by in wheelchairs) through the streets lined with religious tchotchke shops.

Daily flights from Paris to Pau can be had for as little as €50 each way, and the local train station will ferry you in from Bordeaux or Toulouse in 2.5 hours.

Local ski bus service SKIBUS64 makes it easy to become a regular on the local slopes, offering roundtrip service to the resorts with pass included for between €22 and €30. (Some buses even throw in a free coffee and croissant for the ride up.) Twenty-five ski resorts are within a three-hour drive of central Pau; just over the other side of the Pyrénées sits Spain, a popular getaway destination for not only those hankering for authentic tapas washed down with glasses of Rioja but a change of language and scenery. Some Palois, as locals are called, prefer to stay put, and why not? Pau is a self-contained city that feels like a vacation destination. You'll discover nearly 800 hectares of parks and gardens within the city limits—20 percent of the overall city space—which has earned the city a coveted "Greenest Cities of France" designation. Mayor (and former presidential candidate) François Bayrou reiterated his commitment to keeping Pau green throughout his election campaign in 2014, which might be one of the reasons he won the city's top spot.

Exploring Pau on foot is the best way to get a feel for the city. By car, the one-way streets and dead-end roads can be both confounding and confusing, and the hills can be daunting for cyclists new to the area. On foot, you can explore the pedestrian streets of the *centre ville* in a relaxed way, popping inside shops that catch your fancy or nipping into a café for an afternoon pick-me-up without being preoccupied with locking your bike or finding parking (though if you do decide to drive, many paying car-parks and individual spaces in the city center are free on weekends).

When taking your first few promenades, you'll undoubtedly make your way to the boulevard de Pyrénées, where palm trees and belle époque apartments face out onto sweeping views of the majestic 9,000-foot Pic du Midi d'Ossau and other impressive peaks of the southerly mountain range. From here, walking west, you'll bump into the local château, which functions as a museum; head east and you'll eventually find yourself at the Palais Beaumont, an arts and music center with an auditorium that hosts classical and other performances. The Palais sits inside the enormous and very pleasant Parc Palais, where locals walk their dogs, play with their kids, and enjoy the delicious air. A picnic beside the lake comes highly recommended.

DAILY LIFE
Employment and Education

If you're considering a move to Pau, the odds are good you've already got a job here—maybe at Centre Scientifique et Technique Jean Féger (CSTJF), otherwise known as the **Total research center,** a sprawling campus in the northwest of Pau staffed with researchers from around the globe, or perhaps at the **Université de Pau et du Pays de l'Adour,** a 20-minute walk or 10-minute bike ride north from the center of town.

The celebrated boulevard de Pyrénées offers all who walk it a palm-tree flanked view of the mountains.

Pau is a popular destination for **students,** who come for a semester or more of study and the promise of weekend skiing adventures in the nearby mountains. The city supports a working population of 36,000 people, who ply their trades at local shops, restaurants, and hotels (Pau is a popular convention spot), and at the local university and hospital network, which are the region's largest employers. If you have a degree in engineering or another skilled qualification, it's worth checking the job boards to see what's available. LinkedIn offers a good selection of Total jobs in Pau that many expats might be qualified for.

For families with children, there's no dearth of **educational possibilities.** Public and private schools abound, including the **International School of Béarn** (www. internationalschoolofbearn.com). The all-in-one preschool/elementary and middle school/high school is a favorite among expat families—especially those employed at Total, which sits just a 10-minute walk away. Classes are taught in English, with French taught as a foreign language. If you prefer to give your kids a full-throttle French immersion education, you'll have nearly 50 schools for all age levels to choose from, including seven private Catholic institutions.

Resources

Meeting fellow expats and mingling with your new neighbors is the best way to get the inside scoop on the best places to educate and entertain yourself, and to get leads on employment opportunities. One organization every newcomer should engage with is **Anglophones of Pau** (www.anglopau.com). This 100-family membership group welcomes you into the fold with potlucks, hiking groups, book clubs, and children-centric activities, all year round. Despite its name, **Pau So British** (www.pausobritish.

Pau's city hall, otherwise known as the *mairie*, is conveniently attached to the office of tourism.

com) is open to non-British anglophones as well as native francophones interested in expanding linguistic borders. The social club hosts conferences and cocktail parties with a British flair, and invites the public to attend its monthly mixer at local Scottish pub Peter's Corner (at restaurant Chez Pierre, 18 rue Louis Barthou). Pau's **mairie** is conveniently located right beside the main tourist office, yet another stellar resource for newcomers who want to learn more about Pau's rich cultural heritage.

WHERE TO LIVE
North Pau

North Pau is popular among the Palois for a slew of good reasons, including proximity to the university, hospitals, and other major regional employers. There's also a good selection of schools in this area, plus public swimming pools and community centers for children and adults to enjoy. The ambiance is ideal for **families,** and feels very **suburban** while still within a short cycling commute to the center of town. After Pau Sud, Pau Nord has the highest real estate prices; to buy something here, you'll pay close to €2,000 per square meter. Nowhere near Paris prices, but not cheap, either.

　　Renters will fare rather well here in Pau, where a two-bedroom house with a yard can be had for as little as €800 per month. An apartment of similar size (but without the yard) rents for €600, and offers those much-desired Pyrénées views right out the living room windows. Clusters of McMansion-type dwellings have begun to sprout in North Pau's previously unincorporated areas, but as a potential buyer, you can have space and character if you want it, without an exorbitant price tag, if you choose an apartment over an independent *maison*. Three- and four-bedroom flats regularly sell for less than €100,000, though you can easily find something at half that price or 10

© AURELIA D'ANDREA

Moving to Pau means there's a good likelihood of having gorgeous mountain views outside your window.

times as much. A modern, six-bedroom villa designed by a local architect is currently on the market for €650,000, and comes with a garden so expansive and tree-filled that it might be confused for a local park.

For help finding the perfect place in North Pau, visit regional real estate site www.dmaisons-aquitaine.com and send a query to the English-speaking staff who are eager to help you.

South Pau

The neighborhood of South Pau is the most sought-after place to live in the city, and with good reason: It's lovely, green, safe, and **residential.** Some of the city's finest **old mansions** are here, in the Trespoey quartier, giving modern-day residents a glimpse into a past punctuated by annual visits from the English leisure class. You can live the modern equivalent of that lifestyle if equipped with a generous budget. A recent real estate search yielded no fewer than three châteaux priced at more than €1 million each in this part of town. If you've ever dreamed of opening your own luxury inn or B&B, jaw-dropping options exist here.

For more modest budgets, South Pau offers some decent choices, including a 130-square-meter three-bedroom apartment with parking and a fireplace for €750, and a gorgeous four-bedroom Haussmannian-style flat with a garden, near the commercial shopping center Bosquet (with its sushi restaurants and fashion boutiques) and Collège Marguerite de Navarre, for €990.

GETTING AROUND
Public Transportation

Public transport is encouraged by the municipal authorities, who put their money where their mouths are by making transportation free—or practically free. The mini bus **Coxitis,** which runs on natural gas and works its way around the *centre ville,* is one free form of transport. Another is the **funicular**—a pair of tiny vertical trains that climb up the hill from the Gare de Pau, which sits below the city, next to Gave du Pau River.

Pau doesn't have a Métro, but it does have **IDELIS,** an 18-line bus system that will take you wherever you need to go in the greater Pau area. Tickets cost €1 each and are valid for an hour's worth of travel. A 24-hour travel pass costs €2.70, and €8.20 will buy a *carnet* of 10 tickets. You'll pay a 20 *centime* "eco" tax when buying a transit card, but you don't pay again when topping up. If you're in Pau for the long haul and want to buy a yearly transit pass, count on €260 a year, and about half that if you're a senior, student, or job-seeker.

Bicycle

Pau has its own bike system called **IDECycle.** A yearly subscription costs €25, a week is €7, and a day *abonnement* is €1, which entitles you to a free first half-hour of cycling time on any one of its fleet of 200 bikes spread across 20 city stations. Equipped with baskets and bells, the bikes are great for short shopping excursions or trips across town to return library books. IDECycle offers another attractive option, which is long-term bike borrowing. For €30, you could rent a bike that's yours exclusively for three months. For €30 more, that three-month rental could be upgraded to an electric bike. Learn more about all the eco-friendly transportation options at ww.idecycle.com.

Train

Trains depart the palm-tree flanked Gare SNCF de Pau every day in the direction of Paris, Bordeaux, Toulouse, and beyond. Station hours are 5am to 11:20pm every day of the week, except Fridays, when the station closes ten minutes later, at 11:30pm.

Air

Pau's **airport,** from which you can hop a flight to London, Naples, or Amsterdam, among other destinations, sits 10 kilometers north and slightly west of the city center. Shuttle buses headed for the airport depart Pau's train station every hour, and tickets for the 20-minute trip cost €1.

Toulouse

Close your eyes. Now open them. Look around, and you'll think that Toulouse could *almost* be Paris. It's not just the socialist mayor, the river that runs through it, or the traffic that the city has in common with the French capital—there's a certain spark in the air here. It feels like things are happening, and that's because they are. Dubbed la Ville Rose (the Pink City) for the rosy hue cast by the unique-to-Toulouse brick used in most of the city's architecture, this is the fastest-growing community in France, with a river of 12,000 new residents flowing into the population each year. Bisected by the Garonne River and dotted with tens of thousands of trees, the area is home to several universities and a major airplane manufacturing industry that attracts *beaucoup de* (many) foreigners to Toulouse, giving an already cosmopolitan city a welcoming international flavor. From here, the Mediterranean is a little over an hour away by car or train, and the ski resorts of the Pyrénées are similarly close. Sun, mild temperatures, and friendly locals invite you to linger, and the lively pace, international community, and work potential make this a viable destination for setting up a life in France.

THE LAY OF THE LAND

Toulouse is flat as a pancake and shaped like a giant vertical rectangle, with the Garonne meandering through its west side and a smaller but historically significant body of water, the Canal du Midi, skirting its eastern edge. Most of the action—museums, hotels, train station, *mairie*—lie on the east side of the river, where you'll also find a cluster of five university campuses. On the west side, accessible by bus, Métro,

Having a Ball in Toulouse

They sound like mythical creatures out of a Harry Potter novel: Scrum-half. Wing. Fly-half. Fullback. They're creatures, all right, but of the perfectly human variety—though if you've ever seen a game of rugby, you'd swear they were, perhaps, half bovine. The players really are that big. Rugby, that sport revered by he-men (and women) around the globe, is particularly well loved in Toulouse, the undisputed rugby capital of France. The hometown team, Stade Toulousain, has earned many ardent fans, which you'll no doubt discover if you're within proximity of the *stade* (stadium) after any home-game win. Though Toulouse has two stadiums, the home team plays its matches at Stade Ernest Wellon, the smaller of the two, with "just" 19,000 seats. If you decide to brave the crowds and see what a game is all about, it's advisable to bring earplugs—it can get plenty noisy in the observer's trenches.

In rugby, the big, beefy fellows playing the game aren't allowed to wear protective gear. When someone gets tackled, the whole team joins in the pile-up. This fact alone can be disturbing for first-time viewers. Be prepared for some serious physical pummeling to take place right before your eyes.

In rugby, the ball is never thrown forward but rather tossed from side to side between each team's 15 players. (Kicking the ball forward is allowed.) And if a player is tackled while holding the ball, he must release it or risk a penalty. The object of the game, as in football, is the touchdown, which is worth five points. Points are also scored through various kicks—conversion place kicks and drop kicks—and the winning team is the one that has scored the most points when the two 40-minute halves are up.

Not the slightest bit interested in sports? You might want to follow the local season matches in the newspaper anyway, so you know who's playing when, if only to make sure you don't accidentally find yourself in the midst of a winning team's revelry (or, worse, the losing team's ire).

bicycle, or on foot, the streets are wide and airy, and new housing developments are being built among the old orangey-pink stone buildings. The riverside park, Prairie des Filtres, was once Toulouse's original rugby-playing field, and today you can still toss a ball around and have a picnic *sur l'herbe* (on the grass) on a sizzling summer day.

Point your compass south and sally forth for an hour, and you'll hit the Pyrénées. In the summer, Alpine lakes and hiking trails beckon, and during the winter, the ski train ferries you to the mountains for stress-free snow time. To the southeast of Toulouse, past the splendid medieval castle city of Carcassonne, lies Narbonne, the nearest swimmable Mediterranean beach. To the west, the Atlantic coastal city of Biarritz is reachable by train in four hours and Bordeaux in two, and Paris—590 kilometers to the north—is a six-hour journey.

Andorra, that teeny-tiny principality nestled in the Pyrénées, is a favorite destination of Toulousain shoppers on a budget. Because there's no sales tax or VAT, prices are much lower than in France—much, *much* lower. It's not unusual to see cars with French license plates loading up on a year's worth of toilet paper and canned goods at Andorran supermarkets. Many also make this their electronics- and sports-equipment-buying destination, but it's also possible to take a bus from Toulouse to merely enjoy the scenery and change of pace.

DAILY LIFE

The arts play a major part in local culture, and live music is an especially popular form of entertainment. Summer music festivals, including the riverside Rio Loco celebration that recently celebrated its 20th year, draw huge crowds to Toulouse's beautiful outdoor spaces, and year-round you can find indoor musical offerings ranging from punk and flamenco to opera and classical. The city has its own orchestra, and taking in a performance at the Théâtre du Capitole is a rite of passage for every Toulousain. The Association Vélo Toulouse (AVT) also works to promote cycling in the area by hosting events and group rides, as well as advocating for safer, rideable streets.

When the mercury on that thermometer begins its summer ascent, you could hop in a car or onto a train and head for the Mediterranean, or you could stay closer to home and become a local at one of Toulouse's 13 public swimming pools. Tariffs are low—€2.95 per visit, or you can purchase a discount card of 10 for €22.00—and discounts are given to students and seniors.

Toulouse has its share of homeless people, and here the demographic appears to consist solely of young vagabonds, with their dogs and backpacks and sidewalk drinking. They're harmless and generally polite, but don't feel compelled to hand over your hard-earned cash unless you're really motivated.

Climate

In spite of the waterways flowing through it, Toulouse can feel a bit suffocating in the summer. It gets hot, and pollution from the factories dotting the greater suburban area only helps thicken the air, which can settle over the city like a brown blanket. Driving less and relying more on public transport is one way to support cleaner air, but there's

© VILLE DE TOULOUSE.PATRICE NIN

The Canal du Midi is one of many beautiful spots to relax and enjoy life in Toulouse, especially in summer.

A bridge connects the Capitole neighborhood in Toulouse's *centre ville* with St. Cyprien.

nothing like a bike ride along the verdant Canal du Midi to make you feel like you're breathing oxygen-rich country air.

Employment and Education

The cosmopolitan feel of Toulouse is due in large part to its **international student population** and the international community fueling the workforce at the numerous high-tech companies in the area. **Biotechnology** is big business here, but the **aerospace industry** is the dominant economic force: In the Toulouse area alone, **Airbus** employs nearly 12,000 people, representing 100 nationalities, many of whom are Anglophones from the UK, Canada, and the United States.

The locals work hard for a living, but like the rest of their compatriots, they know how to find balance between work and personal life. Weekends are sacrosanct among Toulousains, who congregate at sidewalk cafés for long lunches with family and friends, flock to the scads of cinemas for an afternoon flick, hit one of nearly 20 open-air markets, and wander the cool corridors of the city's many museums.

WHERE TO LIVE

For ideas on where to settle, it's worth talking to other local expats to learn from their experiences. Try English in Toulouse's Friday-night gatherings or **Tuesday teatime Meetups** (www.englishintoulouse.com), and visit the **Americans in Toulouse International Club** (AIT I/C) online guide (www.americansintoulouse.com) for newbies in la Ville Rose.

Centre Ville

This shouldn't come as a surprise, but the *centre ville,* encompassing the Place du

© VILLE DE TOULOUSE.PATRICE NIN

Place du Capitole, in Toulouse's *centre ville*

Capitole, is the city's **most desirable place to live**—and therefore its **most expensive.** It's no wonder: The area boasts beautiful architecture, museums, restaurants, several shopping districts, and the giant, attractive square of la Capitole at its heart. If you're looking for access to the best of city living 24/7, take out your checkbook and prepare to pay considerably more for that privilege than you would in any other quartier. One-bedroom apartments, if you can find them, begin at about €700 here, but elsewhere in the city you can get the same space for around €500. A recent search turned up a revamped two-bedroom with bathtub and floor-to-ceiling windows in the living room overlooking a charming shopping street for €800 per month. Métro Line A is a two-minute walk away and there's a Longchamp boutique right outside the door, in case you need an expensive handbag to go with your new French life. Buying a roomy two-bedroom flat with a little *balcon* and period features will cost about €200,000 in this desirable neighborhood, though generally, home prices in Toulouse are lower than the national average. Thought that studio apartment for €50,000 was a misprint? Not in Toulouse, where one-bedrooms average €89,000 and two-bedroom flats can be had for €125,000. But those prices do tend to inch higher in this hot hood.

Amidonniers and St. Pierre

Students tend to congregate in a very specific quartier of Toulouse just to the west of the city center: St. Pierre. Wedged between the Université Toulouse 1 Capitole (UT1) campus and the Garonne River, St. Pierre and Amidonniers, slightly north, are crammed with the one thing that seems integral to student life the world over: **bars.** Nevertheless, this quartier has its own special appeal, with its pedestrian path, strolling lovers, and river view location. On Thursdays—the unofficial "students-go-out" night—the population swells and the revelers take over with zeal. Moving away from the bars a bit, you can find some charming places to call home within walking distance, bus, or Métro to the *centre ville*. Rental prices are what you might refer to as "student-friendly," ranging from €300 for a flavorless, nothing-special studio to €900 per month for a 78-square-meter three-bedroom with remodeled everything inside and a parking space outside. A one-bedroom unit in a modern building (with sliding doors leading onto a balcony big enough for a table and chairs) will cost in the neighborhood of €200,000.

St. Cyprien

A five-minute walk or two-minute bike ride over the *pont* (bridge) St. Pierre will take you to one of Toulouse's **newly trendy areas.** St. Cyprien used to have an edge to it, with its Arab and Asian markets and multiethnic population, but these days it's looking a lot less up-and-coming and a lot more *bobo* (bourgeois bohemian), as twentysomethings who want to settle down are confronted with the reality of housing costs in the more central districts across the river. This neighborhood has everything the other *côté* has—markets, friendly neighbors, Métro, parks—but with a smaller price tag. It's also one neighborhood where buying a single-family dwelling with a pool is a possibility—it was built in the 1930s, and the interior has been given a full modern makeover. The lovely pool is surrounded by a grassy lawn that will feel magnificent underfoot on a hot summer day. The price tag? €400,000. One bedroom apartments in the 30-square-meters range can be had for the bargain starting price of about €70,000, and renting something similar will cost around €500 per month.

Suburbs

Many expats moving to the area settle in the suburbs, particularly **Blagnac, Colomiers,** and **Pibrac** to the northwest. They are equally pleasant, if a bit staid, and accessible by car or by bus. Housing in Blagnac is most often new and relatively affordable, with three- and four-bedroom villas selling for around €200,000. (They'll come with the suburban perk of front- and backyards, too.) A somewhat pedestrian, newly constructed 50-square-meter apartment here rents for between €500 and €800. To the southwest, over on *l'autre côté* (the other side) of the Aéroport Blagnac-Toulouse, modern Colomiers offers affordable housing, decent public transportation, and a short commute to Toulouse. A big (70-square-meter) two-bedroom apartment lacking in charm but close to amenities rents for about €700, and it might even include access to an enclosed communal swimming pool. If you're in the market to buy, you'll have plenty of options for something roomy—say, four bedrooms for less than €250,000. Pibrac is a bit more expensive: Houses in the four-bedroom range sell for about €300,000 (with pool), and a similar-size rental will run you about €1,200 a month.

The southwest corner of Toulouse, including the Reynerie and Basso Campo districts at the end of Métro Line A, can feel a bit rough around the edges and probably aren't the most welcoming areas on the periphery of the city.

GETTING AROUND
Public Transportation

Tisséo, the local transport system, encompasses Toulouse's bus, Métro, and single tramway line, which together can take you deep into the core of suburbia and beyond. The

Expat Experience: Trying on Toulouse

Name: Zoe Levi
Age: 34
Occupation: yoga teacher/ massage therapist
Hometown: Sydney, Australia
Current city: Toulouse
Neighborhood/District: Saint Cyprien

Australia native Zoe Levi moved to Toulouse in 2011 from Germany, where she had lived for three years. Here, Zoe shares her advice for others dreaming of moving to La Ville Rose.

How proficient were you in French when you arrived, and how does that compare to now?
I didn't speak a single word of French when I got here! Terrible impressions of Steve Martin in *The Pink Panther* don't count, right? These days I'm conversational, can understand most of what's happening around me, and navigate French administration (major victory) but am still far from fluent.

What resources have you discovered in Toulouse that have made your life easier?
The only thing that really helped make life easier was to get out and connect with people. Englishintoulouse.com and Internations (www.internations.org) are both useful websites here in Toulouse. Both communities are full of fantastic people.

You started your own business in Toulouse. What advice would you offer to a would-be entrepreneur who dreams of doing the same?
My yoga school/massage practice, Satya–Yoga and Natural Therapies, is my biggest joy here in Toulouse. I get to do what I love every day and share that passion with the really wonderful community that we've built up over the years. It was a pretty tough ride getting set up without understanding the process, the language, the culture around business

bus, called **TAD**—short for "Transport à la Demande"—offers 80 different routes that weave through every nook and cranny of the Toulouse *agglomeration* (greater urban area). The two **Métro** lines are not as far-reaching but ferry travelers to the southwestern *banlieue* quickly. Both Lines A and B operate from 5:15am to midnight (12:45am on weekends). A newish tram line leaves the city center and hits 18 stops all the way out to the Airbus headquarters in suburban Blagnac. Ticket costs for bus, Métro, and tram are the same: €1.60 individually and €13.40 for a *carnet* of 10.

On rugby and football match nights at the Stade de Toulouse and Stade Ernest Wallon, special *navettes* (shuttles) whisk sports fans from the closest Métro and bus stops to the arenas for free, and yet another free ride can be had on the electricity-powered city-center *navette*. A similar free *navette* system serves the *centre ville* from 9am to 7pm Monday through Saturday. To get to the Aéroport Toulouse-Blagnac 30 minutes away, a shuttle bus (€5) departs from the *autogare* next to Gare Matabiau every 20 minutes. From the airport, EasyJet and Air France fly to Paris's Orly Airport several times a day.

and bureaucracy here in France, but with a bucket-load of patience and persistence and more than a few frustrated tears, I managed to do it. To anyone thinking of starting their own business I would say, just do it! Start doing whatever it is that makes you happy and everything else will fall into place along the way. If you try and do all the paperwork first, you'll drown in the system and never get off the ground.

What is it that you love most about your life in Toulouse?

I love the livability of Toulouse, that it's not too big and not too small; that the fruit man at my local market is one of my yoga students and the vegetable lady gives me cooking tips on whatever I buy (and often a few extra peaches or a sprig of rosemary); the girl at the supermarket is a friend; my bank manager comes to me for massages; everyone has time to be human with each other. And at the same time, as France's fourth largest city, there's a lively cultural scene, concerts, shows, etc., so I'm never bored. And whenever you need a break, you can easily get to the beach in summer and the mountains in winter and a bunch of gorgeous French towns just down the road for a day or weekend. It's not at all a touristy place, but it's so easy to live here and get into the rhythm of southwestern French life.

What language do you speak when you're out with friends?

Most of my friends here are French. With the few who don't speak English at all, obviously we speak French. For the ones who understand English, we have a great system where everyone gets to speak their own language. That way we can all express ourselves in the most authentic way. Basically it's a big mess with everyone changing between the two.

How is Toulouse different from other French cities you've visited?

Toulouse has its southern charm, it's colorful and boisterous. Airbus (and the thousands of foreigners who work there) gives the city a very particular international feeling and the university means there's a young vibrancy, which I love. People here are really genuinely warm and welcoming and interested in accepting foreigners into their fold.

Bicycle

Because Toulouse is so flat, cycling is an ideal way to get around. **VélôToulouse,** with 283 stations and nearly 2,600 bicycles, operates like any other public bike system in France, with the exception that you don't have 24-hour access to bikes: The rental cutoff point is 2am (though you can return them 24 hours a day). Plug the AllBikesNow app into your smartphone to help locate a free bike near you, whether you're in Toulouse or Timbuktu.

Train

From **Gare SNCF Matabiau** in the northwest of town, just across the Canal du Midi, trains depart daily for Paris, Bordeaux, and other points in France and Spain. Station hours are 4:45am to 12:45am.

Montpellier

Walking the sun-drenched, palm-tree-dotted streets of this vibrant city of 270,000, you almost feel like you're not in France. And you almost aren't—the Spanish border is a little more than an hour's drive down the A9 toll road. You feel the difference in the architecture, with its arched doorways and squared balconies; you smell it in the hint-of-salt air; and you sense it in the relaxed attitude of the local population. Montpellier is a pleasant place to visit, a popular place to study, and vibrant community you can really put down roots in.

Montpellier has also been a center of learning since the 11th century, when it was established as a trading zone for wine, olive oil, and spices. In the 12th century, the first universities opened here, including a medical school and a law school, modern in-carnations of which still exist. A diverse student body numbering 70,000 divides itself among Montpellier's three primary university campuses (including one of France's Ivy League-esque *grande écoles*), and lends to the city's youthful, dynamic feel. Forty-three percent of residents here are younger than 30, and that's not a bad thing. You'll always find a musical performance, theater production, or art exhibit featuring the work of these youngsters—and their older siblings (and parents), too.

THE LAY OF THE LAND

Montpellier sits on a gently rolling swath of terrain 12 kilometers north of the Mediterranean. Flowing through the east of the city is the flood-prone Lez River,

© AURELIA D'ANDREA

Remnants of medieval times still stand in Montpellier.

which dumps out into the Mediterranean at Lattes. Outside of Montpellier to the northeast and northwest, vineyards stretch across the bright, sunny hills as far as the eye can see. Two hours north of the city via the A9 is the Parc National de Cevennes, an outdoor lover's oasis where you can hike, mountain bike, camp, and otherwise get your nature fix. South of the city, about a 15-minute drive or 45-minute bike ride away, is the Mediterranean. You can swim, sunbathe (sans suit, if you want; there's a nudist beach here), or kite-surf here, and public transportation will carry you if you're not in the mood for cycling. Heading east-ward up the coast by train, you can be in Arles in an hour. The former stomp-ing grounds of Van Gogh are also the gateway to the Parc Naturel Regional de Camargue, with its pink flamingos, wild horses, and unique marshland landscape.

Head south along the coastline, and within four hours, you could be sipping sangria and eating tapas at a bar in Barcelona.

DAILY LIFE

Adding to the eclectic, exuberant feel of the city is the mixed population of North African, West African, Spanish, and American immigrants. Notably, beginning in the 1960s, thousands of Algerians came to Montpellier to seek asylum during their country's War of Independence. They changed the literal and figurative flavor of the city, bringing in new restaurants, bakeries, and *épiceries,* and a cosmopolitan vitality. To meet the needs of this diverse population, Montpellier has nightclubs that close at 5am and open-air markets that start business at the same hour; preschools, art schools, and law schools; fine art and street art. Family-friendly and open-minded, Montpellier is livable, lively, and welcoming, and particularly suited to those in pursuit of higher learning.

Employment and Education

IBM and **Dell** both have campuses here. IBM—which regularly earns "Best Places to Work"-type awards—is the single largest private employer in town, with 1,000 locals on the payroll, many of whom are non-French. And even though the wine-growing region east of Bordeaux gets all the attention, Languedoc—and the areas surrounding Montpellier—is not just France's but the world's top wine-producing region. If you've always dreamed of working in **viticulture,** there's great potential for getting your foot in the door here, though you may have to start from the bottom and work your way up (harvesting grapes, in other words). One of the perks of the grape harvester's job? Yes, of course! Free wine.

This city is powered on gray matter. Look around at the number of **higher-learning institutions** (22 in total) and you can clearly see that intellectual pursuits are the order of the day in Montpellier. A medical school transforms student residents into healthcare specialists at the area's seven **hospitals,** which employ more than 8,000 medical and nonmedical staff combined. **High-tech business complexes** have mushroomed around town in the past couple of decades, attracting a blend of local cyberintelligentsia and techno-savvy expats. Life in Montpellier is many things, but one thing it never is is dull.

Resources

The **French-American Center of Montpellier** (www.frenchamericancenter.com) exists in part to help students get settled in France by introducing them to locals, sharing job leads, and inviting newcomers to social events. Getting in touch with the organization after you land can enhance your first impression of the city for the better. Find them on Facebook and check out their blog (www.frenchamericancenter.com/blog-english) for the latest information.

The **Anglophone Group of Languedoc-Roussillon** (AGLR, www.anglophone-group-languedoc-roussillon.com) was launched in 2011 by a Canadian and an American with the aim of helping other Anglophone expats integrate and feel welcome. Besides hosting film-discussion groups, cultural outings, and coffee Meetups, they're also a solid resource for all things related to a move to the Languedoc-Roussillon region.

Sea to Shining Sea: The Canal du Midi

The idea was relatively straightforward and unquestionably clever: Construct an inland waterway linking the Mediterranean with the Atlantic, and boom! The trip from sea to sea is whittled down to a few days instead of four weeks, plus there are no more pesky pirates to contend with. Well, this simple idea took more than 15 years and the work of many hands and brilliant minds (including Leonardo da Vinci's) to bring to fruition, and today it stands as one of history's brilliant feats of engineering.

The Canal du Midi project, launched during the reign of Louis XIV in 1666, changed the physical, economic, and cultural landscape of the Languedoc region. To dig this 10-meter-wide, 240-kilometer-long canal, thousands of migrant workers were enlisted, with an unprecedented number of women joining their ranks. Contemporary French labor laws that determine fair wages, sick leave, and paid vacation days were born out of this long project.

The canal officially "opened" in 1681, not long after the project's mastermind and chief engineer, Pierre-Paul Riquet, died. Though Riquet never got to see his project's completion, his life and work are celebrated throughout Languedoc with statues, streets named in his honor, and an annual Canal du Midi festival in the city of Beziers.

Designated a UNESCO World Heritage site in 1996, Europe's oldest operating canal still functions as transport waterway for a few barges ferrying goods from the Mediterranean to the Atlantic. More importantly, it has morphed into a tourist zone, welcoming pleasure boaters who cruise from lock to lock in private vessels, stopping along the way to enjoy wineries, castles, and a bit of culture beneath the southern sunshine.

If you don't happen to have your own boat, you can rent one here; or stay overnight at one of the many hotels-on-water; or just enjoy the canal from the shoreline. A path, sometimes paved but often not, skirts its entire length, making it a favorite among cycle tourists and *promeneurs*. Adding to the canal's picturesque allure are 250,000 plane trees that grow in a shady arc over the water. This is postcard-perfect France, that ideal mélange of function and beauty.

The **Montpellier Internationals** Meetup group (www.meetup.com) is an active social club founded in 2013 that arranges outings and events for maximum bilingual fun. If you want to meet fellow expats over a pint of beer to exercise your tongue with language exchange, you're in luck: Thursdays are the network's dedicated conversation-group night. Board games, hiking, and other forms of indoor and outdoor amusement are regular year-round activities.

WHERE TO LIVE

Montpellier is divided into seven primary districts, each with its own personality: hypermodern, utterly ancient, and everything in between. Brand-new neighborhoods sprout up with regularity, usually featuring the hallmarks of 21st-century French construction: energy-efficient housing, children's recreation areas, and commercial spaces that add value to the livability quotient. Over the last few years, 20,000 new dwellings have been constructed throughout the city to accommodate expected growth. Overall, real-estate prices run below the national average in Montpellier, at around €2,700 per square meter. Likewise, renting here is less expensive than many other big cities.

Centre Ville

Not surprisingly, the *centre ville,* also called **l'Écusson,** is where all the main action happens. At the core of this core is the Place de la Comédie, a *promeneur*'s paradise embellished with umbrella-shaded terrace cafés, fountains, and a magnificent opera house, Théâtre de la Comédie. Even if you don't have a backyard or a terrace at your *centre* apartment, it's no bother; the square is a communal front yard. Children zip around on razor scooters, cyclists weave in and out of pedestrian traffic, and inline skaters glide by on their way north to the old city. Living here means living in the **heart of Montpellier life,** and if there's a *manifestation* (demonstration) or a parade, you can't help but hear about it first. This all-access location means you can mosey over to the covered market and fill up your wine bottles at the central *caviste,* shop for bread and cheese, and enjoy your picnic in the nearby Esplanade gardens. Anywhere you settle in this prime hub affords you the luxury of mobility and access—a winning combination when you're looking for a place to call home. So what will that home cost? If you can imagine living in a ground-floor, one-bedroom apartment with a small kitchen and a living-room fireplace, you might be able to imagine paying €700 per month for it. Purchasing an apartment of the same size costs just a *tad* more: around €250,000.

Antigone

Butted up against the northeast corner of the Place, just beyond the tourist office, is the Antigone district, a 1970s experiment in architectural modernity that some call a failed endeavor and others an **urban redevelopment** success. Designed to resemble ancient Greece, the quartier is broad and airy, with good access to public transportation and all the important amenities. A newly constructed, energy-efficient apartment near the giant public swimming pool and grand public library will run about €100,000 for a studio and €230,000 for a one-bedroom. To rent those same dwellings, you'll need to budget €500 and €700, respectively.

Port Marianne

East of the city center is a neighborhood that holds a lot of appeal for newcomers: Port Marianne. It has a sparkling, futuristic feel, with **modern architecture** (some of it downright flamboyant) and plenty of breathing room. You'll have to cross the Lez river, but by bike, it's only a 10-minute ride, and the dedicated bike paths lend a sense of safety to the commute. This quartier is **family-friendly**—especially for **dogs** and kids, who can romp in the green spaces along the river—and close to the brand-new *mairie*'s office/municipal headquarters. If you like the idea of spending sunny afternoons sipping rosé at a contemporary café, or the prospect of jogging along the paved path along the river every afternoon, you'll love this neighborhood. Expect to pay around €200,000 for a two-bedroom apartment in a brand-new building, or approximately €700 to rent a roomy, modern two-bedroom with a balcony.

GETTING AROUND
Tram, Bus, or Car

To use the **TaM** public transport system, which includes four tram lines (with colorful trains designed by Christian LaCroix) and 36 far-reaching bus lines, purchase your tickets online in advance and they'll be mailed to you in advance of your trip (https://

tam.ticket-net.eu/accueil.do). Trams run every five minutes from 5am to 1am, till 2am on weekends; buses run roughly 7am-9pm. One-way tickets are €1.50 and a *carnet* of 10 tickets will set you back €10.

For €43 per month, you get an all-access Modulauto pass good for the tramway, Vélomagg', bus, and Montpellier's Modulauto car-share program. With 30 car-rental stations throughout Montpellier, this is a convenient option for those who need the use of a car only every once in a while. For more information, visit www.modulauto.net.

Bicycle

The gently rolling landscape is perfect for biking, and the city bike paths—140 kilometers of them in total—make it easy for cyclists to get out of town for a day at the beach, at the vineyard, or in the countryside. If you don't have a bicycle, you can rent one from **Vélomagg's** 52 bike stations scattered across the city, which, unlike most of France's public bike-share systems, offers special rates for extended-use bicycles, as well as access to a fleet of electric bikes. Rates begin at €10 per year, with a free first hour of pedaling time.

Train

Montpellier's St. Roche train station is conveniently located a 10-minute walk from the Place de la Comédie. From here, you can board direct trains to Paris (three-and-a-half hours) and Marseille (two hours), as well as local day-trip destinations such as Nîmes, Carcassonne, and Perpignan. Ticket windows are open from 6am to 9pm.

Air

The nearest airport is the **Aéroport de Montpellier-Mediterranée,** with flights to Paris, Madrid, Lyon, and Copenhagen. Recently added destinations include Tangiers and Manchester.

PROVENCE AND THE CÔTE D'AZUR

In the southeast, you'll find the sun-drenched, lavender-fields-and-olive-groves vision of France that romantics have long dreamed about. This is the land of palm trees and sparkling seas, tanned locals sunning themselves on café terraces with fluffy dogs at their heels, and shaded outdoor markets where women in wide-brimmed hats fill their wicker baskets with the summer's harvest. Living in a year-round vacation spot comes at a price. (Oh, the tourists during the summertime! Oh, how overpriced that stone farmhouse is!). It also comes with unbeatable weather, education and employment opportunities, and easy access to southern Europe—so you might very well find Provence and the Côte d'Azur worth the price of admission. If you choose to settle here, expect to live among an eclectic expat mélange of students, retirees, and adventurous sun seekers, as well as a relaxed local population that includes Italians, Spanish, North Africans, and natives of southern France. Everyone is here for a slice of that legendary quality of life that includes breathtaking scenery, relaxed local attitudes, deliciously unique cuisine, and year-round access to the sea and the mountains.

Those familiar with Paul Cézanne's work will already have a visual sense of Provence's varied geography, composed of craggy mountains, scrubby foothills, olive groves, and

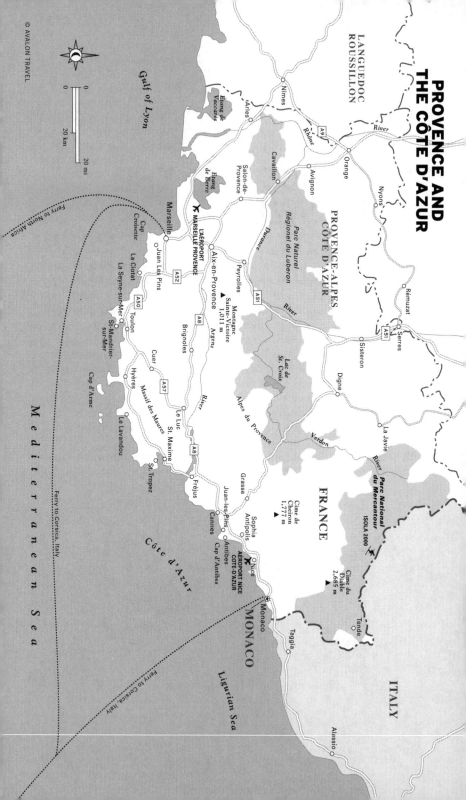

PROVENCE AND
THE CÔTE D'AZUR

LANGUEDOC
ROUSSILLON

PROVENCE-ALPES
CÔTE D'AZUR

FRANCE

ITALY

MONACO

Mediterranean Sea

Ligurian Sea

Gulf of Lyon

Côte d'Azur

Parc National
du Mercantour

Parc Naturel
Régional du Luberon

© AVALON TRAVEL

Nîmes
Arles
Étang de
Vaccarès
Étang
de Berre
Marseille
Cap
Croisette
La Ciotat
Juan Les Pins
La Seyne-sur-Mer
St-Mandrier-
sur-Mer
Toulon
Hyères
Le Lavandou
Cap d'Arme
St. Tropez
Fréjus
Cannes
Cap d'Antibes
Antibes
Juan-les-Pins
Sophia
Antipolis
Nice
Monaco
Grasse
Massif des Maures
St. Maxime
Le Luc
Cuer
Brignoles
Aix-en-Provence
Peyrolles
Salon-de-
Provence
Cavaillon
Avignon
Orange
Nyons
Rémuzat
Serres
Sisteron
Digne
La Javie
Tende
Taggia
Alassio

Montagne
Sainte-Victoire
1,011 m

Cime de
Cheiron
1,777 m

Cime du
Diable
2,685 m

ISOLA 2000

Lac de
St. Croix

Alpes du Provence

Verdon

Rhône River
Durance
River
Argens
River
River
River

AÉROPORT
MARSEILLE PROVENCE

AÉROPORT NICE
CÔTE-D'AZUR

A9
A7
A51
A51
A8
A52
A50
A57
A8

Ferry to North Africa
Ferry to Corsica, Italy
Ferry to Corsica, Italy

0   20 km
0   20 mi

vineyards that stretch for miles. As the hills tumble toward the Mediterranean, the green gives way to definitive signs of civilization that include tourist hotels, oceanfront apartments, and busy harbors bobbing with pleasure boats and massive ferries shuttling passengers back and forth from Corsica, Sicily, and North Africa. A boat ride out to sea to explore the Mediterranean fjords, known as *calanques,* is an ideal way to spend a weekend afternoon. Further east along the water toward Italy, the Côte d'Azur calls out to those who find inspiration in maritime scenery. Henri Matisse, who lived just outside Nice in the early part of the 20th century, worked the captivating beauty of the Riviera onto many of his canvases, bringing the sea, mountains, and palm-tree-fringed hillsides into focus with his muted palette. Even in the dead of winter, the turquoise Mediterranean captivates: Its haunting hue, framed by the snow-capped Alps rising up in the distance, turns the landscape magical.

Aix-en-Provence

Thirty kilometers north of bustling Marseille and a virtual world away sits Aix-en-Provence, better known as the birthplace of Cézanne and the onetime capital of Provence. The Romans first settled here in 125 BC, building their aqueducts, forums (examples of which can still be found in nearby Arles and Nimes), and public baths over the town's thermal hot springs. Today, a thriving arts community has taken root, inspiring would-be Van Goghs and Chagalls (both of whom spent time painting in this area) with its rugged vistas and unspoiled natural beauty. In the city center, the ochre-and-sand-colored Provençal architecture is interspersed with buildings that have distinctly Italianate flourishes, and there's no missing the dozens of sculptural hot- and cold-water fountains that bubble up in the many picturesque squares and quiet corners. When the towering plane trees are in full bloom, this city of 140,000 takes on dreamy appearance best appreciated from the vantage point of a seat at an outdoor café.

In 1904, Frédéric Mistral won the Nobel Prize in Literature for capturing the essence of this area and its people in his body of poetry written in the Provençal language. While the regional dialect—a subdialect of Occitan that more closely resembles Italian and Catalan than French—has been in steady decline over the past 100 years, it is still spoken by some here and understood by many more. A local movement to resurrect the language in the public domain via road signs and media has gained strength in recent years.

Today, Aix attracts thousands of international students each year to its many public universities and private art schools (nearly a third of the entire population is made up of students), and, thanks in part to Peter Mayle's bestselling book *A Year in Provence,* the area also draws dreamers who hanker for a simple life spent restoring one of those elusive old affordable stone cottages, growing vegetables, and perhaps becoming a bee-keeper or a vintner in the process. Wherever you fit into the spectrum, Aix and the surrounding countryside are guaranteed to cast their balmy Mediterranean spell on you.

The tree-lined Cours Mirabeau is Aix's most celebrated street and considered the heart of the city.

THE LAY OF THE LAND

Whether you arrive in the town center by car, train, or bus, you'll know you're in the right place when you spot the town's major fountain, La Rotonde. This round, multi-tiered beauty is a utilitarian traffic circle and art piece in one, surrounded by pairs of sculpted lions and topped by three female figures representing art, agriculture, and justice. To get your bearings from here, look up to Cours Mirabeau, the wide, plane-tree-hemmed boulevard and pedestrian promenade fringed with pop-up art galleries and outdoor cafés.

Heading north on foot takes you into old Aix, a tangle of pedestrian promenades crammed with boutiques, restaurants, *épiceries,* cafés, churches, and small squares. Here is where you'll find the *mairie,* the main post office, and nearly a dozen fountains. South of Cours Mirabeau sits the Mazarin quartier, the "new" part of the city, designed in the mid-17th century by multitasker Michel Mazarin, who was then the archbishop of Aix. With its magnificently muted *hotels particuliers* (mansions) that once housed Aix's aristocratic population, Mazarin has seen those beautiful buildings carved into multifamily dwellings, boutique hotels, museums, and chichi boutiques. Nearby is the international bookstore Paradoxe, near Place des Quatre Dauphins, where you can peruse ads from people looking for roommates or landlords looking for renters. Several cinemas can also be found here.

As you move further south and west from the *centre ville,* you reach the student district, where university life reigns. Here, housing prices tend to be more affordable, but the charm factor decreases: The lovely Renaissance-era architecture has given way to late-20th-century high-rise apartment complexes. Still, for students and others on a budget, settling here makes a lot of practical sense.

Crossing the ring road that circles Aix brings you to a vast and varied world of the great outdoors. Day trips within a 10-kilometer radius will bring you to rivers, hiking trails, olive oil-tasting rooms, ancient chapels, wineries, and prime bird-watching spots. In springtime, wildflowers in bloom make for eye candy on day hikes, and if you mosey east, you can picnic in the shadow of 3,000-foot Montagne Sainte-Victoire, which presides over Aix from its vantage point just north of the city proper and has featured prominently in many a painting over the centuries.

DAILY LIFE

In the summer, Aix belongs to the tourists; the rest of the year, you might say it belongs to students. Academia is the axis upon which this community spins, and you sense it at every turn. Bookstores, student cafés, and the students themselves are reminders that this is an important center of learning. If you haven't come here to study or teach, you're probably a high-tech contract worker or maybe a lucky retiree. Whatever the case may be, you'll need a reliable income to live here, because housing costs are higher than the national average—and the cafés seem to be more alluring than the national average, too.

Climate

Wherever you are in Aix, rest assured it'll be sunny and mild, with a year-round average of 17 degrees Celsius (62 degrees Fahrenheit). Winters rarely dip below freezing, and Aix's sheltered position away from the sea means it's protected from those rough mistral winds that whip through this part of the Mediterranean every winter.

Employment and Education

Aix's **universities** are an obvious channel for exploring employment opportunities here. The robust student body is eager to polish its bilingual proficiency, so marketing yourself as an English-language instructor or tutor could yield some results, if you're motivated to hit the pavement in search of your first clients. Independent-minded techno-whizzes will want to explore all possibilities in Aix's thriving **high-tech industry; contract consulting positions** are there for the taking if you do your homework and start flexing your networking muscles early. Check in with American companies with offices here, blanket the city with your CV, and think creatively. Business ideas you might be mulling over that are related to **tourism** have potential to take root and thrive. Contact the **Chamber of Commerce** (www.ccimp.com) and peruse **Invest in Provence**'s English-language website (www.investinprovence.com) for support in the creation and development of your brilliant idea.

Aix has a higher-than-average concentration of both public and private bilingual and international schools, which can be a burden or a blessing for a parent. Do more choices make the decision about where to enroll your child easier or harder? Joining a parents' group to help you sort out all those niggling questions is a good way to make new friends and be productive in one fell swoop. Try **International Parents** (www. inter-parents.com) and the **English Bubble** (www.englishbubble.fr), the latter of which is also a good place to start your job search as an English teacher.

Almond Joy

You see them at markets all over Provence: *fruits confits* (candied fruits) in a rainbow of colors, looking sweet and luscious and mysterious. What are you supposed to do with them? Many hundreds of years ago, some clever people got the idea to put two of Provence's greatest locally produced flavors—almonds and candied fruit—together to create the sweet regional delicacy known as *calisson*.

Legend has it that *calisson*, an almond-based confection flavored with crystallized melon and topped with a sugary glaze, made its first public appearance at a 15th-century royal wedding banquet held in honor of beloved king René d'Anjou to his second wife, Jeanne de Laval. The pair was betrothed in Aix, and the sweet gift was thought to have been bestowed by an Italian guest. Apparently, it was a hit, even though the treat wasn't manufactured locally until the 19th century, when the first *usines* (factories) opened in town.

Aix claims the top position for the most *calisson* artisans in the world: More than a dozen producers are officially registered with the Union Fabricant de Calissons Aix. A traditional Christmastime treat, *calissons* are served at Provençal dessert tables with the 12 other *desserts provençaux de Noël* (nougat, dried fruits, and nuts in their shells among them).

The teardrop-shaped treats taste sweet and marzipan-y, and once you bite past the crunchy glazed coating, *calisson* are less crunchy and more moist, with a toothsome texture. One well-known fabricator, René Roy, has developed a semisweet, semisalty version in flavors that include basil, ratatouille, and tomato, which earned a coveted prize at the Salon International de l'Alimentation in 2010.

So revered are these local confections that every first Sunday in the month of September, a benediction in their honor is held at Aix's church of St. Jean de Malta to ward off almond blight and to appeal to the heavens for the *calisson*'s continued longevity. You needn't be Catholic nor wait for Christmastime to enjoy it, though. *Calissons* can be found year-round at *confiseries* throughout France.

Healthcare

Healthcare options abound in Aix, making it easy for you to find a hospital or a doctor, dentist, or other medical professional when you need it. The tourist office (www.aixenprovencetourism.com) offers a comprehensive list of health-related services to visitors and residents alike, but when in doubt, dial 15 (emergency medical services), 17 (police), or 18 (fire department) for immediate assistance.

Resources

Before you move, join a few expat organizations so you'll have a welcome wagon there to greet you when you arrive. The **Anglo-American Group of Provence** (www.aagp-provence.com) is an established networking association of 400 expat families who'll show you the ropes and answer your questions, and the **Aix-en-Provence Expat Meetup** (www.meetup.com) offers you the chance to catch up with other nonnatives in a casual atmosphere.

WHERE TO LIVE

Aix is not a cheap city to live in, real-estate wise. The average cost per square meter is €3,800 (slightly less for renters, and slightly more for buyers). Ultimately, where you choose to settle in Aix depends largely on two things: your budget and your livelihood. If you're a student, lucky you—there's a tremendous selection of student housing here, and landlords love you because they know you won't be staying for more than a year or two.

University District

Students on a budget will find the best (otherwise known as cheapest) accommodations on the southern periphery of town, where the university campuses are clustered together. Nearby is the pleasant Parc Jourdan, where you can kick back on a bench and read beneath a shady umbrella of trees or wander among the busts of celebrated dignitaries of yore, including Émile Zola and Frédéric Mistral. The celebrated Théâtre Antoine Vitez is just one of many community resources anyone living in this area will want to take advantage of; tickets are just €16, and students pay half that to watch the next big stage stars in action. Productions run the gamut from stage classic (Moliere, Beckett) to contemporary theater festivals featuring newer playwright's works. The University District feels more suburban than the city center, but you'll still find cafés, restaurants, and other amusements nearby if you don't feel like making the 15-minute walk into the city center. A 25-square-meter studio apartment here will run about €550, and you can count on €700 to €800 for a one-bedroom. Student housing options abound here, and well worth investigating if you plan to attend a local university.

City Center

The obvious choice for a heady Aix experience is the city center, and because the town is compact, you'll have access to all cultural and other amenities whether you choose to settle in Old Aix, Mazarin, or Sextius.

For old-world charm—and heaping helpings of tourists in the summer months—confine your search to **Old Aix.** Here, you could wake up and stroll the flower market in front of the Hotel de Ville, sit for a leisurely *café* at a café on a square tucked deep in the maze of pedestrian-only streets, then get your hair cut at a modern salon. Further east, in the brand-spanking-new **Sextius-Mirabeau** quartier, you could stare out the window of your modern building (painted in the same sandy hues as the nearby 17th-century townhouses) and see Montagne Saint Victoire. In the evenings, you might play billiards at the local pool hall or head to the local nightclub, and weekends might mean poking around for treasures at a *vide-grenier* (communal garage sale) on Cours Sextius. In the quartier **Mazarin,** you could live the chic life among fountains, bookstores, cinemas, and museums, and have easy access

Aix is especially popular with foreign students, who are attracted to local universities by the beautiful weather and rich Provençal culture.

to both the train station and the La Provençal toll road, which will take you to the Mediterranean beaches in no time flat.

If you're hoping to buy a dreamy stone villa with a thicket of bougainvillea, be prepared for a bit of sticker shock; in Aix city limits, private homes are not uncommon (as they are in Paris or Lyon, where nearly everyone lives in an apartment), but they sell for a premium: We're talking €700,000 to more than €1,000,000 for a slice of the Provençal homeowner's pie. Expect a good-size yard for your million euros, almost certainly with a pool plunked in the middle of it. Smaller villas can be found in the €400,000 to €600,000 range, but they go fast, so if you have your heart set on a two-story stone home with periwinkle shutters and room enough for a dog and kids, have that mortgage in order and be prepared to strike a deal *tout de suite* or simply "settle" for a pretty terra-cotta colored apartment in the heart of the city instead.

GETTING AROUND
Bus
In 2011, Aix's public bike share program, V'Hello, bit the dust, making it the first city in the nation to abandon its municipally sponsored two-wheel transport system. That left **Aix en bus** (www.aixenbus.fr), the local bus system, as the primary public transport option for locals. It has more than 20 different bus lines to transport you virtually anywhere you need to go in and around Aix, including the suburbs and areas that border on rural (making it convenient for getting to nature areas for day hikes). Most buses run from 6:30am to 10:30pm, with reduced hours on Sundays and holidays. You can either buy a €1.10 ticket for each leg of your journey from the driver on the bus, or a rechargeable card in advance from the tourist office, kiosks at the Hotel de Ville and at Place Jeanne d'Arc, and at many *tabacs*. A *carnet* of 10 tickets costs €8; don't forget to validate your ticket once you enter the bus. Maps and schedules are available at the tourist office.

Another option, **Flexibus**, is good for people in outlying areas who don't have easy access to a bus stop. With advance warning, a driver will pick you up and take you to the nearest transport hub. A guide to the system is available on the Aix en Bus website. A similar program, **Navette Live** (www.aixenprovence.fr/Navette-Live), was designed for drinkers needing a ride home after a few too many. (Honestly.) It costs €10 per year and only operates during late-evening to early-morning hours.

Car Sharing
Aix has its own *covoiturage* program run through the local automobile association, called **Auto Club Aix** (www.autoclubaix.com). Using the association's online service, you can find cheap (starting at €2.50) rides to Marseille and elsewhere throughout the region.

Train
The **Gare SNCF** (ww.aix-marseille-ter.com) at Place Victor Hugo is a leisurely 10-minute walk from La Rotonde. The ticket office opens at 7am, but you can access the automatic ticket machines between 5:30am and midnight. From here, you can go as far as Pertuis to the north and Marseille to the south; at other stops, you can take connecting trains to get to other stations throughout France. The nearest TGV station, where you can take direct trains to Brussels or Geneva, is a 15-minute bus ride minutes

outside of Aix. To get there, take the Line 40 Navette Aix TGV-Aéroport from the *gare routière* (bus station) on Avenue d'Europe. Tickets are €4.10 to the TGV stop, or pay €7.20 to go to IKEA in Vitrolles and €8.20 to get to the airport right outside Marseille. Download a PDF brochure with more information at www.lepilote.com.

The **Navette Aix-Marseille** (www.navetteaixmarseille.com) will take you from Aix to Marseille for €5.70, where you can also connect with high-speed trains. Tickets can be purchased at the *gare routiere,* where you'll also catch your departing bus. Monthly and weekly passes are also available at discounted rates; discounts are also available to students and seniors.

Antibes

Wandering around the narrow backstreets of old Antibes, it's not hard to see why Picasso parlayed a weekend getaway here into a two-month painter's retreat. The town is quaint in an ancient, seafaring sort of way, with a tiny old town dotted with little restaurants and shops, a pretty harbor and city-center beach, and plenty of cobblestones to support the authentic old-world vibe. The Greeks first settled in Antibes—which they dubbed Antipolis—way back in 1000 BC, choosing this spot among all the others because of its strategic position, perched on an outcrop of rock that rises out of the Mediterranean and shelters the town's harbor. Today, Antibes is a haven for holiday-goers (the population increases dramatically during the summer) and, thanks to the number of vacationing and expat Brits, it definitely feels more English than Greek (but still more French than English!). This means you'll never be without a lifeline to the Anglophone community, if you really need one.

Though Antibes has a village-y feel about it, its population of 75,000 qualifies it as a true city, albeit one with a small-town heart. If France without the hustle and bustle is what you're after, and the idea of a know-thy-neighbor community holds appeal, Antibes is worth a gander.

THE LAY OF THE LAND

Antibes sits 695 kilometers southeast of Paris, but feels light years away from the capi-tal. The sunny seaside town is joined at the hip with Juan-les-Pins, its virtual fraternal twin to the southwest. Whereas Antibes is all cobblestones and history, Juan-les-Pins is a youthful explosion of modernity, complete with nightclubs, bars, and contempo-rary architecture. Further south still is Cap d'Antibes, the Beverly Hills East of the Riviera (Cannes is Beverly Hills West). Think yachts, tans, and pretty little beaches with gorgeous views in every direction. If the Cap—with its gated hillside mansions and almost tropical greenery—feels exclusive, that's because it is.

In Antibes proper, you'll orient yourself by finding the tourist office at Place Charles de Gaulle. The heart is positioned in *vieil* Antibes, the old city, with its narrow, crooked pedestrian passageways, *boulangeries,* and brasseries. In the spring, Antibes' appeal skyrockets as balconies, church walls, and public green spaces erupt in a fragrant riot of bright, colorful blooms—jasmine, wisteria, mimosa—changing the look of the town from lovely to over-the-top gorgeous. Adding to this tangible vision of

The revamped port of Antibes will bring new jobs into the area for years to come.

© M. MONTICELLI/OFFICE DE TOURISME D'ANTIBES JUAN-LES-PINS

heaven are the beaches, which sit south and east of the city center; Plage de la Gravette, the closest beach to the *centre ville,* is, fortunately, a gorgeous little arc of white sand, though many of the *plages* (beaches) around Antibes are of the stone-pebble sort rather than the desirable sable. If you're moving to Antibes with the thought of summer-evening jogs on the beach with Fido, now's the time to cast those dreams aside. Dogs are not allowed on any Antibes beaches, although the fine for getting caught is only €11, should you decide to take the risk.

To the north and a bit west, across the A8 toll road (also known as La Provençale) is Sophia Antipolis, the Silicon Valley of France. Hewlett-Packard, IBM, Air France, American Express, Honeywell, and France Telecom are just a few of the dozens of big-name businesses that have set up shop here since the area was first developed in the late 1960s. Nearby, there's also a campus of the University of Nice, giving the area an interesting mix of young professionals and students. Heading back south toward Antibes, you'll likely see the giant shopping complex with big-box stores like Conforama (hardware), Darty (electronics), and Carrefour (food and household products), plus car dealerships and, of course, a McDonald's, where the Wi-Fi is always free. Within a two-hour drive of Antibes are a host of interesting destinations, including Cannes, 10 kilometers to the west, where you can hit a nude beach *and* an antiques show in one day. To the north is Mercantour, a national park with day hikes amid colorful wildflowers near alpine lakes, deer, and other wildlife (but be sure to bring binoculars if you want to see golden eagles and marmots). In Monaco, 30 kilometers to the east, you can gamble an afternoon (and a week's wages) away at the casino and ogle the parade of fancy cars driving by. The ski resort of Isola 2000 is reachable in 90 minutes by ski bus, and the €50 round-trip ticket includes the cost of a day lift ticket.

DAILY LIFE

Antibes definitely qualifies as a "living the dream" city. It's gorgeous in a bright, sun-shiny, Mediterranean way and neither too big nor too small, with a nearly ideal climate, good schools, hospitals, and amenities galore. Your days here might begin with a jog along the sea, then a morning shopping excursion at the *marché* followed by a leisurely *crème* at your favorite café. Next, you might take a Pilates class before you start your afternoon shift as a server on a tourist yacht docked in the harbor. In the evening, after dinner at an organic restaurant in the old city, you'll head home to your modern, roomy apartment with a view of the hills north of the city to see if any new

For many who move to Antibes, it's all about the beach.

clients have responded to your ad for an English instructor posted at the local English pub. If it's summer, count on this "average" day to take a little longer to get through; you'll be sharing your village with mobs of tourists who'll crowd the market and take your favorite spot at the café. But with that view of the sea, you really can't complain.

Climate

The climate is extremely attractive, with short, wet winters and that fabled Côte d'Azur sunshine that blasts bright 300-plus days of the year. Summers are long—think April to October—and warm enough to allow for continuous outdoor living on your terrace from the beginning of spring straight through to autumn.

Employment

Finding work in and around Antibes probably won't be an epic challenge, provided you speak a bit of French—and, better still, that you have work papers. This area is notorious for its **au pair opportunities** and its **yacht jobs,** which is not surprising considering Antibes has the largest harbor on the entire Mediterranean coast. If you're open to working as a cook, server, or even a housekeeper, you too could spend your days and nights aboard a luxury yacht. Port Vauban is undergoing a major expansion; the project broke ground in 2014, and will be completed in 2021. The project itself has created a slew of new jobs in construction and planning, and once completed, the harbor will fit more boats and create even more employment opportunities for sea-and-sun-loving types. Set your radio dial to **Riviera Radio** (106.5) to hear the latest listings on the Crew Review segment, and check the station's website for more up-to-the-minute job openings: office assistant, international project manager, and everything in between (www.rivieraradio.mc). Another resource worth investigating is

The Crew Network (www.crewnetwork.com), an agency that provides luxury yachts with qualified crew. They're regularly on the lookout for new talent, including chefs, stewards, and deckhands.

Seasonal employment at **cafés** and **restaurants** is another option, but if service-industry work isn't your thing, don't give up. With your high-tech skills, you could land a job at one of those big-name corporations who've set up shop at Sophia Antipolis: **Intel, Dell,** and **IBM.** Openings are posted at www.sophiaantipolis-careers.com, where you can fill out a form and have job listings suited to your qualifications emailed or sent to you by SMS as positions open.

Resources

The cheerful, welcoming English-language bookstore **Antibes Books** (13, rue Georges Clemenceau; www.antibesbooks.com) is quickly becoming the new expat hub for networking. Speaker events give you a chance to meet and mingle with the locals, drink wine, and hear celebrated authors read from their latest books.

WHERE TO LIVE

One of the many nice things about Antibes is its size: It's small enough to navigate on foot but big enough to support all the amenities you'd want in a town—theater, cinema, museums, restaurants, daily market, and shops. Nearly 80 percent of the homes here are **apartments,** so wherever you live, whether in the old town or even ritzy Cap d'Antibes, you'll likely have very close neighbors, and with luck, a sea or mountain view to complete the rosy picture.

Antibes Centre

Antibes Centre, which encompasses *vieil* Antibes, is **where all the quotidian action takes place.** There are cafés, *boulangeries,* schools, doctors' offices, a bus station, and a train station just to the north of the center. From the center, you can access a swimmable beach in five minutes or hop a train or bus to the national parks to the north, Marseille to the west, or Nice to the east. It's pretty, not at all overwhelming, and an obvious choice for those looking for a sense of community on the Riviera. Every day is market day in Antibes; even on Mondays, vendors and buyers crowd the *marché couvert* on Cours Massena, catercorner to the *mairie.* You'll find the usual foodstuffs here, as well as products unique to Provence, including olive-oil soaps and candied fruits. On Saturdays, Place Nationale hosts an antiques market, and during the summer, concerts at the Cathédrale Notre-Dame mean free entertainment for the whole family.

In the center of town, finding a bright studio with a terrace and a communal swimming pool for less than €600 per month is utterly feasible; a similar-size apartment in the old town with a view of the harbor will average approximately €700. Spend a bit more, and you'll get significantly more. For around €1,000, you could get a sunny two-bedroom flat with a terrace, garden, tennis court, and sea views. If you're going to invest in real estate here, expect to spend about €300,000 for a 1970s-built two-bedroom apartment in a complex with a pool and views. Apartments on the *rez-de-chaussée* (ground floor) sell for considerably less than their elevated counterparts, but keep in mind that if it's a sea view you're after, you probably won't find it down there.

© D. VINCENDEAU/OFFICE DE TOURISME D'ANTIBES JUAN-LES-PINS

The backstreets of old Antibes have a fairytale feel that's most pronounced in the warm summer months.

Antibes Ouest

Residential Antibes Ouest has a sleepy feel, away from the hubbub of the city center, and hosts a mix of independent *maisons* and the standard apartments in myriad architectural styles, with a distinctly **suburban** vibe. If you're coming to Antibes with **kids** and want them to have room to run around, this is your hood. Don't expect to find anything too "quaint" or "charming" in these parts, but count on roomy, functional, late-20th century modernity—quite possibly with a sea view. A budget of between €250,000 and €300,000 will afford you a 65-square-meter two-bedroom apartment in a modern building with its own gardener, *gardien(ne)*, and terrace with coveted sea views. Apartment living has its perks—they're low maintenance, and offer a sense of built-in community—though you'll nearly always have to set aside an extra €1,000-2,000 per year to pay for the homeowners association fees. Renters get all the perks without the extra monetary investment; monthly rents on a two-bedroom flat with similar amenities run about €1,000. Prefer the privacy and seclusion of your own personal dwelling? It's best to turn your house-hunt back toward the *centre ville,* where the housing selection is greater and more diverse.

Juan-les-Pins

If you've sought out the Riviera so you can sit on a beach and tan yourself silly 300 days a year, you'll likely *not* want to settle in neighboring Juan-les-Pins, where the beaches have been hijacked by hotel chaises longues and giant beach umbrellas (which you too can use—for a fee). However, if you like amazing sunsets, jazz, and gambling, Juan-les-Pins may be just what you're looking for. Pretty 1960s tower **apartment complexes** will be your likely choice of accommodations; for a sea-view apartment with a terrace in the 75-square-meter range, you can expect to invest around €350,000, minimum. Looking to rent? Studios start at around €600 per month, one-bedrooms around €800, and two-bedrooms around €1,100.

Cap d'Antibes

The closer you inch toward Cap d'Antibes, the more **expensive** the real estate and the fewer choices you'll have. The people who call Cap d'Antibes home are the reason the harbor is loaded with yachts—the rocky hillside overlooking the far southern tip of the Cap secrets away luxury villas that only a select few can afford, unless you happen to have an extra €4 million in the bank. Don't have that many zeros on the end of your asking price? Consider a modest, 45-square-meter, one-bedroom apartment facing the sea for €450,000, or about €150,000 more than the beach-view apartments in the areas to the north. Rentals are hard to come by. But if you restrict your search to the equally lovely areas to the north, you can have your beach and swim in it, too.

GETTING AROUND
Bus
Envibus (www.envibus.fr), the local transport system, holds the title of cheapest transport in the region. Tickets are €1 and valid for one hour. A *carnet* of 10 tickets costs €8, and monthly passes are €22. Seniors ride for a reduced fare. Tickets can be purchased directly from bus drivers, at the tourist office in the center of town, or at the *mairie*. Buses run from 7am to 10pm, and there are 31 bus routes to choose from. If the bus will be your primary form of transport and you foresee using it at least once a day, an annual pass makes sense. It allows you to ride buses and trams along the coast and inland, as far down the coast as Monaco, and it offers unlimited access on the tramways. Flash it at certain movie theaters, restaurants, and boutiques and you'll even get a discount. The Pass Libertè costs €320; students, war veterans, and others pay less.

Train
Trains depart the hard-to-miss brick-red **Gare d'Antibes** at Place Pierre Sémard hourly for Nice, costing an average of €4 euro for the 20-minute journey and between €27 and €40 for the two-hour trip to Marseille's St. Charles station. You can also take direct trains to Paris and Bordeaux from Gare d'Antibes by purchasing tickets directly from station agents (between 5:45am and 10:30pm), from station kiosks, or online at www.sncf.fr.

Bicycle
Bike lanes aren't as prolific here as in other French cities, and there is no communal bike system—but getting about on two wheels makes a lot of sense here, since it's not too hilly nor too big. Public works projects to widen streets and create both bike and pedestrian paths are ongoing, but for now, you'll need to pack your sense of adventure (and your helmet) to *faire des courses* (run errands) by bicycle.

Air
Whether you fly by private jet or EasyJet, you'll be glad to know there's an international airport 13 kilometers northeast of Antibes. From the **Aéroport Nice-Côte d'Azur,** you can fly direct to Sweden, Portugal, or Greece. And if you happen to be flying during the Cannes Film Festival, you can expect to see a French cinema star or two sitting in the departure lounge awaiting a flight back to Paris.

Nice

There's no getting around the cliché: Nice really is nice. What makes France's fifth-largest city so special is that it has the best of big-city living packed into an easy-to-navigate, pretty-to-look-at, midsize *ville*. Adding to Nice's niceness is that marvelous stretch of beach that attracts Speedo-clad swimmers even in the heart of wintertime. It's hard to suppress a smile here, what with all that sunshine, the belle époque architecture, and the fabulous panorama to keep you cheery. What's more, Nice is within reach for all manner of budgets, from the penny-pinching student set straight through to high-rollin' bigwigs. Once the exclusive domain of wealthy holidaymakers and silver-haired sunbirds, Nice has morphed into an all-ages city with a lively old town, a chic city center, and a not-too-shabby selection of outlying neighborhoods where real-estate prices drop but transportation and amenities are still close at hand.

The Greeks first laid claim to Nice in the 4th century BC, but a few centuries later, the Romans staked their own claim to the area, building baths, forums, and amphitheaters, remnants of which can still be found around Nice, primarily in the Cimiez quartier to the northeast. The amalgamation of so many influences is part of what makes Nice so vibrant and interesting. While this city isn't quite a center of learning, there are two universities here, one of which has a strong international student population (University of Nice Sophia Antipolis). What it lacks in adult-learning opportunities, it makes up for in weather, access to leisure activities, and a high quality of life. You'll learn a lot just by exploring the city's many museums and visiting the towns and green oases that skirt the region.

THE LAY OF THE LAND

If you're heading into town by car via La Provençale, you'll likely find yourself pulling off the highway in northern Nice and heading south on avenue Jean-Médecin, which bisects the city center. You'll pass the train station on your way in, as well as Basilique Notre-Dame and the commercial center of modern Nice, with its five-story shopping mall and street-level midrange boutiques. Continuing *tout droit* (straight ahead), you slice right through the area's most desirable living spot, the Carré d'Or (Golden Square), ending up at Place Massena, a pedestrian zone separated from Old Nice by boulevard Jean Jaurès, with its sleek tramway and expansive public promenade.

Cross over into Vieux Nice, a pie-wedge shape of prime real estate where you'll find the city's nicest outdoor market, groovy after-hours bars, and ethnic and regional restaurants galore. The ambience feels vaguely Italian here—not that odd, considering Nice's proximity to the Italian border and who those early local settlers were. Along the coast to the west is the beautiful promenade des Anglais, with its hotels and high-rise apartment complexes overlooking the spectacular Baie des Anges (Bay of Angels), where a steady parade of inline skaters, joggers, and cyclists work up a sweat on the multiuse path skirting the seashore.

Heading back east along the shore past the old town and around the Colline du Château, which bears the crumbling ruins of an old castle and a park with a view, you'll discover the Port de Nice, a picturesque rectangle of water showcasing some

© J. KELAGOPIAN/MÉDIAS OTC NICE

Place Massena is a hub of activity year-round.

pretty swell little boats. If you continue eastward, you'll eventually hit Monaco, then Italy, with some gorgeous towns perched above the sea in between. Tucked into the northern *collines* (hills) behind Nice are charming medieval villages, as well as nature areas with plentiful hiking and wildlife-viewing. Go a little further still and you'll get to winter-sports country, easily accessible by "ski bus" and car.

DAILY LIFE

After a gray December in Paris, a train ride to Nice is a lot like a twister ride to Oz after wintering in Kansas: full of color and a joy to behold. The sun shines brightly here roughly 300 days a year, which means you can put those full-spectrum lights back in the closet and pull up a beach chair as you activate your vitamin D receptors and send the seasonal blues a-packin'. Bustling and vibrant and much cleaner than Paris, Nice has a lot going for it. The Francophone community is friendly and welcoming— they've seen your type here for centuries—and the English-speaking infrastructure will give you a nearly instant sense of security, knowing others have put down roots here and made it work.

Climate

Because its temperature is regulated by the ocean breezes, Nice doesn't get as blisteringly hot in the summer months as cities sitting further inland do. The average temperature is 60 degrees Fahrenheit, and 80 is the norm in summer. When a hankering for snow hits, you'll have to travel for it, but not too far; in 90 minutes, you could be zipping up your ski suit and hitting the slopes. Most don't come here for the winter sports, however, unless your idea of "winter sports" includes swimming laps in the Mediterranean.

Employment and Education

Finding work in Nice probably won't be too challenging, provided you're outgoing, speak a spot of French, and aren't put off by the thought of working in the **service industry**. **Tourism** brings a lot of money into the region, so there are myriad opportunities for tapping into that resource. For **yacht-staffing gigs,** listen to Riviera Radio; for other jobs of particular appeal to expats, read the *Riviera Reporter* (www.rivierareporter.com) and *The Riviera Times* (http://www.rivieratimes.com) for leads.

For families with school-age children, Nice is a hospitable scholastic environment outfitted with the standard *maternelles, lycées,* and *colleges,* plus private preparatory schools offering bilingual instruction (Lycée Albert Calmette), an international elementary school (Auber Elementaire), and a primary school equipped to handle physically disabled students (Acacias Maternelle). The **International School of Nice** (www.isn-nice.com) offers an English-language education for kids aged 4 to 18, and is also a place to consider when searching for employment opportunities, The sprawling **University of Nice Sophia Antipolis** is here as well, making it theoretically possible for the whole family to attend school in Nice.

Healthcare

If you should fall sick or suffer an injury while you're in Nice, you're likely to fall into good hands at one of the city's five hospitals. Surgical clinics, *maternités,* and private doctor's offices are plentiful, and there's a medical university here: Centre Hospitalier Universitaire de Nice (www.chu-nice.fr) where doctors trained in the latest cutting-edge medical technologies are at your service. In an emergency, dial 15—but do your research before disaster strikes.

Opportunities for cultural immersion abound in Nice.

PRIME LIVING LOCATIONS

Resources

The expatriate scene is varied and sizeable in Nice. English speakers congregate at the usual places—the English pub, yoga classes, the American-themed bar—but they're integrated into the French-speaking community, too, so don't be surprised if the woman serving you at the local juice joint is also from Cincinnati. To up your chances of meeting more people like you and learning from their experiences, find a Meetup, join the **English-American library** (www.nice-english-library.org), and tap into the local blogging community to begin your networking journey.

WHERE TO LIVE
Carré d'Or

The **city's modern hub** has its heart in the desirable Carré d'Or, bordered by Victor Hugo to the north, promenade des Anglais to the south, rue Gubernatis to the east, and rue Congrès to the west. Punctuated by healthy-looking palm trees, these neat and tidy streets beckon with their **pretty apartment buildings** in Easter-egg hues, some festooned with belle époque flourishes, others simpler in design with blue or green shutters. What they all have in common is their pleasing aesthetics and their desirability. When people speak of moving to Nice, this is what they're talking about. Sea views? Not necessarily, but your accommodations are guaranteed to be bright and cheerful, with room to breathe and access to all the usual amenities. To rent a one-bedroom, 40-square-meter apartment in this hood, you'll need to budget about €800 per month; to buy something of a similar size, €350,000 should afford you a few possibilities. Within a 10-minute walk, you can be throwing down your beach towel on Lido Plage or shopping for olives at the open-air market on Cours Saleya, in the old town. A 10-minute tram ride will get you to the Gare Nice-Ville or the Musée d'Art Modern.

Quartier des Musiciens

Just north of the Carré d'Or is the Quartier des Musiciens, a similarly attractive neighborhood—think wedding-cake architecture with intricate iron *balcons*—farther from the beach but offering **more affordable real estate.** Look for **vintage one-bedroom apartments** with revamped interiors to sell with a low-end price of €250,000. If you prefer to rent before committing, you could easily find something here in the 40-square-meter range with a balcony for €700 per month. If your French is strong, take a chance on PAP.com; oodles of apartments in this neighborhood and others throughout Nice are available directly from the owners, which can sometimes be an easier transaction than going through an agency. A recent search turned up some real gems, including a gorgeous studio in a Bauhaus-style building flanked by palm trees, and with its own private garden, for €560 per month.

Vieux Nice

In Vieux Nice, the architecture turns moody and dramatic, color-wise; the buildings erupt in reds and oranges, their contrasting turquoise-blue shutters giving the eye a whole lot of stimulus. This is where the young go to socialize, eat, drink, and be merry. The 35-and-up crowd is welcome also, but there is a distinctly **youthful atmosphere** here, surely encouraged by the copious drinking establishments. Amid the baroque churches and modern art galleries are doorways leading to some prime apartment

Socca to Me

© AURELIA D'ANDREA

If you move to Nice, you'll certainly become addicted to *socca*, the local specialty.

The lucky locals on the Côte d'Azur have the *Sarrasins* to thank for their local delicacy, *socca*. At the base of this rich, savory snack is the chickpea, which was brought to Europe from Egypt in the Middle Ages by Arab traders, eventually working its way up through Italy's boot to settle deliciously where the sea meets the southeast corner of France.

Once the working person's breakfast and a menu staple of the poor, *socca* has morphed into a popular street food in Nice, where it is made the traditional way with just four ingredients—chickpea flour, olive oil, salt, and water—blended together to form a batter, then fried on a flat, round griddle. Its final appearance resembles something like a messy crêpe, and the best way to experience it is to visit a restaurant—or several—specializing in *socca*. Ask the nearest Niçois for a recommendation, then sample till your stomach says *"Arrêt!"*

If you're roaming around Vieux Nice (Old Nice), the first place you might happen to stumble upon is Chez Thérèsa, in the middle of the busy Saturday market on Cours Saleya. Here, a crowd gathers around as the *très maquillagée* (elaborately made-up) proprietress pours the rich batter onto a rustic open griddle, barking out the French equivalent of "Who's eating?" before scraping up a serving or two, plopping it on a sheet of paper, and setting it before you with an overzealous hand.

The salt and pepper shakers taking up residence on each of the 10 or so tables are the only condiments on offer, and they're all the *socca* really needs. Season, then eat with your fingers. The taste is savory, rich, and vaguely custardy—the consistency of the *socca* is crunchy at the thinnest sections and spongy at the thickest. It goes down best with cheap and tasty rosé wine served out of a plastic cup.

PRIME LIVING LOCATIONS

living, if ancient character (stairs instead of an elevator and sloping ceilings, for example) is your thing. A roomy one-bedroom with big windows and a balcony can be had for less than €250,000, and a similar rental will run around €700 per month.

Cimiez

If money is no object and high-rise living on the promenade des Anglais holds no appeal, the Cimiez neighborhood might be right up your alley. Perched on a hill northeast of the *gare,* oh-so-close to Nice's Roman ruins and archeology museum, Cimiez is green, pleasant, and **family-friendly,** with several **new housing developments** that hold appeal for those who appreciate newness over old character. It also sits on a main bus line that will take you to the city center, train station, and beaches. Apartments tend to be a little roomier here, and, as you've been warned, more **expensive.** For 60 square meters of modern apartment living, plus a balcony with room for a bistro table and two chairs, you'll pay between €1000 and €1,1100 per month. To buy something to call your own, expect to invest at least €400,000 for a 60-square-meter apartment with views, balconies, an open kitchen, and a communal backyard. Nearby, at the site of the old Gare du Sud, a major public works project is underway to turn the old station into an arts and recreation hub, with a cinema multiplex, community center, shops, and restaurants. The project will be completed by 2018, making right now a good time to invest in the area.

GETTING AROUND
Tram and Bus
A wonderfully efficient and newly expanded tramway glides around Nice, connecting riders with bus lines in areas the tram doesn't reach, which includes more than 20

Nice's public transit system includes trains, buses, bikes, and a far-reaching tramway.

cities and towns around the Nice area. A 31-day adult pass good for unlimited travel on trams and buses throughout the Lignes Azur network costs €40, with discounts for students and seniors. Passes are available for purchase at *tabacs* around the city, and the cards are rechargeable. Whether you're using a temporary ticket or a permanent card, you must validate it on every journey or risk getting slapped with a fine of €30, payable on the spot (it costs even more if you don't have a ticket at all). A single ticket, which you can buy from the conductor, costs €1.50. Slide your ticket into the machine when you enter the bus or tram—or, if it's a card, wave it across the machine until you hear a beep. *Noctambules* (night owls) will be happy to know that the Lignes Azur pass is also valid for transport on the five Noctambus bus lines and one tramline that run after hours, meaning 9:30pm to 1:15am. For a timetable and route, visit www.lignesdazur.com.

To get to the Nice Côte d'Azur Airport, take bus 99, which departs from the main *gare,* and bus 98, from Gare Riquire on the east side of town. Tickets are €5 (not included in the price of your Lignes Azur pass), and buses depart every 20 to 30 minutes, depending on the station.

Bicycle

Moving up and away from the water, Nice can be hilly in spots, which makes its public bicycle system, **Vélo Bleu,** a challenge for those with less than Olympian athletic abilities. Still, the network of 1,750 bikes spread across 175 stations comes in handy for navigating the seaside promenade, as well as the Carre d'Or and broader *centre ville*. To subscribe to the service by the day, week, or year, call tel. 04/30 00 30 01, type in your credit card details, and you're off! Rates are €25 per year (€15 per year for Lignes Azur transport pass holders), €10 per month, €5 per week, or €1 per day. Like all the other public bike-share systems, Vélo Bleu is free for the first half-hour but begins charging €1-2 for subsequent one-hour increments.

Car

Nice's broad-reaching network of buses and trams means relying on a car here is a non-issue, but if you decide to invest in a scooter or automobile, you might want to take advantage of Parcazur, the secure parking zones next to tramlines and bus stops. The Las Planas station is just off the A8 toll road, so you can park and go without having to worry about parking tickets or exorbitant fees. You'll find another Parcazur zone at the Vauban tram stop and another at the Pont-Michel terminus. It's free to park here, but you have to use the local transit system for the privilege.

Train

There are four SNCF train stations spread across Nice, with the main station being the Gare Nice-Ville. The ticket windows at the *gare* are open from 6am to 9pm every day, and tickets can be purchased from automated kiosks during off hours. From here, you can take the 35-minute train to the lovely town of Menton on the Italian border, or plot a five-hour journey to Grenoble (train change required). For more destinations and ideas, scope out the local train network at www.ter-sncf.com.

LYON AND GRENOBLE

With the exception of the Alps and the annual Marché de Noël in Strasbourg, eastern France doesn't attract the same kind of attention from global travel media as its regional neighbors to the west, north, and south do. There's no sparkling sea here, no star-studded film festival, and no Tour Eiffel, but what they do have here—the great outdoors—they have in spades. From snow-capped Alpine mountains to rugged, wildflower-festooned foothills and verdant glacial valleys, southeast France holds particular appeal for athletic types who crave access to nature. Skiing, rock climbing, downhill mountain biking, hiking, river rafting, swimming—all of it and more can be found right here, 365 days a year.

Grenoble is a real winter-sports haven—ski slopes are accessible within 15 minutes of the city center—but outdoor sports aren't the region's only draw. Lyon, France's third-largest city and perhaps one of its prettiest, has long been known as a food lover's paradise. The local specialty? Simple, honest meals prepared with regional ingredients—and *lots* of meat. But the city is cosmopolitan, and even vegans can find something to nosh on here without any fuss. Roman ruins, perfectly preserved Renaissance-era neighborhoods, and exceptional outdoor terrain keep this swath of l'Hexagone intriguing and inviting, and the recreation possibilities invite the adventurous to stay and explore.

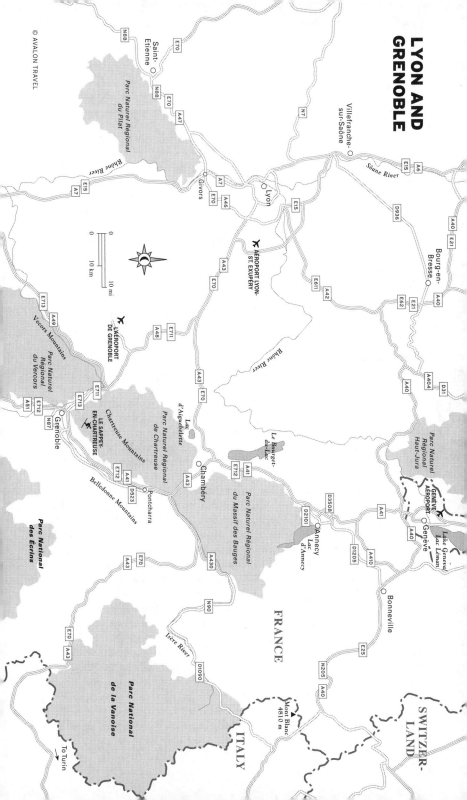

LYON AND GRENOBLE

© AVALON TRAVEL

Saint-Étienne

Villefranche-sur-Saône

Bourg-en-Bresse

Lyon

Givors

AÉROPORT LYON-ST. EXUPÉRY

Rhône River

Sâone River

Parc Naturel Régional du Pilat

L'AÉROPORT DE GRENOBLE

Vercors Mountains

Parc Naturel Régional du Vercors

Grenoble

LE SAPPEY-EN-CHARTREUSE

Chartreuse Mountains

Parc Naturel Régional de Chartreuse

Belledonne Mountains

Pontcharra

Lac d'Aiguebelette

Chambéry

Le Bourget-du-Lac

Lac du Bourget

Parc Naturel Régional du Massif des Bauges

Parc Naturel Régional Haut-Jura

GENÈVE-AÉROPORT

Genève

Lake Geneva/Lac Léman

Annecy

Lac d'Annecy

Bonneville

Parc National des Écrins

Isère River

FRANCE

Mont Blanc 4810 m

ITALY

SWITZER-LAND

Parc National de la Vanoise

To Turin

N88

E70

N88

E70

A47

A7

A7

E15

E15

A7

E70

A46

E15

E15

N7

A6

E15

D936

A40

E21

A40

E62

A42

E611

A404

D31

A40

A43

E70

E70

A48

E711

A43

E70

E713

A49

E711

E713

A51

N87

E712

E712

A41

D523

A43

E70

E712

A41

E712

Ghambéry

A43

D3508

D2101

A41

A40

A410

D1205

D205

A430

N90

E25

N205

A40

Mont Blanc

E70

A43

D1090

0   10 km
0   10 mi

Lyon

The first humans to settle in Lyon were the Romans, who built the city they called Lugdunom on top of Fourvière Hill back in 43 BC. Today, this city of 500,000 still attracts nonnatives in droves. Thirty-eight percent of the population migrated here from elsewhere, and one out of every two newcomers comes from outside the Rhône *département* altogether. This says a lot about the city: Its population is diverse, there is opportunity to be found, and Lyon natives are tolerant of newcomers. In the past decade, the city has grown younger, fueled by an increase in the number of students (currently at 60,000), while the over-60 population has dwindled as retirees move away.

Many tourists come as pilgrims of sorts, to pay a visit and their respects to the many churches, cathedrals, and *basiliques* throughout the city, including the most famous, Basilique Notre-Dame de Fourvière. This city also cares about aesthetics; even Lyon's old slaughterhouse was designed by a famous local architect, Tony Garnier. The structure has since been transformed into La Halle Tony Garnier, one of the city's most popular concert halls.

THE LAY OF THE LAND

From the grassy courtyard beside the Basilique Notre-Dame du Fourvière, 300 meters high on an east-facing hillside, unparalleled views of Lyon bring red-tile roofs and the city's two rivers into focus. Beyond the urban limits, rolling hills, a few of them dotted with those towering symbols of poor planning and rapid growth, the *cite,* stretch as far as the eye can see. Further still, the Alps and western Europe's highest peak, Mont Blanc, preside over the countryside's many mountains and valleys. Italy and Switzerland are right there, too; Geneva is 160 kilometers due east, and the Italian city of Turin is 230.

Rivers, mountains, and proximity to neighboring European nations make Lyon's position particularly strategic. Since the Middle Ages, this regional capital in the heart of the Rhône River Valley has been an important trade hub, and the city continues to thrive as a center of commerce, trade, and industry. Economically, Lyon is robust: Its citizens have larger-than-the-national-average incomes, and the region is number two in France for job creation through international investment. Lyon also embraces new industry, and even has its own Wall Street equivalent and school of economics.

For hundreds of years, Lyon has been an important religious and academic center, and today it draws thousands of international students to its many universities every year. Many come to study but end up staying long past graduation, seduced by the Gallo-Roman architecture; the thriving arts scene, which includes its own opera and theater companies; the world-class cuisine; and the lovely landscape. Some of the loveliest neighborhoods are the oldest—in the St. Jean and St. Paul quartiers, on the west side of the Sôane, the cobblestone alleyways are lined with 17th- and 18th-century *maisons particuliers* that have been transformed into modern storefronts, galleries, restaurants, and neighborhood *épiceries* without losing an ounce of their medieval charm. Hovering overhead is Fourvière Hill, where an ancient Roman amphitheater still welcomes performers onto its thousand-year-old stage.

In the center of town, straddled by the Sôane and the Rhône, the Presqu'ile quartier welcomes strollers and cafégoers to its many picturesque squares, especially Place Bellecour and Place des Terreaux, the city's onetime guillotine grounds. Wherever you are in Lyon, groomed streets lined with perfectly manicured trees, dotted with tidy parks, and—it must be admitted—embellished by a rather generous graffiti presence, give the city its unique accessibility.

DAILY LIFE

Weekday mornings and evenings on Lyon's Métro resemble Paris's rush hour: Students, office staff, doctors, biotech professionals, bankers, and service industry workers crisscross the city, keeping it civil in the crowded confines of public transport. Like Paris 480 kilometers to the northwest, Lyon is fast-paced, as you might expect of the country's number-two business capital. Lyon is also a multicultural community—more than 10 percent of its residents are foreign born—with a strong Anglophone presence. You may have noticed a theme running through all major French cities, and that is their popularity with the student set. That's no different in Lyon, where 12 percent of the university population is represented by international students. Among the four principle campuses is a Catholic university, and the city is also home to a prestigious art and design school and several business universities.

On Sundays in Lyon, the only businesses that seem to welcome commerce are the open-air *marchés* and McDonald's—still, you don't have to spend money to enjoy yourself. The Opéra de Lyon regularly hosts free midday concerts, several free museums are open on weekends, and a stroll through one of the city's many parks and plazas reveals sculpture, fountains, and all the gratis people-watching you could want. Wander Lyon's *traboules* (public covered stair- and passageways), visit its Roman ruins, or step

The Croix Rousse market is a popular morning destination in Lyon.

over the *périphérique* to meander the *marché aux puces* along the Canal de Jonage for a no-cost, visually stimulating Sunday experience.

Climate

In Lyon, you can expect four very distinct seasons: Hot summers; nippy autumns; cold, snowy winters; and brisk, colorful springs. During the warmest months, locals flock to the area's 12 public swimming pools or make the 45-minute drive east to Lac d'Aiguebelette, an hour away by train at the foot of the Alps, for swimming, hiking, and relaxing. In wintertime, everybody heads to the mountains; the nearest ski slopes are 90 minutes away by *voiture* (car). If sports aren't your thing, look for plentiful indoor diversions year-round: theater, cinema, dance, museums, and music.

Employment and Education

For much of the 18th and 19th centuries, Lyon was a manufacturing center for silk and other textiles, but the factories have long closed down, replaced by banks, high-tech office complexes, and schools. Expats tend to gravitate toward the **universities** here as sources of both education and employment. Lyon also welcomes millions of visitors every year, so the **tourism infrastructure** lends itself to job creation within that sector. Many newcomers **teach private English classes** or work as **tour guides,** and **au pair** work is easy to find for qualified caregivers. Because of its reputation as the culinary epicenter of France, Lyon also lures the celebrity chefs of the future, who dream of working alongside Paul Bocuse and learning the tricks of the trade from a Michelin-starred pro. Finding **restaurant work** requires solid language skills and a whole lot of confidence; to see who's hiring, check the online listings of the newspaper dedicated to the restaurant, hotel, and café industry in France (www.lhotellerie-restauration.fr). The website www.francejobs77.com lists English-language or bilingual job openings, mostly in the high-tech sector.

Resources

Lyon's many language-exchange groups supplement the French-immersion and university-level language courses available to nonnative French speakers. Both the **Lyon English Language** and **Franglish** Meetup groups (www.meetup.com) offer informal opportunities to meet and *parler avec* friendly people from around the world who share one common trait: They want to improve their language skills and engage in a fun cultural exchange in an informal setting. The **American Club of Lyon** (www.american-clublyon.org) is a more formal association that hosts many themed events throughout the year, usually tied in with an American national holiday. Its annual International Expat Expo is a prime networking zone that's popular with the English-speaking set.

WHERE TO LIVE

Like Paris, Lyon is carved into small administrative districts—nine in total—called arrondissements. However, unlike Paris, the arrondissements here seem to be randomly scattered throughout the *ville* in no particular order, rather than spiraling out in a neat and tidy fashion. The first five districts were created by decree in 1852, and they have retained the most historic flavor. Between 1867 and 1964, the remaining four districts were mapped out, giving the city its present-day look and feel of ancient-meets-modern.

For an apartment hunt, Craigslist Lyon has a decent selection of housing options in realistic price categories.

3rd Arrondissement

The 3rd arrondissement, especially the quartiers of **Villette** and **Paul Bert,** have seen the biggest shift in the past few years in terms of influx of new residents. There's something to be said for this part of town: It's spacious and easy to navigate, it has all the usual amenities and services, and it has one of Lyon's two major *gares* smack in its center. You'll see a noticeable number of aesthetically challenged **modern apartment complexes** here, but just the right amount of **attractive older buildings** keep it balanced. There's also a lot of **commercial activity** in this part of town, including Lyon's biggest shopping mall, and it's within spitting distance of the Université Jean-Moulin campus. The trend has been toward families moving in, rather than singletons and university-student types, and the number of schools, *crèches* (nursery schools), and outdoor play areas for children support the **family-friendly** atmosphere. Living in a popular neighborhood has its price: You'll pay a few more of your hard-earned euros per month here than you will in the 7th or 4th arrondissements, but finding a space to rent or own for around €2,500 per square meter is entirely possible. A light-filled, 70-square-meter two-bedroom flat on kid-friendly Place Ferrandière costs €300,000. A little farther south, closer to the busy boulevard Honoré de Balzac and near all manner of public transportation, an apartment of the same size will cost closer to 400,000.

4th Arrondissement

North of the city, on a hill in the 4th arrondissement, the **Croix-Rousse** quartier's

Finding a favorite spot to enjoy a glass of wine on a sunny day is one of the great pleasures of Lyon.

rough, artsy charm isn't a result only of the graffiti-adorned streets. This neighborhood has been home to Lyon's labor force for millennia: First the Romans, who built an amphitheater here; then, in more modern times, the factory workers at the city's silk mills and textile manufacturing plants and the builders of the grand *basilique* across the river. This is a prime spot to live if you want to save money on the gym by walking to and from the bus and Métro stops at the bottom of the hill each day. Croix-Rousse is sandwiched between two pleasant green spaces, and the bars, theaters, and art galleries make leaving the neighborhood on weekends a nonstarter. **Housing is in demand** here, as it has been for a few hundred years, but when you do find those rare *à louer* signs, you'll find that they're priced better than in the neighboring 6th arrondissement. And that what you get is **good value** for your money. Roomy one-bedrooms rent for around €750 per month.

6th Arrondissement

The 6th arrondissement is a bit *bobo* (yuppie), but if the words **safe, calm,** and **quiet** strike a positive chord, then focusing your house hunt around well-to-do **les Brotteaux** near the pretty Parc Tete de l'Or will likely yield pleasant results. The atmosphere here is not dissimilar to Paris's 16th—if you've been there, you'll know what to expect here in terms of ambience and amenities. Within a five-minute walk of the park, which you'll come to appreciate on hot summer days for its cooling shade trees and leisure lake, you could find a two-bedroom apartment with a fireplace and skylights for €300,000. A similar apartment on the ground floor will cost about €250,000. To rent, budget about €1,100 for a two-bedroom, 70-square-meter apartment in a building with bike parking and communal garden space.

7th Arrondissement

For something a bit **livelier**, the 7th arrondissement, particularly the quartier called **la Guillotière,** is an interesting possibility. Just across the Rhône from Place Bellecour, la Guillotiere is one of the city's most **ethnically diverse** neighborhoods, with a strong Jewish, Indian, and Chinese presence. There's a bit of urban scourge here—a homeless person here and there, the occasional intoxicated corner-dweller—but if you can handle the blight, the prices are right, especially considering the easy access to the *centre ville.* A 50-square-meter apartment with a new kitchen and a *balcon* will cost you €900 per month; buying an apartment of similar size close to amenities in an eco-constructed apartment complex will run between €250,000 and €300,000.

GETTING AROUND
Public Transportation

Lyon's public transport system, **TCL,** includes the tramway, Métro, Cristalis trolleybus, and funicular lines that zip passengers up the city's steepest hillsides. The city is currently expanding its public transport systems to meet the growing numbers of passengers. As of 2015, not all Métro stations were handicapped-accessible, but elevators are being installed to make those final few stations lagging behind available to all. Tickets cost €1.80 individually, but you must buy them from a station agent or automated kiosk to get that rate. If you need to board the bus and don't have a ticket, the price of buying one from the conductor increases to €2. As always, buying a *carnet* of 10 tickets is more economical, costing €15.90. If you plan to use public transport daily, consider investing in a monthly pass. Discounts are given to students, seniors, couples buying passes together, and big families. It's worth investigating all the possibilities to see if you're eligible for a discount. Once you've settled on the pass or ticket option, point your compass in the direction of the nearest main Métro station, one of the two train stations, or the *gare routière,* where you'll find ticket agents who can sell you what you need. *Tabacs* and the public transport website, www. tcl.fr, are other possibilities.

In Paris, it's not uncommon to see smokers lighting up as they wait on the platform for their trains, but these infractions are treated seriously in Lyon. Smoking is not advisable here—the fine for lighting up on the train or in a station is €81. Also, traveling without a validated

There are many ways to tackle Lyon's hills, including funicular, bicycle—or on foot.

ticket falls under the legal description of "fraud" in Lyon, so don't forget to stick your ticket in the *composteur.* The fine for failing to do so is €33, and you'll be slapped with a payable-on-the-spot-fine of €50 for riding without a ticket.

Bicycle

Now some good news: The **Vélo'v** bike-share program allows anyone—even newcomers who haven't opened a bank account or received a French bank card—to use one of the spiffy red-and-silver bikes from any of the city's 300 stations with any credit card, not just those with a *puce.* The *abonnement* process is pretty straightforward: When renting a bike, you agree to uphold traffic laws and obey the Vélo'v rules, which include not talking on your cell phone while riding, not riding against one-way traffic, and not riding with more than one person per bike. *Abonnement* prices start at €1.50 a day and €5.00 per week, and the first 30 minutes will set you back €0.75.

Train

To leave Lyon by train, you'll likely depart from Gare PRT-Dieu, on the right side of the Rhône, or Gare de Perrache, on the south end of Presqu'ile. Both are TGV and SNCF stations. Trains depart daily for Paris, Geneva, Grenoble, and other destinations within France and neighboring countries. To get to Lyon's international **Aéroport St. Exupéry,** 25 kilometers southeast of the city center, take the Rhône Express tram from the Part-Dieux station (€15.80 or €14.60 if you purchase your ticket in advance online at www.rhonexpress.fr/); in 30 minutes, you'll be standing in line at the check-in counter. Trams run every 15 minutes between 6am and 10pm, 365 days a year.

Grenoble

Grenoble has one of those illustrious, richly transformative histories replete with multiple incarnations, from glove-manufacturing town to revolutionary stewpot to wintersports mecca and high-tech hub. But what really put Grenoble on the modern-day map was the 1968 Winter Olympics. In anticipation of an unprecedented influx of tourists and athletes from around the globe, the city shored up its tourism infrastructure, built new housing, and cleaned up its center, giving Grenoble a bit of well-deserved sparkle. Since then, the city has continued to grow and expand southward, with suburban-looking malls, 21st-century apartment complexes, and *hypermarchés*. Grenoble is a practical town, and the landscape reflects that. It's not fussy or overtly embellished, but rather simple and functional to meet the needs of its citizens.

The pitched roofs and the mountain peaks towering over the landscape will probably give it away: Grenoble is the gateway to the snow country, specifically the Alps. Access to snow sports is as easy and convenient as hopping on a local bus for the 15-minute ride to the nearest resort. In the summer, those same mountains morph into a lollapalooza of a wildflower show, where hiking and mountain biking reign.

Balancing out the ski-bum element is a brainpower contingency. Three University of Grenoble campuses are located here, plus an international graduate school of business, a science research campus (Université Jean Fourier), and several private institutes of higher learning. If life nestled within a community of intellectuals who like to ski on weekends sounds like your cup of tea, you've come to the right place.

Grenoble is neat and tidy but could use a bit of polishing up. Some parts have a well-worn look that might be classified as neglect, and some of the architecture has a definitive Eastern Bloc sensibility. But dig a little deeper, and you'll discover an eclectic community of immigrants, adventurers, outdoor enthusiasts, and left-brain professionals. And if you move here, it helps if you aren't lactose intolerant: *Fromage*—in the form of fondue, raclette, and pizza—seems to play an integral role in most café and restaurant menus.

THE LAY OF THE LAND

Wedged between the Drac and Isère Rivers in a high mountain valley in southeastern France, Grenoble reeks of outdoorsiness in a deliciously invigorating way. Everywhere you look, mountains, trees, and blue sky dominate. To the north are the Chartreuse mountains (the birthplace of that licorice-tasting liqueur); to the south and west, the Vercors; and to the east, the Belledonne, each range resplendent in its own way.

In the *centre ville,* perched above the Isère River, the Bastille fortress looms. Slate-gray ramparts stand 300 meters high against the green hillside, and instead of keeping invading armies out, the Bastille now welcomes hundreds of thousands of visitors each year. Feeling spunky? You could head here instead of the gym, huffing it up the mountain on foot (there are stairs and groomed trails for the fearless), or go the relaxed route and climb into one of *les bubbles,* the cable-line transport pods that shuttle passengers up and down the hill. In either case, magical bird's-eye views of the city await.

To the east of the *centre ville,* the 21-hectare Parc Mistral resembles a bright-green welcome mat. This is the place to go for Bastille Day fireworks, spring picnics beneath the magnolia trees, and leaf-peeping on a cool autumn afternoon. This is also where you'll find the Stade des Alpes, the go-to venue for local football (soccer) matches. Cultural events include the Nature and Environment Film Festival, tai-chi classes, free concerts, and other festivals.

The city's high-tech hood, Polygone Scientifique, with its nuclear research institute, nanotech research lab, and molecular biology labs, is squeezed between the two rivers to the north and west of the city center, off the A48 leading to Lyon. This *technopole* isn't particularly attractive, looking very much like any contemporary office complex off the freeways of Los Angeles, but it's hard to knock one of the region's biggest employers based on aesthetics alone.

University campuses are spread throughout the city, including Sciences Po Grenoble, Stendhal University, and ENSAG, the revered local architecture school. More information can be found on the City of Grenoble's user-friendly website at www.grenoble.fr.

DAILY LIFE

Perhaps the number-one reason people are drawn to this area is access to outdoor recreation: skiing, mountain biking, hiking, rock climbing. The possibilities for amusing yourself *en plein air* are vastly varied and accessible to all ages. Dozens of ski resorts are within a two-hour drive of Grenoble, and the closest—the family-friendly Le Sappey-en-Chartreuse—is just 15 minutes away. English is widely spoken, and you'll likely hear it in accents that suggest Ireland, England, and the United States.

Employment

Life in Grenoble is centered on three primary industries: **high-tech, academic,** and

© LA MÉTRO/VILLE DE GRENOBLE

Bike tours of Grenoble are available every day in the warm-weather months.

Cast Your Net

Want to meet people in Grenoble with whom you share at least a common trait? These international groups hold the promise of fun and friendship, and members are either English speakers or folks who would very much like to be.

· **The Working Women's Network of Grenoble** (www.wwng.net) offers (surprise!) networking opportunities for women in Grenoble.

· **France-États Unis** (www.france-etatsunis-grenoble.com) meets monthly over drinks and snacks to promote Franco-American relations.

· **Open House** (www.openhousegrenoble.com), and its 150 members, welcomes newcomers to Grenoble with a good ol' dose of English-speaking hospitality.

sporting. That's not to say that you couldn't come to Grenoble with the idea of selling homemade soap, freelance writing, or working as a carpenter, but employment opportunities here reveal themselves most often in those three particular genres. Of the dozen or so English-language academies, about half are hiring on a regular basis. Short-term **seasonal jobs** at the **resorts** are plentiful, and students and others with valid work papers will have no trouble finding work if they're qualified. Being bilingual helps, too. Many expats are based in Polygone Scientifique, and you could be, too; check the employment opportunities at the **Le Centre National de la Recherche Scientifique**'s (CNRS) website at www.cnrs.fr.

Resources
The Anglophone community is strong and thriving: It's not hard to find a cultural event produced by English speakers but geared toward all. An annual Irish film festival, an English-language radio show, an Anglophone knitting bee, English libraries and literary events (mostly book readings), and an American-themed restaurant are just a small sampling of the resources that will help you get your fix when the homesickness kicks in.

Once you've got a bit of French under your belt, you can begin taking advantage of all the fabulous cultural events that await in Grenoble. The municipal website dedicated to local happenings (www.culture.grenoble.fr) is your portal to a dance-, music-, and theater-filled universe. Log on and explore the annual music and arts festivals such as July's open-air short-film festival (www.festival.cinemathequedegrenoble.fr) and the electro-pop music party known as the Cabaret Frappé Festival (www.cabaret-frappe.com).

WHERE TO LIVE
Centre Ville
The historic *centre ville* of Grenoble, situated on the south banks of the Isère, is the place to be if you hanker for a **thriving community** with interesting, cosmopolitan neighbors and **access to markets and restaurants.** In the side-by-side Championnet and Notre-Dame quartiers, near the river and *gare de télépherique* that takes you up the mountain to the Bastille, a studio apartment in a 19th- or early-20th century building

averages €500 per month. In this area, you'll find the Place Saint André, called la Place du Trib' by locals (the old courthouse used to be here), a popular destination for leisurely café breaks followed by or preceding an art-film screening at the Cinémathèque de Grenoble. This is Stendhal's (who, like Balzac, Zola, and Moliere, needs only one name for recognition) home zone, and the area oozes with his era's old-timey charm. On the Championnet side, you'll find the pleasant Place Victor Hugo, a comfortable nice-weather hangout with free wireless Internet, statues, and benches.

Chorier-Berriat

A bit farther south and west, moving in the direction of the Drac River, you'll come to the colorful Chorier-Berriat neighborhood. Once the dwelling place of the factory workers who breathed life into the local glove-making industry (try a guided tour at the Musée du Gant), it has become a warm **residential neighborhood** with a **multiethnic population.** This is where you'll go to find your halal hamburger, Vietnamese spring rolls, and tofu. The daily (except Mondays) Marché de l'Estecade, on avenue de Vizille, is a fun and practical place to pick up your daily food supply and acquire a sense of the local characters. Renting here is slightly less expensive than in Notre-Dame; a one-bedroom in Chorier-Berriat costs the same as a studio in that neighboring quartier, so expanding your search to encompass this area means more bang for your buck. Renting a big one-bedroom with two fireplaces, a bathtub, and excellent access to transportation means spending around €700 per month. A budget of €170,000 will buy you a flat in a late-20th century apartment building with parking, an elevator, and a balcony, but you'll probably need to budget a thousand more euros to strip off that dated wallpaper and give the whole place a freshening-up.

St. Laurent

If you've always fantasized about what life might be like in Italy, you may like to settle in the right-bank quartier of St. Laurent. Over the centuries, this neighborhood has been home to waves of **Italian immigrants,** and it still has a decidedly Italian sensibility, enhanced by the many pizzerias along the river. You'll hear a lot of *bon giornos,* and not just in restaurants; there's even an Italian-language radio station broadcast from here. There's something sweet about this neighborhood, where art galleries, cafés, and restaurants rest snugly beneath the shadow of the Bastille. The **tramline doesn't reach this part of town,** which might be why the cost of living is equal to those of less charming neighborhoods on the other side of the river. Look to pay about €500 per month for a studio.

Île Verte

Tucked into the northeast crook of the Isère River is another hospitable quartier called Île Verte. This neighborhood is indeed green (*verte*), as well as a friendly, attractive place to settle down for a while. The architecture is noteworthy: Towering above the 19th- and early-20th-century apartment buildings are three **ultramodern high-rises** that were constructed in anticipation of the '68 Olympic Games. Depending on your sense of aesthetics, they're either an eyesore or retro-hip, but there's no denying their eye-catchiness. Studios are roomier and more **affordable** here than in St. Laurent, and **public transport is excellent,** with tram Line B slicing straight through the middle of the neighborhood. If your budget can stretch to €200,000, you could have yourself a two-bedroom place with a huge kitchen and views looking out over the neighboring mountains. Renters have a lot to choose from, including bright studios for €500 and one-bedrooms for €650.

GETTING AROUND

Even if you're not a tourist, the **tourist office** (14, rue de la République) in the Notre-Dame district is a good place to start your Grenoble adventure. You can buy bus passes and find maps, bus schedules, and tips on accommodations and dining here.

Public Transportation and Bicycle

Besides walking and cycling either on your own two-wheeler or one of 5,000 public **Métrovélo** (www.metrovelo.fr) bikes, the easiest ways to move around Grenoble are by tram and bus, which are grouped together under the city's **TAG** transport system. The tramways four lines (A, B, C, and D) are efficient and far-reaching, and the system's two dozen or so local and regional bus lines fill in the gaps. Single voyages cost €1.50 and a *carnet* of 10 tickets costs €13.40. You can buy tickets at automated kiosks and 140 different *tabacs* and other agents around town. Weekly, monthly, and annual passes are available for a slight discount, as are senior and student passes.

Grenoble's *gare*—which recently underwent a much-needed facelift—sits next door to the *gare routière* on the west side of the city, a 10-minute walk from center. Ticket windows are open 4:30am to 11:05pm Monday to Saturday, and from 5:30am on Sundays and holidays. Tickets to Lyon start at €22.50, and the trip takes 90 minutes. For the three-hour trip to Paris, ticket prices vary considerably, but bargain prices run as low as €37. Tickets for the two-hour journey to Geneva begin at €27.

Air

Low-cost airlines Ryanair and EasyJet fly out of **Grenoble-Isère Airport,** located about 45 kilometers northwest of the city, to destinations including London and Stockholm. Getting there means a 45-minute bus ride on the airport *navettes* that leave from the *gare routière.* Hours are odd and trips infrequent—be sure to plan in advance. One-way tickets cost €12.60, and a taxi trip will cost around €60.

STRASBOURG

If the name "Strasbourg" doesn't have a particularly French ring to it, we can blame the Germans. Before the city became the capital of Alsatian France, it belonged to France's neighbors to the east, and its name bears those Germanic roots.

Today, there's a distinctly international air about the city, due in part to its proximity to Germany and Switzerland, and also to its popularity as a tourist destination, particularly among northern Europeans. The annual Marché de Noël—Europe's largest Christmas market—reels in 3.5 million visitors each holiday season alone. Strasbourg is also one of two meeting places for the European Parliament (Brussels is the other). For four days each month, the streets around the parliament building and the international Conseil d'Europe at the north end of the city center hum with a slightly regal vibration that hints of important decision making and intellectual debate. The only town that has Strasbourg beat in numbers of diplomats per capita is Paris, so if you've ever dreamed of a life in politics, Strasbourg might be a good place to kick off your career.

Thirty-two percent of Alsatians are 25 or younger, and that youthful vitality is palpable. The University of Strasbourg has 40,000 students, 10,000 of which are foreign. The international student population injects a layer of vigor into the city, supporting the flow of information and ideas into the region that keep perspectives fresh and minds open. Another appealing quality is the local arts scene, helmed by Generations

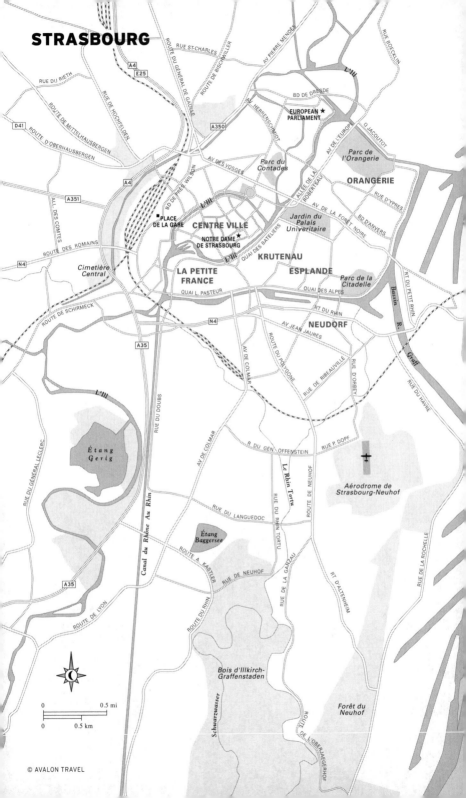

X and Y, that has transformed the city with novel ideas including street art-themed hotels and an exciting contemporary art fairs.

In many ways, Strasbourg feels less French than German—and that's not necessarily a bad thing, even for diehard Francophiles. There's a tidiness and order here, and you can really sense the Germanic history in the half-timbered architecture, the food culture (think sauerkraut and sausages), and the colorful clothing with which Alsatians young and old adorn themselves. The local style offers a welcome break from the French homogeneity, which *is* shifting, but ever so slowly. If you decide to make Strasbourg your home, you'll have made a great choice. For a big city, you get a small-town sense of community coupled with sophisticated attitudes, wrapped up in a beautiful package surrounded by waterways and forest.

The Lay of the Land

To locate Strasbourg on the map, draw a vertical line from Paris eastward toward the border. There, hugging the Rhine River, is where you'll find this vibrant, welcoming city of 280,000. To get your bearings in Strasbourg, you can walk, boat, or—the best choice—ride a bike. This town was made for cycling, and even has slight Amsterdamishness when you consider the canals, bridges, and number of dedicated cycle paths. The most visible monument at the city's core is its celebrated cathedral, Notre Dame de Strasbourg. The gothic structure, which was built over several centuries beginning in 1187, towers over its own square, place de la Cathedral, and draws tour groups in every season who gape and gawk at its rose-colored magnificence. The old church is tall and imposing, which makes it an excellent landmark. If you're ever lost in Strasbourg, just aim your gaze skyward; its spires can be seen from kilometers away.

© AURELIA D'ANDREA

Strasbourg's ancient *centre ville* is actually an island, completely encircled by an oft-photographed waterway resembling a canal, called the L'Ill, which is a tributary of the Rhine. The long, flat Batorama tourist boats ply the canal all year round, giving everyone who climbs aboard for a 70-minute ride spectacular views of the city. Buy a ticket for €12.50 and settle in for a visual feast as you cruise past the UNESCO World Heritage designated neighborhood of La Petite France, or take a second tour focused on a slightly newer urban element: European Parliament. When exploring Strasbourg by bicycle,

Strasbourg's cathedral is an easy landmark; you can spot its tower from kilometers away.

you can see these and other landmarks for free. If you're feeling particularly spunky, head out of the city on a dedicated cycle path toward the German border and beyond to the Black Forest, an oasis of natural beauty and a great day-trip destination.

Not the two-wheel adventuring type? Then point your *voiture* (car) south, in the direction the Alsatian wine-producing region that begins just outside of Strasbourg. The wine route, also known as the D20 highway, meanders through a bucolic river valley and sidles alongside the friendly cities of Mulhouse and Colmar. For oenophiles, this is the ultimate way to develop both a literal and figurative taste of the region. White-wine aficionados, especially, will appreciate the access to so many delicious varieties, including rieslings and the hard-to-pronounce gewürztraminers. If you're doing the tasting, be sure to let someone else do the driving.

From Strasbourg's super-modern train station, you can catch trains that will take you to Stuttgart, Germany (1.5 hours), Bern, Switzerland (2.5 hours), or good ol' Paris (2.25 hours) several times each day.

Daily Life

The day-to-day life of a Strasbourgeois is a lot like that of anyone else's life in cities and towns across France. Each local has his or her favorite market for procuring fruits and veggies. There are 26 weekly outdoor markets in Strasbourg, one of the most popular being the Wednesday and Friday market at place Broglie. After filling up your basket with locally grown goodies, mosey over to the Café de l'Opéra on the edge of the square and sip a glass of Alsatian wine on the sunny terrace. Place Broglie is also a regular spot for other community events, including *vide greniers* and *brocantes,* which draw out the treasure hunters from villages near and far.

CLIMATE

Winter is more "distinct" here than on the Côte d'Azur. Gray skies move in around November and don't move out until March, and the snowfall can be considerable throughout December and January. The annual Marché de Noël helps keep the holiday cheer up citywide, even on the days when the mercury dips below zero, and when blue skies finally do reappear, they herald the triumphant return of the warm season. Spring and summer are divine in this neck of France, with balmy, not-too-hot days and cool evenings. These months are what many

© AURELIA D'ANDREA
Strasbourg is a city full of cyclists.

people who move to Strasbourg live for: the ideal climate suited to every form of outdoor activity. Take the sunshine and cloudless sky as your cue to explore nearby forests, rivers, mountains, and valleys.

EMPLOYMENT AND EDUCATION

Expats will find that securing paid work here is easier than in some other cities in France, based partially on the number of **international employers** seeking polyglot employees. It's also due to the city's **service sector,** which is expanding and therefore in need of bodies (and minds) to fill those important posts at restaurants, hotels, shops, and tourist-oriented businesses. **Teaching English** is a popular expat profession in Strasbourg. Language school **Franglish** (www.franglish.eu) is regularly on the prowl for new talent, as is **Wall Street English** (www.wallstreetenglish.fr/cours-anglais-strasbourg). For more ideas, visit the English Language bookstore the **Bookworm** (3 Rue de Pâques) and peruse the postings on the bulletin board.

To expand your brain power, you might do like some other 55,000 do here and enroll in an institute of higher learning. In 2009, three of the city's universities merged to form the **University of Strasbourg** (www.unistra.fr), which has earned the status of largest university in France. This research university issues doctorates and other degrees, but if you simply want to take some business courses, you might consider the university's school of management. Other educational options include a school of architecture, a drama school, and music conservatory. Not artsy enough for you? Consider the local school of circus arts, where the next stars of the Cirque de Soleil are primed for the stage (www.grainedecirque.asso.fr).

RESOURCES

The member-supported **Americans in Alsace** (www.americansinalsace.com) organization is a great place to start networking. The friendly group is a mixed bag of Americans and Canadians who live, work, and raise families in this special corner of France. Their mission is to help you feel welcome, so help them help you by reaching out and attending one of the many monthly mixers.

Democrats Abroad (www.democratsabroad.org/group/france-strasbourg) has a strong presence in eastern France, and can help liberals feel connected to American politics and give reminders of critical elections and other issues relating to civic life in the United States. The nonprofit organization hosts lectures and various speaker events, and is a worthwhile organization to join even if you're not a registered Democrat.

Where to Live

It's hard to go wrong on neighborhood choice in Strasbourg, where even less desirable quartiers start at an 8 on the 0-10 charm scale. If you're working in the political or NGO arenas or studying at one of the local universities, it makes sense to focus your search on the city center, where you can find quiet, tree-lined streets with a suburban feel within walking distance of all amenities. The area around the train station offers some of the city's most affordable housing options, and is Strasbourg's most ethnically diverse quartier, where the Indian markets, kebab shops, and Thai restaurants hint at the city's cosmopolitan spirit. High-demand, high-price-of-admission neighborhoods such as l'Orangerie, north of the city center, offer prestige and a refined flavor, enhanced by graceful architecture and well-groomed green spaces, making it a popular choice for families.

CENTRE VILLE

If you were wondering what the downsides were to life in Strasbourg, it might be the housing situation. The only thing bad about it is the dearth of options directly in the city center. Plenty of resources for students seeking housing for a semester or two exist, including **Estudines Residence Halls** (www.estudines.com) and **Relais Etudiants** (www.relais-etudiants.com), but what about those of us out in the working world, on a quest for central real estate with long-term appeal?

For singles looking for shared housing opportunities, there's **Appartager** (www. appartager.fr), which helps match you up with the perfect roommate(s) in a variety

© AURELIA D'ANDREA

Café culture is thriving in this eastern metropolis.

of housing situations in and around Strasbourg, with a particularly good selection of housing in the *centre ville*. Options include house-sharing with a married couple in an apartment directly *en face de* (in front of) the cathedral for €365 per month, or, closer to the train station where real estate is cheaper, you could live in a housing co-op with three eco-conscious roommates who enjoy shared meals and even shared bikes (the house bikes are available to all roomies).

The average price per square meter for would-be buyers in Strasbourg is €2,600 for apartments, and €2,800 for houses. In the *centre ville*'s most coveted corners, including la Petite France, prices rise to the top range of the local real estate market, with places selling—quickly, as soon as they become available—for double the local average. That might translate to a

The local tram system is extensive.

remodeled two-bedroom apartment with enviable views over the l'Ill for €318,000 (plus €1,000 a year in communal maintenance charges), or an incredible three-bedroom apartment boasting an interior courtyard and wood beams galore for €468,000. The apartment comes with its own *cave* (storage area) and is being sold with furniture included in the price (and hopefully you're a fan of overstuffed red leather sofas).

KRUTENAU

For **better deals** and a *bobo* feel, Krutenau—wedged between the charming Petite France neighborhood and the super-modern Esplanade quartier in southeast Strasbourg—is a good option. Safe and **family friendly,** the neighborhood is loaded with amenities. Chic wine bars and Korean restaurants, bicycle workshops, and the odd art gallery give the streets a hip vibe without being *trop trop.* It wouldn't be too out of the ordinary to pay less than €200,000 for an average-sized two-bedroom flat here. For renters, budget between €500 and €600 for a one-bedroom flat, and if you're really lucky, you might even land something that says 17th-century charm on the outside, and 21st-century remodel (bathtub, modern kitchen) on the inside.

Getting Around

PUBLIC TRANSPORTATION

Moving around Strasbourg is straightforward, but choosing which form of transport to take can be a challenge. So many choices! Tram, autoshare, bike, and bus are just some of your options, and they each fall under the **CST** (Compagnie des Transports Strasbourgeois) umbrella. Single tickets cost €1.60, and an all-in-one Pass Mobilité costs €49 per month. The 30 bus lines travel far and wide throughout the region, making the pass a good investment for those settling in outlying suburbs. The tramway is France's most extensive, with six lines traveling 60 kilometers of track, and new stretches are currently being added to the eastbound D line, which will stretch toward Kehl at the German border.

BICYCLE

For city commuting in this flat stretch of eastern France, the public bike system called **Vel'hop** (www.velhop.strasbourg.eu) is ideal. For occasional use, you're best off choosing a ride-as-you-go option (€1 per hour, or €5 a day with no extra hourly fees). Another possibility is semipermanent bike rental, which gives you access to your very own bike for a year-long rate of €80. To explore all the pedal-powered options, visit a Vel'hop office when you're in Strasbourg, or head to the website (with English-language menu).

RESOURCES

Consulates and Embassies

UNITED STATES AND CANADA

There are 11 French consulate bureaus in the United States and six in Canada, each presiding over a consular region. Where you go for your in-person appointment depends on which state or province you live in; to figure out which one is your regional HQ, begin your search at the French embassy in Washington, DC, or Ottawa, Canada.

French Embassy in the United States

FRENCH EMBASSY
4101 Reservoir Rd. NW
Washington, DC 20007
tel. 202/944-6000
www.ambafrance-us.org

French Consulates in the United States

ATLANTA
The Lenox Building
3399 Peachtree Rd. NE, Ste. 500
Atlanta, GA 30326
tel. 404/495-1660 _
www.consulfrance-atlanta.org
Jurisdiction: Alabama, Georgia, Mississippi, North Carolina, South Carolina, Tennessee

BOSTON
Park Square Building
31 Saint James Ave., Ste. 750
Boston, MA 02116
tel. 617/435-0418
www.consulfrance-boston.org
Jurisdiction: Massachusetts, Maine, New Hampshire, Rhode Island, Vermont

CHICAGO
205 North Michigan Ave., Ste. 3700
Chicago, IL 60601
tel. 312/327-5200
www.consulfrance-chicago.org
Jurisdiction: Illinois, Indiana, Iowa, Kansas, Kentucky, Missouri, Michigan, Minnesota, Nebraska, North Dakota, Ohio, South Dakota, Wisconsin

HONOLULU
Alii Place, Ste. 1800
1099 Alakea St.
Honolulu, HI 96813|
tel. 808/547-5852
Jurisdiction: Hawaii and the U.S. Pacific Islands

HOUSTON
777 Post Oak Blvd., Ste. 600
Houston, TX 77056
tel. 713/572-2799
www.consulfrance-houston.org
Jurisdiction: Arkansas, Oklahoma, Texas

LOS ANGELES
10390 Santa Monica Blvd., Ste. 410
Los Angeles, CA 90025
tel. 310/235-3200
www.consulfrance-losangeles.org
Jurisdiction: Arizona, Colorado, New Mexico, Southern California, Southern Nevada

MIAMI
Espirito Santo Plaza, Ste. 1050
1395 Brickell Ave.
Miami, FL 33131
tel. 305/403-4150
www.consulfrance-miami.org
Jurisdiction: Florida

NEW ORLEANS
1340 Poydras St.
Ste. 1710
New Orleans, LA 70112
tel. 504/569-2870
www.consulfrance-nouvelleorleans.org
Jurisdiction: Louisiana

NEW YORK
934 5th Ave.
New York, NY 10021
tel. 212/606-3600
www.consulfrance-newyork.org
Jurisdiction: Connecticut, New Jersey, New York

SAN FRANCISCO
40 Bush St.
San Francisco, CA 94108
tel. 415/397-4330
www.consulfrance-sanfrancisco.org
Jurisdiction: Idaho, Montana, Northern California, Northern Nevada, Oregon, Utah, Washington, Wyoming

WASHINGTON, DC
101 Reservoir Rd. NW
Washington DC 20007-2185
tel. 202/944-6195
www.consulfrance-washington.org
Jurisdiction: Delaware, Maryland, Pennsylvania, Washington, DC, West Virginia, Virginia.

French Consulates in Canada
CALGARY
525 11th Ave. SW, Ste. 500
Calgary, AB T2R 0C9
tel. 403-264-1777
www.ambafrance-ca.org
Jurisdiction: Alberta, Saskatchewan. Embassy services are available here.

MONCTON
77 Rue Main, Ste. 800
Moncton, New Brunswick E1C 1E9
tel. 506/857-4191

Jurisdiction: New Brunswick, Nova Scotia, Prince Edward Island, Newfoundland, and Labrador. Visa applications are processed at the general consulate in Montréal.

MONTRÉAL
1501 McGill College, Bureau 1000
Montréal, QC, H3A 3M8
tel. 514/878-4385
www.consulfrance-montreal.org
Jurisdiction: Québec, Nuvanuk

QUÉBEC CITY
25 Rue Saint-Louis
Québec City, QC G1R 3Y8
tel. 418/266-2500
www.consulfrance-quebec.org
Jurisdiction: Québec City. Visa applications are processed at the general consulate in Montréal.

TORONTO
2 Bloor St. E, Ste. 2200
Toronto ON M4W 1A8
tel. 416/847-1900
www.consulfrance-toronto.org
Jurisdiction: Manitoba, Ontario

VANCOUVER
1130 West Pender St., Ste. #1100
Vancouver, BC, V6E 4A4
tel. 604/637-5300
www.consulfrance-vancouver.org
Jurisdiction: Alberta, British Columbia, Saskatchewan, Yukon, and North West Territories

French Embassies in France
Both the American and Canadian embassies in France are good sources of information for new residents in France, offering referrals, services, and information on such topics as how to avoid pickpockets and how to report a lost or stolen passport.

AMERICAN EMBASSY
2, avenue Gabriel
75008 Paris
tel. 01/43 12 22 22
www.France.usembassy.gov

CANADIAN EMBASSY
37, avenue Montaigne
75008 Paris
tel. 01/44 43 29 00
www.canadainternational.gc.ca

Planning Your Fact-Finding Trip

ANGLOINFO
www.paris.angloinfo.com
News and current information for expats and
would-be Parisians in the Île-de-France region.

FRENCH ENTRÉE
www.frenchentree.com
An online guide to living, working, and
vacationing in France.

**FRENCH GOVERNMENT
TOURIST OFFICE**
www.us.franceguide.com.
A useful site with current information on
all things related to tourism in France.

FUSAC (FRANCE USA CONTACTS)
www.fusac.org

A good starting point for finding a short-term
rental during your stay in Paris and beyond.

LE FOODING
www.lefooding.com
Digital dining guide for foodies headed to
the City of Light.

SNCF
www.sncf.fr
The French national railway website,
where you can purchase train and airplane
tickets, book rental cars, and more.

TIMEOUT PARIS
www.timeout.com/paris/en
Current events guide with ideas for sightseeing and eating.

Making the Move

IMMIGRATION AND VISAS
THE CALCULUS GROUP
www.calculusgroup.org
An agency that will file your visa paperwork on your behalf.

CRÉDIT AGRICOLE
www.credit-agricole.fr
This popular French bank's website has
a thorough section on moving to France,
including immigration and visas.

FRENCH LAW
www.frenchlaw.com
A basic site explaining French immigration law.

GLOBAL VISAS
www.globalvisas.com
Immigration specialists who will handle
all your paperwork for a fee.

**OFII (OFFICE FRANÇAIS
DE L'IMMIGRATION ET
DE L'INTÉGRATION)**
www.ofii.fr

New arrivals in France will need to register with this office to complete the temporary residency process.

WORK AND STUDY PERMITS
Working in France
ASSOCIATION FOR INTERNATIONAL PRACTICAL TRAINING
www.aipt.org
The Americans Abroad program helps U.S. citizens who have found jobs in France to acquire work permits.

COUNCIL ON INTERNATIONAL EDUCATIONAL EXCHANGE (CIEE)
www.ciee.org
Offers information for students on working in France.

EUROPEAN-AMERICAN CHAMBER OF COMMERCE (EACC)
www.eaccfrance.com
Provides would-be investors and entrepreneurs with advice and resources for launching a business in France.

JUST LANDED
www.justlanded.com
A useful website that extensively explains the work permit process.

TRANSITIONS ABROAD
www.transitionsabroad.com
This established publication is an excellent resource for job seekers in France.

Studying in France
FRENCH MINISTRY OF FOREIGN AFFAIRS
www.diplomatie.gouv.fr
This government website offers an English-language guide to studying in France.

IES ABROAD
www.iesabroad.com

An informative study-abroad site.

STUDY ABROAD
www.studyabroad.com
A handy, thorough site for anyone thinking of studying in France.

CUSTOMS AND SHIPPING COMPANIES
ERC (EMPLOYEE RELOCATION COUNCIL)
www.erc.org

EURA (EUROPEAN RELOCATION ASSOCIATION)
www.eura-relocation.com

FIDI (INTERNATIONAL FEDERATION OF INTERNATIONAL FURNITURE REMOVALS)
www.fidi.com

GROSPIRON
www.grospiron.com/fr/lien

OMNI (OVERSEAS MOVING NETWORK INTERNATIONAL)
www.omnimoving.com

BLOGS
DAVID LEBOVITZ
www.davidlebovitz.com
Possibly the most popular food blog in all of France, penned by a California transplant who worked in the fabled Chez Panisse kitchen before moving to Paris.

HIP PARIS BLOG
www.hipparis.com
This oft-updated blog is a great resource for shoppers, foodies, and others interested in contemporary French culture.

52 MARTINIS
www.52martinis.com

This fun blog for cocktail lovers focuses on all things boozy and quaffable in the City of Light.

LOST IN CHEESELAND
www.lostincheeseland.com
This popular blog's Franco File Fridays series spotlights expats doing cool things in Paris.

PARIS (IM)PERFECT
www.parisimperfect.wordpress.com
American writer Sion Dayson shares her honest and witty observations about life in the City of Light.

WHERE IS BRYAN?
www.bryanpirolli.com
American journalist and man-about-town Bryan Pirolli's informative blog is loaded with juicy tidbits for locals and those planning a move to France.

GETTING SETTLED
ANGLO INFO
www.france.angloinfo.com
A comprehensive site for expats, including information on jobs, housing, buying a car, having a baby, and finding a builder who speaks English.

THE ESCAPE ARTIST
www.escapeartist.com

Plenty of good, basic information on retiring or otherwise settling abroad can be found here. The site also has a job-search section with employment listings in France.

EXPATICA
www.expatica.com
Detailed job listings, plus useful forums to answer all your move-to-France questions.

FRENCH ENTRÉE
www.frenchentree.com
This site will become your move-abroad bible. It covers everything you'd want to know about life in France, from buying a home to putting your kids in school to dealing with local bureaucracy.

JUST LANDED
www.justlanded.com
As its title suggests, this website offers practical information related to every facet of your move, as well as links to other sites.

TRANSITIONS ABROAD
www.transitionsabroad.com
This established magazine has a thorough, well-organized website loaded with resources for those who want to live, work, or study in France.

Housing Considerations

RENTING
COLOCATION
www.colocation.fr
This is France's top roommate-finding database for renters. Includes detailed information about roommates, such as whether they smoke, keep late hours, or have pets.

CRAIGSLIST
www.paris.fr.craigslist.org
Craigslist is the number-one source for finding almost-no-hassle rental housing. Other cities around France don't have as strong a Craigslist community as Paris does, but it's worth investigating their outposts of the site anyway.

FUSAC

www.fusac.fr

The go-to resource for the Paris Anglophone community for more than 20 years has advertisements for housing, jobs, and other services, plus household items and other things for sale.

PARTICULIER À PARTICULIER

www.pap.fr

This source of for-rent ads is extremely popular, so start making those calls on Thursday morning as soon as the new issue comes out.

RENT A PLACE IN FRANCE

www.rentaplaceinfrance.com

Small but excellent selection of long-term housing for English-speaking renters through English-speaking proprietors.

BUYING
CENTURY 21

www.century21.fr

This well-known name in real estate has a strong presence in France. In addition to buying and selling, the company also lists rentals.

FRANCE THIS WAY

www.property.francethisway.com

Another thorough, easy-to-navigate real-estate database targeting the English-speaking community and encompassing every region of France.

FRENCH ENTRÉE

www.frenchentree.com

This English-language site offers regional listings and detailed articles on buying or renting a home or apartment.

FRENCH PROPERTY

www.french-property.com

This website, which has been providing extensive information for years, offers an excellent database of houses for sale, usually by the Anglophone community for the Anglophone community.

SELOGER

www.seloger.fr

A popular online real-estate service that gives home seekers access to nationwide listings of studios apartments, villas, and even châteaux, along with rental listings.

Language and Education

GENERAL RESOURCES
APPRENDRE LE FRANÇAIS EN FRANCE

www.fle.fr

A comprehensive list of all the public and private French language-learning institutions in France.

FRENCH UNIVERSITIES DATABASE

www.dr.education.fr/Serveurs_Etab/Univ_alpha.html

A complete listing of all the French universities that accept international students.

INTERNATIONAL GRADUATE

www.internationalgraduate.net/eurofrance.htm

Helpful information for students planning to enroll in graduate school in France.

LANGUAGE SCHOOLS
Paris
ALLIANCE FRANÇAISE

www.alliancefr.org

Nonprofit language school and cultural center offers classes at every level, plus events and expositions.

ATELIER 9
www.latelier9.com
A stellar reputation and small classes (no more than nine students per class) are the hallmarks of Atelier 9.

MAIRIE DE PARIS
https://cma.paris.fr
The affordable French language courses offered through the *mairie* are in high demand. Plan ahead to snag a seat.

THE SORBONNE
www.english.paris-sorbonne.fr
If you learn by doing, enroll in a program at the Sorbonne. Classes are in French, so it's sink or swim.

Brittany
INSA RENNES (INSTITUT NATIONAL DES SCIENCES APPLIQUÉES DE RENNES)
www.insa-rennes.fr
This *grande école* offers intensive French-language courses in the summer for incoming students.

OFII (OFFICE FRANÇAIS DE L'IMMIGRATION ET DE L'INTÉGRATION)
www.ofii.fr
Offices throughout France offer referrals for French-language courses.

UNIVERSITÉ DE RENNES 2
www.sites.univ-rennes2.fr/cirefe/
The university runs a popular full-time course for international students who want to learn French.

SPEAK UP FORMATION
www.speak-up-formation.com
Intensive French-language courses for adults and children.

Bordeaux and the Dordogne Valley
ALLIANCE FRANÇAISE BORDEAUX
www.alliance-bordeaux.org
The nonprofit organization has a branch in Bordeaux offering language courses and cultural events year-round.

FRENCH FACTORY
www.ffbordeaux.fr
Small class sizes and a variety of levels to choose from.

UNIVERSITÉ DE BORDEAUX 2
www.langues-vivantes.u-bordeaux2.fr
The university offers courses for doctoral diplomas in life sciences, medicine, and social sciences.

UNIVERSITÉ DE BORDEAUX 3
www.u-bordeaux3.fr
French language courses for international students are available.

Pau, Toulouse, and Montpellier
ALLIANCE FRANÇAISE TOULOUSE
www.en.alliance-toulouse.org
Nonprofit French language and culture institute offers classes for children and adults.

APRE (ASSOCIATION FOR THE PROMOTION OF FRIENDSHIP BETWEEN FRENCH AND FOREIGN STUDENTS)
www.institutfrancaismontpellier.com
For nearly 50 years, APRE has provided French immersion classes in Montpellier. All levels welcome.

DYNAMO FORMATION
www.dynamo-formation-int.fr/en/contact
One- to six-week immersion classes offering special programs geared toward the job transfer.

INSA (INSTITUT NATIONAL DES SCIENCES APPLIQUÉES DE TOULOUSE)
www.insa-toulouse.fr
One of France's *grandes écoles* teaches intensive French-language courses to international students.

INSTITUT LINGUISTIC ADENET
www.ila-france.com
French taught at all levels; housing and meals offered in some curricula.

LANGUE ONZE TOULOUSE
www.langueonze.com
Intensive training courses year-round, and students have access to a multimedia lab that includes books, magazines, and DVDs.

MONTPELLIER ESPACE LANGUES
www.cours-francais-montpellier.com
Offers job placement as well as language training.

UNIVERSITY OF PAU
www.iefe.univ-pau.fr/live/
Intensive-French-courses
A 200-hour intensive French language course open to international students is available through the University of Pau.

Provence and the Côte d'Azur
ALLIANCE FRANÇAISE NICE
www.alliance-francaise-nice.com
Language and culture classes for every level at affordable prices.

CENTRE INTERNATIONAL D'ANTIBES
Antibes
www.cia-france.com
Popular French-language school on the Riviera offers summer courses for teens, adults, and families.

ÉCOLE FRANCE LANGUE
www.france-langue.fr

Offers classes in business French, hotel and tourism industry French, and art history.

INSTITUT D'ÉTUDES FRANÇAISES POUR ÉTUDIANTS ÉTRANGERS
Aix-en-Provence
www.iefee.com
French language and cultural institute welcoming students from around the world.

IS INSTITUTE DE LANGUE
Aix-en-Provence
www.is-aix.com
Long-established language school offers language courses as well as cultural activities.

LANGUAGE INTERNATIONAL
www.languageinternational.fr
Advertises itself as a low-cost alternative to other local language academies.

LANGUE À NICE
www.langanice.fr
Offers semester-, trimester-, and year-long courses at private-college tuition prices.

SCEFEE (SERVICE COMMUN D'ENSEIGNEMENT DU FRANÇAIS AUX ÉTUDIANTS ÉTRANGERS)
Aix-en-Provence
www.sites.univ-provence.fr/wscefee
Multilevel language courses run through the Université de Provence.

Lyon and Grenoble
ALLIANCE FRANÇAISE DE GRENOBLE
www.afgrenoble.org
Five different courses, as well as cultural events and workshops, including cooking classes.

CENTRE INTERNATIONAL D'ÉTUDES FRANÇAISE
cief.univ-lyon2.fr
This international-language institute, run

out of the Université de Lyon 2, provides diploma courses in French.

GRENOBLE INP
www.grenoble-inp.fr
This technical institute has French-language courses for students enrolled in diploma programs.

INFLEXYON
www.inflexyon.com
Language center popular with the under-30 set with affordable French lessons at all levels.

INSA LYON
fle.insa-lyon.fr
This *grande école* offers language courses for international students pursuing degrees in other fields.

UNIVERSITÉ STENDHAL GRENOBLE 3
w3.u-grenoble3.fr/cuef/accueil.php3
This university of Grenoble teaches intensive day and evening courses, plus cooking classes in French.

Strasbourg
ALLIANCE FRANÇAISE STRASBOURG
www.alliance-francaise-strasbourg.fr

CIEL STRASBOURG
www.ciel-strasbourg.org

COLLEGES AND UNIVERSITIES
Paris
AMERICAN GRADUATE SCHOOL IN PARIS
www.ags.edu

AMERICAN UNIVERSITY OF PARIS
www.aup.edu

ÉCOLE SUPÉRIEUR DE CUISINE FRANCAISE
www.egf.ccip.fr

INSTITUT CATHOLIC DE PARIS
www.icp.fr

LE CORDON BLEU PARIS
www.lcbparis.com

SCIENCES PO
www.sciencespo.fr/en

THE SORBONNE
www.english.paris-sorbonne.fr

Brittany
ÉCOLE DES BEAUX ARTS DE RENNES
www.erba-rennes.fr

ESC RENNES SCHOOL OF BUSINESS
www.esc-rennes.fr

L'INSTITUT SUPÉRIEUR DES ARTS APPLIQUÉS
www.lisaa.com

INSTITUT UNIVERSITAIRE DE TECHNOLOGIE
www.iu-vannes.fr

UNIVERSITÉ DE BRETAGNE-SUD
www.univ-ubs.fr

UNIVERSITÉ DE RENNES 1
www.univ-rennes1.fr

UNIVERSITÉ DE RENNES 2
www.univ-rennes2.fr

Bordeaux and the Dordogne Valley
INSEEC BUSINESS SCHOOL
grandeecole.inseec-france.com

**UNIVERSITÉ DE BORDEAUX
MONTESQUIEU**
www.u-bordeaux4.fr

**UNIVERSITÉ DE
BORDEAUX SEGALEN**
www.u-bordeaux2.fr

**UNIVERSITÉ MICHEL DE
MONTAIGNE BORDEAUX 3**
www.iut.u-bordeaux3.fr

Pau, Toulouse, and Montpellier
**ÉCOLE SUPÉRIEURE
D'ART DES PYRÉNÉES**
www.esapyrenees.fr

**ÉCOLE SUPÉRIEUR
DES BEAUX ARTS**
www.esbama.free.fr

**PAU SCHOOL OF BUSINESS
MANAGEMENT**
www.esc-pau.fr

UNIVERSITÉ MONTPELLIER 1
www.en.www.univ-montp1.fr

UNIVERSITÉ MONTPELLIER 2
www.univ-montp2.fr

**UNIVERSITY OF PAU AND
PAYS DE L'ADOUR**
www.univ-pau.fr

**UNIVERSITÉ PAUL VALÉRY
MONTPELLIER 3**
www.univ-montp3.fr

**UNIVERSITÉ TOULOUSE
1 CAPITOLE**
www.univ-tlse1.fr

UNIVERSITÉ TOULOUSE 2
www.univ-tlse2.fr

**UNIVERSITÉ TOULOUSE
3 PAUL SABATIER**
www.univ-tlse3.fr

Provence and the Côte d'Azur
**CENTRE UNIVERSITÉ
MEDITERRANÉE**
www.cum-nice.org

ÉCOLE SUPÉRIEUR D'ART
www.ecole-art-aix.fr

ÉCOLE SUPÉRIEUR DE COMMERCE
www.espeme.com

**INSTITUTE FOR AMERICAN
UNIVERSITIES**
www.iaufrance.org

**UNIVERSITÉ DE LA MEDITERRANÉE
D'AIX- MARSEILLE 2**
www.univmed.fr

**UNIVERSITÉ DE NICE
SOPHIA-ANTIPOLIS**
www.unice.fr

**UNIVERSITÉ DE PROVENCE
D'AIX-MARSEILLE 1**
www.univ-provence.fr

**UNIVERSITÉ PAUL CÉZANNE
D'AIX-MARSEILLE 3**
www.unicaen.fr

Lyon and Grenoble
UNIVERSITÉ CATHOLIC DE LYON
www.univ-catholyon.fr

**UNIVERSITÉ CLAUDE
BERNARD LYON 1**
www.univ-lyon1.fr

UNIVERSITÉ DE GRENOBLE
www.grenoble-univ.fr

UNIVERSITÉ JEAN MOULIN LYON 3
www.univ-lyon3.fr

UNIVERSITÉ JOSEPH FOURIER
www.ujf-grenoble.fr

UNIVERSITÉ LUMIÈRE LYON 2
www.univ-lyon2.fr

UNIVERSITÉ PIERRE-MENDES FRANCE
www.iut2.upmf-grenoble.fr

UNIVERSITÉ POPULAIRE DE LYON
uplyon.free.fr

UNIVERSITÉ STENDHAL GRENOBLE 3
www.u-grenoble3.fr

Strasbourg
L'ECOLE NATIONALE SUPÉRIEURE D'ARCHITECTURE DE STRASBOURG
www.strasbourg.archi.fr

STRASBOURG BUSINESS SCHOOL
www-english.em-strasbourg.eu

UNIVERSITY OF STRASBOURG
http://www.unistra.fr

Health

GENERAL HEALTH AND INSURANCE
ASSOCIATION DENTAIRE FRANÇAISE
7, rue Mariotte
75017 Paris
tel. 01/58 22 17 10
www.adf.asso.fr

ASSURANCE MALADIE
www.ameli.fr

FEDERATION HOSPITALIÈRE DE FRANCE
1 bis, rue Cabanis
75014 Paris
tel. 01/44 06 84 44
www.fhf.fr

FRENCH HOSPITAL GUIDE
www.hopital.fr

SANTÉCLAIR
www.santeclair.fr

EMERGENCY CONTACTS
AMBULANCE
Dial 15

EUROPE-WIDE EMERGENCY NUMBER
Dial 112

FIRE
Dial 18

POLICE
Dial 17

HOSPITALS AND PHARMACIES
Paris
AMERICAN HOSPITAL OF PARIS
63, boulevard Victor Hugo
92200 Neuilly-sur-Seine
tel. 01/46 41 25 25
www.american-hospital.org

**ASSISTANCE PUBLIQUE
HÔPITAUX DE PARIS**
Hopital St. Antoine
184, rue du Faubourg Saint-Antoine
75012 Paris
tel. 01/49 28 20 00

**BRITISH AND AMERICAN
PHARMACY**
1, rue Auber
75009 Paris
tel. 01/42 65 88 29

**GRANDE PHARMACIE
INTERNATIONALE DE PARIS**
17 bis, boulevard de Rochechouart
75009 Paris
tel. 01/48 78 03 01

HÔPITAL ST. LOUIS
1, avenue Claude-Vellefaux
75010 Paris
tel. 01/42 49 49 49

**PHARMACIE DU DRUGSTORE
DES CHAMPS-ÉLYSÉES**
133, avenue des Champs-Élysées
tel. 01/47 20 39 25

Brittany
**HÔPITAL PONTCHAILLOU/
CENTRE HOSPITALIER
UNIVERSITÉ DE RENNES**
2, rue Henri le Guilloux
35033 Rennes
02 99 28 43 21
www.chu-rennes.fr

HÔPITAL PROSPER SCHUBERT
20, boulevard du Général Guillaudot
76017 Vannes
tel. 02/97 01 41 41
www.fhf-bretagne.fr

**HÔPITAL SUD/CENTRE
HOSPITALIER UNIVERSITÉ
DE RENNES**
16, boulevard de Bulgarie
35203 Rennes
tel. 02/99 28 43 21

SOS MEDECINS
Clinique Océane
11, rue du Dr Joseph Audic
56000 Vannes
tel. 08/25 89 89 94

Bordeaux and the Dordogne Valley
**CENTRE HOSPITALIER
JEAN LECLAIRE**
rue Jean Leclaire
24200 Sarlat
tel. 05/53 31 75 75

**CENTRE HOSPITALIER
SAMUEL POZZI**
9, avenue Prof Albert Calmette
24100 Bergerac
tel. 05/53 63 88 88
www.hopital-bergerac-samuelpozzi.fr

CLINIQUE PASTEUR
54, rue Professeur Pozzi
24100 Bergerac
tel. 05/53 61 56 56
www.medi-partenaires.com/clinique-pasteur

GROUP HOSPITALIER PELLEGRIN
Place Amélie Raba-Léon
33000 Bordeaux
tel. 05/56 79 56 79
www.chu-bordeaux.fr

GROUP HOSPITALIER ST. ANDRE
1, rue Jean Burguet
33000 Bordeaux
tel. 05/56 79 56 79
www.chu-bordeaux.fr

RESOURCES

PHARMACIE DES CAPUCINS
30, place des Capucins
33000 Bordeaux
Open 24 hours.

SOS MEDECINS BORDEAUX
www.sosmedecins-bordeaux.com
Dial - 3624

Pau, Toulouse, and Montpellier
CENTRE HOSPITALIER DE PAU
4, blvd Hauterive
tel. 05/59 92 48 48
www.ch-pau.fr

CENTRE HOSPITALIER UNIVERSITAIRE DE TOULOUSE
www.chu-toulouse.fr
Network of nine hospitals in the Toulouse region.

CHU DE MONTPELLIER
191, avenue Doyen Gaston Giraud
34090 Montpellier
04 67 33 05 55

CLINIQUE CLÉMENTVILLE
25, rue de Clémentville
34070 Montpellier
tel. 08/26 88 88 84

PHARMACIE LAFAYETTE DES 7 CANTONS
1, rue Montpensier
tel. 05/59 27 71 91
www.pharmaciedes7cantonslafayette.com
Pau pharmacy that lets customers place orders online.

SOS MÉDECINS TOULOUSE
24, route d'Espagne
31100 Toulouse
tel. 05/61 33 00 00

Provence and the Côte d'Azur
CENTRE HOSPITALIER D'ANTIBES JUAN-LE-PINS
107, avenue de Nice
06600 Antibes
www.ch-antibes.fr

CENTRE HOSPITALIER DE NICE
www.chu-nice.fr
Network of five hospitals in the Nice area.

CENTRE HOSPITALIER DU PAYS D'AIX
avenue des Tamaris
13616 Aix-en-Provence
tel. 04/42 33 50 00

POLYCLINIQUE DU PARC RAMBOT
74 bis, cours Gambetta
13100 Aix-en-Provence
tel. 04/42 23 99 99

SOS MÉDECINS
tel. 04/42 26 24 00 or 04/93 67 20 00

SOS MÉDECINS NICE
tel. 08/10 85 01 01

Lyon and Grenoble
CENTRE HOSPITALIER DE GRENOBLE
tel. 04/76 76 75 75
Network of four hospitals in the Grenoble area.

HÔPITAL DE LA CROIX-ROUSSE
103, grande rue de la Croix-Rousse
69004 Lyon
tel. 08/20 08 20 69

HÔPITAL EDOUARD HERRIOT
5, place d'Arsonval
69003 Lyon
tel. 08/20 08 20 69

HÔPITAL NORD HOTEL-DIEU
1, place de l'Hôpital
69002 Lyon
tel. 08/20 08 20 69

SOS MÉDECINS
5, chemin des Couvents
38 100 Grenoble
tel. 04/38 70 17 01

Strasbourg
LA CLINIQUE SAINTE-ODILE
6, rue Simonis
tel. 08/25 12 45 00
www.steodile.fr
Private clinic offering a variety of healthcare services.

UNIVERSITY HOSPITALS OF STRASBOURG
http://www.chru-strasbourg.fr
A conglomerate of hospital campuses spanning the city, each specializing in unique areas of medicine.

DISABLED ACCESS
ASSOCIATION DES PARALYSÉS DE FRANCE
www.apf.asso.fr
Advocacy organization for people living with paralysis.

AUTISME FRANCE
www.autisme.france.free.fr
Support and resource organizations for families living with autism.

CAISSE NATIONAL DE SOLIDARITÉ POUR AUTONOMIE
www.cnsa.fr
Government-run association promoting independent living for the elderly and disabled.

PERSONNES HANDICAPPES
www.fondationdefrance.org
Organization working to support and uphold French disability laws and better the lives of the disabled public.

Employment

STARTING A BUSINESS
THE AMERICAN CHAMBER OF COMMERCE IN FRANCE
www.amchamfrance.org

APCE (ASSOCIATION POUR LA CRÉATION D'ENTERPRISES)
www.apce.com

BOUTIQUES DE GESTION
www.boutiques-de-gestion.com

CHAMBRE DE COMMERCE ET D'INDUSTRIE DE PARIS
www.ccip.fr

INVEST IN FRANCE
www.invest-in-france.org

NACRE (NOUVEL ACCOMPAGNEMENT POUR LA CRÉATION ET LA REPRISE D'ENTERPRISE)
www.emploi.gouv.fr/nacre

JOB SEARCHES
APEC
www.apec.fr
French-language job-seeking website with listings in multiple industries.

BERLITZ
www.berlitz.fr

An established English-language institute that's always looking for new recruits.

CRAIGSLIST
www.paris.en.craigslist.org
The Paris-focused Craigslist site offers the most employment-related ads of all the French regional sites.

EUROJOBS
www.eurojobs.com
Search engine for job seekers throughout France and the rest of Europe. Emphasis on high-tech industry opportunities.

FAT TIRE BIKE TOURS
www.fattirebiketours.com
American-owned employer that's always on the lookout for qualified staff.

FUSAC (FRANCE USA CONTACTS)
www.fusac.org
Job listings for English teachers, hotel and restaurant workers, and tourism-related industries.

PÔLE EMPLOI
www.pole-emploi.fr
French portal for job seekers in France.

WALL STREET INSTITUTE
www.wallstreetinstitute.fr
Each of the institute's 70 centers throughout France accepts résumés year-round.

VOLUNTEERING

CADIP (CANADIAN ALLIANCE FOR DEVELOPMENT INITIATIVES AND PROJECTS)
www.cadip.org
This Vancouver-based nonprofit aims to support volunteering abroad with humanitarian projects.

CARE FRANCE
www.carefrance.org
Nonprofit French volunteer organization with projects all over the world.

GO ABROAD
www.goabroad.com
This U.S.-based database of volunteer programs includes an extensive selection of possibilities in France.

WWOOF (WORLD WIDE OPPORTUNITIES ON ORGANIC FARMS)
www.wwoof.com
Free food and lodging in exchange for your work on organic farms throughout France. Always welcoming new members.

Finance

BNP PARIBAS
www.bnpparibas.com

CAISSE D'ÉPARGNE
www.caisse-epargne.fr

CRÉDIT AGRICOLE
www.credit-agricole.fr

LA BANQUE POSTAL
www.labanquepostale.fr

PHILIPPE JEDAR
Financial Planner
tel. 06/01 78 35 55

Communications

PHONE AND INTERNET SERVICE
BOUYGUES TELECOM
www.bouyguestelecom.fr
Internet, television, and telephone service.

FNAC
www.fnac.fr
This chain sells a wide variety of mobile phones and other communication devices.

ORANGE
www.orange.fr
Internet, television, and telephone service.

PHONEHOUSE
www.phonehouse.fr
The leading mobile-phone store in France, where you can also buy your *puces*.

SFR
www.SFR.fr
Internet, television, and telephone service.

NEWSPAPERS
LE CANARD ENCHAINÉ
www.lecanardenchaine.fr

THE CONNEXION
www.connexionfrance.com

LE FIGARO
www.lefigaro.fr

FRANCE SOIR
www.francesoir.fr

LIBÉRATION
www.liberation.fr

MÉTRO
www.metrofrance.com

LE MONDE
www.lemonde.fr

NOUVEL OBSERVATEUR
www.tempsreel.nouvelobs.com

LE PARISIEN
www.leparisien.com

MAGAZINES
A NOUS
www.anous.fr

L'EXPRESS
www.lexpress.fr

MARIANNE
www.marianne2.fr

PARISCOPE
http://spectacles.premiere.fr

PARIS MATCH
www.parismatch.com

LE POINT
www.lepoint.fr

RESOURCES

Travel and Transportation

GENERAL RESOURCES
AIR FRANCE
www.airfrance.fr
France's national airline.

COVOITURAGE
www.covoiturage.fr
National public ride-share program.

EUROLINES
www.eurolines.fr
Long-distance bus company.

EUROPECAR
www.europecar.fr
Nationwide car-rental agency.

OPODO
www.opodo.fr
Popular online travel agency.

SNCF
www.sncf.fr
French national railway lines.

REGIONAL TRANSPORTATION
Paris
RATP (RÉGIE AUTONOME DES TRANSPORTS PARISIENS)
www.ratp.fr
Information in English for the bus, Métro, regional trains, and transport passes.

VÉLIB'
www.velib.paris.fr
Paris's public bike-sharing system.

Brittany
STAR (LE SERVICE DE TRANSPORT EN COMMUN DE RENNES MÉTROPOLE)
www.star.fr
Information on Rennes' Métro, bus, and other transportation lines.

LE VÉLO STAR
www.levelostar.fr
Rennes' public bike-sharing system.

Bordeaux and the Dordogne Valley
LA CUB (COMMUNITÉ URBAINE DE BORDEAUX)
www.lacub.fr
Portal to Bordeaux's bus, tram, and public-bicycle system.

TRANS'PERIGORD
www.cg24.fr
Public-transportation hub for the Sarlat region.

TUB (LES TRANSPORTS URBAINS BERGERACOIS)
tel. 05/53 63 96 97
Hours, fares, and other information for Bergerac's bus system.

Pau, Toulouse, and Montpellier
GARE DE PAU
avenue Jean Biray
www.sncf.frl

IDEYCLE
www.idecycle.com
Bike-share program.

IDELIS
www.reseau-idelis.com
Pau regional bus network.

TAM (TRANSPORTS DE L'AGGLOMERATION DE MONTPELLIER)
www.montpellier-agglo.com
Public-transportation hub for Montpellier's bus, tram, bike, and car networks.

TISSÉO
www.tisseo.fr
Public-transportation hub for the Toulouse region.

VÉLÔTOULOUSE
www.velo.toulouse.fr
Toulouse's public bike-sharing site.

Provence and the Côte d'Azur
AIX EN BUS
www.aixenbus.com
Hours, schedules, and tariffs for buses throughout the Aix region.

ENVIBUS
www.envibus.fr
Portal to the Antibes area public-transportation network.

LIGNES D'AZUR
www.lignesdazur.com
Bus and tram information for the greater Nice area.

VÉLO BLEU
www.velobleu.org
Nice's public bike-sharing system.

V'HELLO
www.vhello.fr
Information for Aix's public bike-sharing program.

Lyon and Grenoble
MÉTROVÉLO
www.metrovelo.fr
Grenoble's public bike-sharing system.

TAG (TRANSPORTS AGGLOMERATION DE GRENOBLE)
www.semitag.com
Public-transportation hub for the Grenoble area.

TCL (TRANSPORTS COMMUNAL DE LYON)
www.tcl.fr
Public-transportation hub with information on Lyon's tram, Métro, and bus systems.

VÉLO'V
www.velov.grandlyon.com
Lyon's public bike-sharing system.

Strasbourg
CTS (COMPAGNIE DE TRANSPORTS STRASBOURGEOIS)
www.cts-strasbourg.eu
Public network of buses, trams, park-and-ride stations, and bicycles.

GARE DE STRASBOURG
www.gare-strasbourg.fr

Prime Living Locations

PARIS
General
PARIS CONVENTION AND VISITORS BUREAU
www.en.parisinfo.com

PARIS MAIRIE DIRECTORY
www.paris.fr

PARIS TOURIST BOARD
www.parisinfo.com

Schools
AMERICAN SCHOOL OF PARIS
www.asparis.org

BILINGUAL INTERNATIONAL SCHOOL OF PARIS
www.bilingualschoolparis.com

LYCÉE HONORÉ DE BALZAC
www.balzac-apesa.org

PARIS.FR
www.equipements.paris.fr/?tid=41
City of Paris's official list of primary schools.

PARIS.FR
www.equipements.paris.fr/?tid=44,55,56
City of Paris's list of *lycées*.

BRITTANY
Rennes General
RENNES MAIRIE
www.rennes.fr

RENNES METROPOLITAN
www.ca-rennes-metropole.demarchesenligne.fr

RENNES OFFICE OF TOURISM
www.tourisme-rennes.com

Rennes Schools
ACADEMIE DE RENNES INTERNATIONAL SCHOOL
www.ac-rennes.fr

LES ÉCOLES
http://lesecoles.fr/rennes-35000
Comprehensive list of public and private primary and secondary schools in Rennes.

Vannes General
VANNES OFFICE OF TOURISM
www.tourisme-vannes.com

Vannes Schools
VANNES MAIRIE
www.mairie-vannes.fr
The office of the *maire* has a comprehensive list of all public and private schools in the Vannes region.

BORDEAUX AND THE DORDOGNE VALLEY
Bordeaux General
BORDEAUX OFFICE OF TOURISM
www.bordeaux-tourisme.com

PERIGORD NOIR-DORDOGNE VALLEY OFFICE OF TOURISM
www.perigordnoir.com

Bordeaux Schools
BERGERAC MAIRIE
www.bergerac.fr
The *mairie* of the city of Bordeaux provides a comprehensive list of public and private schools.

BORDEAUX INTERNATIONAL SCHOOL
www.bordeaux-school.com

Bergerac General
BERGERAC MAIRIE
www.bergerac.fr

BERGERAC OFFICE OF TOURISM
www.bergerac-tourisme.com

Bergerac Schools
PAYS DE BERGERAC
www.pays-de-bergerac.com
The official site of the greater Bergerac area provides a comprehensive listing of public and private schools throughout the Bergerac area.

Sarlat General
SARLAT OFFICE OF TOURISM
www.sarlat-tourisme.com

Sarlat Schools
SARLAT MAIRIE
www.sarlat.fr/edito.asp?Scolarite
Sarlat's office of the *maire* offers a comprehensive listing of the area's public and private schools.

PAU, TOULOUSE, AND MONTPELLIER
Pau General
CITY OF PAU
www.pau.fr

Pau Schools
LYCÉE/COLLEGE IMMACULÉE CONCEPTION
www.icbf.net

INTERNATIONAL SCHOOL OF BEARN
www.isbearn.com

Toulouse General
TOULOUSE CONVENTION AND VISITORS BUREAU
www.sotoulouse.com

TOULOUSE MAIRIE
www.toulouse.fr

TOULOUSE OFFICE OF TOURISM
www.toulouse-tourisme.com

Toulouse Schools
LES ENFANTS TOULOUSE
www.enfant-toulouse.com/scolaire/ecolesprimairestoulouse.php
The city of Toulouse's official list of public and private schools.

INTERNATIONAL SCHOOL OF TOULOUSE
www.intst.eu

Montpellier General
MONTPELLIER MAIRIE
www.montpellier.fr

MONTPELLIER OFFICE OF TOURISM
www.ot-montpellier.fr

Montpelier Schools
ECOLE PRIVÉE INTERNATIONAL BILINGUE
www.ecole-privee-bilingue.fr

VILLE DE MONTPELIER
www.montpellier.fr/24-l-enseignement-et-la-recherche-a-montpellier-toutes-les-ecoles-de-montpellier.htm
The Montpellier *maire*'s office offers a comprehensive list of schools throughout the region.

PROVENCE AND THE CÔTE D'AZUR
Aix-en-Provence General
AIX OFFICE OF TOURISM
www.aixenprovencetourism.com

Aix-en-Provence Schools
AIX-EN-PROVENCE MAIRIE
www.mairie-aixenprovence.fr/-Education
The *mairie's* official list of public and private schools.

INTERNATIONAL BILINGUAL SCHOOL OF PROVENCE
www.ibsofprovence.com

INTERNATIONAL PRIVATE SCHOOL OF PROVENCE
www.epim-mis.com

Antibes General
ANTIBES MAIRIE AND OFFICE OF TOURISM
www.antibesjuanlespins.com

Antibes Schools
ACADÉMIE DE NICE
www.ac-nice.fr/ienantibes/admin/ecoles/ecolant.htm
A comprehensive list of all the public schools in Antibes.

L'ANNUAIRE OFFICIEL DE L'ENSEIGNEMENT PRIVÉ
www.enseignement-prive.info/ecoles/departement/alpes-maritimes/06/1
A comprehensive list of all the private schools in Antibes.

Nice General
NICE MAIRIE
www.nice.fr

NICE OFFICE OF TOURISM
www.nicetourisme.com

Nice Schools
SITE DE LA VILLE DE NICE
www.nice.fr/Education-recherche
The city of Nice's official list of public and private schools.

LYON AND GRENOBLE
Lyon General
LYON MAIRIE
www.lyon.fr

LYON OFFICE OF TOURISM
www.lyon-france.com

RHÔNE-ALPES DEPARTMENT OF TOURISM
www.rhonealpes-tourisme.com

Lyon Schools
CITY OF LYON
www.lyon.fr/vdl/sections/en/enseignement
The city's official list of public and private schools.

THE INTERNATIONAL SCHOOL OF LYON
www.islyon.org

Grenoble General
GRENOBLE LIFE
www.grenoblelife.com

GRENOBLE MAIRIE
www.grenoble.fr

GRENOBLE TOURISM
www.grenoble-tourism.com

Grenoble Schools
THE AMERICAN SCHOOL OF GRENOBLE
www.americanschoolgrenoble.com

CITY OF GRENOBLE
www.grenoble.fr/7-education.htm
The city of Grenoble's education site.

ÉCOLE ST. JOSEPH
www.ecolestjoseph.fr

STRASBOURG
General
CITY OF STRASBOURG
www.en.strasbourg.eu/en/home-en

Schools
STRASBOURG WALDORF SCHOOLS
www.steiner-waldorf.org

NOTRE DAME COLLEGE/LYCEE
www.notredame67.com

BILINGUAL INTERNATIONAL PRIMARY SCHOOL OF STRASBOURG
http://www.lucieberger.com

Glossary

l'addition: restaurant check, bill
aller-rétour: round trip
apéro: snack eaten with a drink before dinner
ascenseur: elevator
assurance: insurance
attestation: written and signed statement or testimonial
auberge: inn
banlieue: suburbs
billet: ticket
bisou: kiss
bobo: bourgeois bohemian, yuppie
boulangerie: bread shop where pastries and other baked goods are often sold
bricolage: DIY, do-it-yourself
brocante: antiques and collectibles sale
café: cup of coffee; establishment where you drink coffee
carte bleue: debit card
carte de séjour: residency card
caviste: wineseller
chariot: personal shopping cart on wheels
chien(ne): male/female dog
cinéma: movie theater
clic-clac: foldout couch-bed
clinique: private hospital
collège: middle school
composteur: ticket stamping machine at train stations, on buses, and at Métro stations
crèmerie: shop that sells dairy products
déménager: to move house
demi: half-pint of beer
distributeur: ATM
dossier: file (n)
école élémentaire: elementary school
encore: again
enfant: child
épicerie: grocery shop
étranger/étrangère: foreigner

étudiant(e): male/female student
facture: bill (n)
garant(e): financial guarantor
gare: train station
gratuit(e): free/no cost
grève: strike (n)
hôtel de ville: town hall, city hall (see also *mairie*)
ici: here
immobilière: real-estate agent
imperméable: raincoat
libre: open/available
lycée: high school
maire: mayor
mairie: mayor's office, town hall (see also *hôtel de ville*)
maison particulier: independent house, usually of grand standing
manifestation: demonstration
marché aux puces: flea market
maternelle: preschool
maternité: maternity hospital
mutuelle: supplemental insurance
notaire: notary
ordinateur: computer
panier: shopping basket
parapluie: umbrella
patisserie: pastry shop
périphérique: ring road
permis de conduire: driver's license
petit(e) ami(e): boyfriend/girlfriend
populaire: working-class/crowded
préfecture: regional headquarters for the Ministry of the Interior
préfecture de police: police headquarters
presque: almost
La Presse: newsstand
quartier: neighborhood
rendezvous: appointment
rentrée: the start of a new school year

rosé: pink wine
rue: street
sac: plastic shopping bag
salariée: employee
sans papiers: undocumented workers
SDF: "sans domicile fixe," homeless
SVP: "s'il vous plaît," please
syndicat: union or association
tabac: tobacco shop that also sells bus

tickets, lottery tickets, and sometimes magazines and beverages
tartine: slice of bread
travail: work
verre: a glass (usually of wine or beer)
vide-grenier: community rummage sale
viennoiserie: breakfast pastry
voiture: car

French Phrasebook

French is an intimidating language. It isn't so much the rolling *R*s and figuring out how the accents work that makes it so–it's the fear of sounding silly, saying things "wrong," and potentially not being understood. But rest assured that the French will always meet you halfway if you at least *try*, even if your response to *"merci"* ends up as *"beaucoup."* Set those feelings of vulnerability aside and let 'er rip. You'll be rewarded for your efforts! Remember to begin all requests and queries with *"Excusez-moi, s'il vous plaît"* (ex-cue-zay MWAH, see voo play) and end them with *"Merci, madame/monsieur"* (mair-SEE mah-DAHM/muh-SYUH).

PRONUNCIATION

Before you start practicing your French, relax. This isn't rocket science, though it does take a bit of diligent practice. Getting a grip on French accents will help you read the language–as will pronouncing the consonants and vowels–and let you avoid ordering a cold meat terrine (*pâté*, pah-TAY) when you really want pasta (*pâte*, PAHT).

Vowels

Accents do not always change the sound of the vowel. French is tricky like that.

é   *accent aigu*
à, è, ù   *accent grave*
â, ê, î, ô, û   *accent circonflexe*
ë, ï, ü   *le tréma*
a   as the "a" in "also"; *place* PLAHSS (plaza, place, space)

ai   as "ai" in "rain"; *maison* may-ZOHn (house)

ail   as "ai" in "aisle"; *ail* EYE (garlic)

ais, ait   as "e" in "bed"; *voudrais, voudrait* voo-DREH (would like)

au as   "au" in "au pair"; *auberge* oh-BAIRZH (inn)

e   as "e" in "bed" or "e" in "hamlet"; *mec* MECK (guy), *retour* ruh-TOOR (return)

é   as "ay" in "bay"; *café* cah-FAY (coffee, café)

eau   as "o" in "oh"; *bâteau* bah-TOH (boat)

er, ez   as "ay" in "stay"; *regarder* ruh-gar-DAY (to look), *rez-de-chaussée* raid-shoh-SAY (ground floor)

et   as "e" in "bed"; *complet* cohm-PLEH (full)

i   as "i" in "police"; *minute* mee-NEWT (minute); exception: in closed syllables ending in "-in" the "i" is pronounced as a nasal "an"; *vin* vAn (wine)

o   as "o" in "pope" *stop* STOHP (stop)

oi   as "wa" in "water"; *oiseau* wah-ZOH (bird)

ou   as "oo" in "moon"; *bouche* BOOSH (mouth)

u   as "ew" in "stew"; *prune* PREWN (plum)

ui   pronounced "ew-ee"; *fruit* frew-EE (fruit)

Consonants

With a few exceptions, French consonants are pronounced as they are in English. Exceptions: The letters **d, n, p, r, s, t,** and **x** are generally not pronounced at the end of a word. When a consonant is followed by an e, the consonant is pronounced.

c as "c" in "cut"; when followed by e, i, or y, it is pronounced like "s" as in "salad;" *cadeau* kah-DOH (gift), *céréale* say-ray-AHL (cereal), *cycle* SEE-kluh (cycle)

ç *la cédille;* when followed by a or o, is pronounced like "s" as in "salad"; *ça* SAH (that), *façon* fah-SOHn (way, manner)

ch as "sh" in "shower"; *chat* SHAH (cat), *champignon* shahm-peen-NYOHn (mushroom)

g as "g" in "game"; when followed by e, i or y, it is pronounced like the "s" in "leisure"; *gare* GAHR (train station), *guide* GEED (guide) *géant* zhay-AHn (giant, gigantic)

gn as "ny" in "canyon"; *mignon* meen-NYOHn (cute)

j as the "s" in "leisure"; *jus* ZHEW (juice)

h silent when it's the first letter in a word; *hôpital* oh-pee-TAHL (hospital), *horloge* or-LUHZH (clock)

ph as "f" in "film"; *pharmacie* farm-ah-SEE (pharmacy), *philosophe* fee-loh-SOFF (philosopher)

qu as "k" in "kick"; *qui* KEE (who)

s not pronounced at the end of a plural word; *lettres* LETT-ruh (letters)

th as "t" in "tuna" (note that there is no "th" sound in French); *thé* TAY (tea), *théâtre* tay-AH-truh (theater)

NUMBERS

0 *zéro*
1 *un*
2 *deux*
3 *trois*
4 *quatre*
5 *cinq*
6 *six*
7 *sept*
8 *huit*
9 *neuf*
10 *dix*
11 *onze*
12 *douze*
13 *treize*
14 *quatorze*
15 *quinze*
16 *seize*
17 *dix-sept*
18 *dix-huit*
19 *dix-neuf*
20 *vingt*
21 *vingt-et-un*
22 *vingt-deux*
23 *vingt-trois*
30 *trente*
31 *trente-et-un*
32 *trente-deux*
40 *quarante*
41 *quarante-et-un*
50 *cinquante*
51 *cinquante-et-un*
60 *soixante*
61 *soixante-et-un*
62 *soixante-deux*
63 *soixante-trois*
64 *soixante-quatre*
65 *soixante-cinq*
66 *soixante-six*
67 *soixante-sept*
68 *soixante-huit*
69 *soixante-neuf*
70 *soixante-dix*
71 *soixante-et-onze*
72 *soixante-douze*
73 *soixante-treize*
74 *soixante-quatorze*
75 *soixante-quinze*
76 *soixante-seize*
77 *soixante-dix-sept*
78 *soixante-dix-huit*
79 *soixante-dix-neuf*
80 *quatre-vingts*
81 *quatre-vingt-un*
82 *quatre-vingt-deux*
83 *quatre-vingt-trois*
84 *quatre-vingt-quatre*
85 *quatre-vingt-cinq*
86 *quatre-vingt-six*
87 *quatre-vingt-sept*
88 *quatre-vingt-huit*
89 *quatre-vingt-neuf*
90 *quatre-vingt-dix*
91 *quatre-vingt-onze*
92 *quatre-vingt-douze*
93 *quatre-vingt-treize*
94 *quatre-vingt-quatorze*

95 *quatre-vingt-quinze*
96 *quatre-vingt-seize*
97 *quatre-vingt-dix-sept*
98 *quatre-vingt-dix-huit*
99 *quatre-vingt-dix-neuf*
100 *cent*
101 *cent un*
125 *cent vingt-cinq*
200 *deux cents*
300 *trois cents*
1,000 *mille*
2,000 *deux mille*
1,000,000 *un million*
2,000,000 *deux millions*
one billion *un milliard*
one quarter *un quart*
one third *un tiers*
one half *un demi*
three-fourths *trois-quatre*

DAYS AND MONTHS

Neither the days of the week nor the months of the year are capitalized in French.
Monday *lundi*
Tuesday *mardi*
Wednesday *mercredi*
Thursday *jeudi*
Friday *vendredi*
Saturday *samedi*
Sunday *dimanche*
today *aujourd'hui*
yesterday *hier*
tomorrow *demain*
January *janvier*
February *février*
March *mars*
April *avril*
May *mai*
June *juin*
July *juillet*
August *août*
September *septembre*
October *octobre*
November *novembre*
December *décembre*
spring *printemps*
summer *été*
autumn *automne*
winter *hiver*

TIME

France uses the 24-hour clock. Instead of a colon, an "h" is used; so 1am appears as 1h00 and 11:30pm appears as 23h30.
1am *une heure*
2am *deux heures*
3am *trois heures*
4am *quatre heures*
5am *cinq heures*
6am *six heures*
7am *sept heures*
8am *huit heures*
9am *neuf heures*
10am *dix heures*
11am *onze heures*
noon *midi*
1pm *treize heures*
2pm *quatorze heures*
3pm *quinze heures*
4pm *seize heures*
5pm *dix-sept heures*
6pm *dix-huit heures*
7pm *dix-neuf heures*
8pm *vingt heures*
9pm *vingt-et-une heures*
10pm *vingt-deux heures*
11pm *vingt-trois heures*
midnight *minuit*
morning *le matin*
afternoon *l'après-midi*
evening *le soir*
night *la nuit*
What time is it? *Quelle heure est-il?*
one minute *une minute*
two minutes *deux minutes*
early *tôt*
late *tard, en retard*
10 minutes late *dix minutes de retard*

THE BASICS

"Please" and "thank you" are the first steps toward making yourself welcome in France. Once you've mastered those niceties, expand your vocabulary with these quotidian basics.
yes *oui*
no *non*
OK *d'accord*
maybe *peut-être*
I *je*

me *moi*
my *mon, ma, mes*
you *vous (formal)*
your *votre/vos*
he *il*
him *lui*
his *son/sa/ses*
she/her *elle*
her (possessive) *son/sa/ses*
we/us *nous*
our *notre/nos*
they *ils/elles*
them *eux/elles*
their *leur/leurs*
who *qui*
what *quoi*
when *quand*
why *pourquoi*
where *où*
how many *combien*
because *parce que*
thank you *merci*
thank you very much *merci beaucoup*
you're welcome (formal) *je vous en prie*
you're welcome (informal) *de rien*
I'm sorry *je suis desolé(e)*
I don't understand *je ne comprends pas*
open *Ouvert*
closed *Fermé*
closed on Sundays *fermé le dimanche*
push *Poussez*
pull *Tirez*
stop *Arrêt!*
post office *la poste*
bank *la banque*
empty *vide*
full *plein(e)*
happy *heureux/heureuse*
sad *triste*

GREETINGS

Greetings are an important formality and a many-times-a-day ritual. It's imperative that you master these common salutations for successful living in France.
Hello. *Bonjour.*
Hi! *Salut!*
Good evening. *Bonsoir.*
Good day. *Bonne journée.*
Good night. *Bonne soirée.*
Good weekend. *Bon weekend.*

My name is... *Je m'appelle...*
What's your name? *Comment-vous appelez-vous?*
I'd like to introduce you to... *Je vous présente...*
Nice to meet you. *Enchanté(e).*
Goodbye. *Au revoir.*
See you later. *À tout à l'heure.*
See you soon. *À bientôt.*
How are you? *Comment allez-vous?*
How's it going? *Comment ça va?*
It's going well, thanks. *Ça va bien, merci.*
It's going well, and you? *Ça va bien, et vous? (et toi, if informal)*
Enjoy your meal. *Bon appétit.*

GETTING AROUND

Where is...? *Où est...?*
a hotel *un hôtel*
the airport *l'aéroport*
the train station *la gare*
the bus station *la gare routière*
the Métro (subway) *le Métro*
the bus stop *arrêt de bus*
right *à droite*
left *à gauche*
straight ahead *tout droit*
on the corner *au coin*
here *ici*
there *là*
nearby *près d'ici*
for rent *à louer*
for sale *à vendre*
deposit *caution, acompte, consigné*
available *disponible*

ACCOMMODATIONS

Do you have a room available? *Avez-vous une chambre libre?*
We're full. *Nous sommes complets.*
I have a reservation. *J'ai une réservation.*
Combien de nuits? *How many nights?*
I'd like to stay three nights. *Je voudrais rester trois nuits.*
double room *avec un grand lit*
bed *lit*
key *clé*
the price *le prix*
cheap *pas cher*

FOOD

to eat *manger*
to drink *boire*
breakfast *petit-déjeuner*
lunch *déjeuner*
dinner *dîner*
snack *casse-croûte*
water *l'eau* or *une carafe d'eau*
wine *vin*
beer *bière*
menu *la carte*
first course *entrée*
main course *plat* or *plat principal*
I'd like... *Je voudrais...*
I'm vegetarian/vegan. *Je suis végétarien(ne)/végétalien(ne).*
without... *sans*
with... *avec*
the check *l'addition*
supermarket *supermarché/ hypermarché*
fruit *fruit*
vegetables *légumes*
cheese *fromage*
butter *beurre*
milk *lait*
soy milk *lait de soja*
coffee *café*
tea *thé*
hot water *eau chaud*
jam *confiture*
egg *oeuf*
meat *viande*
bread *pain*
noodles *nouilles*
pasta *pâte*
rice *riz*
salt *sel*
pepper *poivre*
ketchup *sauce tomate* or *ketchup*

SHOPPING

Fruits and vegetables are sold by the kilo at French outdoor *marchés* and supermarkets. If you want less than a kilo, ask for *cinq cents grammes* (a half-kilo) or *un quart* (a quarter-kilo).
to go shopping *faire les courses*
How much does this cost? *C'est combien?*

I'm looking for... *Je cherche...*
I'd like to buy... *Je voudrais acheter...*
I'd like a half-kilo, please *Je voudrais cinq cents grammes, s'il vous plaît*
That's too much. *C'est trop.*
It's too small/big. *C'est trop petit/ grand.*
Do you have any others? *Vous en avez d'autres?*
Do you accept bank cards/credit cards? *Est-ce que je peux payer avec une carte bancaire/carte de crédit?*

SHOE SIZES

M	W	European
3.5	5	35
4.5	6	36
5.5	7	37 1/2
6.5	8	38 1/2
7.5	9	40
8.5	10	42
10.5	12	44

BANKING

bank card *carte bancaire (CB)*
savings account *compte d'épargne*
checkbook *carnet de chèque/chèquier*
account *compte*
checking account *compte chèque*
overdraft *découvert*
withdrawal *prélèvement*
bank statement *relevé bancaire*

HEALTH

an emergency *un urgence*
pain *douleur*
I'm sick. *Je suis malade.*
sharp pain *douleur vive*
swelling *des oedèmes*
flu *grippe*
stomach flu *gastro*
prescription *un ordonnance*
to refill a prescription *renouveler un ordonnance*
diagnosis *diagnostic*
X-ray *une radio*
ultrasound/sonogram *une échographie*
examination of heart, lungs, ears *l'auscultation du cœur, des poumons, des oreilles*
pap smear *un frottis*

pregnancy/pregnant *grossesse/ enceinte*
midwife *sage-femme*
ophthalmologist *ophthalmologiste*

cardiologist *cardiologue*
physiotherapist *kinésithérapeute*
dentist *dentiste*
homeopathy *homéopathie*

Suggested Reading

Ernest Hemingway did it best: write about the French experience from an American's perspective, albeit with a candid pen fueled by copious amounts of alcohol. Honest yet romantic, he made legions of dreamers yearn for their own Lost Generation era in Paris's Left Bank. Hemingway left big shoes for others to fill and boy, have they tried. These tomes, written by scholars, cultural and social critics, cooks, and other France aficionados, will get you revved up (and duly warned) in anticipation of your move.

HISTORY AND CULTURE

Lebovitz, David. *The Sweet Life in Paris.* New York: Broadway Books, 2009. A delicious introduction to France from a top blogger, cookbook author, and Paris expat.

Nadeaux, Jean-Benoît and Julie Barlow. *Sixty Million Frenchmen Can't Be Wrong.* Chicago: Sourcebooks, Inc., 2003. An insightful look at French history and contemporary French society.

Druckerman, Pamela. *Bringing up Bébé.* New York: Penguin Press, 2012. The first book to examine French childrearing tactics has spawned a slew of copycats. The original is smart and humorous.

Timoney, Charles. *Pardon My French.* New York: Gotham, 2008. A funny look at all the French-language errors you'll probably make during your stay in France.

MEMOIRS

Child, Julia and Alex Prud'homme. *My Life in France.* New York: Anchor, 2007. The late, great, mid-century American chef recounts her amazing life in France and her ascent to culinary superstardom.

Baldwin, James. *Notes of a Native Son.* Boston: Beacon Press, 1984. Among these essays by the revered American writer are tales of his years in France.

Beach, Sylvia. *Shakespeare and Company.* New York: Harcourt, 1959. The owner of the famous Paris bookstore reminisces about her exciting literary life in Paris's Left Bank and beyond.

Lebovitz, David. *The Sweet Life in Paris.* New York: Broadway Books, 2011. A delightful mélange of recipes and humorous personal stories illustrating the Franco-American culture clash from a popular writer/chef David Lebovitz.

Corbett, Bryce. *A Town Called Paris.* New York: Broadway Books, 2008. A saucy Australian finds true love with a showgirl in the City of Light.

Gershman, Suzy. *C'est La Vie.* New York: Viking, 2004. A woman of a certain age moves to France and begins anew after her husband's death.

If Your French Is Up to Snuff . . .

You should really try reading some of these authors' works in their own language but if you can't tell your *voilà* from your viola, you can still find semi-decent translations of some of France's most revered writers.

- Guillame Apollinaire
- Charles Baudelaire
- André Breton
- Albert Camus
- Colette
- Simone de Beauvoir
- Alexandre Dumas
- Gustave Flaubert

- Stéphane Hessel
- Michel Houellebecq
- Victor Hugo
- Guy de Maupassant
- Anaïs Nin
- Marcel Proust
- Jean-Paul Sartre
- Voltaire

Gopnik, Adam. *Paris to the Moon.* New York: Random House, 2001. A *New Yorker* writer spent several years in Paris with his family; these are his memories.

Hemingway, Ernest. *A Moveable Feast.* New York: Scribner, 1964. Classic Hemingway about writing, writers, drinking, and adventure in France.

Mayle, Peter. *A Year in Provence.* New York: Knopf, 1990. The quintessential move-to-rural-France tale, full of humor and insight.

Rochefort, Harriet Welty. *French Toast.* New York: St. Martin's Press, 1997. An American moves to France, marries a Frenchman, and pens the delicious details.

Sedaris, David. *Me Talk Pretty One Day.* Boston: Back Bay Books, 2001. Humorous essays detailing Sedaris's language foibles and other funny disasters in France.

Stein, Gertrude. *Paris, France.* New York: Liveright, 1970. The famous 20th-century author's homage to life in France.

Turnbull, Sarah. *Almost French.* New York: Gotham Books, 2002. Another Australian moves to France, settles in Paris, and shares the witty details.

FICTION

Barbery, Muriel. *The Elegance of the Hedgehog.* New York: Europa Editions, 2008. A precocious 12-year-old protagonist is the heart and soul of this story set in contemporary Paris.

Clarke, Stephen. *A Year in the Merde.* New York: Bloomsbury, 2005. The goofy tale of a middle-aged Englishman's adventures in the City of Light.

Gavalda, Anna. *Hunting and Gathering.* New York: Riverhead Books, 2007. A cast of disparate characters cometogether in a Paris apartment and unforgettable drama ensues in this poignant novel by a French writer.

Guene, Faiza. *Kiffe Kiffe Tomorrow.* Orlando: Harcourt, 2006. The story of a young North African immigrant girl's life in the Paris suburbs.

Hugo, Victor. *The Hunchback of Notre Dame.* A dramatic, sorrowful tale of lives intertwined in the heart of medieval Paris.

Hugo, Victor. *Les Misérables.* A riveting story of perseverance, revenge, and survival by one of France's most revered writers.

McClain, Paula. *The Paris Wife.* New York: Ballantine Books, 2011. A fictionalized "memoir" in the voice of Hadley Richardson, Ernest Hemingway's wife.

Nemirovsky, Irene. *Suite Française.* An edge-of-your-seat story set in Paris and the French countryside during World War II.

Suggested Films

The Lumière brothers are credited with inventing the final link in cinema technology, bringing the art form to life in France at the turn of the 19th century. (The Institut Lumière, dedicated to the work of the Lyon-born siblings, should not be missed.) Since then, French filmmaking has evolved into an honored and honorable tradition, and France boasts a long list of directors whose films are consistently compelling: Jacques Demy, Jean-Luc Godard, François Ozon, Jacques Chabral, Marcel Pagnol, Jean Renoir, François Truffaut, Ousman Sembène, Louis Malle, Agnes Varda, and many more. A (very) short list of must-sees includes:

DRAMAS AND COMEDIES

Amélie. Directed by Jean-Pierre Jeunet, 2001. Burbank, CA: Buena Vista Home Entertainment, 2002.

Amour. Directed by Michael Haneke, 2012. Paris, France: TFI Video, 2013.

Betty Blue. Directed by Jean-Jacques Beineix, 1986. United States: Cinema Libre Studio, 2009.

Breathless. Directed by Jean-Luc Godard, 1960. Livingston, NY: Criterion Collection, 2007.

Le Cercle Rouge. Directed by Jean-Pierre Melville, 1970. New York: Criterion Collection, 2004.

City of Lost Children. Directed by Marc Caro and Jean-Pierre Jeunet. Culver City, CA: Columbia Tri-Star Home Video, 1995.

Delicatessen. Directed by Marc Caro and Jean-Pierre Jeunet, 1991. Hollywood, CA: Paramount Home Video, 1992.

Elevator to the Gallows. Directed by Louis Malle, 1958. New York: Criterion Collection, 2006.

The Grand Illusion. Directed by Jean Renoir, 1937. Chicago, IL: Home Vision Cinema, 1999.

La Haine. Directed by Mathieu Kossovits, 1995. Irvington, NY: Criterion Collection, 2007.

l'Intouchables. Directed by Olivier Nakache and Eric Toledano, 2011. Paris, France: Gaumont, 2011.

Suggested Music

There's nothing like the sound of Edith Piaf's warbling to put you in the mood for France. Here are other French musical "arteests" worth getting to know:

- Air
- Arielle Dombasle
- Ben l'Oncle Soul
- Blossom Dearie
- Daft Punk
- Françoise Hardy
- Serge Gainsbourg
- Keren Ann

- Les Innocents
- Louise Attack
- Nouvelle Vague
- Les Nubians
- Paris Combo
- Phoenix
- Rhinôçérôse
- Superbus

Hollywoo. Directed by Frédéric Berthe and Pascal Serieis, 2011. Paris, France: StudioCanal, 2011.

Midnight in Paris. Directed by Woody Allen, 2011. New York, NY: Sony Pictures Classics, 2011.

Paris, je t'aime. Directed by Olivier Assayas et al, 2006. Los Angeles: First Look Home Entertainment, 2007.

Pauline at the Beach. Directed by Eric Rohmer, 1983. Santa Monica, CA: MGM Home Entertainment, 2003.

The Red Balloon. Directed by Albert Lamorisse, 1956. New York: Janus Films, 2008.

The Triplets of Belleville. Directed by Sylvain Chomet, 2003. New York: Sony Picture Classics, 2004.

The Town Is Quiet. Directed by Robert Guédiguian, 2002. Agat Films & Cie/Canal+, 2000.

Umbrellas of Cherbourg. Directed by Jacques Demy, 1964. Port Washington, NY: Koch Vision, 2004.

DOCUMENTARIES

The Gleaners and I. Directed by Agnès Varda, 2000. New York: Zeitgeist Video, 2002.

Kings of Pastry. Directed by Frazer Pennebaker and Flora Lazar, 2009. New York: First Run Features, 2011.

Man on Wire. Directed by James Marsh, 2008. United States: Magnolia Home Entertainment, 2008.

A Year in Burgundy. Directed by David Kennard, 2013. Los Gatos, California: Netflix, 2014.

Index

Acknowledgments

I'm so grateful to the many generous and patient people who supported this project in so many wonderful ways: Jeff Rogers, Steve Kocheran-Letrouit, Chris Horton, Jennifer Eric, Dr. Cindy Davis, Elisabeth Lyman, Isabelle Valentin, Zoe Levi, Concetta Antonelli-Lapeyre, Erin Quirk, Asia Chantal Aniwanou, Sion Dayson, Vanessa Merina, Elissa Villines Shaw, Jadis Armbruster, Ross Husband, Jake Braunecker, and Fanny, my beloved dog. If I missed anyone, let me make it up to you over a glass of bubbly—my treat!

Photo Credits

Also Available

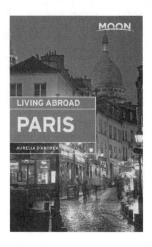

MAP SYMBOLS

▰▰▰▰ Expressway	○ City/Town	✖ Airfield	▰ Archaeological Site
──── Primary Road	◉ State Capital	✈ Airport	⛪ Church
▰▰▰▰ Secondary Road			⛽ Gas Station
▪ ▪ ▪ ▪ Unpaved Road	✦ National Capital	▲ Mountain	Mangrove
············ Ferry	★ Point of Interest	⋏⋏ Park	Reef
▰▰▰ Railroad	▪ Other Location	⛷ Skiing Area	Swamp

CONVERSION TABLES

°C = (°F - 32) / 1.8
°F = (°C x 1.8) + 32
1 inch = 2.54 centimeters (cm)
1 foot = 0.304 meters (m)
1 yard = 0.914 meters
1 mile = 1.6093 kilometers (km)
1 km = 0.6214 miles
1 fathom = 1.8288 m
1 chain = 20.1168 m
1 furlong = 201.168 m
1 acre = 0.4047 hectares
1 sq km = 100 hectares
1 sq mile = 2.59 square km
1 ounce = 28.35 grams
1 pound = 0.4536 kilograms
1 short ton = 0.90718 metric ton
1 short ton = 2,000 pounds
1 long ton = 1.016 metric tons
1 long ton = 2,240 pounds
1 metric ton = 1,000 kilograms
1 quart = 0.94635 liters
1 US gallon = 3.7854 liters
1 Imperial gallon = 4.5459 liters
1 nautical mile = 1.852 km

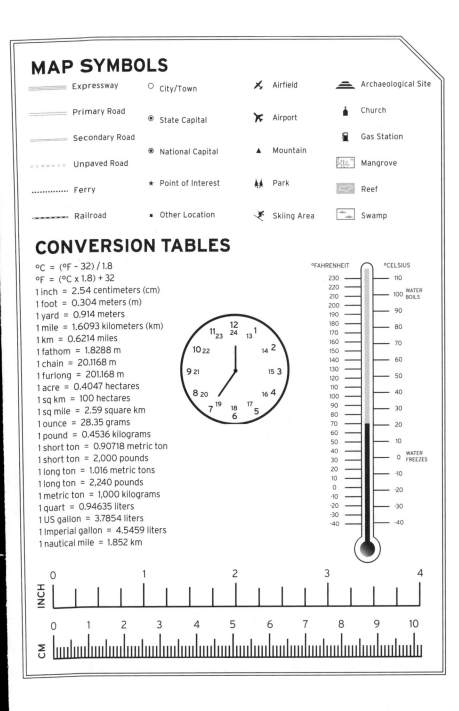

MOON LIVING ABROAD FRANCE
Avalon Travel
a member of the Perseus Books Group
1700 Fourth Street
Berkeley, CA 94710, USA
www.moon.com

Editor: Nikki Ioakimedes
Copy Editor: Kim Runciman
Graphics Coordinator: Darren Alessi
Production Coordinator: Darren Alessi
Cover Design: Faceout Studios, Charles Brock
Moon Logo: Tim McGrath
Map Editor: Kat Bennett
Cartographer: Brian Shotwell
Indexer: Rachel Kuhn

ISBN-13: 978-1-63121-163-8
ISSN: 1534-5890

Printing History
1st Edition – 2005
3rd Edition – November 2015
5 4 3 2 1

Front cover photo: © Elissa Gabriella Photography
Back cover photo: © Keith Levit/123rf.com
Title page photo: © J. Kelagopian/Médias OTC NICE

Printed in Canada by Friesens

All recommendations are based on each author's individual judgment. We do not accept payment for inclusion in our travel guides, and our authors don't accept free goods or services in exchange for positive coverage.

Although every effort was made to ensure that the information was correct at the time of going to press, the author and publisher do not assume and hereby disclaim any liability to any party for any loss or damage caused by errors, omissions, or any potential travel disruption due to labor or financial difficulty, whether such errors or omissions result from negligence, accident, or any other cause.

KEEPING CURRENT

Although we strive to produce the most up-to-date guidebook that we possibly can, change is unavoidable. Between the time this book goes to print and the time you read it, the cost of goods and services may have increased, and a handful of the businesses noted in these pages will undoubtedly move, alter their prices, or close their doors forever. Exchange rates fluctuate—sometimes dramatically—on a daily basis. Federal and local legal requirements and restrictions are also subject to change, so be sure to check with the appropriate authorities before making the move. If you see anything in this book that needs updating, clarification, or correction, please drop us a line. Send your comments via email to feedback@moon.com, or use the address above.

What I Love About France

- The fact that chocolate—in the form of *tartine* spread, cereal, a stuffed croissant, or a hot drink—is an entirely acceptable way to start the day.

- Those first glorious, sunshiny days of spring, when even the frowniest Parisians can't help but smile as they bask in the sun at terrace cafés across the city.

- The way every two-year-old child gleefully cries out *"petit chien!"* as I stride past with my dog.

- Stepping out of my neighborhood *boulangerie* with a still-warm baguette tucked under my arm.

- The genuine feelings of solidarity among French men and women in times of national trouble.

- Sampling regional specialties like Alsatian wines, Perigordine truffles, and the fruits confits from Provence and the Côte d'Azur in the name of cultural exploration.

- The freedom that comes with knowing that Copenhagen, London, the Italian Riviera, and Budapest are within a two-hour journey from Paris.

- Buying hot chestnuts and mulled wine from street vendors at Christmastime.

- Unabashed topless septuagenarians sunbathing at the public swimming pool.

- *Brocantes* (antiques markets), *marchés aux puces* (flea markets), and *vide-greniers* (rummage sales), where scoring secondhand treasures is a popular weekend sport.

- Mid-November, when all of France gets gussied up with twinkling lights, decorated trees, and *marchés de Noël* that usher in the holiday season.

- Conversations with friends over perfectly quaffable €3 glasses of rosé at a local *bar à vins*.

- The first Sunday of every month, when many museums in Paris (including the Louvre, the d'Orsay, and Pompidou) are open to the public for free.

fisherman's sweater, tapping and squeezing a heartstring-tugging rendition of "La Vie en Rose," a beret at his feet awaiting the toss of a few coins.

Up the street, past the *fleuriste*, the *crémerie*, and the 13th-century cathedral, the warm glow of a café summons you indoors. From behind the zinc bar, the owner calls out, "Bonjour, mademoiselle!" (You can always tell if he's flirting by whether he addresses you as "mademoiselle" or "madame.") You make a beeline for the terrace to take in the last rays of sunshine on this fading spring afternoon.

A hyperbolized rendering of a day in your French life? As disarming as it may seem, the truthful answer is a definitive *"non."* Even as it struggles to adapt to 21st-century growing pains—an aging population, stagnant birth rates, and burgeoning unemployment—France rises to the challenge while retaining the traditions that give the country its flavor.

Stimulating? *Absolument.* Survey the expatriate community, and odds are people will tell you that the "danger" Eliot warned us against is a risk worth taking.